HUMAN RIGHTS: INTERNATIONAL PROTECTION, MONITORING, ENFORCEMENT

Human Rights: International Protection, Monitoring, Enforcement

Edited by
JANUSZ SYMONIDES
University of Warsaw, Poland

ASHGATE   UNESCO Publishing

Published by
Ashgate Publishing Limited
Gower House
Croft Road
Aldershot
Hants, GU11 3HR
England

Ashgate Publishing Company
Suite 420
101 Cherry Street
Burlington, VT 05401-4405
USA

Ashgate website: http://www.ashgate.com

Published jointly with the United Nations Educational, Scientific and Cultural Organization 7, place de Fontenoy, 75352, Paris 07 SP

UNESCO website: http://www.unesco.org

British Library Cataloguing in Publication Data
Human rights
    Vol. 3: International protection, monitoring, enforcement
    1.Human rights
    I.Symonides, Janusz
    323

Library of Congress Cataloging-in-Publication Data
Human rights : international protection, monitoring, enforcement / edited by Janusz Symonides.
        p.   cm.
    Includes bibliographical references and index.
    ISBN 0-7546-2301-7 -- ISBN 0-7546-2302-5 (pbk.)
        1. Human rights. 2. International agencies. I. Symonides, Janusz.

    K3240.H8575 2003
    341.4′81—dc21   2002043700

Ashgate ISBN 0 7546 2301 7 (Hbk)
            ISBN 0 7546 2302 5 (Pbk)

UNESCO ISBN 92-3-103883-4

Typeset by Manton Typesetters, Louth, Lincolnshire, UK.
Printed and bound in Great Britain by MPG Books Ltd, Bodmin, Cornwall.

Contents

PART II   REGIONAL SYSTEMS

List of Tables

Preface

The present volume – *Human Rights: International Protection, Monitoring, Enforcement* – is the third and last in the series which began in 1998 with *Human Rights: New Dimensions and Challenges* and continued in 2000 with *Human Rights: Concept and Standards*. Thus, the initiative aimed at the preparation and publication of the UNESCO manual for teaching human rights at the higher education level comes to a successful conclusion.

The international protection of human rights may be presented in many ways: from the point of view of organs, instruments, means of protection, or from the point of view of the protection of specific categories of human rights or persons belonging to vulnerable groups. This volume adopts a method which may be qualified as institutional. It gives, first, the presentation of the United Nations system of protection which may be seen as universal, followed by an analysis of regional systems.

Article 1 of the 1945 Charter of the United Nations lists among its purposes '... promoting and encouraging respect for human rights and for fundamental freedoms'. It further provides that the General Assembly shall initiate studies and make recommendations for the purpose of '... assisting in the realization of human rights and fundamental freedoms' (Article 13), whereas the Economic and Social Council may make recommendations '... for the purpose of promoting respect for, and observance of human rights and fundamental freedoms for all' (Article 62). It also entitles the Economic and Social Council to set up commissions for the promotion of human rights (Article 68). This led to the establishment of the Commission on Human Rights which plays an important role in the protection of human rights.

Although the Charter can be seen as the starting point for the creation of the United Nations machinery and system of human rights protection, many years nevertheless elapsed before a system comprising reports, State complaints and individual communications, as well as establishing treaty bodies, came into being. It is enough to note that the Universal Declaration of Human Rights of 1948 did not foresee any procedure or organ to monitor its implementation.

The first chapter of this volume gives a comprehensive, holistic view of the United Nations human rights machinery and procedures, including the very important role played by the Commission on Human Rights, the treaty bodies and the Office of the United Nations High Commissioner for Human

Rights. The United Nations system also comprises specialized agencies of which two, in the context of human rights protection, deserve special attention – namely, the International Labour Organization (ILO) and the United Nations Educational, Scientific and Cultural Organization (UNESCO). The former because it is the oldest international organization, established in 1919, which developed, long before the United Nations, a very elaborate system of promotion and protection of human rights in its field of competence, including the monitoring of the implementation of conventions adopted by it. As far as UNESCO is concerned, it is worth noting that the Organization has created a permanent system of reporting on education for peace, human rights, democracy, international understanding and tolerance. It also instituted, in 1978, a special procedure for individual communications concerning alleged violations of human rights in UNESCO's fields of competence. The right to present communications does not result from any special human rights instrument adopted by the Organization; communications may be directed at any Member State of UNESCO. Although not mentioned specifically in this manual, we should not forget that other members of the United Nations system, such as the Food and Agriculture Organization (FAO), the World Health Organization (WHO), the United Nations High Commissioner for Refugees (UNHCR), the United Nations Development Programme (UNDP) and the United Nations Children's Fund (UNICEF) play an important role in the promotion and protection of human rights.

Part II of this volume is devoted to the presentation of regional systems of human rights protection. The trend towards closer political, economic and cultural cooperation has led to the creation of regional organizations and regional systems of human rights protection. It has already brought to life three regional systems: the first was created by the Council of Europe in 1950 based on the European Convention for the Protection of Human Rights and Fundamental Freedoms; the second was created in 1969 by the Organization of American States (OAS) on the basis of the American Convention on Human Rights; and the third was created in 1981 on the basis of the African Charter on Human and Peoples' Rights, by the Organization of African Unity (now the African Union). The fourth regional system which may be qualified as *in statu nascendi* is that of the League of Arab States, dated 1994. The Vienna Declaration and Programme of Action of 1993 gives a positive evaluation of regional arrangements, noting that they play a fundamental role in the protection of human rights. Indeed, the regional systems reinforce, develop and advance the universal standards. Suffice it to observe that the Council of Europe has adopted nearly 30 regional human rights instruments including the European Convention for the Protection of Human Rights and Fundamental Freedoms and the European Social Charter.

The regional procedures differ as far as their organs and ways and means of protection of human rights are concerned. The most advanced is the European system which gives individuals the right to present cases of alleged violations of human rights to the European Court of Human Rights.

The importance of this development cannot be overestimated as, for the first time in the history of international law, a very important precedent has been set. The European Court of Human Rights is open to individuals who can take their States before an international tribunal because of alleged violations of their rights. This procedure is not optional; the ratification or accession to the European Convention makes it binding for the States. As one can also learn from the chapter on this question, the European system referred to in the singular is composed of several systems of protection: the system of the Council of Europe; the human dimension system established by the Organization for Security and Cooperation in Europe (OSCE); the European Union; and sub-regional systems.

The American system is based on the possibility of presenting petitions to the Inter-American Commission on Human Rights. The Inter-American Court of Human Rights, created by the American Convention on Human Rights, can judge cases presented to it by the Commission and by States. Individuals have no direct access to the Court. However, this question of access, already accepted by the Council of Europe, is now being discussed in the Organization of American States.

The African system is based on petitions which may be presented to the African Commission on Human and Peoples' Rights. The Organization of African Unity (OAU) attempted to follow the examples of the other systems and establish an African Court on Human and Peoples' Rights. The Protocol to the African Charter on Human and Peoples' Rights on the establishment of an African Court on Human and Peoples' Rights was adopted by the OAU in 1998. Until now, it has only been ratified by five States and has not yet entered into force.

The populous Asian region has no regional or sub-regional procedures for the protection of human rights. The World Conference on Human Rights (Vienna, Austria, 1993) strongly emphasized the need to establish regional and sub-regional arrangements for the promotion and protection of human rights where they do not already exist. The General Assembly, as well as the Commission on Human Rights, adopted a series of resolutions in which they confirmed the value of regional arrangements for the promotion and protection of human rights in the Asian and Pacific region.

An analysis of universal and regional systems of human rights protection allows the observation of differences in the scope of the protection of various categories of human rights. The reasons for this are manifold and can be traced back to the time of the Cold War and the contradictions and polemics concerning the importance and legal character of economic, social and cultural rights. For this very reason, neither the European nor the American Convention on Human Rights has embraced all human rights; they are limited to civil and political rights. Consequently, these systems of protection were limited to these rights. The situation was remedied with the adoption, in 1961 by the Council of Europe, of the European Social Charter (revised in 1996) and the introduction in 1995 of a procedure of collective complaints concerning non-implementation of the Charter. The American system was also extended to these rights after the adoption of the

Additional Protocol to the American Convention on Human Rights in the Areas of Economic, Social and Cultural Rights of 1998. The only system of protection which, from the very beginning, grants equal status to all categories of human rights is that based on the African Charter on Human and Peoples' Rights. It is worth noting that, on 7 December 2001, the European Union adopted the European Charter of Fundamental Rights which also follows the principle of unity of all human rights: civil, cultural, economic, political and social.

Differences in the scope of protection can be seen in the case of the International Covenant on Civil and Political Rights (ICCPR) and the International Covenant on Economic, Social and Cultural Rights (ICESCR). As clarified by the Committee on Economic, Social and Cultural Rights in Comment No. 3 of 1990, the concept of 'progressive realization' of economic, social and cultural rights formulated in Article 2 of the ICESCR embraces obligations of conduct and obligations of result binding upon States Parties. This article, speaking about all appropriate means to be undertaken by States, covers not only legislative but also administrative, financial, educational, social and other measures. Although the justiciability of these rights is challenged, the Committee stressed that at least some of them are justiciable and can be guaranteed by judicial remedies. For this reason, the adoption of the Optional Protocol to the ICESCR, now under consideration in the Commission on Human Rights, and the establishment of a new procedure for communications which will allow individuals to present petitions concerning alleged violations of their economic, social and cultural rights, are of paramount importance. Bearing in mind that the possibility of individual communications already exists in the case of civil and political rights, in accordance with the Optional Protocol to the ICCPR the principle of the indivisibility of human rights leads to the logical conclusion that both categories of human rights – civil and political and economic, social and cultural – should have the same guarantees.

The unquestionable progress achieved by the United Nations, its specialized agencies and regional organizations in the development of the international system of protection of persons belonging to vulnerable groups does not mean that this system as a whole can be recognized as fully satisfactory. The advancement and development of the protection is uneven. No doubt, recent years have witnessed the further strengthening of the protection of women's and children's rights, both on the universal and regional levels. Suffice it to note that the Committee on the Elimination of Discrimination against Women, after the entry into force in 2000 of the Optional Protocol, is authorized to receive communications from individuals concerning alleged violations by States Parties to the Convention on the Elimination of All Forms of Discrimination against Women.

In some cases, such as that of the rights of migrant workers and their families, attempts to establish a system of protection have been blocked for several years. The International Convention on the Protection of the Rights of All Migrant Workers and Members of Their Families, adopted by the General Assembly in 1990, entered into force in July 2003. It took thirteen years to obtain the 20 ratifications needed. This Convention foresees, in order to monitor its implementation, the establishment of a Committee on the Protection of the Rights of All Migrant Workers and Members of their Families which should become the seventh human rights treaty body.

Sometimes the protection of certain groups is more advanced on a regional than on a universal level. Thus, the rights of persons belonging to minorities are far better protected in the European system by the Organization for Security and Cooperation in Europe and the Council of Europe, as well as by a number of treaties concluded among Central and Eastern European States, than by the United Nations.

The non-effectiveness of the protection of some vulnerable groups is often demonstrated by the fact that, as in the case of disabled persons, aliens, prisoners or the elderly, their rights are formulated by non-binding declarations or they are, like people with HIV/AIDS, not protected at all by any specific instrument.

Part III, containing five chapters, raises the question of how international human rights protection can be further strengthened. It starts with reflections on the importance of national systems of protection which should involve legislative, judiciary and executive powers. It goes without saying that the very existence of a national system of protection is *conditio sine qua non* of the effectiveness of a universal or a regional system. Claims to international mechanisms can be presented after the exhaustion of all domestic remedies. Creation of national mechanisms is therefore an obligation of States formulated by international instruments. In recent years in many countries, national institutions such as ombudspersons, human rights commissions and, in some cases, even special human rights ministries have been established.

For the protection of human rights, for their defence and for the elimination of impunity of violators, the adoption of the principle of criminal responsibility for the crime of genocide, crimes against humanity or war crimes is of great importance. This new approach is reflected in the establishment of the International Criminal Tribunals for the Former Yugoslavia and for Rwanda and the adoption of the Rome Statute of the International Criminal Court (ICC) which entered into force on 1 July 2002. It will now act as a deterrent against massive violations of human rights making this a great step forward in the international protection of those rights. No doubt its effectiveness will depend on its universality and the support of all permanent members of the Security Council.

In the post-Cold War period the United Nations Security Council is increasingly taking action to deal with massive human rights violations by imposing sanctions foreseen by Chapter VII of the United Nations Charter. Although it advances the cause of human rights, sometimes it raises questions about the ultimate result of sanctions and, in particular, unilateral ones, which often victimize populations rather than the decision-makers responsible for wrongdoings.

A step which might strengthen protection is linked with the elaboration of a set of human rights indicators. They could provide treaty bodies with a means for measuring the progress in the implementation of human rights and a method for determining difficulties or problems encountered by States. Indicators could also help to reveal the extent to which certain rights are, or are not, enjoyed in practice and to provide a means to measure and compare the performance of individual countries.

The volume ends with reflections concerning the role of non-governmental organizations in the protection and enforcement of human rights. They are the essential part of the 'human rights movement' which, to a great extent, brought about the advancement of human rights and the reinforcement of their protection. Non-governmental organizations participate in the monitoring procedures, collect and disseminate information on human rights violations, mobilize international public opinion, condemn and exert pressure on human rights violators, and create human solidarity.

It is worth noting that, on 10 December 1998, the United Nations General Assembly adopted the Declaration on the Right and Responsibility of Individuals, Groups and Organs of Society to Promote and Protect Universally Recognized Human Rights and Fundamental Freedoms. The Declaration contains an enumeration of different legal guarantees if there is a human rights violation, the right for an effective remedy and protection, public hearings, independent judicial authorities and compensation. It states in Article 2: 'Each State has a responsibility and duty to protect, promote and implement all human rights and fundamental freedoms, *inter alia*, by adopting such steps as may be necessary to create all conditions necessary in social, economic, political and other fields.' In this context, we may also recall that the Universal Declaration of Human Rights, in its Article 28, proclaimed: 'Everyone is entitled to a social and international order in which the rights and freedoms set forth in the Declaration can be fully realized.'

This volume is presented to readers in the hope that it will be used not only as a source of information on the protection of human rights but also as a practical guide on how to use existing procedures for the defence of those rights.

The editor would like to express his warmest thanks to the authors – well-known specialists from different countries and regions – for their readiness to cooperate and update their contributions. The volume could not have been published without the support, professional help and fruitful collaboration, over many years, of Ashgate Publishing and UNESCO. From the long list of persons who in various ways contributed to the preparation of this volume, words of special gratitude should be directed to Pierre Sané, Assistant Director-General of the Sector of Social and Human Sciences, to Vladimir Volodin, Chief of the Human Rights and Development Section of the Division of Human Rights within the same sector and to Gillian Whitcomb, Chief of the Communication, Information and Publication Section of the sector. Deepest thanks are also expressed to Sheila Bennett for her devotion to the manual and her close cooperation in the preparation of all three volumes.

JANUSZ SYMONIDES

About the Contributors

Hugo Caminos Member of the International Tribunal for the Law of the Sea since October 1996. Professor Emeritus in the School of Law and Social Sciences, University of Buenos Aires. Ambassador of Argentina to Brazil (1981–1984). Under-Secretary for Legal Affairs and Legal Counsel, Organization of American States (1984–1994). Lecturer at The Hague Academy of International Law (1987 and 1998). Visiting Professor of International Law and Law of the Sea, University of Miami School of Law (1995–present). Member of the Institute of International Law. Author of numerous publications on public international law, the law of the sea, human rights and international organizations.

Daniel D.C. Don Nanjira Former Ambassador and Permanent Representative of Kenya to the United Nations. Representative of Kenya, *inter alia*, to the Food and Agriculture Organization of the United Nations, the International Fund for Agricultural Development, the World Food Programme, the World Food Council and various international organizations in Geneva, as well as the International Atomic Energy Agency and the United Nations Industrial Development Organization. Representative of the World Meteorological Organization to the United Nations and other United Nations system organizations in North America. Has been involved in human rights issues for many years and has published widely on the human rights situation in Africa.

Bahey el Din Hassan Director of the Cairo Institute for Human Rights (CIHRS). Author and editor of various books, articles and papers on human rights and democratic transformation in the Arab region, as well as on contextual challenges facing the human rights movement and education.

Klaus Hüfner Professor Emeritus of International Economics at the Freie Universität Berlin; since 1993 Honorary President of the World Federation of United Nations Associations (WFUNA). President of the German Commission for UNESCO (1998–2002). Member of several UNESCO Advisory Committees.

Zdzislaw Kedzia Leader, Policy Planning and Methodology Team in the Office of the United Nations High Commissioner for Human Rights in

Geneva. Rapporteur of the World Conference on Human Rights, Vienna, 1993. Author of numerous publications on human rights.

Michael Kirby   Justice of the High Court of Australia. Awarded the Australian Human Rights Medal in 1991. Former President of the International Commission of Jurists and the Special Representative of the United Nations Secretary-General for Human Rights in Cambodia. Member of the UNESCO International Bioethics Committee and member of the Australian National Commission for UNESCO. In 1998, awarded the UNESCO Prize for Human Rights Education.

Jean-Bernard Marie   Research Director at the Centre National de la Recherche Scientifique (CNRS, France). Former Secretary-General of the International Institute of Human Rights and former Director of the International Center for University Human Rights Teaching (CIEDHU), Strasbourg. Has organized training sessions on human rights in various regions of the world; has lectured in universities in several countries and teaches at the University of Strasbourg. Expert at the United Nations Sub-Regional Centre for Human Rights and Democracy in Central Africa, Yaoundé, Cameroon. Author of over 100 publications on human rights.

Karl Josef Partsch   Professor of International Law at the Universities of Kiel and Mainz and Professor Emeritus at the University of Bonn, died on 30 December 1996. As one of the most prominent German international lawyers, devoted a major part of his work to the cause of human rights, both in his many publications and in his practical activities. Member of the Committee on the Elimination of Racial Discrimination (1970–1990). Member of the German delegation to the Geneva Diplomatic Conference (1974–1977).

William A. Schabas   Holds the Chair in Human Rights Law at the National University of Ireland, Galway, Director of the Irish Centre for Human Rights. Author of *Genocide in International Law* (2000), *Introduction to the International Criminal Court* (2001) and *The Abolition of the Death Penalty in International Law* (2nd edn, 1997). Editor-in-Chief of the Criminal Law Forum.

Lee Swepston   Chief of the Equality and Employment Branch, and Human Rights Coordinator, in the International Labour Standards Department of the International Labour Organization which he joined in 1973. Took his legal degree at Columbia University in New York. Former Regional Adviser on International Labour Standards in English-speaking Africa and in the Caribbean. Has been responsible for the supervision of the ILO's standards concerning equality, indigenous and tribal peoples and employment policy issues, as well as coordination relations with other intergovernmental organizations on human rights questions. Author of a number of books and articles on international human rights, international labour standards, indigenous and tribal peoples, child labour and related subjects.

Janusz Symonides Professor of International Law at Warsaw University and Nicolaus Copernicus University, Torun. Director, UNESCO Division of Human Rights, Democracy and Peace (1989–2000). Director, Polish Institute of International Relations (1980–1987). Member of many editorial boards and scientific councils. Has lectured in many countries, including the Hague Academy of International Law (1988) and the International Institute of Human Rights, Strasbourg (1993). Author of over 500 articles and publications on human rights, international law and international relations.

Maxime Tardu Has taught international law of human rights, University of Grenoble and University Paris XIII. Former Head of Research Unit, United Nations Centre for Human Rights. During his career concerning human rights activities within the United Nations (1952–1986), worked on the preparation on numerous instruments including the Convention against Torture and Other Cruel, Inhuman or Degrading Treatment or Punishment (1984) and the Convention on the Rights of the Child (1989). Author of many publications on human rights.

Katarina Tomaševski Professor of International Law and International Relations, Faculty of Law, University of Lund, and the Raoul Wallenberg Institute of Human Rights and Humanitarian Law. United Nations Special Rapporteur on the Right to Education since 1998. Previously worked at the Danish Centre for Human Rights, Copenhagen, the McGill Centre for Medicine, Ethics and Law, Montreal, and the Institute for Social Research, Zagreb. Has also taken part in the Global Programme on AIDS of the World Health Organization. Author of more than 150 articles and a number of books.

Laurie S. Wiseberg Political scientist. Graduate of McGill University (BA), University of London (M.Sc.Econ) and University of California Los Angeles (PhD). Has taught at universities in the United Kingdom, the United States, Canada and Nigeria. Founder of the international NGO, Human Rights Internet (HRI). Has edited the quarterly *Human Rights Tribune* and the annual report, *For the Record: The United Nations Human Rights System*. NGO Liaison Officer in the Office of the High Commissioner for Human Rights for the World Conference Against Racism (Durban, 2001). Has written extensively on the role of non-governmental organizations in the protection and promotion of human rights.

PART I
THE UNITED NATIONS SYSTEM

1 United Nations Mechanisms to Promote and Protect Human Rights

ZDZISLAW KEDZIA*

INTRODUCTION

Lessons drawn from the Second World War, especially those concerning the inability of the pre-war international community to prevent the plans of those whose actions tragically affected millions of lives, led political, social, and intellectual leaders to the conclusion that an effective protection of human rights was indispensable if future generations were to be spared a similar experience. It was also recognized that to achieve this end, human rights standards should not remain simply 'law in books' – just a beautiful promise. The rule, already in place at the domestic level, that appropriate organs and procedures are necessary to make them 'law in action' was also accepted at the international level. The critically evaluated weakness of the League of Nations in this regard was fairly helpful in outlining the place of human rights in the United Nations system. Though varying political interests and visions as to the role of the international community in the field of human rights made it impossible to go further, the United Nations Conference on International Organization (San Francisco, USA, 1945) gave expression to the principle of the internationalization of human rights in the Charter of the United Nations.[1] The subsequent months and years showed the internal dynamics of human rights, embodying the dreams of people, and brought amazing progress not only in standard-setting but also in creating organs and procedures to protect these rights. While looking at the results achieved in building this machinery, a human rights student might indeed be astonished that, despite the Cold War, despite diverging political and economic interests and despite cultural differences, such an impressive international human rights framework has been developed.

3

About 30 human rights treaties, as well as 50 declarations and resolutions – the latter sometimes referred to as 'human rights soft law' – have been adopted. The opinion is widely held that the 'codification' of human rights has by and large been completed; this does not mean, of course, that, in some cases, further drafting of human rights norms is, or will no longer be, necessary. Since about 1976 (the year when the International Covenants on Human Rights entered into force), the international community has, however, attached primary importance to the implementation of these rights. Initially, emphasis was placed on international monitoring of the observance of, and *ex post* measures addressing, violations of human rights. At that time, particular importance was attached to the activities of intergovernmental bodies, in particular the Commission on Human Rights, and the system of reporting by states to the established bodies about the fulfilment of their human rights commitments. Later, the communications procedures protecting individuals claiming to be victims of human rights violations or addressing mass and gross human rights violations[2] gained increasing importance. At present, especially since the 1993 World Conference on Human Rights in Vienna, the previous approach to the protection of human rights has been supplemented by the emphasis placed on the prevention of human rights violations and a proactive attitude to their protection (human rights advocacy). At the 54th session of the Commission on Human Rights, commemorating the 50th anniversary of the Universal Declaration of Human Rights, the Secretary-General of the United Nations appealed to the international community to make the twenty-first century the age of prevention.[3] It is important to bear in mind this evolution in order to understand problems related to the effectiveness of international human rights mechanisms.

The consensus around human rights achieved at the 1993 World Conference in the post-Cold War spirit was reinforced by the United Nations Millennium Declaration in which all states declared to spare no effort to promote respect for all internationally recognized human rights and fundamental freedoms, including the right to development.[4] The Vienna Declaration and Programme of Action adopted by the 1993 Conference recognized the necessity for a continuing adaptation of the United Nations human rights machinery to the current and future needs with a view, in particular, to improving its coordination, efficiency and effectiveness.[5] This process launched at the General Assembly session in the same year by the the establishment of the post of the High Commissioner continues. The remarks below will refer to its essential elements.

Principles of the Machinery

The Vienna Declaration and Programme of Action reaffirms and/or develops the following principles which should guide the international human rights machinery:

- Human rights are universal. The Vienna Declaration and Programme of Action stresses that 'The universal nature of these rights and freedoms is beyond question' and continues 'While the significance of national and regional particularities and various historical, cultural and religious backgrounds must be borne in mind, it is the duty of States, regardless of their political, economic and cultural systems, to promote and protect all human rights and fundamental freedoms';[6]
- The promotion and protection of human rights constitute a legitimate concern of the international community;[7]
- Member states are obliged to develop international cooperation, including cooperation with the United Nations, to promote human rights;[8]
- All human rights are indivisible, interdependent and interrelated. The Vienna Declaration and Programme of Action calls on the international community to treat them 'globally in a fair and equal manner, on the same footing, and with the same emphasis'.[9] It also emphasizes that 'Democracy, development and respect for human rights and fundamental freedoms are interdependent and mutually reinforcing'.[10]

Looking at these principles as a whole, one can observe that they produce a consistent body, the components of which are logically interconnected. However, this harmony is fragile and sensitive to a preferential emphasis placed on one or another principle. The debates in the Third Committee of the General Assembly and in the Commission on Human Rights concerning the reform of the human rights machinery should be consulted to discover related problems. Some of them will be highlighted below.

HUMAN RIGHTS MACHINERY

The Main Structure of the Machinery

The human rights machinery may be perceived in a narrow and broad sense. First, this notion embraces organs and procedures dealing explicitly and directly with human rights in the framework of the United Nations. This category includes:

1 intergovernmental organs established on the basis of the Charter of the United Nations (policy-making organs): the General Assembly, the Security Council, the Economic and Social Council, and the Commission on Human Rights. The Commission on the Status of Women and the Commission on Crime Prevention and Criminal Justice also address human rights issues within their respective mandates;
2 bodies established by human rights treaties;
3 reporting, communications, and investigating procedures established by policy-making organs and treaty-based bodies;

4   the parts of the United Nations Secretariat responsible for human rights activities, especially the United Nations High Commissioner for Human Rights. The Division for the Advancement of Women and the Centre for International Crime Prevention have also human rights responsibilities. The Office of the High Commissioner for Human Rights and the Division for the Advancement of Women adopt joint work plans.

In the broad sense, the notion 'human rights machinery' also includes those organs and procedures which have been established within the United Nations specialized agencies and programmes and deal, *inter alia*, with human rights or with specific aspects of human rights. Such organs and procedures exist in the framework of the International Labour Organization, UNESCO, the United Nations High Commissioner for Refugees, UNICEF, the United Nations Development Programme, and the United Nations Congresses on the Prevention of Crime and Treatment of Offenders. In this context, the International Criminal Tribunal for the former Yugoslavia, the International Criminal Tribunal for Rwanda, and the International Criminal Court also need to be mentioned because of their competence to address the accountability of the perpetrators of human rights violations.

Policy-making Bodies

The General Assembly

While the General Assembly has an overall competence to deal with all the matters covered by the Charter of the United Nations,[11] human rights issues are subject primarily to debate in its Third Committee (Social, Humanitarian and Cultural Committee). Nevertheless, decisions taken by other main committees of the General Assembly may also have an impact on this area. For instance, the Fifth (Administrative and Budgetary) Committee, while adopting the budget of the Organization, decides about an important part of the financial framework of United Nations human rights activities.[12] The Sixth Committee participates in the standard-setting process. The auxiliary bodies of the General Assembly frequently deal with human rights, thus contributing to development in this area. For example, the International Law Commission participates in standard-setting, and special committees of the General Assembly dealt, or are dealing with, decolonization, apartheid, the situation in Namibia and the rights of the Palestinian People.

The General Assembly adopted the Universal Declaration of Human Rights, both International Covenants on Human Rights, all other United Nations human rights treaties and all the major declarations concerning this field which, before adoption, were subject to drafting within the United Nations system, including the Committees of the General Assembly themselves. Yet drafting international instruments does not exhaust the activities of the General Assembly in the field of human rights. It also makes the most important decisions in this area. Among others, the General Assembly has convened both World Conferences on Human Rights (Tehran, 1968 and Vienna, 1993), established the post of the High Commissioner for Human Rights (1993), proclaimed United Nations Decades, such as the Decade for Human Rights Education (1995–2004), the Decades for Action to Combat Racism and Racial Discrimination (1973–1983, 1983–1993, 1993–2003), and the International Decade of the Rights of Indigenous People (1994–2004).

Matters considered by the General Assembly may be categorized in the following groups:

1   substantive human rights issues;
2   'human rights situations' (this notion is used by the United Nations bodies to refer to situations of alleged human rights violations on a large scale);
3   draft conventions or declarations; and
4   organizational matters.

For example, the agenda of the Third Committee of the General Assembly at its 56th session in 2001, included under agenda item 12 the following issues:[13]

- implementation of human rights instruments
- human rights questions, including alternative approaches for improving the effective enjoyment of human rights and fundamental freedoms
- human rights situations and reports of Special Rapporteurs and representatives
- comprehensive implementation of and follow-up to the Vienna Declaration and Programme of Action
- report of the United Nations High Commissioner for Human Rights.

In addition, the following items of the General Assembly agenda were related to the United Nations human rights programme:

- promotion and protection of the rights of children (item 8)
- programme of activities of the International Decade of the World's Indigenous People (item 9)
- elimination of racism and racial discrimination (item 10)
- right of peoples to self-determination (item 11).

The resolutions of the General Assembly reflect not only the assessments of this body but also – most frequently – include recommendations for further action by the international community as a whole, and specifically by governments, components of the United Nations system, and non-governmental organizations and the wider civil society.

At its 56th session, the Third Committee of the General Assembly dealt with thematic issues in more than 50 resolutions. Country-specific human rights situations were subject to 11 resolutions in which the General Assembly articulated its position regarding the human rights problems in a given country and formulated recommendations for the respective governments. While the majority of the General Assembly resolutions are adopted by its Third Committee without a vote, country-specific resolutions in the majority of cases need a vote, since consensus is often impossible.

To handle its agenda, the Third Committee may create working groups which usually have an open-ended character. Such a working group was established after the World Conference on Human Rights (48th session) '… to discuss the ways and methods of implementation of the Vienna Declaration and Programme of Action'. The Group, *inter alia*, drafted the resolution concerning the establishment of a High Commissioner for Human Rights.

The Security Council

Article 24 of the Charter of the United Nations confers on the Security Council '… primary responsibility for the maintenance of international peace and security'. For many years, this crucial decision-making body refrained from specifically recognizing human rights as a determining factor in its considerations, noting their controversial nature in international relations. Human rights issues were usually referred to as humanitarian problems. The situation gradually changed in the 1990s. The human rights abuses have been recognized as one of the root causes of contemporary armed conflicts and, at the same time, the protection of human rights as one of essential elements of peace-making and peace-building. Tragedies of this period, such as those in Rwanda and in the Balkans with thousands of victims of the most serious violations of human rights, were not without influence on this process. Today, Security Council decisions frequently address human rights issues in the context of peace and security.[14] Peace accords supported by the Security Council contain references to human rights. It has become a rule that the Security Council, when establishing a peace operation includes a human rights component in it (see also the section, 'United Nations High Commissioner for Human Rights: from Headquarters to the Field'). Reports of the Secretary-General to the Security Council contain human rights related analysis and recommendations. The Security Council has also requested reports of the Office of the High Commissioner of Human Rights when human rights violations posed a threat to peace and security. On some occasions, the Security Council established missions to carry out inquiries into human rights violations (1992 Commission of Experts on the Former Yugoslavia and 1994 Commission of Experts on Rwanda).

Special arrangements (the so-called Arria formula for informal meetings) are used to invite human rights experts to address members of the Security Council. For example, the Special Rapporteur on the Human Rights Situation in the Democratic Republic of the Congo was invited several times to provide a briefing. It seems that the next step may be a more regular appearance of the High Commissioner before this body. So far, this has been rather exceptional, but such an exchange might enhance the input by the human rights mechanisms to the work of the Security Council.

The Economic and Social Council (ECOSOC)

Pursuant to Article 62, para. 2, of the Charter of the United Nations, the promotion and protection of human rights are among the main areas of the mandate of ECOSOC.[15] In this framework, ECOSOC makes '… recommendations for the purpose of promoting respect for, and observance of, human rights and fundamental freedoms for all', prepares draft conventions to be submitted to the General Assembly and convenes international conferences on subjects within its competence. ECOSOC's 2001 agenda[16] included the consideration of the reports of the following bodies: the Commission on Human Rights on its 57th session; the Human Rights Committee; the Committee on Economic, Social and Cultural Rights; and the United Nations High Commissioner for Human Rights.

ECOSOC is also the main United Nations coordinating organ in the economic and social field. For instance, at its session in 1998, within the framework of the so-called co-ordinating segment, it discussed the implementation of recommendations adopted by the 1993 World Conference on Human Rights by the United Nations agencies and programmes. The resolutions adopted by ECOSOC as a result of such debate are aimed to serve as a framework and guide for the work of the entire Organization.[17]

Under Article 68 of the Charter of the United Nations, ECOSOC has set up commissions in the economic and social fields. Two of them have been established to deal with matters falling in the area of human rights – namely, the Commission on Human Rights and the Commission on the Status of Women. They report to ECOSOC annually, prepare relevant draft decisions and recommendations, as well as draft conventions and declarations. Resolutions of the Commissions that have financial implications, need to be approved by ECOSOC before implementation. In addition to these two bodies, other functional Commissions of the ECOSOC are also relevant to the human rights area, in particular Commission on Crime Prevention and Criminal Justice, Commission on Sustainable Development, and Commission for Social Development. The Office of the High Commissioner for Human Rights is developing cooperation with ECOSOC regional economic commissions.

ECOSOC made an important contribution to the development of procedures for dealing with human rights matters in the Commission on Human Rights and the Commission on the Status of Women. For instance, subsequent ECOSOC resolutions have marked the history of the communications procedures, which provide the framework for how the Commission on Human Rights deals with alleged human rights violations.

ECOSOC also decides about the consultative status that selected non-governmental organizations can enjoy under ECOSOC resolution 1996/31. This is relevant in the discussed context because of the fundamental contribution that these organizations make to the work of the UN human rights mechanisms (see the last section).

The Commission on Human Rights

Status and composition   The Commission on Human Rights was created in 1946[18] with the initial task of preparing the draft of the International Bill of Rights. It is most probable that, at that time, only a few expected the dynamism and spectacular turns in the development of this body in subsequent years. Although the Commission continues to occupy the same place within the United Nations system as an auxiliary body to ECOSOC, its actual role and position have become substantially more important. What began as a rather quiet, small body of experts representing various countries is today almost as big as ECOSOC itself. Initially composed of 18 Member States, the Commission has gradually increased its membership to 53. Its profile has developed to one of a fully intergovernmental body, which gives the Commission an important standing in international relations, although it also has its political costs. It could also be expected that sooner rather than later, the Commission will come across the issue of its status. Its link to the Charter of the United Nations is evident, since Article 68 of the Charter provides for setting up a commission for the promotion of human rights as a subsidiary body of ECOSOC. However, for some time already, some commentators have been raising the question whether, in the context of the advancement of human rights on the international and domestic agenda, the Commission's position within the United Nations system should not be more important. It is striking that the international human rights parliament in which the Commission has grown up during the last five decades, occupies a rather modest place within that system.

The composition of the Commission is based on the principle of regional balance. In view of geographical distribution, the seats in the Commission are currently distributed as shown in Table 1.1.

Table 1.1   **Distribution of seats in the Commission on Human Rights**

African Group	Asia Group	Eastern European Group	Latin and Caribbean Group	Western European and Other Groups
15	12	5	11	10

This allocation results from decisions adopted in 1990[19] when the membership was increased by ten seats. At that time, a better representation of the numerous African countries, which had become independent in the framework of the decolonialization process, was pursued. This arrangement also served the strengthening of the representation of developing countries in general. One has to note in this context, however, that changes in the composition of the Eastern European Group – the emergence of several new countries in the 1990s – have so far had no impact on the geographic distribution of seats in the Commission.

Mandate and methods of work   The Commission's mandate ranges from participation in standard-setting, monitoring and shaping the implementation of human rights through technical cooperation to '… any other matter concerning human rights'. The Commission submits proposals, recommendations and reports to ECOSOC, helping it coordinate United Nations activities in the field of human rights.[20] Looking at the Commission's legacy, one can see the merit of the observation made by the High Commissioner for Human Rights that: 'the Commission on Human Rights has been the central architect of the work of the United Nations in the field of human rights.'[21]

The work of the Commission is basically framed by the Rules of Procedure of the Functional Commissions of the Economic and Social Council.[22] During the 1990s, the Commission on Human Rights made considerable efforts to reform its organization and methods of work. The World Conference on Human Rights forcibly stressed the need for 'a continuing adaptation of the United Nations human rights machinery to the current and future needs'.[23] In this context, the Conference also specifically referred to the elements of the Commission system, including the Sub-Commission and special procedures (see below). Responding to this call, the Commission launched its reforms, including the establishment of a special Working Group, already at its 50th session (1994), but failed to produce tangible results because of differences among the members. Nevertheless, these initial attempts generated a certain dynamic for the process and helped it move ahead with a largely successful reform that was launched by the statement of the Chairperson of the Commission's 55th session, Ambassador Selebi from South Africa, on 28 April 1999. By virtue of this statement, a Working Group on Enhancing the Effectiveness of the Mechanisms of the Commission on Human Rights was established, and it presented its report to the Commission at its 56th session. The Commission, chaired at that time by Ambassador Anderson from Ireland, approved the proposals contained in this report by its decision 2000/109, 'Enhancing the effectiveness of the mechanisms of the Commission on Human Rights'.[24] The reform encompassed the work of the Commission itself, the Sub-Commission and the system of special procedures. The unanimous support for it was based on some important conceptual considerations referred to in the report of the Working Group, in particular that:

- none of the component parts of the United Nations human rights machinery function in isolation from each other;
- preference should be given to the maintenance of approaches which are perceived to be more democratic and representative than alternatives;

- a balance between the benefits of continuity and the benefits of renewal should be sought;
- a balance should be struck between civil and political rights and
  economic, social and cultural rights – the equal importance of both
  sets of rights should find a broad reflection in the United Nations
  human rights machinery.

The Commission holds its annual six-week long sessions between mid-March
and the end of April.[25] They are attended by governmental delegations of up
to 50 members. Even if this number is exceptional, the size of delegations has
indeed increased since the role, tasks and organization of the Commission's
work demand it. The agenda of a regular session of the Commission usually
remains basically unchanged for long periods, which is understandable since,
in a way, it reflects a balance of interests and preferences. After the 1993
World Conference on Human Rights, attempts to 'rationalize' the agenda
remained central to various proposals targeting the reform of the Commission. Being, to a certain extent, a product of a spontaneous process over the
years, the agenda was criticized for being too long, leading to an overloaded
debate and frequent night sessions. Eventually, the Commission's new agenda
was introduced at its 55th session. The aforementioned Working Group recommended[26] that the question of agenda reform should be kept under review,
regarding *inter alia*, further re-clustering of its items.

The agenda of the Commission on Human Rights at its 58th session could
be divided as follows:

1   organization of work, including election of officers and adoption of the
    agenda;[27]
2   the work of the United Nations human rights organs and bodies, includ-
    ing the promotion of human rights;[28]
3   thematic human rights issues;[29] and
4   country-specific human rights situations.

To ensure more time for in-depth debate on different issues, attempts continue to biannualize some of the agenda items.

Since the late 1990s, the Commission on Human Rights has dedicated one
meeting for a Special Dialogue on a so-called annual theme chosen by the
Chairperson in consultation with the Bureau. Decision 2000/109 endorsed
this practice and recommended that the selection of the annual theme should
take into consideration the one decided on by the General Assembly for its
activities. The subjects of the Special Dialogues were 'Tolerance and Respect' at the 57th session, 'Poverty and the Enjoyment of Human Rights' at
the 56th session and 'Rights of the Child' at the 55th session. Unfortunately,
members of the Commission could not agree on the theme for the Special
Dialogue at its 58th session. Hopefully, this will remain an exception and
not become a precedent.[30]

At its 58th session, the Commission was faced with constraints resulting
from some rather surprising budgetary cuts. Evening and night sessions

were almost entirely suppressed and the time at the disposal of the Commission was thus reduced to 70 per cent of that available during the previous session of the Commission in 2001. It was eventually possible to complete work on the agenda but at the expense of the time granted to different categories of speakers. As a consequence, it was stressed by many speakers, including the Chairperson and the High Commissioner, that steps were necessary to ensure appropriate presentation by holders of special procedures of their findings and to provide a timeframe for their dialogue with the Commission. Equally strong was the emphasis placed on guaranteeing time for the participation in the debate of non-governmental organizations commensurate with their role in the promotion and protection of human rights.

At each session the Commission elects its Chairperson, three Vice-Chairpersons, and a Rapporteur who form the Bureau and who, together with the coordinators of regional groups, constitute its Expanded Bureau. While electing the Chairperson, the Commission follows the principle of regional rotation. It should be noted that the Bureau of the Commission plays a far more important role than in the past, when its activities were limited to the duration of the Commission's session and to a meeting, following its closure, convened to discuss observations about the organization of the work and to carry out consultations on such other matters as, for example, the appointment of Special Rapporteurs. As of the 56th session, the Bureau has developed into a permanent organ, holding meetings throughout the year. This change coincided with the Bureau's involvement in the Commission's reform – a process of a largely inter-sessional character. It was also, however, a response to those voices which asserted that, in view of the increasing role of human rights in international relations, a certain continuation of the Commission's work is necessary between sessions. At its 58th session, the Commission decided to elect the Bureau before the session at a special meeting held on the third Monday in January.[31] This will enable the Bureau of the next session to lead in the preparation of the substantive agenda.

In the framework of the recent reform of the Commission's work, a decision was taken to convene the Commission in September for a one-day informal meeting to facilitate the exchange of information just before the session of the General Assembly. This decision was guided by the fact that the agenda of, and attendance in, the Commission and the Third Committee of the General Assembly overlap significantly; this merits an enhanced preparation to the General Assembly in the framework of the Commission. These informal meetings do not have a formal outcome. Their programme of work combines issues on the agenda of the Commission's previous session and those placed on the provisional agenda of the Third Committee. Both members and observers highly appreciate these meetings that have also become a bridging element between the Commission's regular sessions.

Resolutions and decisions   To conclude the discussion on thematic issues or country-specific situations, the Commission usually adopts a resolution.

Sometimes, mainly in organizational matters, it takes a decision. A statement by the Chairperson always presents the consensus position of the Commission (see Table 1.2).

Table 1.2   Resolutions, decisions and Chairperson's statements

Session	Number of resolutions	Number of decisions	Number of statements by the Chairperson
58th	92	18	3
57th	82	19	3
56th	87	13	4

From among all the resolutions and decisions adopted at its 58th session, 71 (almost 60 per cent) were adopted without a vote and 39 were voted on. A request from a Commission member is necessary for a vote. An analysis of voting results provides students with analytical material for mapping current human rights controversies and identifying borderlines. It is also an important source of information for both diplomatic relations and campaigns by non-governmental organizations at the international and national levels.

The coordination of consultations on the text of a resolution is usually in the hands of the delegation or group of delegations, which initiated the item. To propose a resolution, a State delegation does not need to be a member of the Commission. However, for formal submission, a draft resolution must be sponsored by at least one member of the Commission. The mode of consultation on resolutions has an important impact on the Commission's democratic nature. The large number of consultations taking place in parallel to the Commission's meeting often makes the participation of smaller delegations, in particular, very difficult. Not surprisingly, voices highlighting the need for transparency and appropriate organization of the consultation process are vociferous from this corner. This is indeed a major problem for the Commission's collective, participatory work. Some organizational steps, including the announcement of the time and location of consultations, the early launching of consultations, as well as making the Commission's documentation, particularly the relevant reports, available well in advance before a given item is on the agenda, are examples of this type of corrective measures, recommended by decision 2000/19. It was agreed, among other things, that the intention to bring a thematic resolution to the attention of the Commission should be announced in advance of the session. In the case of resolutions addressing the human rights situation in a country, the delegation of that country should be informed no later than during the first week of the session.

Standard-setting   From its very establishment, the Commission on Human Rights has been the main United Nations body drafting international human rights standards and related procedural norms. Whether it is a draft human rights treaty or a draft declaration, the product of the Commission is forwarded through ECOSOC to the General Assembly for final adoption. In the opinion of the Working Group on Enhancing the Effectiveness of the Mechanisms of the Commission on Human Rights, '… standard-setting will continue to be one of the central functions of the Commission on Human Rights'. Unsurprisingly, the Working Group dedicated much attention to this issue and recommended the following rules, adopted subsequently by the Commission on Human Rights:

1 proposals concerning standard-setting should be forwarded to the Sub-Commission on the Promotion and Protection of Human Rights with the request to undertake a comprehensive analysis of the instrument envisaged and to prepare a draft text;
2 in order to pursue the objectives of the working group drafting an instrument, its Chairperson should be entitled to enter into informal contacts and consultations between meetings of the group;
3 the Commission should consider a specific timeframe (in principle not exceeding five years) for the completion of the work of a working group drafting an instrument.

The Commission also decided to consider the extension of the mandate of a working group, if necessary. Alternatively, the Commission could decide to provide a period of reflection (one to two years) that could be used by the Chairperson for further consultations or to examine the working methods applied by the working groups concerned.

Making the standard-setting process more effective and, in particular, shorter would be a major contribution to the promotion and protection of human rights and to the position of the Commission in general. It may be recalled that in the cases of both the 1992 Declaration on the Rights of Persons Belonging to National or Ethnic, Religious and Linguistic Minorities and the 1998 Declaration on the Right and Responsibility of Individuals, Groups and Organs of Society to Promote and Protect Universally Recognized Human Rights and Fundamental Freedoms, commonly known as the Declaration on Human Rights Defenders, it took 13 years for the respective working groups to complete the drafting process. This observation should not, however, prompt any conclusions which would question the respectable achievements of the international community in human rights standard-setting during the last 50 years.

Country situations   If a human rights situation in a country is on the Commission's agenda, or a member or group of members is expected to propose that the Commission take action on a country situation, the delegation of the country concerned may, in fact, take one of the following positions:

1   join the consultations and subsequently agree or disagree with the nego-
    tiated position of the Commission;
2   refuse to participate in the consultation process which does not exclude
    its public statements;
3   object to the consideration of the human rights situation in its country
    through a formal 'no action motion', which must be voted immediately.

A consensus position of the Commission can be articulated in a statement
of the Chairperson that replaces a resolution. Since it is a negotiated text
between interested delegations and the delegation of the country concerned
and expresses the consensus position of the whole Commission, the Chairperson's statement is perceived as a softer step vis-à-vis a country's human
rights situation than a resolution even though for the same reasons, it can
have greater impact on future developments than a resolution which may
be stronger in its language but rejected by the government concerned. This
dilemma is not unusual for the Commission's members.

    It goes without saying that the agenda items related to country situations
are the most spectacular moments of the session, drawing the attention of
the delegations, non-governmental organizations and the media. Nor is it
surprising that governments are ready to develop campaigns at different
levels to avoid this sort of public scrutiny over their human rights record. It
is widely said that the debates on country situations are highly politicized,
but it is nevertheless the Commission's responsibility to react impartially to
serious human rights violations. The High Commissioner for Human Rights,
in her closing address to the Commission on 26 April 2002 stressed:

> I am particularly worried about a possible trend seeking to weaken the role of
> protection that this Commission has been exercising. One could see this in the
> voting on country situations, where there has been, at this session, a preference
> for an approach excluding action if consensus was not possible. The core role of
> the Commission in protecting human rights through drawing attention to viola-
> tions and abuses must be retained. But it is clear that, in the future, it needs to be
> matched by a much more significant commitment to provide resources for tech-
> nical co-operation and advisory services to assist countries in building and
> strengthening their national capacity in the rule of law, the administration of
> justice, and adherence to human rights norms and standards. Criticism will then
> be perceived as constructive and forward-looking, not finger-pointing in a judg-
> mental way.[32]

Controversies around the human rights situations in specific countries often make it indispensable to vote on the respective resolutions. Unfortunately,
it also happens that governments refuse to recognize a resolution addressing them. Such an attitude of the government does not deprive, however,
the resolution of its applicability. Reports requested are prepared and other
steps undertaken. What sometimes takes place is a refusal by the government concerned to cooperate with a Special Rapporteur established for the
country or to follow on other steps recommended by the Commission.
Characteristically, however, governments usually, sooner or later, are inclined

to cooperate, even if initially opposed. The authority of the Commission and the attitude of the public informed about the process are important factors in this regard.

Reaction to emergencies   In 1990, in reaction to the Commission's sessional mode of working and also to the need to equip this central human rights body with the opportunity to promptly react to large scale human rights emergencies, ECOSOC created the possibility of convening the Commission for special sessions.[33] Since then, the Commission has been convened five times for such sessions: twice in 1992 regarding the situation of human rights in the territories of the former Yugoslavia; in 1994 regarding the situation of human rights in Rwanda; in 1999 regarding the situation in East Timor; and in 2000 regarding the situation of the human rights of the Palestinian people. Special sessions are convened if a request, which can be submitted by a member (or members) of the Commission, is endorsed by a minimum of half of its members. All requests for a special session have so far been successful. At a special session, the Commission exclusively debates the situation which provided the rationale for its convening. The Commission may adopt resolutions expressing its views and determining further measures to address the situation. Examples of such measures are: the nomination of a Special Rapporteur for the situation under discussion (former Yugoslavia, Rwanda); the establishment of a commission of inquiry into alleged human rights violations (East Timor, the Middle East); and the request to the Secretary-General or High Commissioner for Human Rights to report on the situation to the Commission and the General Assembly.

The Commission's system   In carrying out its mandate, the Commission benefits from the input by its bodies and procedures that have now developed into quite a sophisticated system. ECOSOC empowered the Commission on Human Rights to establish two Sub-Commissions: the Sub-Commission on Freedom of Information and of the Press and the Sub-Commission on the Prevention of Discrimination and Protection of Minorities. The Commission elected both Sub-Commissions at its 1st session in 1947. The mandate of the first expired in 1952.

The Commission on Human Rights may also establish working groups which meet inter-sessionally. The objective of such working groups is to draft human rights treaties or declarations concerning human rights standards, to analyse substantive issues or deal with organizational matters. At present, the following working groups support the Commission: the Working Group on the Right to Development; the Working Group on Guidelines on Structural Adjustment Programmes and on Economic, Social and Cultural Rights; the Working Group on a draft United Nations Declaration on the Rights of Indigenous Peoples; and the Working Group on Situations established under item 9(b) to examine human rights situations referred to the Commission by the Working Group on Communications.[34] If the matter under consideration permits, which is most frequently the case, these working groups have an open-ended character, which means that all those who participate in the work of the Commission are entitled to take part in their work in accordance with the same principles. Only the meetings of the Working Group on Situations are open exclusively to the members. The working groups drafting human rights instruments usually meet once a year for two weeks. An essential tool of the Commission on Human Rights constitutes its special mechanisms established to monitor the implementation of specific human rights standards (see 'Non-conventional procedures' below). They include, among others, two Working Groups: on Arbitrary Detention and on Enforced or Involuntary Disappearances.

Assessment   Any assessment of the Commission on Human Rights must recognize its centrality within the United Nations human rights organs and bodies. The High Commissioner pointed out that the Commission 'has a history of solid achievement in both defining the content of international human rights norms and in their promotion and protection ... The effective functioning of the Commission is a legitimate concern for all of its participants, and more importantly for all those who rely on it'.[35]

The Commission has provided the institutional framework for drafting most of the human rights treaties and international declarations developing human rights standards, including the Universal Declaration of Human Rights and the International Covenants on Human Rights. Human rights treaties and declarations, hammered out since 1948, produce not only an impressive picture but are, indeed, the fundamental tool in the hands of the international community. The Commission has elaborated major strategies and procedures for the promotion and protection of human rights. Debates in the Commission have contributed to the broadening of the United Nations' agenda concerning human rights. Finally, it has been the Commission that has responded to major human rights violations in different regions of the world and has provided a platform for victims and their advocates to address the international community. However, it is not only its substantial output that proves the importance of the Commission; one can also see its importance in such indicators as the increasing number of high-ranking representatives of Member States and important world personalities who come to the Commission as guest speakers.[36] Many representatives of international and regional organizations, and a remarkable number of actively participating non-governmental organizations,[37] also give evidence of the role played by this organ. The reform of the Commission in the follow-up to the World Conference on Human Rights (see above) proves that the Commission can mobilize its potential to reflect on its own work.

Anyone who follows the developments in the Commission on Human Rights is also aware of the problems that affect this organ. As an intergovernmental body, it is sensitive to the political processes that influence the environment in which it addresses human rights problems. Otherwise it would be difficult to explain why, even with regard to questions which already seem to be resolved, tensions return and sometimes dominate the debate. Hence, from different corners one can hear calls for a depolitization of the human rights area, close cooperation between states and the

Commission on Human Rights, and a comprehensive understanding of the principle that the promotion and protection of human rights constitute a legitimate concern of the international community as stressed by the World Conference on Human Rights. It is noteworthy that the Secretary-General recognized it purposeful to make a strong statement on the role of the Commission in his report to the 57th session of the General Assembly:

> The Commission on Human Rights is a vital part of the Organization, with a glorious history ... People all over the world look to it for protection of their rights and for help to win for themselves the better standards of life in larger freedom referred to in the Preamble to the Charter. I strongly urge Member States to keep in mind the true purpose of the Commission, and to seek ways of making it more effective. They must realize that, if they allow elections and debates to be dictated by political considerations, or by block positions, rather than by genuine efforts to strengthen human rights throughout the world, the credibility and usefulness of the Commission will inevitably be eroded.[38]

The Sub-Commission on the Promotion and Protection of Human Rights

Mandate and composition   This Sub-Commission, formerly known as the Sub-Commission on Prevention of Discrimination and Protection of Minorities, was created in 1947 as a relatively small body of 12 members who were '... to undertake studies, particularly in the light of the Universal Declaration of Human Rights, and to make recommendations to the Commission on Human Rights concerning the prevention of discrimination of any kind relating to human rights and fundamental freedoms and the protection of racial, national, religious and linguistic minorities'. It was also expected to perform other functions entrusted to it by ECOSOC and the Commission on Human Rights.[39] While the formal description of the main functions of the Sub-Commission has remained the same, its composition, agenda and overall profile have evolved significantly over the years. The Sub-Commission now has 26 members who have the same number of alternates and who are elected for a period of four years based on the principle of an equitable geographical representation.[40] At present, seven experts come from Africa, five from Asia, five from Latin America and the Caribbean, three from Eastern Europe and six from Western European and other states.

Evolution and reform   The legacy of the Sub-Commission is widely respected. It includes numerous drafts, studies, and proposals submitted to the Commission on Human Rights for further action. The findings and ideas elaborated by the Sub-Commission have frequently stimulated not only the Commission to take action, but also other parts of the United Nations human rights programme. The Sub-Commission's contribution to the drafting of all the most important human rights standards is unquestionable. Finally, it has developed into an important component of the international monitoring of the implementation of human rights, especially within the '1503 procedure'.

In the course of time, however, the Sub-Commission has been exposed to quite strong criticism for departing from its original mandate and profile. It has been pointed out that its discussions increasingly involve political components. The large participation of government's representatives, United Nations organs and bodies, and non-governmental organizations has complicated the preservation of the expert nature of this body, making its sessions similar to those of the Commission. Its growing workload has also caused concern, since analysis and studies expected from an expert body require more time for reflection and evaluations than that available. It was in this context that, in the framework of the recent reform of the Commission on Human Rights, the Working Group on Enhancing the Effectiveness of its Mechanisms reviewed extensively the work of the Sub-Commission and formulated several fundamental recommendations that have now been largely implemented.[41] While recognizing the contribution of the Sub-Commission to the human rights work of the United Nations, the Working Group stressed the need for clarification and adjustment of its mandate. Taking into consideration that the Sub-Commission agenda had already included many elements which go well beyond the initial tasks of the prevention of discrimination and protection of minorities, the Working Group recommended renaming this body to the Sub-Commission on the Promotion and Protection of Human Rights.

Studying the documents of the Working Group one gets the impression that two main considerations guided the reform of the Sub-Commission. First, the Working Group endeavoured to reinstall the Sub-Commission as an indubitably auxiliary body of the Commission, while avoiding overlapping of agendas and methods of work of both organs. Second, the Group was guided by a rather common criticism of the Sub-Commission for having lost much of its independency, and thus credibility and influence, as result of its increasingly political profile. Reform proposals therefore sought the reinforcement of the Sub-Commission's independence as an expert body.[42]

The Working Group called upon the Commission on Human Rights to strengthen its role in setting priorities for the work of the Sub-Commission and to ensure that duplication with work of other competent bodies and mechanisms was avoided. The Sub-Commission should concentrate on studies, research and providing expert advice requested by the Commission. Research and studies carried out by the Sub-Commission on its own initiative should comprise a modest fraction of its workload. It can debate only those country situations which are not dealt with by the Commission. It can also address serious violations of human rights in any country if they are of an urgent nature. However, such debates cannot be concluded by country-specific resolutions and can only be reflected in the summary records. The Working Group stressed that, while considering this question, it was aware that '… resolutions on country situations risk duplication with the work of the Commission and creating a perception of politicization of independent experts'.[43] Furthermore, the Sub-Commission was recommended not to adopt thematic resolutions, which contain references to specific countries. Finally, its involvement in the communication procedure ('1503') has been substantially limited (see below).

The reform of the Sub-Commission envisages that this body will continue to play an important role in standard-setting. Before establishing a working group to draft a new human rights instrument, the Commission on Human Rights should '... where the necessary groundwork has not otherwise been undertaken, consider requesting the Sub-Commission to undertake a study on the question at hand and to prepare a draft text which should include a comprehensive analysis, with substantive comments'.[44]

Although it was recognized by the Working Group that the membership should be as small as possible, it was decided to maintain the present number of members (26) with a view to ensuring the effectiveness of this body and the appropriate representation of different regions and legal systems. In view of the existing electoral practice, it was not surprising that the Working Group linked the issue of elections with the question of the independence of this organ. The fact that candidates to the Sub-Commission had sometimes been designated from among high-ranking officials of governments, including ambassadors, was widely criticized. The Working Group also observed that the election of the members through the Commission was more transparent and democratic than the appointment of candidates. However, it refrained from indicating which categories of employment should be perceived as incompatible with membership in the Sub-Commission, recognizing this issue to be too complex. The Working Group only emphasized that '... persons putting their candidacies forward for membership, and governments in electing the membership, should be conscious of the strong concern to ensure that the body is independent and is seen to be so'. One can only agree with the Working Group's conclusion that 'Members of the Sub-Commission should maintain the highest integrity and impartiality and avoid acts which would affect confidence in their independence'.[45]

Organization of work   The organization of work is based on 'Guidelines for the application by the Sub-Commission on the Promotion and Protection of Human Rights of the rules of procedure of the functional commissions of the Economic and Social Council and other decisions and practices relating thereto'.[46] The annual sessions are convened, at present, for three weeks in August (previously four weeks). They are attended by observers from states, United Nations agencies and programmes and other intergovernmental and non-governmental organizations in consultative status with ECOSOC. The agenda of the 53rd session (2001), which was the result of the reform of the Sub-Commission, nevertheless remained very, or even too, lengthy. It addressed numerous substantive items under the following general headings:

1   the question of the violation of human rights and fundamental freedoms;
2   the administration of justice;
3   economic, social and cultural rights;

4   the prevention of discrimination; and
5   other human rights issues.

The Sub-Commission placed 51 specific themes under these headings.

To illustrate the work of the Sub-Commission, one should also refer to the studies and analysis on its agenda. In 2001 the following six studies entrusted to its Special Rapporteurs were ongoing:

- globalization and its impact on the full enjoyment of all human rights
- the concept and practice of affirmative action
- the rights of non-citizens
- traditional practices affecting the health of women and the girl child
- terrorism and human rights
- human rights and human responsibilities.

The Sub-Commission also completed a study on 'Indigenous peoples and their relationship to land' and recommended to the Commission on Human Rights a study on 'Promotion of the realization of the right to drinking water and sanitation'. In addition, the preparation of 16 working papers was entrusted to members of the Sub-Commission.

The work of the Sub-Commission is supported by its working groups. At present, the pre-sessional working groups include: the Working Group on Contemporary Forms of Slavery (established in 1974),[47] the Working Group on Indigenous Populations (established in 1982),[48] and the Working Group on the Rights of Persons belonging to National or Ethnic, Religious and Linguistic Minorities (established in 1995). A sessional working group deals with the administration of justice, another one with the working methods and activities of transnational corporations, and still another one with communications, which addresses a consistent pattern of gross and reliably attested violations of human rights within its terms of reference (see below).

Assessment   Looking at the recent changes in the work of the Sub-Commission, it appears that they have brought this organ much closer to its initial mandate as a body of independent experts constituting a think tank within the system of the Commission on Human Rights. Free from political constraints resulting from the representation of governmental standpoints, the Sub-Commission can play a very important role as a forum for analytical work, as well as in assisting the Commission in standard-setting and in efforts aimed at the full implementation of international human rights standards.

The Commission on the Status of Women

The Commission on the Status of Women was established in 1946 with the same status as the other functional commissions of ECOSOC.[49] The initial number of 15 members has been gradually increased to 45.[50] Commission members are elected for a term of four years and represent member states. The Commission's composition is based on the principle of equitable geographical distribution. In 1989, ECOSOC took the decision to replace the biannual cycle of the Commission's sessions by annual sessions.

The Commission's mandate includes the preparation of recommendations and reports to ECOSOC on the promotion of women's rights in the political, economic, civil, social and educational fields. In 1987, ECOSOC decided to specify further this mandate by including the promotion of the objectives of equality, development and peace, the monitoring of the implementation of measures aimed at the advancement of women, and the evaluation of the progress made at the international, regional and domestic levels in this regard.[51] Consideration of confidential and non-confidential communications concerning violations of the status of women[52] also constitutes a part of the Commission's mandate. In the follow-up to the 1995 Fourth World Conference on Women in Beijing, China, the Commission integrated into its work programme the implementation of the Platform for Action adopted by the Conference.

At its 45th session in 2001, two main themes headed the Commission's agenda:

- women, the girl child and human immuno-deficiency virus/acquired immuno-deficiency syndrome (HIV/AIDS)
- gender discrimination and all other forms of discrimination, in particular racism, racial discrimination, xenophobia and related intolerance.

The Commission is the main forum within the United Nations system, which elaborates and implements programmes concerning the human rights and equal status of women. Its sessions are attended not only by governments, but also by representatives of United Nations agencies and programmes, regional organizations and non-governmental organizations. The Commission adopts its own resolutions and drafts to be considered by ECOSOC. It is also a catalyst for the coordination of efforts made by various organizations to develop the protection of women and facilitate their advancement.[53]

United Nations High Commissioner for Human Rights

The genesis of the institution

During the preparatory process to the World Conference on Human Rights between 1991 and 1993, in the convenient political climate of the end of the Cold War, Amnesty International re-introduced the idea of a High Commissioner for Human Rights.[54] However, it soon turned out that doubts and fears accompanying the concept of the new institution from the moment it was first proposed in 1948 had not disappeared, and the debate appeared again to be highly controversial. Nevertheless the World Conference managed to recommend '... to the General Assembly that, when examining the report of the Conference at its 48th session, it begin, as a matter of priority, consideration of the question of the establishment of a High Commissioner for Human Rights for the promotion and protection of all human rights'.[55] In early October 1993, the Third Committee of the General Assembly established an open-ended Working Group '... to discuss the ways and methods of implementation of the Vienna Declaration and Programme of Action'. In fact, the Working Group concentrated at that time on the recommendation concerning the High Commissioner. After a long and controversial debate, the participating delegations finally reached consensus shortly before the end of the autumn part of the 48th session. The General Assembly created the post of the High Commissioner for Human Rights on 20 December 1993, by resolution 48/141.[56] The seat of the High Commissioner is located in Geneva. By giving consensus support to the creation of this new institution, the international community has empowered it with a strong moral and political legitimation.

The first United Nations High Commissioner for Human Rights, José Ayala Lasso (Ecuador) took up his duties in Geneva on 5 April 1994. The second High Commissioner, Mary Robinson began her tenure on 12 September 1997. Sergio Vieira de Mello (Brazil) became the third High Commissioner on 12 September 2002.

The status of the High Commissioner

The High Commissioner is appointed by the United Nations Secretary-General, subject to approval by the General Assembly. This procedure gives the mandate-holder high authority in contacts with governments, as well as United Nations organs and bodies. During the appointment process, due regard should be given to geographical rotation. The High Commissioner is expected '... to be a person of high moral standing and personal integrity and shall possess expertise, including in the field of human rights, and the general knowledge and understanding of diverse cultures necessary for impartial, objective, non-selective and effective performance of the duties [...]'.[57] The term of office is four years and the incumbent may be re-appointed once only.

In accordance with resolution 48/141, the High Commissioner '... shall function within the framework of the Charter of the United Nations, the Universal Declaration of Human Rights, other international instruments of human rights and international law, including the obligations, within this framework, to respect the sovereignty, territorial integrity and domestic jurisdiction of states to promote the universal respect for and observance of all human rights, in recognizing that, in the framework of the purposes and principles of the Charter, the promotion and protection of all human rights is a legitimate concern of the international community'.

The High Commissioner enjoys the rank of an Under-Secretary General of the United Nations. The function of '... the United Nations official with principal responsibility for United Nations human rights activities ...' places him/her at the centre of the United Nations human rights programme in general, not only within the Secretariat of the Organization itself. In the implementation of the mandate, the High Commissioner acts '... under the direction and authority of the Secretary-General' and '... within the framework of the overall competence, authority and decisions of the General Assembly, the Economic and Social Council and the Commission on Human Rights ...' In other words, the competence of the High Commissioner may not go beyond the competencies of these organs. The General Assembly, the ECOSOC and the Commission on Human Rights can also address their recommendations to the High Commissioner.

The High Commissioner's close association with the main United Nations organs relevant to human rights is also reflected in the competence to make recommendations to the '... competent bodies of the United Nations system in the field of human rights ... with a view to improving the promotion and protection of all human rights'.[58] In this way, the High Commissioner has been equipped with a strong practical instrument for the implementation of his/her mandate. In practice, the incumbents regularly address the General Assembly, ECOSOC, the Commission on Human Rights and other human rights organs and bodies to share their views and present proposals for action.

The responsibilities of the High Commissioner

Resolution 48/141 provides for the High Commissioner's specific responsibilities[59] which may be categorized as follows:

- *Promotion and protection of human rights*:
  - promoting and protecting the effective enjoyment by all of all civil, cultural, economic, political and social rights;
  - promoting and protecting the realization of the right to development;
  - enhancing international cooperation for the promotion and protection of all human rights;
  - providing advisory services and technical and financial assistance with a view to supporting actions and programmes in the field of human rights.
- *Reaction to situations challenging human rights*:
  - playing an active role in removing the current obstacles and in meeting the challenges to the full realization of all human rights and in preventing the continuation of human rights violations throughout the world;
  - engaging in a dialogue with all governments with a view to securing respect for all human rights.
- *Co-ordination and adaptation to the existing needs of the United Nations system of human rights protection*:
  - co-ordinating activities for the promotion and protection of human rights throughout the United Nations system;

- co-ordinating relevant United Nations education and public information programmes in the field of human rights;
- strengthening the United Nations machinery in the field of human rights with a view to improving its efficiency and effectiveness.

The High Commissioner should take action, on his/her own initiative, to promote or protect human rights, wherever and whenever required. He/she is also obliged to carry out the tasks assigned by the competent bodies of the United Nations in the field of human rights,[60] including the United Nations Secretary-General, the General Assembly, ECOSOC and the Commission on Human Rights. However, the mode of action, whether public or confidential, whether including an on-the-spot mission, the establishment of a monitoring system or the offering of good offices, lies within the discretion of the High Commissioner.

The High Commissioner should '... report annually on his/her activities, in accordance with his/her mandate, to the Commission on Human Rights and through the Economic and Social Council, to the General Assembly'.[61] These reports are a useful source of information about the High Commissioner's activities and his/her views concerning crucial human rights issues.[62] In addition to annual reports, the High Commissioner submits, at the request of the Commission on Human Rights or the General Assembly or on his/her own initiative, reports on specific human rights issues or country human rights situations. These reports are prepared on the basis of information received from governments, various parts of the United Nations system, regional and international organizations and non-governmental organizations and collected by his/her Office. They can be of a factual or analytical nature. Sometimes, a visit by the High Commissioner or a representative or a fact-finding mission precedes the report. This increasing reporting activity coincides with reports of the Secretary-General to the various bodies which exclusively, or partially, cover human rights issues which are thematic or country related.

In some cases, the High Commissioner is requested, '... to keep Member States informed' of the human rights developments in a country. In such situations, it is for the High Commissioner to choose the form of providing relevant information; it may be oral information or a part of a written general report, or a written specific report. In view of the recently developed permanent system of work of the Bureau of the Commission and the newly introduced informal meetings of the Commission in September, the High Commissioner also uses these opportunities to keep the Commission informed.

The Office of the High Commissioner (OHCHR) provides support to the High Commissioner and the United Nations human rights programme in general. Its responsibilities are determined by both the High Commissioner's mandate and the tasks of the former United Nations Centre for Human Rights that had assisted human rights bodies and mechanisms until 1997 before it was integrated into the OHCHR.

The usual mutual influence between a programme and its secretariat is particularly strong in case of the OHCHR and the United Nations human rights programme. This is understandable in view of the wide programmatic mandate of the High Commissioner and his/her central position within the programme. The outline of the main trends in the evolution of the UN human rights programme below takes the indicated linkage as a point of departure.

From standard-setting to standard-implementation   The value of human rights is largely tested by their implementation. Now that the main body of international human rights law has been established, the attention of the international community has shifted towards the impact of its standards on real life. It is inside the follow-up to the 1993 World Conference on Human Rights that the implementation efforts are more equally addressing all human rights. The United Nations human rights machinery embraces an increasing number of mechanisms serving economic, social and cultural rights. The agenda of the Commission on Human Rights today reflects, to a much larger extent, the balance between various categories of rights. The Office of the High Commissioner for Human Rights also strongly advocates this approach in its activities. Among the more recent projects, that related to the human rights aspects of poverty reduction programmes, which has led to the elaboration of draft guidelines, provides an example.

The indicated shift of attention does not mean that standard-setting belongs to the past only. Needs in this regard exist and will continue to exist. Among new instruments currently under discussion, the Optional Protocol to the International Covenant on Economic, Social and Cultural Rights, the Convention on Human Rights of Disabled Persons, a draft legally binding normative instrument for the protection of all persons from enforced disappearance, and the Declaration on the Rights of Indigenous Peoples can be mentioned.

From a reactive approach to prevention of human rights violations   The United Nations human rights programme was initially conceived, in addition to standard-setting and the promotion of human rights, as a mechanism to report on developments in the field of human rights and follow-on recommendations of policy-making bodies. The present emphasis on prevention means a doctrinal shift, which is guided by the recognition that compensation to victims always comes somewhat too late. In the context of conflict prevention, the Secretary-General called for the United Nations to move 'from a culture of reaction to a culture of prevention' and formulated ten principles for a future approach, which *mutatis mutandis* may also be applied to the area of human rights.[63] Measures undertaken by the United Nations, which may have a deterrent impact on human rights violations include *inter alia*: 'urgent appeals' by special procedures (see below); requests by treaty bodies for emergency reports; the urgent discussion of situations in bodies such as the Committee on the Elimination of Racial Discrimination; the urgent dispatch of personal envoys of the Secretary-

General, the High Commissioner for Human Rights, or of other organizations; the dispatch of human rights and humanitarian observers or fact-finders; the establishment of international courts; and proposals for the establishment of a rapid reaction force.[64] The OHCHR, as well as special procedures of the Commission on Human Rights, treaty-based bodies and other parts of the human rights machinery, monitor situations involving a high human rights risk factor, contribute to early warning mechanisms of the United Nations, as well as provide expert advice regarding measures aimed at the resolution of human rights problems.

It has also been widely recognized that combating impunity is essential for the prevention of human rights violations. The United Nations human rights programme has carried out several inquiries into such breaches of international law. For example, under the mandate of the Commission on Human Rights, the Joint Investigative Mission of Special Procedures for the DRC was established in 1997, the International Commission of Inquiry on East Timor in 1999, and the Human Rights Inquiry Commission pursuant to resolution on violations of the human rights of the Palestinian people by Isreal in 2001. In 1997, the Secretary-General established an Investigative Team for the DRC and in 2002 sent a forensic mission to Afghanistan. The General Assembly decided to establish a UN Investigation Team for Afghanistan in 1998. In 1999, the High Commissioner carried out an inquiry into human rights violations in the former republic of Yugoslavia, Kosovo. Finally, the government concerned can also ask for an inquiry, as was the case in 2000, when the International Commission of Inquiry was established for Togo. In almost all such situations, the OHCHR provides secretariat support.

From service to advocacy   The establishment of the mandate of the High Commissioner opened new opportunities to the United Nations Secretariat in the area of human rights. A substantial part of this mandate is human rights advocacy – needless to say, a particularly complicated challenge in a multiple diversified world. Although the very notion of 'advocacy' does not appear in resolution 141, several provisions of this document determine the High Commissioner's responsibilities in this regard. In particular, two of them need to be mentioned here – namely those which establish the responsibility of the High Commissioner to play 'an active role in removing the current obstacles and in meeting the challenges to the full realization of all human rights and in preventing the continuation of human rights violations throughout the world ...'[65] and to engage 'in a dialogue with all Governments in the implementation of his/her mandate with a view to securing respect for all human rights'.[66]

Advocacy means an active advancement and defence of human rights in all countries, following the principle that 'nobody is perfect'. Advocacy also consists in supporting those who work for human rights, including organs and bodies of the United Nations, non-governmental organizations and other partners, which entails facilitating dialogue between governments and the United Nations human rights machinery, in particular special procedures and treaty bodies.

The High Commissioner's dialogue for human rights may take different forms. While on missions, the High Commissioner always addresses human rights problems encountered in the visited country. This could include structural problems, for example, gender discrimination, the existence of penalties unacceptable from the human rights points of view, access to education, or interventions on behalf of, for example, human rights defenders or those imprisoned for their political views. On some occasions, the High Commissioner appoints a personal envoy to undertake missions to facilitate the achievement of human rights goals. This happened, for example, with a view to addressing the situation of persons deprived of liberty in the context of the Kosovo crisis. While performing his/her advocacy function, the High Commissioner also refers to the public at large through statements, press releases and interviews.

From formal scrutiny to technical cooperation   One of the major changes in the human rights programme has resulted from the recognition that reviewing and commenting on country human rights records, though vital, is not enough. Without national capacities to promote and protect human rights, comments and advice coming from the human rights bodies may remain ineffective. The United Nations human rights programme is, therefore, increasingly involved in assistance to countries to develop national infrastructures for human rights.

The United Nations Voluntary Fund for Technical Cooperation in the field of human rights, established in 1987, is annually funding projects in approximately 35 countries, which include a variety of activities, ranging from constitutional and legislative reform assistance to training for relevant professional groups, such as the administration of justice, police and prison officials. Support for national human rights institutions established in accordance with the Paris Principles[67] is one of its central sub-programmes. To cope with the increasing demand, OHCHR cooperates with UNDP, UNICEF, UNESCO and other organisations.

From Headquarters to the field   One of the most striking changes the United Nations human rights programme launched in the 1990s was with its operationalization. Twenty-six human rights field presences have been deployed around the world, from Cambodia to Colombia, from the Great Lakes of Africa to the Balkans and Mongolia. At the beginning of this process, the impartial, independent and objective monitoring of the human rights situation on the ground, in direct contact with victims, witnesses and authorities, was seen as the particular contribution of field presences. Over time, this function has usually been combined with technical assistance, as, for example, in Colombia, Cambodia, and Abkhazia/Georgia.

More recently, however, new important developments have taken place. First, following the review of peace operations at the request of the Secretary-General,[68] human rights components have become an integral part of peace operations established by the Security Council. OHCHR provides substantive and, to some extent, organizational support to them (for example, in Sierra Leone, Angola, DRC). Second, United Nations country teams are getting increasingly involved in human rights work. Here the OHCHR plays the role of the substantive resource unit. And, finally, the OHCHR is building up a network of its regional/subregional advisors who must cooperate with regional organizations, United Nations agencies and programmes, governments and civil society.

From isolation to an integrated approach and partnerships   Initially, human rights was perceived as a specialized area with few links to other major United Nations activities. The end of the Cold War and the 1993 World Conference on Human Rights gave an important impetus to further advancing human rights on the United Nations agenda. The aforementioned Secretary-General's 'United Nations: Programme of Change' integrated human rights into the programme of all the most important management structures of the United Nations. The High Commissioner for Human Rights is present in all four Executive Committees: Peace and Security, Social Affairs, Development, and Humanitarian Affairs. Examples of programmatic changes are provided by the documents issued by developmental organizations, for example, the UNDP and the World Bank.[69] This structural process, sometimes called 'mainstreaming human rights', is supported by OHCHR, which develops links with partners within and outside the United Nations. Particularly important is that an understanding emerges among OHCHR partners that integrating human rights into their programmes does not mean just adding new tasks to their existing workload, but rather may help them to carry out their mandates more effectively since human rights standards provide an internationally agreed set of criteria for the orientation and assessment of their work.

Treaty Monitoring Bodies

General

Ratification of human rights treaties   The implementation of the six core human rights treaties is monitored by special bodies established for that purpose. These are:

- the Committee on Economic, Social and Cultural Rights (CESCR) for the 1966 International Covenant on Economic, Social and Cultural Rights (ICESCR);
- the Human Rights Committee (HRC) for the 1966 International Covenant on Civil and Political Rights (ICCPR);
- the Committee on the Elimination of All Forms of Racial Discrimination (CERD) for the 1965 International Convention on the Elimination of All Forms of Racial Discrimination (ICERD);
- the Committee on the Elimination of All Forms of Discrimination against Women (CEDAW) for the 1979 International Convention on

the Elimination of All Forms of Discrimination against Women (ICEDAW);
- the Committee against Torture (CAT) for the 1984 International Convention against Torture and Other Cruel, Inhuman or Degrading Treatment and Punishment (ICAT);
- the Committee on the Rights of the Child (CRC) for the 1989 International Convention on the Rights of the Child (ICRC).

The real position and the impact of the treaty-based bodies are basically determined by the level of ratification of the treaties. As of 8 February 2002, the overall number of ratifications of the six core conventions reached 941 (see Table 1.3):

Table 1.3   The status of ratifications of human rights treaties

ICESCR	ICCPR	CERD	CEDAW	CAT	CRC
145	148	161	168	128	191

The independent expert on enhancing the long-term effectiveness of the United Nations human rights treaty system, Philip Alston, named by the Commission on Human Rights,[70] recommended the following with a view to improving the ratification process:

1 consultation with the leading international agencies to explore their potential involvement in a ratification campaign;
2 appointment of special advisers on ratification and reporting, and the setting aside of funds for those purposes; and
3 examination of special measures to streamline the reporting process for states with small populations.[71]

On the occasion of the 50th anniversary of the Universal Declaration of Human Rights, the Secretary-General and the High Commissioner called on all governments for the universal ratification of the six core human rights treaties by the year 2003. A call for universal ratification of human rights treaties was also included in the documents of the Millennium Summit of September 2000.[72]

Mandate   The establishment of the treaty monitoring bodies, composed of independent experts elected by State Parties and not acting as government agents, was a breakthrough in the approach to the control mechanisms in the field of human rights at the international level. The implementation of fundamental rights and freedoms has been put under the scrutiny and guidance of independent bodies which not only monitor how governments comply with their obligations deriving from the ratified human rights treaties, but also contribute to the interpretation of the relevant standards, advise on their implementation and assist in the protection of victims of human rights violations. This has been achieved through mandating treaty bodies to:

1   examine the obligatory periodical reports delivered by governments;[73]
2   develop jurisprudence through the adoption of General Comments (see below); and
3   consider communications concerning alleged human rights violations (with exceptions referred to below).

The mandate of treaty bodies is also determined by the fact that they have adopted a comprehensive approach in the interpretation of the states' treaty obligations. The jurisprudence indicates that under the treaties, States Parties have the obligation to respect, fulfil and protect human rights. This means that treaty bodies do not exclusively examine whether the reporting government has interfered with the rights protected by a given treaty, but also review other action to which the State Party is obliged under the treaty.

The treaty bodies report annually about their activities to the General Assembly. In the case of the Committee against Torture, the relevant Convention also mentions States Parties in this context. The Committee on Economic, Social and Cultural Rights reports to ECOSOC which forwards the report to the General Assembly, and the Committee on the Rights of the Child reports every two years to the General Assembly. The concluding observations made by treaty bodies while considering States Parties' reports, together with possible comments thereon made by States Parties, constitute parts of the annual reports.

Composition   The membership of the treaty bodies has a great impact on their standing and work. Members are elected for four years and can be re-elected. To ensure their unbiased and multifaceted approach, the requirements of equitable geographical distribution of membership, of the representation of the different forms of civilization, and of the principal legal systems, are taken into account during the election process. Another principle states that one nationality can be represented by only one member in a given treaty body. Unfortunately, as stressed on various occasions, the composition of the treaty bodies does not always reflect a geographical and gender balance and, in this context, proposals are sometimes made to introduce quotas, for example, for different regions.[74]

The fact that States Parties often make an effort to elect outstanding specialists to sit on the treaty bodies, and the independent behaviour of experts, are basic premises on which these bodies may build their prestige and authority. Almost 100 experts – members of the Committees – constitute a unique resource group of expertise for the United Nations human rights programme and the wider human rights community.

Organization of work   The treaty bodies work in sessions which take place two or three times a year for two or three weeks. Meetings of the treaty bodies are accessible to the public with the exception of those which deal with communications about human rights violations, and the parts of the proceedings that the rules of procedure, or the chairperson, recognize as private.[75] There is a general rule that the concluding debate on a State Party report is also held in private. The only exception here is the Committee on the Elimination of Racial Discrimination (see below). In order to prepare the meetings and give the participants, particularly reporting states, the necessary time before the debate, the treaty bodies establish pre-sessional working groups convened in advance. In addition to the preparation of the review of the state reports (adoption of list of issues – see the section, 'Reports to the treaty bodies', below), such working groups may also focus on other aspects of the preparation of the session of the Committee as, for example, the allocation of time, the response to supplementary reports containing additional information, and draft General Comments.[76]

Some treaty bodies have decided to dedicate one or more of their meetings to a general discussion on an issue of particular importance to their area of competence. In the case of the Committee on Economic, Social and Cultural Rights, such a discussion takes place at each session, usually on the Monday of the third week. As the Committee itself explains: 'The purpose is twofold: the day assists the Committee in developing in greater depth its understanding of the relevant issues; and it enables the Committee to encourage inputs into its work from all interested parties.' The Committee selected the following issues for its general discussions: the right to adequate food; the right to housing; economic and social indicators; the right to take part in cultural life; the rights of the ageing and elderly; the right to health; the role of social safety nets; human rights education and public information activities relating to the Covenant; the interpretation and practical application of the obligations incumbent on States Parties; a draft Optional Protocol to the Covenant; the revision of the general guidelines for reporting; the normative content of the right to food; globalization and its impact on the enjoyment of economic, social and cultural rights; the right to education; and, recently, the right of everyone to benefit from the protection of the moral and material interests resulting from any scientific, literary or artistic production of which he/she is the author.[77] The Committee on the Rights of the Child held, both in September 2000 and September 2001, a two-day general discussion on 'Violence against children'. The meeting, which was attended by a large circle of participants, including experts, representatives of governments, intergovernmental and non-governmental organizations, produced an important set of observations and recommendations calling for action at the international and national levels.[78]

General Comments   The treaty bodies are empowered to make General Comments as considered appropriate. In practice, such comments deal with fundamental human rights issues, both in the form of the Committee's views on the content of human rights standards or an evaluation of typical manifestations of state or international practice relevant to the implementation of these standards. In their General Comments, the Committees are inclined to take a comprehensive approach reflecting different aspects of the subject. Considerations concerning the content of the right in question are usually placed in a broad comparative normative framework involving both universal and regional regulations and jurisprudence. The General Comments indicate the consequences of violations of a given right and determine vulnerable groups; they are explicit in interpreting obligations resulting from the treaty for states and other relevant actors; and formulate clear recommendations.[79] Although General Comments adopted by one treaty body are not binding on other human rights organs and bodies, with regard to either the interpretation or implementation of standards, they constitute an important point of reference and, in fact, influence the perception of the binding human rights law and the assessment of its application. The majority of the treaty bodies take advantage of such opportunities quite often (see Table 1.4) and, today, it would be difficult to interpret the standards contained in human rights treaties without placing them within the background of General Comments.[80]

Table 1.4   **Number of General Comments by treaty-based bodies**

CESCR	HRC	CAT	CERD*	CRC	CEDAW*
14	29	1	27	1	24

* CERD and CEDAW adopt 'General Recommendations'.

Dialogue with partners   While executing their monitoring functions, the treaty bodies are guided by the principle of cooperation with states. The dialogue is helpful for both a better understanding of problems encountered in the process of implementation of human rights standards and providing adequate advice on how to resolve them. For example, the Committee on Economic, Social and Cultural Rights emphasized that the reporting obligations are designed to assist States Parties in fulfilling their obligations under the Covenant, enable monitoring States Parties' compliance with these obligations, and facilitate the realization of economic, social and cultural rights in accordance with the provisions of the Covenant. Although the treaty bodies consequently draw the attention of the governments concerned to deficiencies in their human rights record, they refrain from public campaigns in specific cases. To strengthen their impact, however, some treaty bodies have adopted follow-up procedures allowing them to watch the implementation of their recommendations.[81]

United Nations agencies within their own mandates have also become an important partner of the treaty bodies. Many instances illustrate this observation. The Human Rights Committee reports, for example, on its collaboration with the United Nations Development Programme, in the context of the Memorandum of Understanding signed by the latter and OHCHR. On the one hand, the Committee notes that UNDP draws guidance from the Committee's conclusions addressing State Party reports while developing its technical assistance programmes. On the other hand, the Committee benefits from the UNDP input while drawing up lists of issues on State Party reports.[82] CERD decided already in 1972 to develop cooperation with the International Labour Organization (ILO) and the UNESCO and invited both organizations to attend its sessions.[83] The ILO Committee of Experts on the Application of Conventions and Recommendations makes its reports submitted to the International Labour Conference available to the members of the Committee. UNHCR submits comments to the members of the Committee on reports of States Parties if this organization is active in the country concerned.[84] Annual reports of treaty bodies and reports from annual meetings of chairpersons of these bodies provide other instances of this practice.

One can also observe an increasing involvement of civil society in the work of treaty bodies, in particular of non-governmental organizations (NGOs). Generally speaking, NGOs are an important source of information for members of the Committees. National NGOs are sometimes involved in the preparation of governmental reports. In some cases, the Committees receive separate reports from NGOs, parallel to state reports. Equally important is the fact, however, that the dialogue between governments and the Committees may stimulate an internal dialogue in countries based on international human rights standards and jurisprudence of the treaty bodies. The importance of NGOs in the work of the Committees has been reflected in rules of procedure adopted by these bodies. The Committee on Economic, Social and Cultural Rights was the most precise body in this regard by establishing criteria to be met by information provided by NGOs, according to which such information should: '(a) focus specifically on the provisions of the International Covenant on Economic, Social and Cultural Rights; (b) be of direct relevance to matters under consideration by the Committee; (c) be reliable; (d) not be abusive.' The Committee also decided to make available any written information formally submitted to it by individuals or NGOs in relation to a State Party report as soon as possible to the representative of the state concerned.[85]

Conditions of work   For a long time, the treaty bodies have been facing serious problems concerning how to cope with their growing workload. The very limited time spent by the treaty bodies on sessions, the rapidly growing number of reports and individual communications to be considered and, in addition, the very limited resources available to support the treaty-bodies system have led to long delays in different procedures. The consequences may, of course, be serious; that is a diminishing impact of the treaty bodies and the treaty system in general. In response to this situation, the High Commissioner for Human Rights has taken steps to strengthen the support of the United Nations Secretariat for the treaty bodies through the following Plans of Action:

- for Strengthening the Implementation of the International Covenant on Civil and Political Rights, the International Convention on the Elimination of All Forms of Racial Discrimination and the Convention against Torture and Other Cruel, Inhuman or Degrading Treatment or Punishment
- for Strengthening the Implementation of the International Covenant on Economic, Social and Cultural Rights
- for Strengthening the Implementation of the Convention on the Rights of the Child.

The Plans' central objectives are: '(a) to reduce the time lapse between the submission of reports by States Parties and their consideration by the respective Committees; (b) to reduce the backlog in complaints under the Human Rights Committee; and (c) to improve the follow-up to treaty body recommendations and observations by States Parties.' The Plans have permitted, *inter alia*, the deployment of additional staff to service the treaty bodies, an increase in the analytical capacity of these bodies, the development of a database and other information technology facilities, and even the holding of additional meetings of some bodies.[86] In addition, the High Commissioner has also established a 'Petition Team'. However, the barrier to such attempts is finance. The very modest resources allocated to treaty bodies from the United Nations regular budget make it necessary to rely on voluntary funding. In turn, this does not guarantee a sufficient stability of the established capacities. According to a widely shared opinion, the Plans of Action should, therefore, be seen as temporary measures which should be replaced by an increase in funding from the United Nations regular budget.

The need for reforms   In his recent report, the Secretary-General stated that

> The existing treaty bodies and human rights mechanisms and procedures constitute a large and intricate network. The growing complexity of the human rights machinery and the corresponding burden of reporting obligations strain the resources of Member States and the Secretariat. As a result, the benefits of the current system are not always clear.[87]

The problems faced by the treaty bodies have recently been the subject of comprehensive studies.[88] Various proposals have been made to make the treaty monitoring system more effective and less burdensome. Some of them appear to be rather radical, as, for example, the possibility of merging all the treaty bodies into one single Committee with overall competence, or the establishing of a human rights court to consider cases of human rights violations and, thus, eliminating the communication procedures from the agenda of the treaty bodies and reducing their workloads. Other proposals envisage consolidating state reports to different treaty bodies into one overarching report, reducing the scope of requested information, and better coordinating the periodicity of reports.[89]

Substantial reforms would however, require, involvement and approval by States Parties. One can expect such a process to be long and complicated, given the highly differentiated levels of ratifications and subsequently com-position of State Parties to specific treaties. These differences, as long as they exist, would rather speak in favour of self-contained implementation mechanisms for each of the treaties. Bearing this in mind, the aforemen-tioned independent expert called for changes in the relevant procedural provisions of the human rights treaties to make them more susceptible to amendment.[90]

Cooperation between treaty bodies   Despite differences in their mandates and methods of work, all treaty bodies manifest significant similarities. Already in 1988, the meetings of the Chairpersons initiated closer cooperation be-tween the treaty bodies. At the beginning biannual, since 1995 the meetings have been convened annually by the Secretary-General. To illustrate the profile of the meetings – the 13th meeting, held from 18 to 22 June 2001,[91] addressed such issues as: support for the work of the treaty bodies; coop-eration between them and the Sub-Commission for the Promotion and Protection of Human Rights; various aspects of reform of the treaty body system; and the implementation of treaty body recommendations at the national level. The meeting also provided a framework for one-day consul-tations with representatives of governments. This informal dialogue was appreciated by both sides. For the Chairpersons, it was an opportunity to draw the attention of governments to the problems encountered by the treaty bodies; for governments, it was an important source of information and an occasion to present their concerns to the treaty bodies. The Chair-persons also met holders of the mandates of the special mechanisms of the Commission on Human Rights to discuss cooperation and to exchange experiences. This meeting recommended, *inter alia,* enhanced exchange of non-confidential information as well as mutual briefing on activities (in-cluding studies and country visits), cooperation in disseminating the expertise accumulated in the jurisprudence and other work of the treaty bodies and of mandate-holders of special procedures. The Chairpersons met the expanded Bureau of the Commission and representatives of the Sub-Commission to discuss cooperation with these bodies. They also re-ceived visits from representatives of the United Nations agencies and programmes and from NGOs.

The meetings of Chairpersons increasingly play the role of a *sui generis* coordinating forum for the treaty bodies.[92] It seems, however, that the mem-bers of these bodies still feel the need for closer contacts. The Chairpersons endorsed the idea of inter-Committee meetings to develop common ap-proaches to specific issues important to all the bodies and held the first such meeting in 2002 to address methods of work and reservations to the human rights treaties.[93]

Individual treaty bodies

Committee on Economic, Social and Cultural Rights   The Committee on Economic, Social and Cultural Rights monitors the implementation of the International Covenant on Economic, Social and Cultural Rights. It is the only treaty-monitoring body which was not established by the respective treaty. The General Assembly, while adopting the Covenant decided that periodical reports on its implementation by States Parties would be considered by ECOSOC. In 1976, ECOSOC established a working group to assist it in considering the reports which, since 1981, was called the 'Sessional Working Group of Governmental Experts on the Implementation of the International Covenant on Economic, Social and Cultural Rights'. In 1985, this group was replaced by the Committee on Economic, Social and Cultural Rights which is similar in character to the treaty-based bodies but anchored in an ECOSOC resolution. The 18 members of the Committee are elected by ECOSOC, not by the States Parties to the Covenant. They meet twice a year for three-week sessions in Geneva. This annual cycle was extended in 2000 and 2001 to a third extraordinary session (see below).

The mandate of the Committee embraces:

1   monitoring the implementation of the Covenant by States Parties through the consideration of their periodic reports and advising them on the means needed to ensure full compliance with the standards laid down in the Covenant; and
2   the adoption of General Comments concerning the implementation of the Covenant.

In light of the ongoing theoretical and political disputes concerning the legal meaning of various standards laid down in this Covenant, the role of the Committee in the determination of their specific content and, thus, the treaty obligations, has gained particular importance.

The Committee thus often issues General Comments not only to articulate its opinion on various aspects of the implementation of the Covenant, but also to explore the content of the standards laid down therein. In 1999, the Committee adopted an Outline for Drafting General Comments on specific rights of the International Covenant on Economic, Social and Cultural Rights,[94] according to which such comments should include the following sections:

1   introduction (general context);
2   normative contents of the right;
3   the obligations of the State Party;
4   obligations of other relevant actors, such as other States Parties, ECOSOC, other United Nations organs, the relevant specialized agencies, and civil society;
5   violations; and
6   recommendations to States Parties.

In its General Comments, the Committee on Economic, Social and Cultural Rights up to November 2002 has addressed 15 issues.[95] At present, the Committee is working on three further General Comments: on Article 3 – equal rights of men and women; Article 15, para. 1(a) – the right to take part in cultural life; and on Article 15, para. 1(c) of the Covenant – intellectual property.

The controversies concerning the nature of economic, social and cultural rights have so far hindered the establishment of the procedure of individual communications and the Committee is not entitled to consider individual cases of alleged human rights violations. The World Conference on Human Rights encouraged '... the Commission on Human Rights, in cooperation with the Committee on Economic, Social and Cultural Rights, to continue the examination of optional protocols to the International Covenant on Economic, Social and Cultural Rights'.[96] However, despite advanced projects elaborated within the academic community and a thorough analysis of a draft by the Committee,[97] the Commission on Human Rights has not yet been able to begin formal drafting of the Optional Protocol. At its 57th session, the Commission decided to appoint an independent expert to examine this question. His mandate was renewed at the 58th session and the Commission asked him to report to its next session on the following issues:

1   the nature and scope of the obligations of States Parties under the Covenant;
2   conceptual issues regarding the justiciability of economic, social and cultural rights;
3   the benefits and the practicability of a complaints mechanism under the Covenant and the complementarity between different mechanisms.

At its 58th session, the Commission also decided to establish an open-ended working group of the Commission with a view to considering options regarding the elaboration of an optional protocol to the International Covenant on Economic, Social and Cultural Rights.[98]

An important role is played by the Committee in international dialogue on economic, social and cultural rights. Examples are provided by the general discussion on intellectual property and human rights, organized together with the World Intellectual Property Organization in November 2000, and a consultation on human rights and trade and development with the participation of relevant United Nations agencies and programmes, other international organizations, national human rights institutions, and NGOs in May 2001. The Committee is developing dialogue with the World Bank and the International Monetary Fund, for example, regarding poverty reduction strategies. Its comments were submitted to the Convention drafting the European Charter of Fundamental Rights in Nice, adopted on 7 December 2000 by the European Union.[99] These examples demonstrate that the Committee applies a broad interpretation of its mandate while looking for different methods to enhance the implementation of the Covenant.

The Committee's constant policy is to encourage the participation of NGOs in its activities. They provide the Committee with valuable information on the one hand and, on the other, give publicity to its findings at the country level. In May 1993, the Committee adopted rules[100] by which NGOs are invited to provide written information relevant to its work any time. At the beginning of each session of the pre-sessional Working Group discussing preparations to review country reports, NGOs may submit relevant oral information. Finally, during the first afternoon of each session, the Committee offers an opportunity to NGOs to make oral presentations; those that wish to benefit from this arrangement have to inform the Committee in advance.

The Committee has undertaken measures to strengthen the impact of its work. Its Rules of Procedure allow it to examine compliance with treaty obligations in the absence of reports from the governments concerned. During 2000–2001, this happened twice. The present follow-up procedure to the Committee's concluding observations was established in 2000.[101] The Committee may request a State Party to provide information in its next periodic report (or at an earlier date) about steps taken to implement the recommendations contained in the concluding observations. Such information is considered at the next meeting of the Committee's pre-sessional Working Group, which may recommend additional concluding observations in response to that information; or that further information be sought; or that the chairperson inform the State Party that the Committee will take up the issue at its next session. When the Committee considers that it has not received relevant information, it may request the State Party concerned to accept a mission consisting of one or two members of the Committee. Such a decision is of an exceptional nature and is taken only if the Committee concludes that no adequate alternative approach is available. The purpose of an on-site visit is: '(a) to collect the information necessary for the Committee to continue its constructive dialogue with the State Party and to enable it to carry out its functions in relation to the Covenant; (b) to provide a more comprehensive basis upon which the Committee might exercise its functions in relation to Articles 22 and 23 of the Covenant concerning technical assistance and advisory services'. The Committee's mission may gather information from all available sources and should analyse whether it should recommend to the State Party making the technical cooperation programme of the OHCHR available in this connection. If the State Party does not accept the proposed mission, the Committee may address related recommendations to ECOSOC. The Committee has applied the follow-up procedure in relation to two States Parties and has found it very useful.

To address problems arising from the growing workload, the Committee took the initiative of holding extraordinary sessions in August 2000 and August 2001. These sessions were financed from voluntary contributions under the aforementioned Plan of Action and helped to reduce the average delay in examining reports after submission by half, that is to between 12 and 18 months instead of the previous delay of 30 to 36 months. To address further this issue, the Committee has recently considered the possibility of reducing the number of meetings dedicated to initial reports to three and, in the case of periodic reports, to two. In this way, the Committee hopes that it will be in the position to address six instead five reports per session. Finally, the Committee also decided to apply a flexible approach to the rigid five-year interval for periodic reports.

Human Rights Committee   The Human Rights Committee was established in 1976 under the International Covenant on Civil and Political Rights. Its 18 members are elected by the States Parties and meet three times a year in Geneva for three-week sessions. Its mandate is laid down both in the Covenant itself and in the first Optional Protocol to the Covenant. It includes:

1   examination of periodical reports submitted by the States Parties on the measures adopted to give effect to the rights recognized by the Covenant and on the progress made in their enjoyment;
2   adoption of General Comments concerning the implementation of the Covenant;
3   consideration of state and individual communications concerning alleged violations of the commitments of the States Parties under the Covenant.

General Comments adopted by the Human Rights Committee are not only instrumental in the implementation of this Covenant, but also provide an essential input to the development of the concept of human rights in general. On average, the Committee has adopted more than one General Comment annually which is a considerable achievement during 26 years.[102]

The International Covenant on Civil and Political Rights is the only treaty which does not determine the periodicity of State Party reports, leaving decisions in this regard with the treaty body itself. In accordance with the new consolidated guidelines on States Parties' reports, the initial report should be prepared on an article-by-article basis. Subsequent periodic reports should focus primarily on issues raised in the Committee's concluding observations on the previous report.[103] In addition, the State Party can be requested to inform the Committee within a specified period on measures taken to implement the Committee's concluding observations. Such information is analysed by a group of Committee members who, accordingly, may propose to the Committee a definitive time limit for the submission of the next report.[104]

In situations where a State Party has failed to provide any report despite reminders received, the Committee may inform the government concerned that on a date or at a session duly specified, it intends '... to examine in a private session the measures taken by the State Party to give effect to the rights recognized in the Covenant, and to proceed by adopting provisional concluding observations which will be submitted to the State Party'.[105] The Committee can also examine a report submitted by a State Party if the representative of the latter did not attend a scheduled meeting on two or more successive occasions.[106]

To improve the follow-up to the adopted views in the framework of the communication procedures, the Committee designates a Special Rapporteur who monitors the measures taken by states and make recommendations for further action by the Committee. The Committee gives information about follow-up activities in its annual report.[107]

The Committee resorts to the establishment of working groups to address issues requiring particular attention.[108] Two regular working groups which meet before each of the Committee's sessions deal with communications under the Optional Protocol and with the preparation of lists of issues to be presented to States Parties submitting their reports.

Another important development consists of the Committee's advanced cooperation with the special procedures of the Commission on Human Rights, relevant agencies and programmes of the United Nations and NGOs. In its last report, the Committee noted that, in particular, the International Labour Organization, the United Nations High Commissioner for Refugees and the World Health Organization shared information with the Committee which was relevant to the consideration of reports submitted by States Parties. The regular working groups were also offered presentations by Amnesty International, Human Rights Watch, PEN International, the International Service for Human Rights, the International League for Human Rights, the Lawyers' Committee for Human Rights and several national human rights NGOs.

On 30 October 2000, the Committee held its first meeting with representatives of States Parties to the Covenant.[109] This meeting was attended by 55 representatives of States Parties and observers to discuss, *inter alia,* the following issues: difficulties related to the country reporting process; duplication in reporting to different treaty bodies; cross-cutting issues for the entire system of treaty bodies; difficulties with the communication procedure; resources for the work of the Committee; and dialogue between States Parties and the Committee. Both the Committee and States Parties found this dialogue important and decided to hold a similar consultation in October 2002, during the Committee's 76th session.

The Human Rights Committee suffered in particular over the lack of sufficient resources and this led to delays in the consideration of reports and communications. The establishment of the Petitions Team within the Office of the High Commissioner for Human Rights has considerably accelerated the processing of individual communications. However, the Committee remains rightly concerned that these and other improvements are financed from voluntary contributions under the aforementioned Plan of Action, which may be insufficient to ensure a stable financial basis for support for its work.

The Committee on the Elimination of Racial Discrimination   Created by the International Convention on the Elimination of All Forms of Racial Discrimination in 1969, the Committee on the Elimination of Racial Discrimination was the first ever human rights treaty-based body. It has 18 members elected by the States Parties who meet twice a year for three weeks in Geneva. Its mandate includes:

1   examination of periodical reports submitted by the States Parties;
2   adoption of General Recommendations based on the examination of the reports and information received from the States Parties;
3   consideration of State and individual communications concerning alleged violations of the commitments of the States Parties under the Convention.

'Racial discrimination' is interpreted rather broadly both by the Convention and the Committee's own jurisdiction. Pursuant to the Convention, 'racial discrimination' means: 'any distinction, exclusion, restriction or preference based on race, colour, descent, or national or ethnic origin which has the purpose or effect of nullifying or impairing recognition, enjoyment or exercise, on an equal footing, of human rights and fundamental freedoms in the political, economic, social, cultural or any other field of public life.' While examining country reports, the Committee is thus interested not only in racial discrimination in a narrow 'traditional' sense, but also in other dimensions of combating discrimination, including, for example, measures taken to protect national or ethnic minorities.

In 1991 the Committee established a special procedure which is applied if a state report is more than five years overdue. In such a case, a member of the Committee is requested to present information instead of the report, and the Committee reviews the state's compliance with the treaty obligations on this basis and other information available. The Committee has recently noted that the possibility of the application of this procedure has prompted many States Parties to submit a report or to reassure the Committee of their willingness to submit a report within a specific time. With a view to improving further its work despite the insufficient time at its disposal, the Committee has taken a more flexible approach to the periodicity of the reports (see the section, 'Reporting under human rights treaties'). It is also interesting that the Committee decided to continue adopting concluding observations in public meetings. The wish to maintain the transparency of its debates prevailed in this case.

The Committee is a precursor among the treaty-based bodies in that it developed a special preventive procedure to deter or stop the continuation of violations of the human rights standards enshrined in the Convention. At its 41st session, it already had decided to introduce the prevention of racial discrimination as one of its regular agenda items. At its next session, the Committee adopted a working paper that foresaw the following preventive modalities of action:

1   early-warning measures – 'aimed at addressing existing problems so as to prevent them from escalating into conflicts and [which] would also include confidence-building measures to identify and support structures to strengthen racial tolerance and solidify peace in order to prevent a relapse into conflict in situations where it has occurred';

2   urgent procedures – 'aimed at responding to problems requiring immediate attention to prevent or limit the scale or number of serious violations of the Convention'.

The working paper also elaborates on criteria for the application of these measures. So far, on the basis of the working paper, the Committee has considered the situations in Algeria, Australia, Bosnia and Herzegovina, Burundi, Côte d'Ivoire, Croatia, Cyprus, Democratic Republic of the Congo, Israel, Liberia, Mexico, Papua New Guinea, Russian Federation, Rwanda, Sudan, the former Yugoslav Republic of Macedonia and Yugoslavia. It also adopted a statement on Africa and on the human rights of Kurdish people and declared its willingness to send its representatives to Liberia to enter into a dialogue with the government with a view to assisting it in fulfilling its obligations under the Convention.[110]

The Committee often refers to General Recommendations (Comments) to explain its position on the content of the provisions of the Convention or on its implementation, including the functioning of mechanisms established under this treaty. The full list of General Recommendations adopted so far is presented in the notes section at the end of this chapter.[111]

In August 2000, the Committee followed the practice of some other treaty bodies by holding its first thematic public discussion dedicated to discrimination affecting the Roma; this was attended by representatives of other human rights organs and bodies, United Nations agencies and international organizations, as well as NGOs. In the follow-up to this discussion, the Committee adopted a General Recommendation on Discrimination against Roma and declared its intention to continue to organize such thematic discussions in the future.

The Committee against Torture   Established in 1987 by the Convention against Torture and other Cruel, Inhuman or Degrading Treatment or Punishment of 1984, the Committee against Torture is composed of 10 members elected by the States Parties and meets twice a year for a two-week session in Geneva. The Convention describes in detail the obligations of States Parties regarding the prohibition of the relevant human rights violations, the punishment of perpetrators and the protection of potential and actual victims of torture. As in the case of other treaty-based bodies, the Committee's principal tasks consist of the consideration of the periodical reports submitted by the States Parties, the elaboration of suggestions and general comments, and the consideration of communications related to alleged violations of the commitments resulting from the Convention.

The Committee against Torture has a particular competence which goes beyond the usual mandate of the treaty bodies.[112] It can undertake urgent action if it receives reliable information that torture is systematically practised in the territory of a State Party.[113] It means that this procedure can be applied neither to torture appearing incidentally nor to 'other cruel, inhuman or degrading treatment or punishment'. When undertaking urgent action, the Committee invites the state concerned to cooperate in the examination of the allegations and provide comments. After having considered the contribution submitted by the state and other available information, the Committee may decide to launch an inquiry by one or more of its members (including a visit to the country) who should urgently report back to it. The Committee then forwards to the State Party the findings of the inquiry and its related comments and suggestions. All stages of this procedure are confidential but, with the consent of the State Party, a summary account of the case may be included in the Committee's annual report. From its 4th to 26th session, the Committee dedicated 93 meetings to action under this regulation. A recent case presented in the annual report was related to Peru and included a country visit by two Committee members.[114]

Unlike the Committee on Economic, Social and Cultural Rights, the Human Rights Committee and the Committee on the Elimination of Racial Discrimination, the Committee against Torture did not spend much time on General Comments. The first General Comment was published in 1997 and dealt with the implementation of Article 3 of the Convention (the prohibition of expelling, returning (*non-refoulement*) or extraditing a person to a country where there is substantial ground to believe that he/she would be in danger of being subjected to torture). Yet, the Committee recently decided to make a wider use of this possibility and established working groups to discuss the drafting of General Comments on the definition of torture, the follow-up to individual communications and overall procedures.

The World Conference on Human Rights, while reaffirming the need to eradicate torture, stressed that efforts to that end should, first and foremost, be concentrated on prevention, and called for '... the early adoption of an optional protocol ... which is intended to establish a preventive system of regular visits to places of detention'. This was a reference to an initiative of the Delegation of Costa Rica in the early 1980s which, supported by a number of other countries and some NGOs, proposed to the Commission on Human Rights that it elaborate a new procedure of regular preventive visits to places of detention. This proposal was motivated by the fact that, in the case of torture, there was no possibility of restitution because the damage caused to victims cannot be erased. In 1992, the Commission on Human Rights established an inter-sessional Working Group which was charged with drafting an Optional Protocol. The drafting process was not easy, and it took the Commission until its 58th session (2002) to adopt it. The General Assembly adopted the new instrument on 18 December 2002. However, to come into force, the Optional Protocol needs to obtain 20 ratifications.

The Protocol provides for the establishment of a Subcommittee on Prevention of Torture and Other Cruel, Inhuman or Degrading Treatment or Punishment of the Committee against Torture, comprised of ten members who would be entitled to visit places where persons deprived of liberty are held. It is a particular and important feature of this instrument that it is speaking in parallel about national preventive mechanisms to the establishment of which State Parties to the Optional Protocol will have obligations. The Protocol also lays down principles of cooperation between the Subcommittee and national mechanisms. The States Parties commit themselves under the Protocol to guarantee to the Subcommittee and national mechanisms free access to all places of detention and to all relevant persons (including those deprived of liberty). The proceedings of the Subcommittee will remain confidential unless the State Party concerned wishes otherwise. If the State Party refuses to cooperate with the Subcommittee, or refuses to improve the situation in the light of the Subcommittee's recommendations, the Committee against Torture would be able, at the request of the Subcommittee, to decide whether to make a public statement on the matter or publish the Subcommittee's report.[115]

In the opinion of its members, the Committee does not have sufficient time and resources to perform its mandate appropriately. In this context, the Committee welcomed the strengthening of the capacities of the Secretariat through the Plan of Action mentioned above, in particular, the establishment of the Petition Team to handle individual communications (see the section, 'Individual communications'). The Committee itself is in the process of examining its working methods with a view to releasing some capacities, but it has been stressed by its members that more basic changes are necessary.

The Committee on the Rights of the Child   The Committee on the Rights of the Child has been in place since 1991. Initially, it was composed of 10 experts, but an amendment to Article 43, para. 2 of the Convention adopted in 1995, which has recently come into force, increased this number to 18. The Committee meets twice a year in Geneva for a three-week session. It is the most universal treaty body, on the one hand, because the 1989 Convention on the Rights of the Child has the largest number of ratifications (191 by 2002). On the other hand, the Convention lays down the standards of the rights of the child related to all human rights: civil, cultural, economic, political, and social. In this way, the Committee is not limited to specific categories of rights as is the case with regard to the Committees dealing with the International Covenants.

The Committee's mandate comprises both the consideration of the periodic reports of States Parties on the measures taken to implement the Convention and the progress made in this respect, and the adoption of suggestions and General Comments. The Convention, like the International Covenant on Economic, Social and Cultural Rights, does not introduce a specific communication procedure. The Committee on the Rights of the Child faces a backlog of state reports awaiting examination (approximately 50 reports – resulting in a delay of approximately two years before a report is reviewed). The Committee decided, therefore, to make an effort to increase the number of reports reviewed during a session to nine. Recently, it set up a working group to review its working methods, as well as its guidelines on the preparation of periodic reports, in order to further facilitate the preparation of the reports and reduce the related burden. The issue of the periodicity of the reports is also on the Committee's agenda.

For a long time, the Committee was reluctant to develop its jurisprudence in the form of General Comments. The first and only General Comment so far adopted was in 2001 and addressed 'The aims of education'. Perhaps the Committee preferred first of all to consolidate its work and will now elaborate General Comments more often. Recently, it decided to begin, in consultation with partners, drafting two General Comments on:

1   the role of national human rights institutions with regard to the rights of the child; and
2   HIV/AIDS and the rights of the child.[116]

It is interesting that it called on outside resources to produce its first General Comment. In addition to debates within the Committee itself, the drafting was undertaken with the assistance of a consultant and through a meeting organized by a NGO with the participation of the Rapporteur of the Committee on Economic, Social and Cultural Rights and representatives of UNICEF and UNESCO.

The Committee also organizes one-day general discussions on fundamental issues attended by governmental delegations, United Nations agencies and programmes, NGOs and experts. The theme of the September 2000 debate was 'State violence against children'. In September 2001 it was followed by a discussion on 'Violence against children within the family and in schools'.

The Committee appears as a pro-active body, catalysing and stimulating system-wide United Nations activities in respect of the rights of the child. To enhance international cooperation, the Convention entitles the specialized agencies, UNICEF and other United Nations organs to be represented when the Committee considers the implementation of the rights falling within its competence and to be invited to provide expert advice on its implementation, as well as to submit relevant reports. Examples in this regard provide recent invitations to the Special Rapporteurs on Adequate Housing and on the Right to Food of the Commission on Human Rights. The Committee may also transmit to these bodies state reports along with its own observations and suggestions if the reports identify a request or a need for technical advice or assistance. The Committee has developed a particularly close working relationship with UNICEF. Finally, the Convention states that the Committee may recommend to the General Assembly that studies on issues relating to the rights of the child be undertaken by the Secretary-General. Experience so far confirms that the Committee has, indeed, taken advantage of these competences.

Committee on the Elimination of Discrimination against Women   The Committee on the Elimination of Discrimination against Women was established in 1982 on the basis of the Convention on the Elimination of All Forms of Discrimination against Women of 1979. Initially, it comprised 18 members but, since the ratification of the Convention by 35 states, this number has increased to 23. It meets annually for one two-week session, alternately in Vienna and New York. United Nations specialized agencies can be represented during the consideration of matters relevant to them.

The Convention defines the term 'discrimination against women' as: '... any distinction, exclusion or restriction made on the basis of sex which has the effect or purpose of impairing or nullifying the recognition, enjoyment or exercise by women, irrespective of their marital status, on a basis of equality of men and women, of human rights and fundamental freedoms in the political, economic, social, cultural, civil or any other field'. The Committee's mandate includes the consideration of the periodic reports submitted by States Parties and the adoption of suggestions and general recommendations based on the analysis of the reports and other information submitted by the States Parties. The Committee is competent to consider individual communications concerning alleged non-compliance by States Parties with the obligations laid down in the Convention and carry out inquiries into alleged violations of the rights protected under the Convention.

The Committee has frequently benefitted from the possibility of articulating its position through General Recommendations that address different aspects of the human rights of women and factors having an impact on them, as well as the execution of its mandate. The average annual number of General Recommendations is comparable with that of the Human Rights Committee and exceeds one per year.[117] Recently, the Committee on the Elimination of Discrimination against Women also started work on a general recommendation on Article 4, para. 1 of the Convention regarding temporary special measures aimed at accelerating *de facto* equality between men and women.

This Committee also suffers from the backlog of state reports to be reviewed. To deal with this problem, it has adopted a temporary measure giving the states concerned the opportunity to combine overdue and current reports. It also requested the General Assembly to authorize an additional session of 30 meetings in 2002 to review outstanding reports.[118]

The World Conference on Human Rights called for the adoption of an Optional Protocol to the Convention, which would introduce a communications procedure. It recommended that: 'The Commission on the Status of Women and the Committee on the Elimination of Discrimination against Women should quickly examine the possibility of introducing the right of petition through the preparation of an optional protocol to the Convention on the Elimination of All Forms of Discrimination against Women.' The Optional Protocol entered into force on 22 December 2000.[119] The procedure has been launched in 2002 after the 26th session of the Committee.

The Optional Protocol also introduced another important procedure to be undertaken by the Committee, namely, the inquiry into alleged grave or systematic violations by a State Party of the rights set forth in the Convention. The procedure follows closely the one established under Article 20 of the Convention against Torture and Other Cruel, Inhuman or Degrading Treatment and Punishment. The Committee, on receiving reliable information on such violations, in this case as well, shall request the State Party to participate in its examination and submit observations. On this basis, the Committee is entitled to invest one or more of its members with the responsibility to conduct an inquiry and report to it. With the consent of the State Party, the designated members may visit the country and hold hearings. Findings and recommendations resulting from the inquiry are shared with the State Party. The Optional Protocol also establishes rules concerning the response of the State Party and subsequent communications with the Committee, as well as the protection of persons who communicated with the Committee against related ill-treatment and intimidation. After having consulted the State Party, the Committee includes summary information on the inquiry into its annual report. Otherwise, all stages of the procedure are confidential.[120] The approval of the inquiry procedure automatically follows the ratification of the Optional Protocol, unless the State Party has made a declaration that it does not recognize this competence of the Committee.

Like other Committees, the Committee on the Elimination of Discrimination against Women and its members do not confine themselves to scrutiny over the implementation of the Convention on the Elimination of All Forms of Discrimination against Women. For example, the Committee participated in the process of the Fourth World Conference on Women in Beijing, China, in 1995, and now is actively involved in the follow-up to that summit. The members of the Committee also declared their willingness to act in the framework of expert group meetings preparing sessions of the Commission on the Status of Women and as members of panels held during its sessions.[121]

Non-conventional procedures: Special Rapporteurs and Working Groups

Status and mandates

The Commission on Human Rights has the competence to establish special mechanisms (called 'special procedures') to deal with either selected substantive human rights problems ('thematic procedures') or with the human rights situation in a given country ('country-specific procedures'). This competence originates from ECOSOC resolution 1235(XLII) that has empowered the Commission on Human Rights in appropriate cases to 'make a thorough study of situations which reveal a consistent pattern of violations of human rights' (see also the section 'Communications Procedures' below). Started in 1967,[122] special procedures are widely appreciated as one of the main pillars of the United Nations human rights programme. The Secretary-General, in a recent report, underlined that: 'These procedures are vital instruments and, over the years, have helped to advance the cause of human rights.'[123] Special Rapporteurs of the Commission, Special Representatives of the Secretary-General, Independent Experts, or Working Groups may be established as a special procedure. The Commission in its choice in this regard is guided by the nature and requirements of the mandate.

In 1993, the World Conference on Human Rights underlined '… the importance of preserving and strengthening the system of special procedures, rapporteurs, representatives, experts and working groups of the Commission on Human Rights and the Sub-Commission on the Prevention of Discrimination and Protection of Minorities' and called on all states to cooperate fully with them. Indeed, the rapid development of special procedures, particularly during the 1990s, has become one of the most striking changes in the United Nations human rights programme. It is sufficient to recall that, since the 58th session of the Commission, its work is supported by 37 special procedures, among which 12 have country specific mandates.

The overall function of special procedures is to assist the Commission on Human Rights and the General Assembly in their activities, in particular through reporting on and reacting to serious human rights violations and exploring methods for an improved implementation of human rights. In spite of their originally auxiliary character, special procedures have developed into a system with a high degree of autonomy. The holders of the mandates have the status of independent experts who can freely decide on the content and mode of action, including views and assessments presented publicly. They should be guided only by the relevant norms of the United Nations and the, usually rather general, stipulations of the Commission's resolutions which establish a given mandate. The General Assembly has adopted Regulations Governing the Status, Basic Rights and Duties of Officials other than Secretariat Officials, and Experts on Mission,[124] which could also be applicable to the holders of the discussed mandates.

The independence of mandate-holders is guaranteed, *inter alia*, by the applicability of Article VI of the 1946 Convention on the Privileges and Immunities of the United Nations. Under this Convention, while executing their mandates they act as experts on missions for the United Nations and thus enjoy privileges and immunities necessary for the purpose of the mission, including: immunity from personal arrest and detention and from seizure of their personal baggage; immunity from a legal process of any kind in respect of words spoken or written, and acts undertaken by them in the course of performing their mission; inviolability for all papers and documents; the right to use codes and to receive papers or correspondence by courier or in sealed bags; and immunities and facilities in respect of their personal baggage, as accorded to diplomatic envoys.[125]

With regard to the main objective of their mandates, one can differentiate between the following functions of thematic special procedures:

- protective function – informing the Commission on the occurrence and practice of human rights violations. This function may also embrace assistance to victims, if this is possible;
- promotional function – reporting to the Commission (and to the General Assembly, if so decided) on the status of the realization of a given right and promoting its implementation;
- analytical function – analysing specific human rights issues and offering the findings and recommendations to the Commission (and to the General Assembly, if so decided).

The mandates of thematic procedures in the majority of cases embrace different functions and thus a typology of the mandates using the criterion of their functions is hardly possible.

The main task of the thematic procedures is to collect information concerning the worldwide implementation of a given human right. They identify typical patterns of violations of human rights, locate and analyse sources of such violations and the most suitable methods of countering them. The thematic procedures also make recommendations addressed to both the international community and national actors regarding improvements in the implementation of human rights. One can say that they act both in the area of diagnosis and of cure.

Initially thematic procedures were established exclusively in the area of civil and political rights. The first thematic procedure, the Working Group on Involuntary Disappearances, was established in 1980. Mandates dealing with economic, social and cultural rights or related areas are relatively new.

Country mandates are established with a view to providing the Commission on Human Rights and the General Assembly with a reliable assessment of the human rights situation in a given country. This happens when the Commission decides to keep the situation under scrutiny and to establish a Special Rapporteur or an Independent Expert under the advisory services programme. Country Rapporteurs and Experts, on the basis of available information and their visits to countries, if feasible, make recommendations to the Commission and other United Nations organs and bodies, and provide advice to the governments concerned. The nomination of a Special Rapporteur is interpreted as a stronger measure than the appointment of an Independent Expert. While the former is perceived more as a 'scrutiny mechanism', the latter is conceived rather as an 'advisory mechanism'. Moving a country from the former mandate to the latter is also interpreted as easing the Commission's attitude. Another group of country mandates embraces Special Rapporteurs established under the '1503 procedure'.[126]

Establishment of the mandate and appointments Mandates of special procedures are created by the Commission on Human Rights, subject to approval by ECOSOC. Sometimes the idea of creating a mandate remains pending for some time in order to await conducive conditions for support from the Commission's members. The timeframe is identified in the resolution establishing a given mandate and is usually set for one or three years with a possible renewal. The Working Group on Mechanisms, mentioned above, recommended that the Commission conduct periodically an objective and thorough review of all mandates to establish which should be continued in view of evolving needs. The Working Group also observed that:

> The Commission clearly must be responsive to human rights imperatives; where human rights violations exist, mechanisms focus attention and have the potential to bring about important improvement. At the same time, the increasing number of mandates can create difficulties in terms of overlap and inadequate support services, as well as straining the capacity of States to absorb the output.

It proposed that decisions concerning creating or terminating mandates should take into consideration the following:

> (i) Mandates should always offer a clear prospect of an increased level of human rights protection and promotion; (ii) The balance of thematic mandates should broadly reflect the accepted equal importance of civil and political rights and economic, social and cultural rights; (iii) Every effort should be made to avoid unnecessary duplication; (iv) In creating or reviewing mandates, efforts should be made to identify whether the structure of the mechanism (expert, rapporteur or working group) is the most effective in terms of increasing human rights protection; (v) Any consideration of merging mandates should have regard to the content and predominant functions of each mandate, as well as to the work-load of individual mandate-holders.[127]

Special Rapporteurs and independent experts are appointed by the Chairperson of the Commission on Human Rights, who takes the decision after having formally consulted the Commission's Bureau and the five regional groups on this matter. The opinions gathered in this way are, however, not binding for the Chairperson. In his/her selection, the Chairperson should be guided by the professional and personal qualities of the individual – expertise and experience in the area of the mandate, integrity, independence and impartiality are of paramount importance. Due regard should also be given to an overall geographical and gender balance among the mandate-holders, as well as to the representation of different legal systems. The OHCHR has been requested to maintain a list of possible candidates for the mandates of special procedures. The list should be updated continuously, contain candidates representing different regions and legal systems, and be gender-balanced. Proposals can be made by states and other sources, including NGOs having consultative status with ECOSOC and the Secretariat of the United Nations. The list can be visited on the website of the OHCHR. While appointing a mandate-holder, the Chairperson should essentially draw on this list, but exceptions are possible if the requirements of a particular post so justify. The Secretary-General appoints the Special Representatives if such mandates have been established by the Commission on Human Rights. The principle has been formulated that one person can hold only one mandate of no longer than two terms of three years.

Current mandates according to their subject   In 2000 the Commission, following the recommendations of the Working Group on Mechanisms, took several steps regarding existing mandates. Although of an incidental nature, they seem to be an important indicator of the concepts which prevailed in the Commission's approach to its special procedures. The Commission decided to:

- Merge the mandate of the independent expert on structural adjustment and the Special Rapporteur on Foreign Debt because of the synergies between the mandates. The new mandate is one of an independent expert on structural adjustment and foreign debt.

- Maintain the Working Group on Arbitrary Detention (as opposed to a proposal to transform it into a post of a Special Rapporteur on Arbitrary Detention) and the Working Group on Enforced and Involuntary Disappearances (as opposed to a proposal to transform it into a post of a Special Rapporteur on Disappearances). In these cases, the Commission recognised that the benefits of the present solutions were more important than savings by replacing a working group by an individual mandate holder.

Most of thematic mandates can be divided in two groups related to the categories of rights:

- In the area of economic, social and cultural rights: Special Rapporteur on the Right to Education; Special Rapporteur on the Right to Food; Special Rapporteur on Adequate Housing as a Component of the Right to an Adequate Standard of Living; Independent Expert to examine the question of a draft Optional Protocol to the International Covenant on Economic, Social and Cultural Rights; Independent Expert on Human Rights and Extreme Poverty; Independent Expert on Structural Adjustment Policies and Foreign debt; Special Rapporteur on the Adverse Effects of the Illicit Movement and Dumping of Toxic and Dangerous Products and Wastes on the Enjoyment of Human Rights.
- In the area of civil and political rights: Working Group on Arbitrary Detention; Working Group on Enforced or Involuntary Disappearances; Special Rapporteur on Extra-Judicial, Summary or Arbitrary Executions; Special Rapporteur on the Question of Torture; Special Rapporteur on Violence against Women, Its Causes and Consequences; Special Rapporteur on the Promotion and Protection of the Right to Freedom of Opinion and Expression; Special Rapporteur on Freedom of Religion or Belief; Special Rapporteur on Contemporary Forms of Racism, Racial Discrimination, Xenophobia and Related Intolerance; Special Rapporteur on the Use of Mercenaries as a Means of Impeding the Exercise of the Right of Peoples to Self-Determination; Independent Expert to Examine the Existing International Criminal and Human Rights Framework for the Protection of Persons from Enforced or Involuntary Disappearance.

Some of the mandates remain outside these groups, involving elements of different categories of human rights, namely: Independent Expert on the Right to Development; Special Rapporteur on the Sale of Children, Child Prostitution and Child Pornography; Special Rapporteur on the Situation of Human Rights and Fundamental Freedoms of Indigenous People; Special Rapporteur on the Human Rights of Migrants; Special Representative of the Secretary-General on Internally Displaced Persons; and Special Representative of the Secretary-General on the Situation of Human Rights Defenders.

As a result of the 58th session of the Commission on Human Rights, Special Rapporteurs monitor the human rights situation in the following countries: Afghanistan (since 1984); Bosnia and Herzegovina and the Federal Republic of Yugoslavia (a Special Rapporteur was nominated for the region in 1992); Burundi (since 1995); Cambodia (since 1993); Democratic Republic of the Congo – former Zaire (since 1994); Haiti (since 1995); Iraq (since 1991); Myanmar (since 1992); Palestinian territories occupied since 1967 (since 1993); Somalia (since 1993); and Sudan (since 1993).

Information gathering   In order to fulfil their mandates, Special Rapporteurs develop contacts with governments, United Nations agencies and bodies, especially those within the human rights machinery, and other actors. NGOs, other segments of civil society and individuals, including victims, their families and other persons close to them are a significant source of information. For obvious reasons, visits to countries undertaken by Special Rapporteurs play an essential role. Such a visit, however, requires an invitation from the government concerned or, at least, as is sometimes the case, the willingness of the government to tolerate the visit without actively helping in its realization. Frequently, therefore, the Commission in its resolutions calls on governments to invite Special Rapporteurs and offer them full cooperation. An important initiative has already been undertaken by more than 40 governments, which have extended a standing invitation to holders of thematic mandates. Such an invitation is not only evidence of the willingness of governments to cooperate with a crucial part of the United Nations human rights machinery, but also facilitates the implementation of mandates and paves the way towards a better coordination of work between mandate-holders. Most often, mandate-holders themselves enter into a dialogue with the government concerned to solicit an invitation. Unfortunately, sometimes governments refuse to invite Special Rapporteurs, whether they are country-specific or thematic, even if the Commission explicitly requests for it in a resolution. However, as stated earlier, such a refusal does not prevent Special Rapporteurs from reporting, which is the core of their mandates, but deprives the country concerned of the benefits of such a visit (see below). It also forces the Special Rapporteur to rely on other sources than first-hand observations.

Communications – urgent appeals   Action by special procedures frequently originates from numerous communications on human rights violations coming from victims or from persons or organizations acting on their behalf. Although interventions to governments by special procedures do not, of course, prejudge the outcome of the case, they can have an important protective impact. Simply the very fact that state authorities note the signal of international scrutiny can be helpful.

The Working Group on Mechanisms agreed on a crucial point, namely that '... the human rights machinery of the United Nations is particularly tested at a time when there are allegations of an urgent situation of serious human rights violations requiring immediate attention in any part of the world'.[128] In four cases, namely, the Working Group on Enforced or Involuntary Disappearances, the Special Rapporteur on Summary and Arbitrary

Executions, the Special Rapporteur for Torture and the Special Rapporteur for Religious Intolerance, the Commission on Human Rights decided to empower the mandate-holders to take urgent action, if necessary. These particular regulations do not prevent other special procedures from taking such steps, but they do so on a much smaller scale. The most immediate tool for special procedures in response to communications indicating an emergency are 'urgent appeals' addressed to governments by thematic and country mandate-holders. In an urgent appeal, the Special Rapporteur draws the attention of the government to the information concerning alleged human rights violations, requests urgent measures to master the situation and restore respect for human rights and asks for comments and information from the government. To accelerate the process, an urgent appeal is sent directly to the Foreign Minister of the country concerned (other correspondence follows the usual diplomatic routes).

The average annual number of such appeals is large. It is necessary to ensure that they are dealt with expeditiously and that action taken by various Special Rapporteurs on the same case benefits from some form of coordination. Although each Special Rapporteur has an independent mandate, knowledge of action taken by other special procedures can help to achieve a more targetted, and thus effective, intervention. Sometimes Special Rapporteurs issue joint urgent appeals to demonstrate a coordinated interest in a case and thus strengthen the impact of their action. The responsibility for support for urgent appeals, including the adequate flow of information, rests with the Office of the High Commissioner for Human Rights which services the special procedures. To cope with this task, the Office has recently established an Urgent Appeal Desk. For its part, the Working Group on Mechanisms has stressed that the governments concerned should respond to urgent appeals as quickly as possible bearing in mind the importance of this tool. It was also stressed that, in the absence of a satisfactory response, the High Commissioner should facilitate the dialogue and cooperation between the government and the relevant special procedures.

No formal procedure has been established to deal with communications (petitions). To facilitate their submission, some of the special procedures have adopted 'Model questionnaires for communications/complaints'.[129] However, the communication does not need to follow this model and is processed if it provides the following basic information: '... identification of the alleged victim(s); identification of the perpetrators of the violation; identification of the person(s) or organization(s) submitting the communication; a detailed description of the circumstances of the incident in which the alleged violation occurred.' From these requirements, formulated by the Office of the High Commissioner on its website, a communication can be submitted on behalf of a victim (not necessarily by the victim personally). Nevertheless, anonymous communications are treated as inadmissible. Communications addressed to special procedures have also been released from the condition of the exhaustion of domestic remedies before submission, which is applicable in the case of other communication procedures. It must also be stressed that communications can be considered by all special procedures, country-specific and thematic, not just the six mentioned in the aforementioned guidelines.

Reports   The report to the Commission on Human Rights is the basic form of communication between the holder of a special procedure mandate and this body. In addition to annual reports to the Commission, some of the mandate-holders have been requested to report to the General Assembly. Missions to countries are usually reported separately. Reports are normally very detailed and include analyses, the presentation of specific cases and recommendations.[130] The latter are addressed to the states concerned, the High Commissioner, including the field operations and the technical cooperation programme of the Office of the High Commissioner, and to other components of the United Nations system. In the past, the way in which the reports have been introduced to the Commission has been criticized for its rather formal character, being reduced to a short oral statement. In the framework of its reform, the Commission decided to give the consideration of the reports more significance and greater prominence. With a view to facilitating the preparation of delegations before the debate, the reports should have an executive summary and be made available in advance in an unedited version. Reports referring to specific countries should be made available to the governments concerned a minimum of six weeks before the presentation of the report at the Commission meeting. This should provide interested governments with 'a reasonable opportunity'[131] to submit comments that can be distributed as an official document. The Working Group on Mechanisms also encouraged more interaction between the Special Rapporteurs and the participants in the meeting of the Commission. To that end, it recommended allocating time for the debate on the report immediately after its introduction. The Commission did follow this recommendation but this practice was, unfortunately, interrupted at its 58th session due to the financial and, subsequently, time constraints referred to in the previous section, 'The Commission on Human Rights'.

The need for reform   The Working Group on Mechanisms of the Commission on Human Rights agreed that the institution of special procedures was '… in need of rationalization and strengthening and that this requires a multi-pronged approach'.[132] Demand for reforms has also been stressed frequently by the mandate-holders themselves. Underlying these views is the hope for a better utilization of the potential of special procedures.

Two tracks have been identified in the approach to a possible reform of the special procedures. The first was oriented towards a higher degree of geographical and professional balance in the composition of mandate-holders and to a system of rotation imposing limits on the number of years in office of an individual mandate-holder. Steps taken in this regard have already been addressed in this section. The second track was oriented towards strengthening support for special procedures. Already in 1998, that is, parallel to the intergovernmental discussions on the Commission's mechanisms and, in support of this process, two mandates-holders of special procedures, Thomas Hammarberg and Mona Rishmawi, examined ways through which the Office of the High Commissioner could contribute to improving the effectiveness of the special procedures. As well as concluding that the system urgently required better support based on adequate resources, both experts proposed several organizational measures that could strengthen the system. These proposals included, among others, establishing an Urgent Appeal Desk and an emergency response team, developing analytical capacities available to the special procedures, and providing better general assistance to the mandate-holders.[133] It should be noted that the Commission, in a resolution adopted at its 58th session, placed the reform of special procedures on its agenda for the next session.

As was the case concerning treaty bodies, it needs to be repeated here that the system of special procedures is generally under-resourced and this factor weighs substantially on the output. To refer to only one example – according to the aforementioned experts, supported by other mandate-holders – each Special Rapporteur should be assisted by at least one staff member of the Office of the High Commissioner. However, under the regular budget for the biennium 2002–2003, only 15 posts have been designated to service all 37 special procedures, including working groups with considerable workloads. Moreover, the Commission sometimes establishes new mandates without determining their financial implications and this further exacerbates an already uneasy situation. There is also a shortage of resources for special procedures missions and for necessary analytical support. Responding to this need, the High Commissioner decided to launch a project to support the special procedures from voluntary contributions. In the 2002 Annual Appeal of the Office of the High Commissioner, the chapter related to this project was budgeted at US$ 2,607,080, almost 5 per cent of the requested voluntary funding. This facilitated meeting some of the most urgent needs related to special procedures, including the maintenance of the Urgent Appeal Desk and other assistance for mandate-holders. The emergency task force proposed by the above-mentioned experts was established without additional funding.

In his programme for reform, the Secretary-General calls for two sets of measures related to the special procedures:

1 the improvement of the quality of the reports and analyses produced by the special procedures through setting clear criteria for the use of this institution, the selection of appointees and better guidelines for their operations and reporting functions;
2 the strengthening of the support for the special procedures, including the appointment of more senior professionals, as well as better administrative support.[134]

Special mechanisms as a system   The authority stemming from special procedures draws increasingly on their work as a system, in addition to the input by individual mandate-holders. Already in 1994 their first meeting called for '... more efficient sharing of information and pursuing the possibilities of joint missions ... Holders of country and thematic mandates should enhance co-operation in the discharge of their mandates'.[135] There are instances of Special Rapporteurs' coordinated action, for example, in the form of joint urgent appeals, joint press releases drawing the attention of international public opinion to a certain problem, or joint country visits to address different aspects of a human rights situation in an orchestrated manner. Joint missions of Special Rapporteurs have already taken place, for example, in Colombia, East Timor, former Yugoslavia and Rwanda. On some occasions, the Commission on Human Rights appealed to different special procedures to address the same human rights situation. An intersectional approach, as such, could, indeed, provide an added value. For instance, in a conflict situation with the transfer of great numbers of people, a joint assessment of needs and recommendations from the perspective of the Special Rapporteur on Extra-Judicial, Summary or Arbitrary Executions, the Special Rapporteur on Torture, the Special Rapporteur on Violence against Women, the Special Rapporteur on the Right to Food, the Special Rapporteur on the Right to Health, and the Special Representatives of the United Nations Secretary-General on Children in Armed Conflicts and Internally Displaced Persons could produce unique material of great relevance to international decision-making bodies and thus contribute to dealing with the emergency situation. It can be assumed that the impact of such an action would be greater than that of steps taken in isolation. Yet, it is remarkable that some governments tend to be reluctant in extending such joint invitations.

The potential opportunities resulting from coordinated action were recognized by the World Conference on Human Rights which recommended convening annual meetings of the mandate-holders. Such meetings have been organized by the Office of the High Commissioner since 1994 and their agendas include basic substantive issues of importance for special procedures (for example, the gender perspective, internally displaced persons, corporate responsibility for human rights violations), coordination between mandate-holders and between them and other partners within and outside the United Nations, and questions of organization of work and support received. Particular attention is paid to the relationship with the Commission on Human Rights and cooperation with human rights treaty bodies, the Office of the High Commissioner and NGOs.[136] To ensure a certain continuity of the work undertaken during the meetings, participants elect a chairperson and a rapporteur for a one-year term.

It is a view shared by both members of treaty bodies and holders of special procedures' mandates that a considerable potential consists in closer cooperation between them. And, indeed, progress can be noted during recent years in respect of the flow of information and intensive direct contacts, in particular in cases of similar substantive mandates such as, for example, between the Special Rapporteur on Torture and the Committee against Torture; the Special Rapporteurs on the Right to Food and Adequate Housing and the Committee on Economic, Social and Cultural Rights; and the Special Rapporteur on Racism, Racial Discrimination and Xenophobia and the Committee on the Elimination of Racial Discrimination. The already mentioned holding of parallel annual meetings of the chairpersons of treaty bodies and holders of special procedures mandates provides a suitable framework for further fostering of this process.

PROCEDURES

Reporting under Human Rights Treaties

Reporting by State Parties is widely assessed as an indispensable component of the overall strategy of the implementation of the human rights treaties and an important contribution to the promotion and protection of these rights at the national level. The consideration of the reports on legislative and other relevant measures by the treaty bodies is seen as the basic method of the independent international monitoring of the compliance by State Parties with their obligations. The role of the reporting system is enhanced through the public character of the examination. In this way, the law and practice of a State are scrutinized by the international community and the society involved.

Some commentators stress that governments may be predisposed to evaluate the situation in their own countries in a more positive light than it actually merits. However, the treaty bodies are not passive recipients of the governmental 'products' but, on the contrary, are active and inquiring examiners. In addition, the treaty bodies themselves have developed some practical solutions to counteract the potential misuse of the reporting system. In its General Comment No. 1 of 1989, the Committee on Economic, Social, and Cultural Rights pointed out that: '… it would be incorrect to assume that reporting is essentially only a procedural matter designed solely to satisfy each State Party's formal obligation to report to the appropriate international monitoring body.' The Committee identified the following seven objectives of the reporting system (also reflecting the purposes of the reporting under other human rights treaties):

- to ensure that a comprehensive review is undertaken [by the State Party] with respect to national legislation, administrative rules and procedures, and practices in an effort to ensure the fullest possible conformity with the Covenant;
- to ensure that the State Party monitors the actual situation with respect to each of the rights on a regular basis and is thus aware of the extent to which the various rights are, or are not, being enjoyed by all individuals within its territory or under its jurisdiction;
- to provide the basis for the elaboration of clearly stated and carefully targetted policies, including the establishment of priorities which reflect the provisions of the Covenant;
- to facilitate public scrutiny of government policies with respect to economic, social and cultural rights and to encourage the involve-

ment of the various economic, social and cultural sectors of society in the formulation, implementation and review of the relevant policies;

- to provide a basis on which the State Party itself, as well as the Committee, can effectively evaluate the extent to which progress has been made towards the realization of the obligations contained in the Covenant;

- to enable the State Party itself to develop a better understanding of the problems and shortcomings encountered in efforts to realize progressively the full range of economic, social and cultural rights;

- to enable the Committee, and the States Parties as a whole, to facilitate the exchange of information among states and to develop a better understanding of the common problems faced by states and a fuller appreciation of the type of measures which might be taken to promote effective realization of each of the rights contained in the Covenant. This part of the process also enables the Committee to identify the most appropriate means by which the international community might assist states, in accordance with Articles 22 and 23 of the Covenant.[137]

As it results from the presented goals of the reporting system, the Committees do not expect States Parties to report only about legal norms. The country report should provide conclusive information on both law and practice. For example, in its Guidelines for the preparation of reports by States Parties, the Committee on the Elimination of Discrimination against Women recommends: '… that the reports not be confined to mere lists of legal instruments adopted in the country concerned in recent years, but should also include information indicating how those legal instruments are reflected in the actual economic, political and social realities and general conditions existing in the country.'[138]

The reports are delivered and distributed among the members well in advance of the sessions of the Committees. To better prepare their sessions, the majority of treaty bodies develop a list of issues to be presented to the government before the public examination of the report. This list is approved by a pre-sessional Working Group or by the Committee itself. There is a tendency, however, to benefit from the first option and thus save time.[139] The Working Group meetings also offer the opportunity to work more closely with other partners in the preparation of the review of a report by the Committee, since the timeframes of the sessions are very tight. Recently, the Committee against Torture has also decided to establish such a pre-sessional Working Group in the biennium 2002–2003.[140]

The pre-sessional procedure to the examination of the reports gives the States Parties an opportunity to prepare responses to be presented either in writing before the Committee's meeting or orally at the meeting. It is interesting that the Human Rights Committee indirectly discouraged States Parties to submit written answers to the list of issues in order to better facilitate a constructive discussion at the meeting.[141]

The consideration of a report before a Committee often exceeds two days. Recently however, some Committees have attempted to cut the time dedicated to one report with a view to reducing the backlog of reports awaiting review. At the beginning of the examination, the government representatives present the report and answer questions raised. Afterwards, members of the Committee ask additional questions which are subsequently answered by the governmental delegation. This stage often develops into a real discussion between the Committee and the government, going far beyond the formal presentation of positions and views. This should be stressed, because such a discussion makes the reporting system an instrument of assistance to states, whose representatives can draw on the expertise of the Committee members and also seek their advice. Equally, it also enables the Committee to understand better the problems faced by the country under review. The Human Rights Committee stressed that: 'Central to the consideration of States Parties reports is the oral hearing, where the delegations of States Parties have the opportunity to answer specific questions from Committee members.'[142] While examining the report, the Committee takes advantage of information received from NGOs, United Nations organs and bodies, and from other sources. Questions raised by members of the Committee usually evidence a solid bank of knowledge related to the reporting country. As a consequence, governments send high-level and well-prepared delegations to present their reports.

Finally, the Committee holds a debate in private and formulates concluding observations which are presented to the government. However, the dialogue sometimes continues after the meetings dedicated to the consideration of the report. In some instances, governments provide further information on issues raised during the meeting or the Committee applies follow-up measures.

Conclusions reached by the Committees should be implemented by States Parties. Although the Committees do not have any executive power to ensure this, they establish their own mechanisms to monitor the follow-up on their recommendations and thus be able to continue their dialogue with State Parties.[143]

The reporting process has, however, some weak points which, to a certain extent, are related to the inherent limits of such a system. The treaty bodies have already responded to several shortcomings. Some of the problems are presented below in more detail.

In view of the report by the Secretariat for the 13th Meeting of Chairpersons of the Human Rights Treaty Bodies in 2001, the accumulated backlogs of submitted reports awaiting examination by the treaty bodies and the delays in submitting reports by states are major issues.[144] There are also States Parties which fail to deliver reports at all. In its last annual report, the Human Rights Committee warned that 28 initial reports had not yet been presented.[145] As of 31 March 2001, the number of overdue reports reached a total of 1277, distributed among the different human rights treaties as shown in Table 1.5.

The treaty bodies take a more rigid approach in cases of great delays in reporting. For example, the Committee on the Elimination of Racial Discrimination: '... decided that it would continue to proceed with the review

Table 1.5   Overdue reports

ICESCR	ICCPR	CERD	CEDAW	CAT	CRC
180	143	433	250	126	145

of the implementation of the provisions of the Convention by the States Parties whose reports were excessively overdue by five years or more.' This review would draw on the previous reports submitted by the State Party. If the State Party failed, over a period of five years or more, to submit its initial report, the Committee would review the implementation of the provisions of the Convention on the basis of: '... all information submitted by the State Party to other organs of the United Nations or, in the absence of such material, reports and information prepared by organs of the United Nations.' The Committee may also benefit in such a situation from information received from other sources, including NGOs. It should be noted that the Committee's announcement of its decision to review the compliance by several named countries in the absence of their reports, prompted some governments to either submit the reports or to ask for the postponement of the discussion for the time necessary to prepare the report.[146] Other treaty bodies apply similar measures to that effect.[147] The Committee against Torture has decided to continue to present during the press conferences at the end of its session a list of States Parties whose reports are more than four years overdue.[148]

As the Independent Expert of the Commission on Human Rights on enhancing the long-term effectiveness of the United Nations human rights treaty system pointed out,[149] non-reporting had reached chronic proportions. In the case of the International Covenant on Economic, Social and Cultural Rights, the percentage of overdue initial reports concerned 40 per cent of the States Parties. On the other hand, he noted that the present reporting system only functioned because of the delays in delivery of the reports. If all the reports had been delivered on time, existing backlogs would be further exacerbated. To effectively tackle this and other problems faced by the treaty bodies, the independent expert called for consideration of both the reform of the system of treaty bodies and of specifically targeted measures. Among the former, he mentioned the preparation of 'consolidated reports' to be considered by all treaty bodies; individualizing the requirements for periodic reports for each state; and a reduction in the number of treaty bodies. Among the latter, he proposed that:

1   a new project of technical cooperation be designed to assist governments in their reporting obligations; and
2   all treaty bodies adopt a procedure which would enable them to review a state's compliance with the treaty obligations in the case of persistent delinquency in delivering the report.[150]

The idea of the replacement of separate reports to each of the treaty bodies by one overarching report on the implementation of human rights standards to be submitted by a government to all the Committees is apparently one meeting the greatest interest. On the basis of this report, the Committees would be in a position to formulate more specific questions relating to their spheres of interest. This would also reduce the reporting burden on governments and, at the same time, make comparable the information available to all the Committees.

In the report on the consultations conducted by the independent expert, the Secretary-General stated that:

> While no clear consensus has yet been reached on the desirability of consolidating reports due under the various treaties, a number of treaty bodies have moved towards a more focused examination of States Parties' reports. This is most apparent in the lists of issues or questions formulated by most treaty bodies requesting clarification on specific parts of States Parties' reports or on specific rights. Practical difficulties, however, remain in reducing the reporting burden on States Parties at the point where it would be most useful, namely *before* the preparation of their reports. There is, therefore, a need for further reflection on ways to streamline the reporting process.[151]

In his report submitted to the 57th session of the General Assembly, the Secretary-General explicitly called on the treaty bodies to adopt a more coordinated approach to their activities and standardize their varied reporting requirements, as well as making it possible for states to provide a single report summarizing their adherence to the full range of the relevant international human rights treaties.[152]

Discussions concerning possible improvements in the reporting system currently focus on the periodicity of the reports. Countries which are parties to several human rights treaties frequently refer to serious difficulties in providing their reports in an appropriate, timely and qualitative manner. It must also be borne in mind in this context that various parts of the United Nations human rights machinery, especially the Commission and the Sub-Commission, the thematic and country Special Rapporteurs, and working groups also request information and comments from governments concerning specific issues. The above-mentioned report by the Secretary-General underlines that a better coordination of the timing of the reports to different Committees will significantly improve the working conditions of treaty bodies and, at the same time, reduce the burden on States Parties related to the preparation of the reports for various human rights organs and bodies.

A fundamental reform of the periodicity of the reports would require, however, coordinated amendments in different treaties, since they determine the timeframes for reports. Only the Human Rights Committee decides freely when the State Party should submit a periodic report and ECOSOC decides about this matter with regard to the Committee on Economic, Social and Cultural Rights. Meanwhile, the treaty bodies have adopted several amendments to their rules of procedures which, in fact, lead to adjustments of procedural treaty norms to present requirements through '... *de facto* departures from the strict periodicities set out in many of the treaties'. For example, the Committee on the Elimination of Racial Discrimination decided that, if there is less than two years between the consideration of a periodic report and the scheduled date for the following one, the Committee can propose to the State Party to combine the two.[153] Other treaty bodies also adopt a similar approach.[154] It is now up to the treaty bodies to analyse to what extent further reforms, focusing in particular on the rationalization of the procedure from the perspective of the drafters of reports, could be undertaken through their coordinated action.[155]

The concept of periodical reports creates a certain tension between the monitoring function of treaty bodies and their limited ability to respond to the evolving human rights situations, in particular in the case of emergencies. To address this problem, the Committees have decided to move beyond the normal procedure and, in emergencies, ask the government concerned for an ad hoc report to consider the situation as a matter of urgency. For instance, the Rules of Procedure of the CEDAW refer specifically to reports requested on an exceptional basis, the substantive scope of which should be limited to those areas mentioned in the Committee's request.[156] Such a practice responds to the widely shared demand that the human rights machinery should be able to take preventive or responsive action without unnecessary delay. However, the independent expert expressed some scepticism concerning the effectiveness of special reports and urgent procedures. In his view, it is important to maintain the division of labour between the treaty bodies and the special mechanisms.[157]

For many years, the technical cooperation programme of the Office of the High Commissioner for Human Rights has been involved in the training of governmental officials responsible for reporting to treaty bodies. Regional workshops are organized, and sometimes specific projects are developed, for selected countries.[158] In the framework of the 'Hurist' project of the United Nations Development Programme and the Office of the High Commissioner, one of the six windows is dedicated to assistance in the ratification of human rights treaties and reporting. Core information embracing fundamental data concerning individual states, including their legal systems and domestic human rights machinery, is being distributed to States Parties to give them the possibility of no longer including this type of information in each report. A *Manual on Human Rights Reporting* has also been published by the Office and UNITAR. Some other publications by the Office also assist the human rights treaty system, namely: *Recent Reporting History of States Parties under the Principal International Human Rights Instruments;*[159] *Compilation of Guidelines on the Form and Content of Reports to be Submitted by States Parties to the International Human Rights Treaties;*[160] *Compilation of Rules of Procedure adopted by Human Rights Treaty Bodies;*[161] and *Compilation of General Comments and General Recommendations adopted by Human Rights Treaty Bodies'.*[162] All these documents are also available at the website of the OHCHR, alongside the basic documentation of the treaty bodies.

The impact of the reporting system does not only result from the scrutiny by the human rights treaty bodies. Moreover, it seems that the control function, albeit crucial, is no longer dominant. In parallel, the dialogue between experts sitting on the Committees and the States Parties has gained importance. As it has already been said, the purpose of this dialogue is not only to take stock of the human rights record of a country, but to assist the country in improving its human rights performance. Consequently, in view of the growing number of governments, the Committees are not perceived so much as international supervisors, but as attractive partners who, given their own expertise and place in the human rights machinery, may provide valuable guidance in the fulfilment of national human rights obligations.

Procedures Related to Human Rights Violations

The evolution of the procedures in the framework of the Commission on Human Rights

The problem of how to react to human rights violations reported to the Commission was present in the debates of this organ from its very first session. A Sub-Committee on the Handling of Communications set up by the Commission in 1947 concluded its work by saying that '… the Commission has no power to take any action in regard to any complaints regarding human rights'.[163] Nevertheless, the Commission agreed that the Rapporteur should draw the attention of ECOSOC to the situation resulting from this gap.

It is interesting to note that, at the same time, the Commission on the Status of Women, while examining its own competence, arrived at the opposite conclusion. A Sub-Committee created by this Commission found it possible to recommend a procedure for dealing with communications complaining about violations of women's rights or demanding action; this was finally endorsed by the Commission. Despite the above-mentioned differences, ECOSOC refused to recognize that either the Commission on Human Rights or the Commission on the Status of Women had adequate power to take action on communications.[164]

Despite the early debate on communications in the Commission on Human Rights and several attempts to change the conclusions adopted in 1947, it took 12 years before, in 1959, ECOSOC adopted its first resolution – 728F (XXVIII) – establishing a procedure for handling communications. While reiterating once again its previous position concerning the missing competence of the Commission to take action on complaints concerning violations of human rights, ECOSOC requested the Secretary-General to distribute among the Commission's members, before each session, a non-confidential list of communications dealing with the principles involved in the promotion of universal respect for, and observance of, human rights. At the same time, the Secretary-General was requested to distribute among the Commission's members a confidential list of other communications concerning human rights.[165] The lists contained only a summary of the communications, whereas the full text remained accessible to the Commission's members and was sent to the states concerned. In accordance with the wishes of states, their replies to communications were presented to the Commission in full or in summary form. An analogical procedure was adopted with regard to communications dealing with discrimination and minorities. The distribution of the non-confidential list was discontinued in 1977.

In 1967 this relatively weak procedure, which continued to prevent the Commission from considering specific cases of human rights violations, was supplemented, on the Commission's initiative, by ECOSOC resolution 1235 (XLII) which, in fact, departed from the rigorous position taken in 1947 and empowered the Commission and the Sub-Commission to '... examine ... information relevant to gross violations of human rights and fundamental freedoms'. Pursuant to this resolution, the Commission could also: '... make a thorough study of situations which reveal a consistent pattern of violations of human rights [situations affecting a large number of people over a protracted period of time] and report, with recommendations thereon, to the Economic and Social Council.'

In 1970, in its resolution 1503 (XLVIII), ECOSOC acting on the basis of the draft submitted by the Commission on Human Rights[166] established a 'Procedure for dealing with communications relating to violations of human rights and fundamental freedoms'. Widely known as the '1503 procedure', it applies to situations '... which appear to reveal a consistent pattern of gross and reliably attested violations of human rights and fundamental freedoms'.

Examination of the human rights situation in a country under ECOSOC resolution 1235 (XLII)

In the 1970s, the Commission commenced to place on its agenda an item, 'Human rights situations ...', which, since then, has for many years evoked strong emotions and tensions. Under this agenda item (at present number 9), participants in the debate can comment on human rights situations in all countries. In practice, some delegations review the situation in several countries, whereas others focus on one or two country situations or remain silent in the debate. Subsequently, members of the Commission, who can be supported by states observers, may table draft resolutions proposing that the human rights situation in a given country remain under consideration by the Commission. The Commission can also decide to terminate the consideration on a specific case under the '1503 procedure', and continue its examination in public under ECOSOC resolution 1235. This usually happened when, in the Commission's view, the situation had not improved and/or the government was not willing to cooperate with the Commission to its satisfaction.

In country-related resolutions, the Commission identifies its matters of concern and recommends appropriate steps to be taken to the government in question, with a view to stopping human rights violations. The Commission may also establish a special mechanism to follow the situation, which could be a Special Rapporteur, Special Representative or Independent Expert – depending on the nature of the situation – while the appointment of a Special Rapporteur is perceived as the strongest measure. Such a mechanism reports to the Commission and, in some cases, to the General Assembly. The Commission always invites the government to cooperate closely with the special mechanisms.

Having expressed its concern about a country situation, the Commission usually keeps it on the agenda until the situation improves sufficiently. Sometimes, countries remain under the direct scrutiny of the Commission for many years. Member states pay close attention to the government's willingness to cooperate with the Commission and its special mechanisms since, as experience has taught, this cooperation may significantly facilitate the resolution of human rights problems.

The public character of the procedure under ECOSOC resolution 1235 often prompts the governments concerned to seek a solution in direct consultations between interested delegations, leading to a compromise on the final position taken by the Commission. This compromise can lead to an agreed text of the resolution or to the concluding of the issue by a statement of the Commission's Chairperson, which is construed to be softer than a resolution. Occasionally, a delegation aiming to interrupt the debate on the human rights situation in its country, submits a so-called 'no action motion' which, if adopted, stops the proceeding. This approach, although formally in accordance with the Rules of Procedure,[167] has been criticized for being inappropriate in the case of alleged human rights violations. Critics maintain that doubts in such a case require examination.

The consideration of a situation under resolution 1235 is discontinued if the Commission so decides in view of improvements in the country's human rights record. A situation can also be dropped from the agenda if the majority/minority balance in the Commission changes. Quite often country resolutions have been adopted by a tiny majority and it can happen that, at the next session, this majority diminishes. Unfortunately, the results of voting do not always reflect the real human rights situation in a country, but sometimes bear witness to the political preferences of the Commission's members. In some cases, the Commission decides to move the consideration of the human rights record of a country from the agenda item concerning situations of gross human rights violations to the item dealing with technical cooperation in the field of human rights. This happens when the Commission continues to show its particular interest in the human rights developments in the country, but estimates that the situation has improved and therefore no longer justifies scrutiny under the previous agenda item. In such a situation, the Commission recommends a programme of technical cooperation and requests the High Commissioner or a Special Rapporteur to report on its implementation.

Communications procedures

General   Communications procedures enable states and individuals to bring violations of and/or other forms of states' non-compliance with human rights standards to the attention of the competent organs or bodies. The notion of 'communications' has been carefully selected. It indicates that lodging such a motion does not initiate a judicial proceeding but opens an examination of a case with a view to stating facts as to whether the violation or another form of non-compliance has taken place. There are a variety of communications procedures within the United Nations machinery and all of them play an important role in the protection of human rights, both in a preventive and reactive sense. They can be differentiated according to one of the following criteria:

- The legal basis of the procedure – one category comprises procedures based on the human rights treaties; the other includes those based on ECOSOC resolutions.
- Legal foundations of communications – in the case of procedures based on a treaty, human rights standards laid down therein provide the legal foundation for a communication; in the case of the procedures based on ECOSOC resolutions, human rights standards, as referred to by the Charter of the United Nations and proclaimed in the Universal Declaration of Human Rights, provide the terms of reference for a communication.
- The organ competent to consider communications – a treaty-based body is competent to consider communications submitted in the framework of the respective treaty; the Commission on Human Rights and its Sub-Commission are organs competent within the procedures based on ECOSOC resolutions.
- The subject submitting communication – it can be a state, which claims that another state has violated human rights or in another way did not comply with its human rights obligations (so-called state communications), or an individual/group of individuals (so-called individual communications).

Treaty-based communication procedures have been established by the International Covenant on Civil and Political Rights, the Convention on the Elimination of All Forms of Racial Discrimination, the Convention against Torture and Other Cruel, Inhuman or Degrading Treatment and Punishment, and the Convention on the Elimination of All Forms of Discrimination against Women. Two other human rights treaties, which have their own monitoring mechanisms, do not allow for the consideration of communications: the International Covenant on Economic, Social and Cultural Rights and the Convention on the Rights of the Child. Yet, the Commission on Human Rights is already engaged in the examination of the communication procedure under the Covenant (see the section, 'Committee on Economic, Social and Cultural Rights,' above).

To facilitate the lodging of communications and further proceedings, the Human Rights Committee and some of the special procedures have adopted model questionnaires.[168] However, the authors of such submissions need to be aware that, while they may wish to benefit from these questionnaires, it is not obligatory to do so and communications that do not follow a questionnaire will be processed provided that they meet relevant substantive criteria. All communications need to be sent to the OHCHR, either directly or through other United Nations offices.

The '1503 procedure'   The '1503 procedure' is a channel for individuals and groups to bring their concerns about alleged human rights violations directly to the attention of the Commission on Human Rights. It has been exposed to some serious criticism from two opposite directions. On the one hand, the Commission's slow pace due to a complicated procedure and large number of communications, as well as its cycle of work, has prompted some critics to express doubts as to whether this procedure was an adequate response to communications alleging serious human rights violations. It is to be noted here that the '1503 procedure' processed 98,799 communications in 2000; 29,726 in 2001; and 18,492 in 2002.[169]

On the other hand, for some governments, this procedure interfered too much with states' claims to be protected against external scrutiny in the area of human rights perceived as a domestic affair. Nevertheless, the Working Group on Mechanisms reinforced the value of the '1503 procedure' and reaffirmed its basic principles, that is: objectivity, impartiality and confidentiality.[170] The Working Group decided, however, to propose several changes to eliminate existing shortcomings. These should simplify the preparatory process and make the Commission's examination of the communication, including its decision-making process, more effective. The following presentation of the procedure reflects these changes, as adopted in ECOSOC resolution 2000/3 which contains a revised 'Procedure for dealing with communications concerning human rights'.[171]

Communications can be declared admissible if there are reasonable grounds to believe that they may '... reveal a consistent pattern of gross and reliably attested violations of human rights and fundamental freedoms within the terms of reference of the Sub-Commission'.[172] It is of fundamental importance for its admissibility that a communication be based on credible information. It cannot refer, for example, to the mass media as an exclusive source of information. Replies from the governments concerned are taken into account when the admissibility of communications is under consideration. The aim of the communication must not be inconsistent with the principles of the Charter of the United Nations or the Universal Declaration of Human Rights. Furthermore, the communication can be declared inadmissible if it is submitted for political motives alone. The Secretariat has been empowered to screen manifestly ill-founded communications, but its findings require the approval of the Chairperson of the Working Group on Communications (established by the Sub-Commission).

Communications may be submitted by: individuals and groups who claim to be victims, and individuals and groups who have direct, reliable knowledge of violations. The relevant rules provide that a communication coming from a NGO may be declared admissible if this organization '... acts in good faith and in accordance with recognized principles of human rights, not resorting to politically motivated stands contrary to the provisions of the Charter'. The approval of *actio popularis* was an important decision that has made the procedure not only a remedy in the hands of victims, but also a tool which may be used by human rights advocates. However, anonymous communications are inadmissible.

A communication must reveal relevant facts, determine its purpose and identify human rights that have allegedly been violated. Abusive language, in particular insulting references to the state concerned, by the author may be grounds for declaring a communication inadmissible. As in many other international complaints procedures, the '1503 procedure' is based on the rule that, before an effective submission of the communication, domestic remedies must be exhausted. The lack of effectiveness of these remedies may, however, justify an exception to this principle. As a rule, a communication is declared inadmissible if it has already been subject to the same, or another, international procedure.

Communications should be sent to the Commission on Human Rights, addressed to the Office of the High Commissioner. On receipt of an admissible communication, the Office sends it to the government concerned for comments which, together with the communication, are considered by the Working Group on Communications. All members of the Working Group receive monthly confidential summaries of communications.

The following organs and bodies are currently involved in the consideration of the communications under the '1503 procedure': the Working Group on Communications; the Working Group on Situations; the Commission on Human Rights; and ECOSOC. The Working Group on Communications is elected by the Sub-Commission on the Protection and Promotion of Human Rights from among its members and represents all the regional groups. It meets for one week immediately after the session of the Sub-Commission and examines communications received and any government's responses thereto. In its report, it recommends communications which should be referred to the Working Group on Situations.[173]

The Working Group on Situations comprises five members nominated from among the members of the Commission on Human Rights by the regional groups, with due attention to rotation in membership. The Working Group meets at least one month prior to the Commission. On the basis of the report of the Working Group on Communications, the Working Group on Situations decides which situations under consideration should be referred to the Commission. It can recommend to the Commission one of the following options:

(i) To discontinue consideration of the matter when further consideration or action is not warranted; (ii) To keep the situation under review in the light of any further information received from the government concerned and any further information which may reach the Commission under the '1503 procedure'; (iii) To keep the situation under review and to appoint an independent expert who reports to the next session of the Commission; (iv) To discontinue consideration of the matter under the confidential procedure governed by Council resolution 1503 (XLVIII) in order to take up consideration of the same matter under the public procedure governed by Council resolution 1235 (XLII).[174]

ECOSOC resolution 1503 also empowered the Commission to appoint, with the consent of the state concerned, an ad hoc committee to investigate the situation. This type of action has never been applied and is not included in the revised 'Procedure for dealing with communications concerning human rights'.

Like all the communications procedures, the '1503 procedure' is also based on the principle of a dialogue with the government concerned. The Working Group on Situations informs the government about its recommendations and, subsequently, the government's representatives are invited to attend the Commission's meetings during which the human rights situation in their country is examined. Usually, governments send high-level delegations who participate actively in the meeting.

The Commission holds two separate closed meetings to consider a human rights situation placed before it by the Working Group on Situations, as well as the situations still under review. At the first meeting, the consideration of a human rights situation in a country includes the presentation of comments by the government concerned if it so wishes, and a discussion between members of the Commission and the government's delegation. This is based on confidential files on the case and the report of the Working Group on Situations. During the second session, the Commission takes action on draft resolutions or decisions. The time between the two sessions can be used by the members of the Commission for submitting alternative proposals or amendments to the proposal of action made by the Working Group on Situations. On completion of the procedure, the Chairperson of the Commission announces at a public session which countries have been examined under the '1503 procedure', as well as the names of countries with regard to which the Commission decided to conclude its proceedings under this procedure.[175]

An important rule of the '1503 procedure' is the principle of confidentiality which covers the entire proceeding, including the meetings of both Working Groups and of the Commission; all relevant correspondence and dossiers; and the appointment and work of independent experts established under this procedure. There are two exceptions to the rule of confidentiality: First, if the government concerned wishes to wave this principle; second, when ECOSOC so decides, whether acting on its own or on the Commission's initiative. It should be noted that the second exceptional ruling, which is, in a way, a sanction, has been applied on several occasions.[176]

Communications procedures under the human rights treaties   The communications procedures under the human rights treaties are optional, that is, they are applicable only to those states which have approved them by accession or ratification. The only exception to this rule is the procedure of state communications under the Convention on the Elimination of All Forms of Racial Discrimination, which is applicable to all States Parties to the treaty.[177] The approval of an optional communication procedure may take place either at the time of ratification or at any time thereafter.

The treaty-based communications procedures embrace two categories of communications: those lodged by states and those submitted by private individuals. The relevant rules are similar in the case of all treaties. Since the procedures established under the International Covenant on Civil and Political Rights have been approved by the largest number of States Parties by far, they will be presented here as examples. It should be stressed that no state has so far submitted a communication claiming that another State Party does not comply with its treaty obligations.

State communications   If a State Party claims that another State Party to the International Covenant on Civil and Political Rights does not comply with its obligations under this treaty, it could lodge a communication with the Human Rights Committee. This procedure is applicable exclusively when both states have recognized the competence of the Committee to consider such communications.[178] The procedure comprises the following steps:

- A written communication is brought to the attention of the state concerned that should provide its response within three months; if the matter is not settled between the two states within six months from the time of submission of the communication, either state may refer the matter to the Committee.
- The Committee offers its good offices to the States Parties involved based on human rights and fundamental freedoms laid down in the International Covenant.
- The Committee may request the States Parties to supply any relevant additional information.
- The States Parties concerned are entitled to be represented and make oral or written submissions during the Committee's meetings when the matter is under consideration.
- Not later than 12 months after the submission of the matter to the Committee, it should adopt a report containing a brief statement of the facts and, if possible, the solution reached. If the matter continues to be a subject of dispute, the report should include written and oral submissions made by the States Parties concerned.

With the exception of the Committee's report, the proceedings are confidential.

In case of the Convention on the Elimination of All Forms of Racial Discrimination, when the matter has not been resolved to the satisfaction of both parties within the six months following the submission of the communication, the Committee on the Elimination of Racial Discrimination forms a Conciliation Commission which continues to deal with the matter.

Individual communications   Through the direct or indirect access of those who claim to be victims of human rights violations to the communications procedures, the international protection of human rights laid down by various human rights treaties has ceased to be an instrument at the disposal of states alone, and has also become a tool in the hands of individuals. A situation in which the subject of human rights and the state are put on equal footing before an independent international organ has been a breakthrough in the traditional approach of international law to the relationship between the individual and the state. In the view of many, this has been either the most, or one of the most, significant changes in international law since 1945. It is also fascinating to see how rapidly a significant number of countries have recognized that this is an appropriate step towards granting recourse to the international protection to those who complain that their rights have been infringed upon. Before this happened at the international level, individuals could acquire access to regional human rights commissions and courts in the framework of the European and Inter-American systems for the promotion and protection of human rights. The present status of accession to the four existing procedures of individual communications as of April 2002 is shown in Table 1.6.

Table 1.6   Accessions to the procedures of individual communications

ICCPR	CERD	CAT	CEDAW
103	38	45	35

A communication received by the Human Rights Committee is forwarded to the State Party concerned for a written reply within six months, both on the admissibility and the merits of the communication. Within two months, the State Party may, however, apply for the communication to be recognized as inadmissible for the reasons set out in its reply. The Committee may also request additional comments from the state concerned and from the author of the communication. While the final consideration of the case is in the hands of the entire Committee, its preparatory stage, including the examination of the admissibility of the communication, is handled by the Committee's Working Group on Communications.[179] A communication may be declared admissible under the following conditions:

- the author, being subject to the jurisdiction of a State Party to the Protocol, is the victim of a violation of any of the rights set forth in the Covenant. The communication could also be submitted by a victim's representative. The communication may also be accepted if submitted on behalf of the victim when a submission of the communication by the victim personally is impossible.

- The communication does not constitute an abuse of the right of submission.
- The communication is compatible with the provisions of the Covenant.
- The matter is not under consideration by another international procedure of international investigation or settlement.
- Domestic remedies have been exhausted.

The Working Group declares a communication admissible by consensus. If unanimity has not been achieved or the Working Group believes that it would be appropriate for the Committee to decide upon admissibility, the case is referred to the Committee.

A set of procedural rules have been developed which govern the conduct of affairs in the Committee when considering the communications.[180] Among them, the following are of fundamental importance to the overall concept of communications procedure:

- the procedure is based on a dialogue with parties placed on an equal footing
- the parties present their views to the Committee in writing; there is no hearing before the Committee
- the Committee is not mandated to carry out fact-finding
- the burden of proof cannot rest on the author of the communication alone[181]
- the procedure is confidential, although the Committee's opinions are announced publicly.

The Committee adopts its Views on Communications (the final position in the case) after having given the state concerned and its author the opportunity to comment on the communication and on the government's views. The decision is limited to the statement whether, in the view of the Committee, the state concerned complied with its obligations under the International Covenant or not. The Committee also makes explanatory comments. Individual opinions may be attached to express the specific observations of the Committee members about the case. The Views are communicated to the parties and their summary is published in the Committee's report.

While considering individual communications, the treaty-based bodies have developed a unique jurisprudence. Besides the impact on an individual case, the Views on Communications influence more generally the law and practice of states, not only those of the parties to the given proceeding. Moreover, through commenting on the content of international standards and evaluating the domestic law and practice from this perspective, the treaty bodies contribute to the development of the body of the international human rights law in general.

Although an evident achievement of the international community, the communication procedures suffer because of their length. While this is certainly not a weak point of international procedures alone, in the case of the Human Rights Committee, it took in the past three to five years for the Committee to conclude the consideration of a communication. Through the recent merger of the admissibility and merits stages, it has been possible to cut this time to two to three years. This is still a long period that not only tests the patience of victims, but also frustrates those who expect the international community to offer timely and effective protection as a matter of principle. However, the Committee can request the State Party to take interim measures (without prejudice to the final decision), if, otherwise, irreparable damage might be done to the rights or fundamental freedoms of the interested person. For instance, the Committee may recommend that the state refrain from deporting a person seeking asylum, examine the state of health of an alleged victim or postpone the execution of a penalty. However, in light of the Committee's present workload, its sessional mode of work whereby its meets annually for only nine weeks, and the increasing number of communications, a radical acceleration of the procedure seems impossible unless the time at the Committee's disposal is extended and support from the Secretariat is strengthened. In 2002, the Human Rights Committee has 1153 registered cases and some 245 pending.[182]

With a view to ensuring more expeditious and highly professional handling of communications, the Office of the High Commissioner created a 'Petition Team' in 2000. The responsibilities of this new team cover screening and evaluating incoming correspondence, registering cases, assisting treaty bodies in preparing draft decisions on admissibility and on the merits of individual cases, providing uniform legal advice to the treaty bodies regarding communications procedures and assisting in the follow-up to Committees' recommendations.[183] As stressed before, however, this solution is based on a fragile basis of voluntary funding.

Comparison of the '1503 procedure' and the treaty-based communications procedures   The existence of various communications procedures before the various human rights organs and bodies sometimes leads to confusion. Clarity in this regard is, however, important, particularly in the context of specific human rights violations. There is a general rule of conduct according to which a person who feels that his/her rights have been infringed upon is well advised to choose only the remedy which promises the best results. It is important that a case pending in the framework of one international procedure should not, as a matter of principle, be taken up in the framework of another. In this context, the choice between the international and, if available, regional procedures should also be taken into consideration. In practical terms, at the international level, most important is the distinction between the '1503 procedure' and the individual communications procedures under the human rights treaties. Taking the Optional Protocol to the International Covenant on Civil and Political Rights as an example, one can draw the following comparisons:

The '1503 procedure'	The procedure under the Optional Protocol to the International Covenant on Civil and Political Rights
The procedure is established by an ECOSOC resolution	The procedure is established by an international treaty. The obligations deriving therefrom are legally binding
The procedure is applicable to all states	The procedure is applicable only to States Parties
The procedure covers situations of consistent patterns of gross human rights violations	The procedure can be applied only to cases of human rights violations affecting a specified person or persons
The procedure can be applied to all categories of human rights	The procedure covers only rights protected by the International Covenant
The communication can be submitted by a victim/group of victims of human rights violations, or in the framework of *actio popularis*	The communication can be lodged only by victims or a person acting on behalf of a victim
The authors of communications do not take part in the procedure. They are not informed about the course of action unless the Commission makes a public announcement. The authors are only informed about the mode of procedure applied in such cases.	The authors of communications participate in the procedure in the form of written statements.

Non-governmental Organizations' Contribution to the Work of the United Nations Human Rights Mechanisms

NGOs are not part of the UN human rights machinery. Yet, they play a very important role in its work, often acting as the voice of victims and wider civil society. However, articulating human rights concerns, although essential, is not the only contribution by NGOs. They also offer to the international community capacities in the area of monitoring, fact-finding, inquiries into human rights violations, analysis, research and training. More specifically, the contribution of NGOs is significant, in particular, in the following areas:

1   The work of the Commission on Human Rights and the Sub-Commission – representatives of NGOs participate in the discussions of these organs, presenting their views, assessments and postulates. Equally important is the NGOs' lobbying. Disseminating information and analysis, NGOs often successfully attempt to influence negotiations. Finally, they take an active part in the proceedings of working groups established to negotiate draft treaties or declarations.

2   The work of treaty bodies – NGOs are an important source of information, next to governments and UN agencies and programmes.

3   The work of special procedures – this is also largely based on information coming from NGOs. For example, a large part of urgent appeals sent by special procedures to governments follows information made available by NGOs.

4   Human rights work in the field – NGOs are involved in human rights monitoring and investigations and provide the United Nations and the wider International Community with materials resulting therefrom. NGOs are also increasingly involved in the programme of technical cooperation carried out by the OHCHR as implementing partner.

5   The work of international conferences – the mode of NGOs' participation in such conferences often generated disputes about applicable and workable solutions. While the concept of world summits as essentially governmental meetings prevailed, NGOs held their own parallel meetings and provided input to the governmental level.

Among NGOs, those with consultative status with the ECOSOC enjoy a privileged position. For example, they are entitled to designate United Nations representatives, to make proposals regarding the agenda of the Commission on Human Rights and the Sub-Commission, attend meetings of these bodies and present written and oral statements, be commissioned with the preparation of studies, participate in international conferences organized by the United Nations and in the preparatory processes to such conferences, and have facilitated access to the documentation system and support from the secretariat. In view of the particular empowerment of NGOs with consultative status, the principles ruling this status are also important for the work of the UN human rights machinery.[184]

The participation of NGOs in the work of the United Nations human rights programme continues to give rise sometimes to controversies between the advocates of a very broad presence of NGOs and those who are inclined rather to narrow it. While repeating, once again, that the participation of NGOs in the work of the United Nations human rights machinery is vital, there is also a space for NGOs to make the role of their advocates easier. To that end, NGOs could try to better coordinate their active presence in different United Nations through, for example, broader use of joint statements and other presentations. This would probably further strengthen their impact. On the other hand, one can be afraid that the attempts of administrative restrictions to limit the contribution by NGOs to the United Nations human rights machinery would negatively influence its work and thus be counterproductive.

NOTES

*   This contribution presents the views of the author, who is a staff member of the United Nations, and does not necessarily reflect those of the Organization.

1   Compare Articles 1, para. 3, 55, 56 and Articles 13, para. 1, 62, para. 2, 68 of the Charter of the United Nations.

2   See section on 'Communication procedures'.

3   Statement of 16 March 1998 at the opening of the 54th session of the Commission on Human Rights, UN doc. SG/SM/98/53.

4   GA resolution 55/2, paras. 24 and 25.

5   Part II, para. 17.

6   Part I, paras 1 and 5 respectively of the *Vienna Declaration and Programme of Action*. The quoted para. 5 should be interpreted in light of Articles 1, para 3, 55 and 56 of the Charter of the United Nations. This means that states have the duty to promote and protect human rights both at the national and international level.

7   Part I, para. 4, of the *Vienna Declaration and Programme of Action* lays down, *inter alia:* 'The promotion and protection of all human rights and fundamental freedoms must be considered as a priority objective of the United Nations in accordance with its purposes and principles, in particular the purpose of international co-operation. In the framework of these purposes and principles, the promotion and protection of all human rights is a legitimate concern of the international community.' This was the first time in history that the principle of 'legitimate concern' was recognized unanimously in this context.

8   The *Vienna Declaration and Programme of Action* refers in several places to international cooperation, including cooperation with the United Nations human rights machinery. It is important to recall that in Article 56 of the Charter of the United Nations, member states pledged themselves to take joint and separate action in cooperation with the Organization for the achievement of the purposes set forth in Article 55 which include, *inter alia,* the promotion of universal respect for, and observance of, human rights and fundamental freedoms for all.

9   Part I, para. 5, of the *Vienna Declaration and Programme of Action*.

10   Ibid., para. 8.

11   Exceptions in favour of an exclusive competence of the Security Council are mentioned in Article 12 of the Charter.

12   This is the so-called regular budget which in 2001 reached US$22 million (approx. 1.7 per cent of the overall budget of the United Nations), whereas the budget of voluntary contributions for human rights activities made mainly by member states reached US$46 million.

13   A/C.3/56/1.

14   See, for example, S/PRST/2002/22 and Press Release from Security Council's 4583rd Meeting (PM) on 23 July 2002, SC/7462; S/2003/90 (report of an urgent human rights mission to Côte d'Ivoire).

15   ECOSOC is composed of 54 member states of the United Nations, elected by the General Assembly in accordance with the principle of regional balance – see Article 61 of the Charter and General Assembly resolution 2847 (XXVI) of 20 December 1971. Observer states, United Nations specialized agencies and programmes, and non-governmental organizations may participate in the work of ECOSOC without a right to vote. ECOSOC holds one regular session a year (special sessions may also be convened).

16   UN doc. E/2001/100.
17   See ECOSOC resolution 1998/2 concerning the coordinated follow-up to the *Vienna Declaration and Programme of Action*.
18   ECOSOC resolution 5(1).
19   ECOSOC resolution 1990/48.
20   ECOSOC resolution 9(II) 1946 and 1979/36.
21   Mary Robinson, Address at the opening of the 56th session of the Commission on Human Rights, 20 March 2000, <www.unhchr.ch>.
22   Initially adopted ECOSOC resolution 100 (V) of 12 August 1947. For an updated version consult <www.unhchr.ch>.
23   *Vienna Declaration and Programme of Action*, Article II, para. 17.
24   UN doc. E/CN.4/DEC/2000/109 – thereafter referred to as decision 2000/109.
25   Initially lasting for three weeks, the regular sessions have been extended to six weeks.
26   See Decision 2000/109.
27   The Commission considered the following items: election of officers; adoption of the agenda; organization of the work of the session; rationalization of the work of the Commission; draft provisional agenda for the next session and report to ECOSOC on the 57th session of the Commission.
28   The Commission considered the following items: report of the United Nations High Commissioner for Human Rights and follow-up to the World Conference on Human Rights; report of the Sub-Commission on the Promotion and Protection of Human Rights and election of members of the Sub-Commission; promotion and protection of human rights: status of the International Covenants on Human Rights; human rights defenders; information and education; science and environment; effective functioning of human rights mechanisms: treaty bodies, national institutions and regional arrangements; adaptation and strengthening of the United Nations machinery for human rights; advisory services and technical cooperation in the field of human rights.
29   The Commission considered the following items: the right of peoples to self-determination; racism, racial discrimination, xenophobia and all forms of discrimination; the right to development; economic, social and cultural rights; civil and political rights, including the questions of: torture and detention, disappearances and summary executions, freedom of expression, independence of the judiciary, administration of justice, impunity, religious intolerance, states of emergency, conscientious objection to military service; integration of the human rights of women and the gender perspective; rights of the child; specific groups and individuals, including: migrant workers, minorities, mass exoduses and displaced persons, other vulnerable groups and individuals; indigenous issues.
30   Two themes divided the members of the Commission: 'the human rights of disabled people' and 'human rights and terrorism'.
31   Decision 2002/113.
32   See <www.unhchr.ch/huricane/huricane.nsf/newsroom>.
33   ECOSOC resolution 1990/48.
34   See '1503 procedure' in the section, 'Procedures related to human rights violations'.
35   Sergio Vieira de Mello, Essay 'Their Dignity Will Be Mine, As It Is Yours', *The UN Chronicle*, No. 4/2002.

36   This group encompassed 69 speakers at the 57th session and 78 at the 58th session. On the other hand, how encouraging and welcome it might be, the considerable time allocated to 'dignitaries' also gives rise to concern. Thus proposals have been made to concentrate such statements in the framework of a high-level segment of the Commission. Today, scattered throughout the session, they generate organizational problems in handling the tight agenda of the Commission.

37   250 non-governmental organizations were accredited at the 57th session and 247 at the 58th session. They produced 192 and 205 official documents respectively.

38   Report of the Secretary-General: 'Strengthening of the United Nations: an agenda for further change', UN doc. A/57/387, para. 46. Discussing this issue in her aforementioned statement to the 58th session of the Commission, the High Commissioner quoted one of the principal drafters of the Universal Declaration of Human Rights, Rene Cassin, who stated: 'Finally, I would draw the Working Parties' attention to the advisability of gradually increasing the means of implementation – by urging the importance of preventive measures which depend largely on the collaboration of States with the United Nations and the vigilance of public opinion, and means of redress, or even punishment, of the violations committed.' The topicality of these words is indeed self-evident when one looks at the work of the Commission and the challenges it faces today.

39   Resolution of the Commission on Human Rights adopted at its 5th session in 1949.

40   Subsequent reelections are possible. Half of the members and alternates are elected every two years.

41   See Commission on Human Rights' decision 2000/109.

42   See para. 43 of the report of the Working Group – decision 2000/109.

43   Ibid., para. 51.

44   Ibid., para. 58.

45   Ibid., paras 45 and 46.

46   Sub-Commission resolution 1999/114, annex.

47   ECOSOC resolution 16 (VI).

48   ECOSOC resolution 1982/34.

49   ECOSOC resolution 11(II).

50   ECOSOC resolution 1989/45.

51   ECOSOC resolution 1987/22.

52   ECOSOC resolution 1983/27. See also the section on reporting in the International Labour Organization and UNESCO in this book.

53   The Commission is presented in a detailed manner elsewhere in this volume. Since it plays a central role in the promotion and protection of the human rights of women, it is necessary to make the comments above.

54   See: *Amnesty International, World Conference on Human Rights. Facing Up to the Failures: Proposals for Improving the Protection of Human Rights by the United Nations*, 1992, AI Index: IOR 41/16/92. During the four decades since the first formal submission of a proposal, negotiations were sometimes quite advanced, in particular in the 1970s, but not enough to make the final breakthrough.

55   *Vienna Declaration and Programme of Action*, Part II, para. 18.

56   Thereafter referred to as resolution 48/141; compare also 'New United Nations High Commissioner will champion rights worldwide', *United Nations Chronicle*, March 1994, Vol. XXXI, No. 1, p.84.

57 UN doc. 48/141 para 2 (a).
58 Para. 4 (b) of resolution 48/141.
59 Para. 4 of resolution 48/141.
60 Para. 4 (b) of resolution 48/141.
61 Para. 5 of resolution 48/141.
62 All reports of the High Commissioner are available on the website: <www.unhchr.ch>.
63 See the Report of the Secretary-General to the Security Council Prevention of armed conflict, dated 7 June 2001, UN doc. A/55/985S/2001/574.
64 The Report of the High Commissioner to the 56th session of the Commission on Human Rights, doc. E/CN.4/2000/12. A recent urgent human rights mission to Ivory Coast from 23 to 29 December 2002 by the Deputy High Commissioner for Human Rights provides an example here – see note 14.
65 Para. 4 (f) of resolution 48/141.
66 Para. 4 (g) of resolution 48/141.
67 The Paris Principles were adopted as the conclusions of a workshop, held in Paris in October 1991. These conclusions were transmitted by the Commission on Human Rights, in resolution 1992/54, as the 'Principles relating to the status of national institutions', to the General Assembly. The General Assembly attached the Principles in 1993 as the Annex to resolution 48/134. The Paris Principles affirmed *inter alia* that national human rights institutions should be vested with as broad a mandate as possible set forth clearly in a constitutional or legislative text, and accorded competence sufficient to protect and promote human rights effectively.
68 The Secretary-General Report on the implementation of the report of the panel on United Nations peace operations, UN Doc. A/55/502, and the report of the Panel on United Nations Peace Operations [so-called 'Brahimi Report'], (A/55/305–S/2000/809).
69 See papers by UNDP 'Integrating human rights with sustainable human development' and the World Bank 'Development and Human Rights. The role of the World Bank' published in 1998. UNDP dedicated its Human Development Report 2000 to human rights and development.
70 See reports by the independent expert on enhancing the long-term effectiveness of the United Nations human rights treaty system (Ph. Alston), delivered to the Commission on Human Rights in 1989, 1993, 1997. UN doc. A/44/668; A/CONF.157/PC/62/Add.11/Rev.I; E/CN.4/1997/74 and the report of the Secretary-General on the consultations conducted in respect of the aforementioned reports – UN doc. E/CN.4/2000/98.
71 See UN doc. E/CN.4/1997/74, paras. 14, 31–35 and 111.
72 See the United Nations Millennium Declaration, UN doc. A/55/2; Report of the Secretary-General 'Road map towards the implementation of the United Nations Millennium Declaration', UN doc. A/56/326.
73 See the section, 'Reports under human rights treaties'.
74 Some participants in the 2001 meeting of the Chairpersons referred to this problem, see 'Report of the Chairpersons of the human rights treaty bodies on their 13th meeting': 16/07/2001. A/57/... – advance unedited text, see: OHCHR website <www.unhchr.ch/tbs/doc.nsf/(Symbol)/A.57...> and: the report of the Secretary-General on the consultations conducted in respect of the aforementioned report, UN doc. E/CN.4/2000/98. For the time being, such quotas have been established exclusively for the election of members of the CESCR.

75 Usually the rules of procedures of the treaty bodies lay down that the adoption of concluding observations after the examination of the report takes place in a private meeting. An exception provides here that the CERD, after having recently reexamined this issue, recognized that the adoption of concluding observations in public meetings serves the interest of transparency and decided to continue its present practice in this regard, Report of the Committee on the Elimination of Racial Discrimination, 58th and 59th sessions, UN doc. A/56/18, p.119.

76 Para. 37 of the Report on the 22nd, 23rd and 24th sessions of the Committee on Economic, Social and Cultural Rights, UN doc. E/C.12/2000/21. See also the section on 'Reports under human rights treaties'.

77 Para. 50 of the CESCR report (note 76).

78 See Committee on the Rights of the Child: the Report on the 28th session (24 September–2 October 2001), UN doc. CRC/C/111, pp.227–53. The previous general discussions focused on children in armed conflict; economic exploitation of children; the role of the family in the promotion of the rights of the child; the girl child; the administration of juvenile justice. See also Rule 55 of the Rules of Procedure of the Committee on the Elimination of Discrimination against Women, UN doc. A/56/38.

79 See 'Outline for drafting General Comments on specific rights of the International Covenant on Economic, Social and Cultural Rights', adopted by the CESCR at its 21st session, 15 November–3 December 1999.

80 See 'Compilation of General Comments and General Recommendations', UN doc. HRI/GEN/1/Rev.5, published on 26/04/2001 by the Office of the High Commissioner for Human Rights.

81 See below comments on CESCR, HRC and CEDAW.

82 See paras 59–60 of the Report of the Human Rights Committee, UN doc. A/56/40 (Vol. I); see also, for example, rules 45–7 of the CEDAW Rules of Procedure – UN doc. A/56/38.

83 CERD decision 2 (VI) 'Co-operation with the International Labour Organization (ILO) and the United Nations Educational, Scientific and Cultural Organization (UNESCO)', adopted by the Committee on 21 August 1972.

84 CERD Report, p.13 (note 75).

85 Paras 34 and 35 of the Rules of Procedure of the CESCR.

86 See the Report by the Secretariat to the 13th Meeting of Chairpersons of the Human Rights Treaty Bodies Geneva, 18–22 June 2001: 'Review of Recent Developments Relating to the Work of the Treaty Bodies, Status of the Annual Appeal 2001 of the Office of the United Nations High Commissioner for Human Rights and of the Plans of Action Strengthening Support to and Enhancing the Effectiveness of the Treaty Bodies', UN doc. HRI/MC/2001/2. See also Annual Appeals 2001 and 2002 by the Office of the High Commissioner for Human Rights.

87 Para. 52 (note 38).

88 See the reports of the independent expert, Philip Alston, on enhancing the long-term effectiveness of the United Nations human rights treaty system (note 70). See also A. Bayefsky, 'Report – the United Nations Human Rights Treaty System: Universality at the Crossroads', April 2001, comprehensive report from a study conducted under the direction of the author, which included, *inter alia,* an in-depth analysis of 20 countries.

89 See section on 'Reports under human rights treaties'.

90 See UN doc. E/CN.4/1997/74, para. 101.

91 Report of the Chairpersons of the human rights treaty bodies on their 13th meeting, 16/07/2001 (advance unedited text) – see: <www.unhchr.ch/tbs/doc.nsf/(Symbol)/A.57...>.

92 The Human Rights Committee has recently stressed that it '... continues to find value in the meeting of persons chairing the human rights treaty bodies as a forum for the exchange of ideas and information on procedures and logistical problems, particularly the need for sufficient services to enable the various treaty bodies to carry out their respective mandates', The HRC Report (Vol. I), p. 56 (note 82).

93 Para. 83 of the CESCR Report (note 75). See also UN doc. HRI/MC/2001/2, paras 24–26.

94 The Committee on Economic, Social and Cultural Rights, 21st session, 15 November–3 December 1999.

95   1. Reporting to States Parties on 24/02/89
     2. International technical assistance measures (Article 22) on 2/02/1990
     3. The nature of obligations of States Parties on 14/12/1990
     4. The right to adequate housing on 13/12/1991
     5. Persons with disabilities on 9/12/1994
     6. The economic, social and cultural rights of older persons on 08/12/1995
     7. The right to adequate housing (Article 11, para. 1; forced evictions) on 20/5/1997
     8. The relationship between economic sanctions and respect for human rights on 12/12/1997
     9. The domestic application of the Covenant on 8/12/1998
    10. The role of national human rights institutions in the protection of human rights on 14/12/1998
    11. Plans of action for primary education (Article 14) on 10/5/1999
    12. The right to adequate food (Article 11) on 12/5/1999
    13. The right to education (Article 13) on 8/12/1999
    14. The right to the highest attainable standard of health on 11/08/2000
    15. The right to water on 26/11/2002.
Texts of the General Comments can be found in the compilation UN doc. HRI/GEN/1/Rev.5 and on the Office of the High Commissioner for Human Rights website.

96 *Vienna Declaration and Programme of Action*, Part II, para. 75.

97 See the Report of the Committee on Economic, Social and Cultural Rights to the Commission on Human Rights on a draft optional protocol for the consideration of communications in relation to the International Covenant on Economic, Social and Cultural Rights, published in the annex to the Note by the Secretary-General 'Draft optional protocol to the International Covenant on Economic, Social and Cultural Rights', UN doc. E/CN.4/1997/105.

98 Commission on Human Rights resolution 2002/24, para. 9 (c) and (f).

99 Paras. 644–50 of the CESCR Report (note 76).

100 E/1994/23, para. 354. At its 24th session, the Committee updated the procedure for the participation of non-governmental organizations in the Committee's activities, UN doc. E/C.12/2000/6. See also paras 651–52 of the CESCR Report (note 76) and the general part of the section on 'Treaty monitoring bodies' for criteria for information provided by non-governmental organizations. -

101 See para. 43 of the CESCR Report (note 76).

102   1. Reporting obligation on 27/7/1981

2. Reporting guidelines on 28/07/1981
3. Implementation at the national level (Article 2) on 29/07/1981
4. Equality between the sexes (Article 3) on 30/7/1981
5. Derogation of rights (Article 4) on 31/7/1981
6. The right to life (Article 6) on 30/4/1982
7. Torture or cruel, inhuman or degrading treatment or punishment (Article 7) on 30/5/1982
8. Right to liberty and security of persons (Article 9) on 30/6/1982
9. Humane treatment of persons deprived of liberty (Article 10) on 30/7/ 1982
10. Freedom of expression (Article 19) on 29/6/1983
11. Prohibition of propaganda for war and inciting national, racial or religious hatred (Article 20) on 29/7/1983
12. The right to self-determination of peoples (Article 1) on 13/3/1984
13. Equality before the courts and the right to a fair and public hearing by an independent court established by law (Article 14) on 13/4/1984
14. Nuclear weapons and the right to life (Article 6) on 9/11/1984
15. The position of aliens under the Covenant on 11/4/1986
16. The right to respect of privacy, family, home and correspondence, and protection of honour and reputation (Article 17) on 8/4/1988
17. Rights of the child (Article 24) on 7/4/1989
18. Non-discrimination on 10/11/1989
19. Protection of the family, the right to marriage and equality of the spouses (Article 23) on 27/7/1990
20. Replaces General Comment concerning the prohibition of torture and cruel treatment or punishment (Article 7) on 10/3/1992
21. Replaces General Comment 9 concerning humane treatment of persons deprived of liberty (Article 10) on 10/4/1992
22. The right to freedom of thought, conscience and religion (Article 18) on 30/7/1993
23. The rights of minorities (Article 27) on 8/4/1994
24. Issues relating to reservations made upon ratification or accession to the Covenant or the Optional Protocols thereto, or in relation to declarations under Article 41 of the Covenant on 4/11/1994
25. The right to participate in public affairs, voting rights and the right of equal access to public service (Article 25) on 12/7/1996
26. Continuity of obligations on 8/12/1997
27. Freedom of movement (Article 12) on 2/11/1999
28. Equality of rights between men and women (Article 3) on 29/3/2000
29. States of Emergency on 31/8/2001.

Texts of these General Comments can be found in a compilation – UN doc. HRI/GEN/1/Rev.5 – and on the OHCHR website.

103   See para. 51 of the HRC Report (note 82). Compare the Guidelines for Reporting, UN doc. CCPR/C/66/GUI/Rev.2, 26 February 2001, para 66.

104   See para. 53 of the HRC Report (note 82); Rule 70A of the Rules of Procedure. It is interesting that the Committee has been adopting concluding observations since its decision of 24 March 1992. Sometimes, states send comments on concluding observations that are published in a separate document, see para. 55 of the Report.

105   Rule 69A of the Rules of Procedure of the Human Rights Committee, UN doc. CCPR/C/3/Rev.6.

106 See para. 53 of the HRC Report (Note 82); para. 68.
107 Ibid., para. 95. See also the section on 'Non-conventional procedures' on the
practice of the follow-up procedure. The Committee stresses that:

> '... follow-up information has been systematically requested in respect of all
> Views with a finding of a violation of the Covenant. At the conclusion of the
> Committee's 72nd session, follow-up information had been received in re-
> spect of 198 Views. No information had been received in respect of 75 Views.
> In 10 cases, the deadline for receipt of follow-up information had not yet
> expired. In many instances, the Secretariat has also received information
> from authors of communications to the effect that the Committee's Views
> had not been implemented. Conversely, in rare instances, the author of a
> communication has informed the Committee that the State Party had given
> effect to the Committee's recommendations, although the State Party had
> not itself provided that information ... Roughly 30% of the replies received
> could be considered satisfactory in that they display the State Party's will-
> ingness to implement the Committee's Views or to offer the applicant an
> appropriate remedy. Other replies cannot be considered satisfactory because
> they either do not address the Committee's recommendations at all or merely
> relate to one aspect of them. Certain replies simply indicate that the victim
> has failed to file a claim for compensation within statutory deadlines and
> that no compensation can therefore be paid to the victim ...'

The remainder of the replies either explicitly challenge the Committee's findings, on either factual or legal grounds, constitute much-belated submissions
on the merits of the case, promise an investigation of the matter considered
by the Committee or indicate that the State Party will not, for one reason or
another, give effect to the Committee's recommendations, paras. 176–79.
108 See Rules 62 and 89 of its Rules of Procedure.
109 Para. 25 of the HRC Report (note 82).
110 See the CERD Report, pp.15–16 (note 75).
111   1.   States Parties' obligations (Article 4) on 25/2/1972
          2.   States Parties' obligations (Article 9) on 26/8/1972
          3.   Apartheid (Article 3) on 24/8/1973
          4.   Demographic composition of the population (Article 9) on 25/8/1973
          5.   Demographic composition of the population (Article 9) on 14/4/1977
          6.   Overdue reports (Article 9) on 19/3/1982
          7.   Legislation to eradicate racial discrimination (Article 4) on 23/8/1985
          8.   Identification with a particular racial or ethnic group (Article 1, paras 1
               and 4) on 22/8/1990
          9.   Independence of experts (Application of Article 8, para. 1) on 23/8/1990
         10.   Technical assistance on 24/3/1991
         11.   Non-citizens (Article 1) on 19/3/1993
         12.   Successor States on 20/3/1993
         13.   Training of law enforcement officials in the protection of human rights
               on 21/3/1993
         14.   Definition of discrimination (Article 1, para. 1) on 22/3/1993
         15.   Organized violence based on ethnic origins (Article 4) on 23/3/1993
         16.   References to situations existing in other states (Article 9) on 24/3/1993
         17.   Establishment of national institutions to facilitate the implementation of
               the Convention on 25/3/1993

18. Establishment of national institutions to facilitate the implementation of the Convention on 18/3/1994
19. Racial segregation and apartheid (Article 3) on 18/8/1995
20. Non-discriminatory implementation of rights and freedoms (Article 5) on 15/3/1996
21. Right to self-determination on 23/8/1996
22. Article 5 and refugees and displaced persons on 24/8/1996
23. Indigenous peoples on 18/8/1997
24. Reporting of persons belonging to different races, national/ethnic groups, or indigenous peoples (Article 1) on 27/8/1999
25. Gender-related dimensions of racial discrimination on 20/3/2000
26. Article 6 of the Convention on 24/3/2000
27. Discrimination against Roma on 16/8/2000.

Texts of the General Recommendations can be found in a compilation – UN doc. HRI/GEN/1/Rev.5 and on the OHCHR website.

112 A similar competence has also been given to the Committee on the Elimination of Discrimination against Women by virtue of the Optional Protocol to the Convention on the Elimination of Discrimination against Women (see below).
113 Article 20 of the Convention against Torture and Other Cruel, Inhuman or Degrading Treatment or Punishment.
114 See the Report of the Committee against Torture, 25th and 26th sessions, UN doc. A/56/44, pp.72 and subseq.
115 Commission on Human Rights resolution 2002/33.
116 The CRC Report, pp.253–54 (note 78).
117   1. Reporting by States Parties on 21/3/1986
       2. Reporting by States Parties on 10/4/87
       3. Education and public information campaigns on 11/4/1987
       4. Reservations to the Convention on 12/4/1987
       5. Temporary special measures on 4/3/1988
       6. Effective national machinery and publicity on 5/3/1988
       7. Resources on 6/3/1988
       8. Implementation of Article 8 of the Convention on 7/3/1988
       9. Statistical data concerning the situation of women on 3/3/1989
       10. 10th anniversary of the adoption of the Convention on the Elimination of All Forms of Discrimination against Women on 4/3/1989
       11. Technical advisory services for reporting obligations on 5/3/1989
       12. Violence against women on 6/3/1989
       13. Equal remuneration for work of equal value on 7/3/1989
       14. Female circumcision on 2/2/1990
       15. Avoidance of discrimination against women in national strategies for the prevention and control of acquired immunodeficiency syndrome (HIV/AIDS) on 3/2/1990
       16. Unpaid women workers in rural and urban family enterprises on 2/1/1991
       17. Measurement and quantification of the unremunerated domestic activities of women and their recognition in the gross national product on 3/1/1991
       18. Disabled women on 4/1/1991
       19. Violence against women on 29/1/1992
       20. Reservations to the Convention on 30/1/1992
       21. Equality in marriage and family relations on 4/2/1994

22. Amending Article 20 of the Convention on 3/2/1995
23. Political and public life on 13/1/1997
24. Women and health on 2/2/1999.
Texts of the General Comments can be found in a compilation – UN doc. HRI/GEN/1/Rev.5 and on the website of the Office of the High Commissioner for Human Rights.

118   Decision 25/I. See also the Report of the Committee on the Elimination of Discrimination against Women, 24th and 25th sessions, United Nations doc. A/56/38, para. 23. A request for an additional session has been formulated since 2000.

119   The Protocol was adopted by General Assembly resolution A/54/4 on 6 October 1999 and opened for signature on 10 December 1999, Human Rights Day.

120   Articles 8 to 12 of the Protocol. See also the chapter 'Proceedings under the inquiry procedure of the Optional Protocol' (Rules 76–91) of the revised Rules of Procedure adopted by the Committee on the Elimination of Discrimination against Women.

121   Decision 24/III 'Links with the Commission on the Status of Women'.

122   The first special procedure was established in 1967 – the Ad-hoc Working Group of Experts on Human Rights in southern Africa – to investigate the charges of torture and ill treatment of prisoners, detainees or persons in police custody in South Africa. The first thematic special procedure was the Working Group on Enforced or Involuntary Disappearances created in 1980.

123   'Strengthening of the United Nations: an agenda for further change' (note 38), para. 55.

124   ST/SGB/2002/9, General Assembly resolution 56/280.

125   The applicability of privileges and immunities to the mandate-holders to ensure the independent exercise of their functions has been confirmed in two advisory opinions by the International Court of Justice in 1989 in the case of Mr. D. Mazilu, Special Rapporteur of the Sub-Commission on Prevention of Discrimination and Protection of the Minorities, and in 1999 in the case of Mr. D. P. Cumaraswamy, the Special Rapporteur on Independence of Judges and Lawyers.

126   See the section on '1503 procedure'.

127   Decision 2000/109, paras 12 and 13.

128   Decision 2000/109, para. 26.

129   The Working Group on Arbitrary Detention; the Working Group on Enforced or Involuntary Disappearances; the Special Rapporteur on Extra-Judicial, Summary or Arbitrary Executions; the Special Rapporteur on Violence against Women; the Special Representative on the Situation of Human Rights Defenders; the Special Rapporteur on the Promotion and Protection of the Right to Freedom of Opinion and Expression. See <www.unhchr.ch>.

130   The Working Group on Arbitrary Detention is also formulating its views on individual cases being shared with the governments concerned and being part of the reports.

131   Decision 2000/109, para. 30.

132   See Decision 2000/19, para. 5.

133   These recommendations were discussed at the meeting of special procedures in 1999, UN doc. E/CN.4/2000/5, paras. 32–46.

134   'Strengthening of the United Nations: an agenda for further change' (note 38), paras 56 and 57.

135   See para. 26 of the Report on the meeting of Special Rapporteurs/representa-

tives/experts and chairpersons of working groups of the special procedures of the Commission on Human Rights and of the advisory services programme, Geneva, 30 May–1 June 1994; UN doc. E/CN.4/1995/5.

136   Compare, for example, the agenda of the meeting of special procedures in 1999 in UN doc. E/CN.4/2000/5.

137   See UN doc. E/1989/22. See also Consolidated guidelines for State reports under the International Covenant on Civil and Political Rights adopted by the Human Rights Committee, dated 29 September 1999, UN doc. CCPR/C/66/GUI; Guidelines for preparation of reports by States Parties adopted by the Committee on the Elimination of Discrimination against Women, 26 July 1996, UN doc. CEDAW/C/7/Rev.3.

138   See the note 137 for the source, para. 5.

139   For instance, Rule 4 of the Rule of Procedure of the Committee on the Elimination of Discrimination against Women states that 'The pre-sessional working group shall formulate a list of issues and questions on substantive issues arising from reports submitted by States Parties in accordance with Article 18 of the Convention and submit that list of issues and questions to the States Parties concerned', see UN doc. A/56/38.

140   See the CAT Report, p.12 (note 114).

141   See para para. 50 of the HRC Report (note 82).

142   Ibid.

143   See the section on 'Treaty monitoring bodies'.

144   'Review of recent developments relating to the work of the treaty bodies. Status of the Annual Appeal 2001 of the Office of the United Nations High Commissioner for Human Rights and of the plans of action strengthening support to and enhancing the effectiveness of the treaty bodies', UN doc. HRI/MC/2001/2, para. 30.

145   See para. 67 of the HRC Report (note 82).

146   See the CERD Report, p.119 (note 75).

147   See, for example, paras 47–49 of the CESCR Report (note 76).

148   See the CAT Report, p.19 (note 114).

149   See reports by the independent expert (note 70).

150   UN doc. E/CN.4/1997/74, paras 37–45, 47–52, 81–97, 112 and 120.

151   E/CN.4/2000/98, p.70.

152   Para. 54 (note 38).

153   See UN doc. HRI/MC/2001/2, paras 27–36.

154   See, for example, the decision taken by the Committee on Economic, Social and Cultural Rights to apply a flexible approach to the rigid five-year interval for periodic reports, in view of which the Committee may reduce this period on the basis of the following criteria and taking into account all relevant circumstances:

   (a)   The timeliness of the State Party's submission of its reports in relation to the implementation of the Covenant;

   (b)   The quality of all the information, such as reports and replies to lists of issues, submitted by the State Party;

   (c)   The quality of the constructive dialogue between the Committee and the State Party;

   (d)   The adequacy of the State Party's response to the Committee's concluding observations;

   (e)   The State Party's actual record, in practice, regarding implementation of the Covenant in relation to all individuals and groups within its jurisdiction.

Paras. 636–7 of the CESCR Report (note 76); see also para. 65 of the HRC Report (note 82).

155 See UN doc. HRI/MC/2001/2, paras 27–36.

156 See Rule 48, UN doc. A/56/38.

157 UN doc. E/CN.4/1997/74, paras 78–79 and 119.

158 See also Report of the Secretary-General 'Advisory services and technical co-operation in the field of human rights', UN doc. E/CN.4/2001/104. It should be pointed out that the independent expert criticized the effectiveness of regional and sub-regional training courses on reporting. He postulated designing a special programme in this regard, see: UN doc. E/CN.4/1997/74, paras 72–77 and 118.

159 UN doc. HRI/GEN/4/Rev.1.

160 UN doc. HRI/GEN/2/Rev.1.

161 UN doc. HRI/GEN/3.

162 UN doc. HRI/GEN/1/Rev.5.

163 E/CN.4/14/Rev.2, para 3.

164 ECOSOC resolutions 75(V) and 76(V).

165 The authors' names remained secret unless otherwise agreed by them.

166 This draft was based on the concept worked out by the Sub-Commission.

167 Rule 50 of the Rules of Procedure of the Functional Commissions of ECOSOC, UN doc. E/5975/Rev.1.

168 See also 'Treaty monitoring bodies' and. 'Non-conventional procedures'.

169 The strong fluctuation of the numbers of communications results, among others, from so-called mass campaigns when hundreds of communications concern one gross violation of human rights.

170 See Commission on Human Rights decision 2000/109.

171 See also OHCHR Fact Sheet No.7/Rev.1, Complaint Procedures, Part II, 2000 (in print and on the OHCHR website <www.unhchr.ch>.

172 The Sub-Commission on the Promotion and Protection of Human Rights has established criteria for the admissibility of communications, Sub-Commission resolution 1 (XXIV), 13 August 1971.

173 Previously it was the Sub-Commission that decided about forwarding a communication to the Commission on the basis of the Report of the Working Group on Communications which met one week before the session of the Sub-Commission. This was recognized as an unnecessary complication of the '1503 procedure'.

174 ECOSOC resolution 2000/3, para. 7 (d).

175 It was late 1978 when the Chairperson of the Commission publicly named the countries under examination, differentiating between pending human rights situations and those dropped from the agenda.

176 This happened with regard to Argentina and Uruguay in 1985, the Philippines in 1986, Haiti in 1987.

177 Article 11 of the Convention.

178 See Article 41 of the International Covenant on Civil and Political Rights.

179 Rules 89 to 91 of the Rules of Procedure of the Human Rights Committee, UN Doc. CCPR/C/3/Rev.6.

180 Ibid., rules 78 to 98.

181 In this context, the Committee has considered that the author of the communication can have difficulties in obtaining access to evidence.

182 For comparison: in the case of the CAT complaints procedure, 227 cases were registered as of 30 January 2003 and 57 pending; of the CERD procedure: 27 registered cases, 9 pending.

183   See the Report by the Secretariat to the 13th Meeting of Chairpersons of the Human Rights Treaty Bodies Geneva, 18–22 June 2001, 'Review of Recent Developments Relating to the Work of the Treaty Bodies. Status of the Annual Appeal 2001 of the Office of the United Nations High Commissioner for Human Rights and of the Plans of Action Strengthening Support to and Enhancing the Effectiveness of the Treaty Bodies', UN doc. HRI/MC/2001/2.
184   See ECOSOC resolution 1996/31 'Consultative relationship between the United Nations and Non-Governmental Organizations.' Visit also <www.un.org> where, under ECOSOC, precise information on the consultative status of non-governmental organizations is provided.

BIBLIOGRAPHY

Alfredsson, Gudmundur (2001) (ed.), *International human rights monitoring mechanisms: essays in honour of Jakob Th. Möller*, Martin Nijhoff.
Alston, Philip and Crawford, James (2000) (ed.), *The future of UN human rights treaty monitoring*, Cambridge University Press.
Bayefsky, Anne (2001) *Report – the United Nations Human Rights Treaty System: Universality at the Crossroads*, Transnational Publishers.
Buergenthal, Thomas, Shelton, Dinah and Stewart, David (2002) *International Human Rights in a Nutshell*, 3rd ed., West Law School.
English, Kathryn and Stapleton, Adam (1995) *The Human Rights Handbook*, UK Human Rights Centre.
Hanski, Raija and Suksi, Markku (1999) *An Introduction to the International Protection of Human Rights. A Textbook*, Abo Akademi University.
Haynes, Christof and Viljoen, Frans (2002) *The impact of the United Nations Human Rights Treaties on the Domestic Level*, Kluwer Law International.
Lempinen, Miko (2001) *Challenges facing the system of special procedures of the United Nations Commission on Human Rights*, Abo Akademi University.
Minnesota Advocates for Human Rights (Weissbrodt, D. and Parker, P.) (1993) *The U.N. Commission on Human Rights, its sub-commission and related procedures: an orientation manual.*
National Commission for UNESCO (2002) *Germany, How to file complaints on human rights violations: a manual for individuals and NGOs*, 3rd ed.
Nowak, Manfred (1993) *UN Covenant on Civil and Political Rights. CCPR Comment*, Kehl, Strasbourg, Arlington, N.P. Engel.
Ramcharan, Bertrand (2002) *The United Nations High Commissioner for Human Rights: The Challenges of International Protection*, Kluwer Law International.
Ramcharan, Bertrand G. (2002) *Human rights and human security*, Martinus Nijhoff.
Shelton, Dinah (1999) *Remedies in International Human Rights Law*, Oxford University Press.
Symonides, Janusz (2000) (ed.), *Human Rights: Concepts and Standards*, UNESCO Publishing/Ashgate Publishing.
UNESCO (2001) *A guide to human rights: institutions, standards, procedures.*
University of Oslo/Norwegian Institute of Human Rights (1997) *Manual on human rights monitoring: an introduction for human rights field officers.*
Winter, Jane (1999) *Human wrongs, human rights: a guide to the human rights machinery of the United Nations*, 2nd ed., British Irish Rights Watch and the Northern Ireland Human Rights Commission.

2 The International Labour Organization's System of Human Rights Protection

LEE SWEPSTON

INTRODUCTION

The International Labour Organization (ILO) has the most effective and well-developed mechanisms for human rights protection in the international system. Based on the adoption of a wide range of international conventions, it includes the regular examination of reports, input from non-governmental organizations and both technical and political review. It has been supplemented in the last few years by the addition of promotional tools applicable to human rights, even if governments have not ratified conventions. The process is then rounded off by the fact that the ILO's technical assistance is available to help correct any problems that may occur.

It should be made clear that the supervisory procedures outlined below apply to all ILO conventions, whether they deal with human rights or not. Questions of discrimination and forced labour are handled in much the same way in the supervisory process as safety and health questions, or the payment of wages. Human rights problems do, of course, receive a higher degree of attention, and additional procedures have been adopted in the last few years to supplement the ILO's work in this area.

THE ILO'S HISTORY AND STRUCTURES

The ILO was established in 1919 as part of the settlement of the First World War. Its first Constitution was part of the Treaty of Versailles, and it was one of the two international organizations created as a result of that conflict. The League of Nations was responsible for political and military peace, and

91

the ILO was established to be responsible for social peace. As the Constitution of the ILO states, '... there can be no lasting peace without social justice'.

The ILO survived the demise of the League of Nations to become the first specialized agency of the United Nations system in 1945. It won the Nobel Peace Prize in 1969, on the occasion of its 50th anniversary, for its work in promoting peace and justice throughout the world. In 1994, as it celebrated its 75th anniversary, it launched a searching examination of its working methods and objectives, from which has emerged a renewed commitment to human rights and to social justice.

The method by which the ILO fights for social justice is based on the adoption and supervision of international labour standards, consisting of conventions and recommendations. This has resulted, up to the end of the 2001 session of the International Labour Conference, in the adoption of 184 conventions and 192 recommendations on different subjects – mostly directly to do with the world of work, but a few are of wider application. They are known collectively as the International Labour Code.

In 1998 the ILO also adopted the Declaration on Fundamental Principles and Rights at Work, which adds a promotional approach to the supervisory one, and vastly increases the ILO's capacity to assist countries to apply these rights. This joined a large-scale assistance programme on child rights, the International Programme for the Elimination of Child Labour (IPEC).

TRIPARTISM: A FUNDAMENTAL CONCEPT

The great strength of the ILO, and the characteristic which distinguishes it from all other international organizations, is that it is *tripartite*. This means that decisions in the ILO are not made by governments alone, but by representatives of workers and employers as well. Each member state of the ILO is required to send to the annual conference a tripartite delegation, consisting of two government delegates and one delegate each from the most representative organizations of employers and of workers in that country.

The ILO's organs are thus composed of all three partners. In the conference, there are four votes for each member state, two from the government and one each from the employers and workers. In conference committees, the system goes even further, and the groups comprising the government, employers and workers each has one-third of the votes.

The governing body of the International Labour Office[1] is also tripartite, with 28 government members, 14 employers and 14 workers.

This tripartite concept thus extends, at the level of the ILO itself, to the adoption and supervision of standards, to the taking of all fundamental decisions on the Organization's programme and budget[2] and to the day-to-day supervision of its work through the governing body. In the member states it means that all decisions relating to the ILO and its standards should be taken on a tripartite basis. Many of the standards explicitly require the involvement of representatives of employers and workers in their implementation, and this is implicit even where it is not contained in the text of the relevant convention.

THE CONCEPT OF FUNDAMENTAL HUMAN RIGHTS IN THE ILO

The ILO was founded before the term 'human rights' became current in the international world. Neither the ILO Constitution nor the other fundamental documents of the Organization use the term, and the Constitution speaks instead of 'social justice' as the basis of the ILO's work. While there is no contradiction between these terms, there is certainly a difference. The term 'human rights', as used by the United Nations in particular, may sometimes seem to express human aspiration as a struggle between the individual and the state: rights may be asserted only in the context of a legal system which recognizes them and provides a means of redress for their violation. The concept of 'social justice' is wider. Certainly, many ILO conventions lay down fundamental human rights, such as the rights to be free from forced labour and discrimination, the right to organize and bargain collectively, and many others. These are, however, expressed in the ILO more often in terms of obligations of states to provide for the protection and implementation of these conditions than in terms of a basis of claims by the individual against the state, or rights that may be claimed from it.

In addition, the ILO's instruments do not suppose that important human relations exist only between the state and individuals. The tripartite nature of the ILO and its mandate for economic questions mean that most ILO instruments are directed towards employment or service relations, in which the state exists as guarantor rather than as a direct player (except when the state itself is the employer, of course). For this reason, ILO instruments most often speak of an obligation of a ratifying state to 'ensure' or 'promote' the situation posited in a Convention. They contemplate a situation in which employers must be regulated or assisted in their relations with their employees, or oblige the state to regulate other human relationships or needs, such as contracting for work or ensuring that vocational training is provided.

The concept of fundamental human rights has nevertheless found a place in the ILO's normative action for two reasons. The first is that this is the expression used by the United Nations system to refer to the protection of certain basic values, and that the ILO is part of that system. Second, it defines the basic values that must be preserved and promoted in all aspects of the ILO's work.

DEFINITION OF FUNDAMENTAL HUMAN RIGHTS IN THE ILO

There are four main fundamental human rights subjects protected by the ILO, although many others are relevant to human rights. Although these subjects have been recognized informally for many years, they were given formal recognition first in the World Summit on Social Development held in Copenhagen in March 1995 and then in the Declaration on Fundamental Principles and Rights in 1998, both on the basis of ILO conventions and recommendations.

The World Summit made explicit reference to the need for all states to ratify and implement the ILO's fundamental human rights conventions, which it stated were those dealing with freedom of association and collective bargaining, discrimination, forced labour and child labour. The governing body decided in April 1995 that these instruments would be the targets of a campaign for the promotion of the fundamental human rights conventions of the ILO.[3]

The Declaration of Fundamental Rights and Principles at Work codifies the ILO's long understanding of the fundamental human rights contained in its Constitution and standards, as comprising: freedom of association and the right to bargain collectively; freedom from forced labour; freedom from child labour; and freedom from discrimination. It provides that all states, even if they have not been able to ratify the conventions which embody these principles, have 'an obligation, arising from the very fact of membership in the Organisation, to respect, to promote and to realise, in good faith and in accordance with the Constitution, the fundamental rights which are the subjects' of the eight ILO conventions recognized as fundamental.

There are two conventions on each of these subjects, building on the basic protections found in the ILO Constitution. First, freedom of association and protection of the right to organize is protected principally in the Freedom of Association and Protection of the Right to Organise Convention, 1948 (No. 87) and the Right to Organize and Collective Bargaining Convention, 1949 (No. 98).

Freedom from forced labour is covered by the Forced Labour Convention, 1930 (No. 29) and by the Abolition of Forced Labour Convention, 1957 (No. 105).

Child labour, in turn, is covered by the Minimum Age Convention, 1973 (No. 138), and by the Worst Forms of Child Labour Convention, 1999 (No. 182).

Freedom from discrimination is the fourth great subject of human rights protection in the ILO. The basic instrument is the Discrimination (Employment and Occupation) Convention, 1958 (No. 111). It was preceded in time by the more specialized Equal Remuneration Convention, 1951 (No. 100), which covers equal remuneration between men and women for work of equal value.

In most cases, there is an accompanying recommendation which spells out more fully measures which may, or should, be taken to implement the provisions of the convention.

It is only very recently that the ILO has found it necessary to adopt an official position designating some conventions as those covering 'fundamental human rights', since, unlike the United Nations, all ILO instruments are adopted and supervised in the same manner. However, when the ILO adopted a policy of integrating its standards and technical cooperation activities, starting in about 1989, it was necessary to begin to assign a certain priority to the ILO instruments which were to form the basis for this relationship. It was obvious that the details of all the ILO instruments on such subjects as safety and health could not be integrated into all the Organization's work in developing countries, as this is sometimes beyond states' capacity to implement and they may have different approaches to such issues as social security. Nevertheless, it was essential to promote the ILO's basic values as found in its Constitution and developed more fully in its conventions and recommendations.

The need has also become more acute recently in the context of the relationship between international trade and human rights, and the globalization of the world's economy. Based primarily on initiatives from the United States and the international trade union movement, there has been an effort to include, in international trade agreements, a 'social clause' to link 'basic workers' rights' or 'internationally recognized workers' rights' to trading privileges. We will return to this below.

INTERNATIONAL LABOUR STANDARDS: ADOPTION AND SUPERVISION

As indicated above, the foundation of the ILO's work for human rights is the standards adopted by the Conference. It is therefore necessary to examine briefly the mechanisms by which the ILO works.

The Adoption of Standards

There is no need, in this chapter, to examine in detail the means by which international labour standards are adopted. Briefly, the subjects are included in the agenda of the International Labour Conference by the governing body. Written consultations are then undertaken by the Office, leading to a first discussion in a tripartite committee of the conference two years after the subject is included in the agenda. After a second round of written discussions, the conference again discusses the subject, and a new convention and/or recommendation is adopted.

The ILO's Supervisory System

What distinguishes the ILO's human rights protection system from most others is its supervisory mechanisms. It is not productive to adopt an international instrument without ensuring that its application will be supervised. The ILO has the most sophisticated supervisory system in international law although many in the human rights field are unaware of this, as most ILO conventions focus on labour matters – an aspect of international human rights law that has until lately been largely neglected. The system was radical when it was first developed, between 1919 and 1927; in some ways, it is even more so now.

The supervisory system is based on Article 22 of the ILO Constitution. Ratifying states are required to send reports to the ILO, at regular intervals of between one and five years, depending on various factors.[4] At the same time, they are required (Article 23 of the Constitution) to send copies of these reports to workers' and employers' organizations, which have their own right to comment, stating, for example, that the government is misrepresenting the situation or has not provided full information, or even that they agree with the government's report.

These reports are examined by the Committee of Experts on the Application of Conventions and Recommendations, which meets annually. This Committee is a purely technical body made up of eminent jurists from around the world, representing all major legal, social and economic systems. It examines nearly 2000 government reports each year – a massive workload. The Committee makes any comments it feels are necessary – asking questions about application, or indicating that the national law and practice are not in conformity and requesting changes. This is done in two forms:

- *Direct requests* are not published[5] and consist of less serious or more preliminary points. They request further information or ask for minor adjustments.
- *Observations* are published comments which appear in the annual reports of the Committee of Experts[6] and are submitted to the International Labour Conference for possible discussion. They deal with more serious matters than do direct requests.

The Report of the Committee of Experts is already a powerful tool for those who want to compare their country's performance with its international obligations. The process does not stop there, however. The International Labour Conference meets every June and has a Committee on the Application of Standards composed of representatives of governments, employers and workers. This Committee will usually decide to discuss, in public session, about 30 cases of the several hundred published in the report of the Committee of Experts. The Committee invites the representative of the government concerned to appear before it and explain the reasons for the problem in question. This representative then takes part in a dialogue with the Committee, usually led by the employers' and workers' own representatives. The government representative is asked to clarify statements, to indicate a timetable for the implementation of measures requested by the Committee of Experts, or to commit the government to inviting the International Labour Office to carry out 'direct contacts' or technical assistance to resolve the problems. These sessions can be very difficult for government representatives, but often result in promises of improved performance.

There are also two main complaints procedures in the ILO supervisory machinery. Under Article 26 of the Constitution, any government which has ratified the same convention, any delegate to the International Labour Conference or the governing body of the ILO can file a *complaint* alleging the violation of a convention by a country which has ratified it. This results in the establishment of a Commission of Inquiry which holds hearings in Geneva, visits the country concerned, and makes findings as to whether the convention is being violated. Under Article 24 of the Constitution, a *representation* may be filed by any workers' or employers' organization, alleging violation of a ratified convention. This results in the appointment of a tripartite Governing Body Committee, which decides the case, usually on the basis of an exchange of correspondence; it is thus particularly used in cases where the facts are not in doubt. In both complaints and representations, the responsible bodies make recommendations for improved application, in addition to their findings; the cases are then referred to the Committee of Experts for follow-up.

The Committee on Freedom of Association

There is another complaints body operating on a very different basis in the ILO. The Committee on Freedom of Association was created in 1951 by agreement with the Economic and Social Council of the United Nations. Originally intended to be a screening body for the Fact-Finding and Conciliation Commission on Freedom of Association, it became in time the main body receiving complaints of violations of freedom of association. These complaints may be filed by organizations of employers and workers, regardless of whether the country concerned has ratified the ILO conventions on the subject.

The Committee is tripartite, unlike the Committee of Experts, and is made up of three employers' members, three workers' members and three government members of the governing body. It meets three times a year, and has dealt with more than 2000 cases. Its decisions and recommendations are almost always accepted by governments, and have led over the years to innumerable cases of freeing trade unionists from prison or returning them from exile, as well as reforms in labour law and industrial relations, and many other improvements in various situations.

The Fact-Finding and Conciliation Commission is a much more formal procedure, involving an investigative panel of three persons who visit the country and make detailed recommendations. In a recent instance of its use, a Commission went to South Africa in 1991, with the government's permission, and made detailed recommendations concerning the changes which would have to be made in the country's industrial relations system with the approaching end of apartheid. This illustrates the fact that the Fact-Finding and Conciliation Commission may also be used even in cases in which the country concerned is not a member state of the ILO (South Africa was not at that time). In all cases, the approval of the government concerned is required before this procedure can be instituted – the only one of the ILO's procedures requiring consent.

Follow-up to the Declaration

The Declaration on Fundamental Principles and Rights at Work was adopted in 1998, together with a follow-up. The Declaration is a promotional instrument and not binding; therefore the Organization did not adopt a 'supervisory' mechanism. Under the follow-up, each year a country which has not ratified all the eight conventions communicates a report on what it is doing to apply the principles of the Declaration covered by the unratified conventions – not the Declaration itself, which it is not obligatory. These reports provide a baseline against which countries can measure their own progress. The Annual Review is introduced by a group of independent expert-advisers whose task is to draw attention to aspects for further discussion by the ILO governing body. In addition, the ILO Director-General submits a Global Report on one of the four categories of Fundamental Principles and Rights at Work to the tripartite International Labour Conference each June. The discussion of the Global Report is then the basis on which the governing body adopts or updates an action programme for the ILO to implement the rights covered by that Report.

THE RELATIONSHIP BETWEEN ILO HUMAN RIGHTS STANDARDS AND OTHER UNITED NATIONS INSTRUMENTS ON HUMAN RIGHTS

It is generally accepted that the Universal Declaration of Human Rights (1948), together with the International Covenant on Economic, Social and Cultural Rights (1966) and the International Covenant on Civil and Political Rights (1966) contain the fundamental expression of human rights for the United Nations system. These have been supplemented in the United Nations by a number of other fundamental conventions, including: the Convention on the Elimination of All Forms of Discrimination against Women (1979); the Convention on the Elimination of Racial Discrimination (1965); the Convention against Torture and Other Cruel, Inhuman or Degrading Treatment or Punishment (1984); the Convention on the Rights of the Child (1989); and, finally, the Convention on the Protection of the Rights of All Migrant Workers and Members of their Families (1990).[7]

The two 1966 International Covenants, as well as the other instruments cited above, were adopted after all of the basic ILO conventions on human rights had been adopted; and, in so far as they cover the same territory, they are in fact condensations of much of what was already contained in ILO standards. Articles 6 to 9 of the International Covenant on Economic, Social and Cultural Rights, in particular, are very close to being a summary of the ILO standards which already existed on the same subjects. Indeed, Article 8 refers explicitly to the ILO's Freedom of Association and Protection of the Right to Organize Convention (No. 87). The other United Nations instruments also coincide in some respects with ILO standards and, in almost all cases, are fully consistent with them.[8]

The relationship between these instruments and those of the ILO is that the United Nations instruments are, in most cases, general statements of human rights in a form which enters into little detail, but rather lays down the fundamental principle and leaves it to states to apply it. ILO instruments, on the same or overlapping subjects, tend to be considerably more detailed, containing more guidance on means of implementation. While still drafted in more general terms than national law on the same subject, they tend to provide more guidance as to method and acceptable variation than do United Nations instruments. It is also worth noting that, unlike other international conventions, they are not subject to reservations.

A good example of this comparison is the Convention on the Rights of the Child. It was the intention of the United Nations to achieve a broad and general statement of the rights of the child which could be applied widely across the entire world. Indeed, this has been remarkably successful, with the Convention having been ratified by almost all countries since its adoption in 1990. This Convention contains one article (Article 32) which prohibits economic exploitation of children and requires the establishment of a minimum age for employment. The ILO, in contrast, has adopted 11 detailed conventions on minimum age for employment or work, together with a large number of other standards laying conditions of work for young people in various economic sectors and activities.[9] The International Covenant on Economic, Social and Cultural Rights is another example. As indicated above, Articles 6 to 9 reflect a number of ILO conventions already adopted in 1966, and by now there are more than 75 ILO conventions covering and developing the various concepts laid down in brief statements of principle in the International Covenant.

Both approaches are valid, and indeed both are necessary. It is the ILO's task to explore in detail the requirements for establishing social justice within its mandate. It is able to do this in large part because of its tripartite structure, and because of its conception of permanent dialogue between the Organization itself and its tripartite constituents. The United Nations, on the other hand, defines the general principles guiding human rights and human relationships across the entire range of ideas. Its instruments are necessarily more general, of broader scope and less detailed. The relationship is a healthy one, even if it is not always easy to carry out.

OTHER WORK WITH INTERNATIONAL ORGANIZATIONS ON HUMAN RIGHTS

ILO standards have formed the basis for much of the work of other organizations on the human rights of workers, and in relation to the economy. It is equally important that the ILO participates actively in the work of these other organizations and that they take part in the ILO's work. The ILO believes that it is vital that there should be a single system of human rights law among international organizations, and that both the standards and their interpretation should be as consistent as possible.

The International Labour Office therefore takes an active role with the treaty bodies, created to supervise the six United Nations covenants and conventions. A detailed summary can be found in each report of the Committee of Experts indicating that the ILO has taken part in the discussions of the treaty bodies, or has furnished them detailed reports on the findings of its supervisory bodies in relation to the countries being examined by the treaty body. For instance, the ILO takes part in the discussions in the Human Rights Committee, the Committee on Economic, Social and Cultural Rights, and the Committee on the Rights of the Child. This frequently leads the United Nations committees to raise questions already raised by ILO bodies and vice versa, thus reinforcing the effect of international supervision. This is particularly important since different ministries are usually concerned with the ILO and with the United Nations; and it is rarely remarked that national ministries have as much trouble coordinating their approaches as do international organizations.

At the regional level also, the ILO takes an active role in the supervision of the European Social Charter and its Additional Protocol, as well as the European Code of Social Security and its Protocol.[10] It should also be mentioned that there is one instrument which has been adopted jointly by the ILO and UNESCO: the 1966 joint ILO/UNESCO Recommendation Concerning the Status of Teachers. There is a joint supervisory mechanism, meeting periodically, which then reports to the annual sessions of the ILO Conference as well as to UNESCO.

Finally, there are many practical steps being taken between the ILO and other international organizations. A number of ILO conventions, for instance, have been adopted with the active participation of other organizations, such as the United Nations, UNESCO and other specialized agencies, with International Maritime Organization for maritime instruments and even with the Inter-American Indian Institute for the Indigenous and Tribal Peoples Convention, 1989 (No. 169). Fieldwork and training may also be carried out jointly, as often has been the case with the Office of the United Nations High Commissioner for Human Rights on matters of common interest. It is necessary to increase and develop this kind of cooperation among all the different parts of the international system.

LINKS BETWEEN TECHNICAL COOPERATION AND ILO STANDARDS

Another aspect of the ILO human rights work is through its technical assistance and advisory services with member states. When technical assistance began to be a part of the ILO's work after the Second World War, a new kind of expertise began to be developed. After some years, however, it was noted that this sometimes did not take full account of the ILO's own standards. Therefore, at the end of the 1980s, the ILO began to develop an approach which is now fully in place. This ensures that no ILO assistance may take place which is in contradiction with ILO's fundamental human rights standards, and that account is always taken of relevant standards in any advisory or assistance work. At the same time, the assistance work has the objective – not necessarily the primary one – of enabling the country either to apply conventions it has already ratified or to ratify those it has not been able to. This approach is implemented in particular through the multidisciplinary teams which are located in 14 offices of the ILO in all the developing regions of the world.

This is reinforced by the two large programmes in the ILO created specifically to implement ILO human rights standards: the IPEC programme for child labour and the Declaration programme to provide assistance to implement the 1998 Declaration, both operating on the basis of voluntary contributions. Over the last few years the proportion of ILO technical assistance spending on human rights has increased exponentially, so that it now accounts for more than half the technical cooperation budget.

THE IMPACT OF THE ILO'S WORK FOR HUMAN RIGHTS

Although it is often difficult to quantify, it is certain that the ILO's standards and assistance have a great impact on human rights in member states. They are the basis for labour legislation adopted around the world, especially for countries which have recently attained independence or are undergoing democratization. Furthermore, the ILO's regular work includes helping countries to rewrite labour and human rights legislation on the basis of its standards.

In many other cases, the ILO supervisory system returns to problems over and over again before obtaining results. This happened with questions of forced labour and trade union rights in the Soviet bloc before political changes finally set these countries free to adopt the changes which the ILO had been recommending for years. This still happens with such issues as forced labour, child labour, discrimination against women and minorities – deeply entrenched problems which will not be eradicated by a simple legislative decision.

In many cases we can clearly see the influence of ILO standards. The following are some examples.

Cases of Progress: More than 2000 Noted in 35 Years

Every year the ILO Committee of Experts lists cases in which countries have taken measures, requested by the Committee, to bring their law and practice into conformity with conventions. There are typically more than 40 cases affecting some 30 countries noted in each report. These cases cover everything from fundamental human rights (for example, freedom of association, discrimination, forced labour and child labour) to the highly technical subjects dealt with in many ILO conventions. The Committee has recently added another measurement tool: cases of 'interest', in which are noted examples of measures taken to improve the level of application of conventions, even in the absence of a specific request by the supervisory bodies for those measures. Some examples of recent cases are given below.

Brazil

The Committee of Experts and the ILO Conference had severely criticized Brazil under Convention No. 111 for failing to prevent employers from demanding sterilization and certificates of non-pregnancy before they will hire women. In early 1995 after an emotional confrontation at the ILO Conference in 1994, the government adopted its promised new law forbidding this practice. Under pressure from the Conference to describe how, in fact, it handled discrimination, it also asked the ILO to work with it to put into place a system for implementing this convention in a programme beginning in 1995. The ILO is now working with the government to evaluate the impact of these measures.

Eastern Europe

In 1992 and 1993 the ILO's Committee of Experts on the Application of Conventions and Recommendations welcomed a series of new labour laws in the former communist bloc, abolishing monopoly trade union systems and discrimination based on political opinion, and basing new labour laws on the ILO's Freedom of Association and Protection of the Right to Organize Convention, 1948 (No. 87) and the Discrimination (Employment and Occupation) Convention, 1958 (No. 111). Progress continues to be made in bringing the new laws into conformity with ILO standards.

Guatemala

In early 1995 the Guatemalan Peace Agreements between the government and the rebels were supplemented by an agreement by Indian rebels to cease hostilities, on the basis of a government promise to ratify and apply the ILO's Indigenous and Tribal Peoples Convention, 1989 (No. 169). ILO supervisory bodies, working to supplement the effect of the United Nations verification mission in Guatemala (MINUGUA) are pressing the government to take more practical measures to implement the Agreement, thus maintaining international pressure.

Nepal

Forced and bonded labour have long been a feature of Nepalese national life. In 2000 the government asked the ILO to establish a broad-based programme to eliminate bonded labour, allowing it to ratify the Forced Labour Convention, 1930 (No. 29).

Myanmar

The practice of forced labour in Myanmar under the military government has long been notorious, and comments have been made by the Committee of Experts for many years. After a complaint on Article 26 and a Commission of Inquiry in 1998, the government still denied the existence of the practice. The Conference then moved to apply, for the first time in ILO history, Article 33 of the Constitution allowing the imposition of other measures. In 2001 the government invited the ILO to carry out a detailed field investigation of forced labour and has agreed to work with the ILO to eliminate the large amount of forced labour found still to exist.

The Russian Federation

The Committee of Experts noted in 1994 that, after many years of difficult discussions on the Forced Labour Convention, 1930 (No. 29), the government had finally removed criminal penalties for 'leading a parasitic way of life'.

South Africa

The ILO was probably the most effective of all the international organizations in fighting apartheid in South Africa through persistent and detailed criticism combined with practical help to workers' organizations, and, since the installation of the new government, to employers' organizations as well. In 1992, two years before the fall of the apartheid system, the government accepted a visit from the ILO Fact-Finding and Conciliation Commission on Freedom of Association and made detailed recommendations for adapting the industrial relations system and labour laws to a non-discriminatory world. This was the only international investigative mission ever allowed into South Africa under apartheid, and its recommendations have formed the basis for the country's policies in this area ever since. The Office continues to work with the government, which in 2000 ratified the Discrimination (Employment and Occupation) Convention, 1958 (No. 111).

Child labour

The ILO points out cases in which such countries as Brazil, Peru, India, Bangladesh, Pakistan and Thailand allow children to be enslaved, to work in brothels and factories, and to be exploited in brick kilns, carpet factories and many other workplaces. Practical help to eliminate these evils is provided to countries through the ILO's International Programme for the Elimination of Child Labour. Progress is slow, but the fight goes on.

Effect on regional organizations

ILO standards have formed the basis of the European Code of Social Security and the European Social Charter, thus increasing social standards in one of the major trading blocs in the world. In Latin America, following ILO advice, the social dimension of the common market between Argentina, Brazil, Paraguay and Uruguay (MERCOSUR) was based on more than 30 ILO conventions.

THE EFFECT GIVEN TO RECOMMENDATIONS OF THE COMMITTEE ON FREEDOM OF ASSOCIATION

This tripartite committee is one of the most effective human rights bodies in any international organization. In recent years the Committee has noted cases of progress which include:

- *Argentina*: restoration of the right of collective bargaining in the national airlines sector
- *Chad*: lifting of various measures dismissing workers for trade union activity
- *China*: release of independent trade unionists from prison
- *Fiji*: legislative amendments allowing the free election of trade union representatives and recognition of a miners' union as a bargaining agent, previously denied to workers in this sector
- *Panama*: reinstatement of trade union leaders dismissed by government fiat
- *Sweden*: repeal of rules that overrode certain collective agreements.

These are only examples of the impact of ILO standards and procedures. There are many more cases in the long history of the ILO, and it is time further research was done on the quantification of the impact of standards. Most definitely, they have had a profound impact on labour law and practice in a large part of the world.

HOW NON-GOVERNMENTAL ORGANIZATIONS CAN BEST MAKE USE OF THE ILO

How may the supervisory procedures of the ILO be used by non-governmental organizations? The first thing to recognize is that the ILO has no procedure for individual submissions of information or complaints. In fact, organizations which are not trade unions or employers' organizations have no formal access to the system at all. However, this does not mean that the ILO does not receive and use information generated by these organizations. There are several ways in which this can come about.

First, of course, the country in question must have ratified the ILO convention concerned to obtain the full benefit of the ILO's supervisory system.

This does not necessarily mean the convention most directly concerned. Ratification is a voluntary act by a government. If a convention is not ratified soon after it is adopted, a great effort by interest groups inside the country may be necessary to achieve ratification. If the country has not ratified a convention, it can still be useful as a reference. No government likes to have it pointed out that it is acting contrary to international human rights law, even where the convention has not been ratified.

How can ILO standards best be used if the convention has been ratified? It helps, of course, if the non-governmental organization concerned is a workers' or employers' organization. For instance, there are workers' organizations in various countries which were formed to represent the occupational interests of workers but which are not trade unions in the usual sense. If so, they may have the same rights as any other workers' organization as far as the ILO is concerned. What does this give such an organization the right to do? First – and this is an option that is often neglected in favour of a formal complaints procedure – the workers' organization has the right to submit information directly to the ILO on the performance of the country's obligations. These 'comments' from employers' and workers' organizations represent a unique possibility for non-governmental bodies to play a formal part in the international supervisory process. The comments are frequently used: in most years, some 300 such comments are received on some 1700 government reports. They are sent, by the ILO, to the government concerned for observations, and are given considerable attention by the Committee of Experts in the examination of the government's report. This can have as great an effect as a formal complaint and is usually much faster.

If an non-governmental organization is not a trade union or employers' organization, it may be able to form an alliance with one. There are several cases in which international trade union organizations have submitted information to the ILO on behalf of a non-governmental organization, when it believed this information was credible.

A new way of taking advantage of the ILO's supervisory power has just emerged in Norway, in connection with the Indigenous and Tribal Peoples Convention, 1989 (No. 169). A Sami parliament was created in this country some time ago, and it has gradually assumed a greater role in managing the internal autonomy of the Sami people. Based on a suggestion made in the 'Report Form' on Convention No. 169,[11] the Norwegian government has begun to send its reports on Convention No. 169 to the Sami parliament for comment and transmits the parliament's comments to the ILO as part of its own report. The government has also asked the ILO to open a parallel dialogue with the parliament, giving the representatives of the Sami people a formal part to play in the supervisory process. While no exactly similar arrangement has emerged in any other country, the ILO Committee of Experts has been urging governments for some years to consult their indigenous peoples in drawing up their reports, and to state what these consultations have yielded.

What if the government has not ratified the convention most directly relevant to the problem? It should be remembered that the ILO has now adopted

182 conventions on different subjects, and that most countries have ratified at least some of them. There are many that can be used, in all the ways described above, to defend the interests of different groups of workers, even if the government has not ratified the most directly relevant one. In many countries, for instance, a disadvantaged group suffers from forced labour and debt bondage. It may be discriminated against in access to employment and after it enters employment. It may not be able to gain access to vocational training programmes and institutions, and is often relegated to the lowest paid forms of migrant agricultural labour. Often, it is not allowed to join or to form trade unions. These are classic ILO issues, and are the subject of existing conventions. Almost all ILO member states have ratified Convention No. 29 on forced labour, Convention No. 87 on freedom of association and protection of the right to organise, and the conventions on the protection of wages (No. 95), minimum wages (Nos 26, 99 and 131), discrimination in employment (No. 111), and others. It may take more research but these conventions can offer a great deal of protection.

THE NEED TO ADAPT

It is often said that the world is changing and that perhaps it is necessary to adapt ILO standards and their supervisory system to a changing world. Change is positive when it responds to real needs, but there are also solid virtues in a system that has been so widely endorsed for more than 80 years. A comprehensive discussion of ILO standards has followed from the Director-General's 1994 report on the future of the Organization, and the programme of review and revision of older standards has been greatly accelerated. The supervisory machinery is also being reviewed from top to bottom, to ensure that it is fair, thorough and constructive. This is one of the periodic reviews the ILO has carried out throughout its history.

Reporting Obligations

There are now well over 7000 ratifications of ILO conventions, plus another 1000 declarations of application to non-metropolitan territories. Governments find the burden of reporting a significant one, and the ILO sometimes finds it difficult to handle adequately all the 2000 or more reports to be examined by its supervisory machinery each year. The continuing rapid increase in ratifications led, in 1993, to a decision to change the intervals for reporting from a two-year or four-year cycle to a cycle of reporting every two years for only 12 conventions on fundamental human rights and five years for all other conventions. Safeguards are built in to allow the supervisory bodies to ask for more frequent reporting if necessary. As part of the review of standards, measures have also been taken to allow the withdrawal or abrogation of out-of-date conventions, and to stop requesting reports on some of them.

The Universality of Application of Standards

This question continues to be posed in many forms, inside and outside the ILO, as countries which have only recently found their voice wish to have their national specificity accepted. The ILO has always rejected the idea of adopting regional standards on the basis that all workers deserve the same protection and that to provide lower protection for workers in some parts of the world might even be racist. In the United Nations system as a whole, the question was posed in the World Conference on Human Rights (Vienna, 1993), and the Vienna Declaration and Programme of Action, adopted on that occasion, included in its paragraph 5 the following:

> All human rights are universal, indivisible and interdependent and interrelated. The international community must treat human rights globally in a fair and equal manner, on the same footing, and with the same emphasis. While the significance of national and regional particularities and various historical, cultural and religious backgrounds must be borne in mind, it is the duty of States, regardless of their political, economic and cultural systems, to promote and protect all human rights and fundamental freedoms.[12]

Globalization and Workers' Rights

The governing body decided in June 1994 to create a Working Party to discuss the subject of 'The social dimensions of the liberalization of international trade', as a way of examining proposals for a 'social clause'. Following the realization that this could not be adopted in the current climate, the Working Party changed its name and now focuses on the discussion of the 'Social dimensions of globalization'.

The proposal for a social clause was based on the conviction of some that fundamental workers' rights should be enforced by the possibility of imposing international trade sanctions, if they are violated. One of the most forceful proponents of the idea is the international trade union movement and, in particular, the International Confederation of Free Trade Unions. The United States is the most active governmental advocate of this idea and itself applies trade sanctions unilaterally through its Generalized System of Preferences (GSP) legislation and others if 'internationally recognized workers' rights' are not respected. The proponents of the idea maintain that it is intended to increase respect for workers' rights and to give some power of enforcement to international supervision in this area.

The idea is vigorously opposed by most of the developing world and has been rejected in various meetings leading up to, and following, the establishment of the World Trade Organization. While these countries have condemned certain labour abuses in international trade, they consider the idea of trade sanctions to be protectionist and aimed at gaining economic or political advantages by removing the competitive advantages of the developing countries. The result has been a recognition that the ILO is the only international institution to set and supervise labour standards, and that its means of action must be strengthened to allow it to do so.

The Promotion of Fundamental Human Rights

There has been a renewed emphasis on the promotion of fundamental human rights, as expressed through ILO standards. In part, this is a reaction to the debate on the relation between international trade and workers' rights, to the effect that, if the objective cannot be achieved by sanctions, it can perhaps be achieved by gentler methods.

However, there is a far more fundamental reason. The ILO itself has re-examined its standards and principles in its 75th anniversary discussions, and has decided that it must concentrate on these rights. This coincided with a series of major international conferences around the 50th anniversary of the United Nations, including the World Conference on Human Rights (Vienna, June 1993), the World Summit on Social Development (Copenhagen, March 1995), the Fourth World Women's Conference (Beijing, September 1995), the World Conference against Racism, Racial Discrimination, Xenophobia and Related Intolerance (Durban, August–September 2001), all of which have reaffirmed more or less explicitly the reliance of the rest of the United Nations system on the standards laid down by the ILO.

Therefore, at its March–April 1995 session, the governing body asked the Director-General to report to it on the reasons why most countries had not yet ratified the ILO conventions on fundamental human rights, and the Director-General stated that he would contact all member states and submit a report on this question in November 1995. This campaign has resulted in more than 350 ratifications of the ILO's fundamental conventions since that time, with a steadily increasing number of member states having ratified all eight of them.

CONCLUDING REMARKS

The ILO system provides significant help to those in every country who wish to protect human rights, particularly workers. The system is under continuous examination and is even challenged by some. More recently, the ILO's work in this area is being threatened by the general climate of financial restrictions weighing on all international organizations.

The ILO's commitment to human rights has never been questioned, and recently has been reinforced. It is changing, as all institutions must change to survive and adapt, but this proven mechanism for the protection of human rights is likely to last as far into the future as it already has in the past.

NOTES

1 The International Labour Office serves as the Secretariat of the International Labour Organization.
2 Except for the Conference examination of the amount of the budget, carried out in a Finance Committee composed exclusively of government delegates.
3 ILO doc. GB.262/LILS/4, March–April 1995 session of the governing body.
4 Similar obligations exist for non-metropolitan territories (NMTs), under Article 35 of the Constitution. Although the number of these NMTs is diminishing, there are still in force nearly 1000 declarations of application of ratified conventions to them.
5 They are not published in book form and are not submitted to the Conference, as are observations. However, they are not confidential and are published in the ILOLEX data base which appears on CD-ROM annually. The separate arrangements are purely a practical matter to deal with the enormous volumes of information. It may be noted that ILOLEX is published in English, French and Spanish (on the same disk) and also includes all the comments of the ILO's supervisory bodies since 1985, the texts of conventions and recommendations and the Constitution, and other material.
6 The Committee's report is published as Report III(1A) to each session of the Conference. It should be mentioned that the Committee of Experts also publishes a 'General Survey' each year, as Report III(1B), many of which concern such human rights subjects as freedom of association, discrimination, migrant workers and so on.
7 This is the only one of the instruments cited here which has not come into force, for lack of a sufficient number of ratifications (17 at the end of 2001).
8 An exception is Article 7(a) of the International Covenant on Economic, Social and Cultural Rights, which provides for 'equal pay for equal work' for women, a notion markedly less beneficial than the 'equal pay for work *of equal value*' required by ILO Convention No. 100 which was adopted 16 years earlier.
9 A comparative analysis of the Convention on the Rights of the Child and ILO Convention No. 138 may be found in Swepston (1994, pp.7–18).
10 Also noted in the annual Report of the Committee of Experts.
11 For each convention, the ILO governing body adopts a 'Report Form' which is designed to help governments make their periodic reports. These forms contain questions to illustrate the kind of information desired under various articles, as well as more general guidelines on reporting on each individual instrument.
12 World Conference on Human Rights (1993).

BIBLIOGRAPHY

ILOLEX data base, published on CD-ROM annually. In English, French and Spanish on the same disk.
Swepston, Lee (1994), 'The Convention on the Rights of the Child and the ILO', *Nordic Journal of International Law* (61–62).
World Conference on Human Rights (1993), *The Vienna Declaration and Programme of Action*, UN doc. A/CONF.157/23, June.

3 UNESCO Procedures for the Protection of Human Rights

KARL JOSEF PARTSCH AND KLAUS HÜFNER*

INTRODUCTION[1]

In the United Nations system, different types of organs for the protection and promotion of human rights are used.[2] They can be distinguished or characterized according to various criteria: the legal basis for their activities, the category of rights to be promoted or protected, the persons or groups having access to the body, the composition of such bodies by government representatives or independent experts, the competence to consider the admissibility of complaints, the requirement of prior exhaustion of domestic remedies, the distinction between Charter-based organs and organs monitoring treaty compliance and, finally, the kind of final decision available.

When, in 1976, the 19th session of the General Conference of UNESCO invited the Executive Board and the Director-General to study the existing comparable organs which could be used as models for a more effective system in UNESCO,[3] they were able to draft a comparative table showing the principal procedures for the examination of individual complaints. Nearly all of the above-mentioned criteria appeared in this table, but no two procedures were entirely identical. One could not even discern a trend to develop a common type of organ for this task. Each system had unique characteristics.

It is remarkable that the question about which persons have access to these human rights bodies was answered only by two universal organizations in the same way, by ECOSOC and UNESCO: 'Victim – other person – non-governmental organization.'

UNESCO AND HUMAN RIGHTS

UNESCO's Constitution

According to Article I(1) of its Constitution, UNESCO has the obligation 'to further universal respect for justice, for the rule of law and for human rights and fundamental freedoms which are affirmed for the peoples of the world, without distinction of race, sex, language or religion by the Charter of the United Nations'. It is, however, added in Article 1(3) that '... the Organization is prohibited from intervening in matters which are essentially within their [the member states'] domestic jurisdiction'.

In this way, the relevant provisions concerning human rights of the Charter of the United Nations, namely Articles 1(3) and 2(7), have been reaffirmed. The Charter already provides for a sub-organ of ECOSOC, a commission for the promotion of human rights (Article 68), the only one mentioned by name for a specific task. When the United States delegation proposed its establishment, some other delegations expressed doubts as to whether the Commission might interfere with matters essentially within the domestic jurisdiction of member states, incompatible with Article 2(7) of the Charter.[4]

The UNESCO Constitution has not followed this example, leaving it to its main bodies (the General Conference and Executive Board) to provide a special organ on the basis of their competence to set up special and technical committees as necessary.[5]

The Need for a Special Organ

The adoption of the Convention against Discrimination in Education[6] made it necessary to examine reports of States Parties and to appoint a committee for this task. This was first done in 1965[7] and repeated when consultations on the implementation of the Convention were organized or when other matters were delegated to the 'Special Committee on Discrimination in Education', as it was called between 1967 and 1969.

Human Rights in UNESCO's Competence

Not all human rights fall within UNESCO's competence. The name of the Organization indicates that education, science and culture are part of UNESCO's fields of competence, to which must be added information/ communication.

When the first communications were received, the need was felt to inform their authors how UNESCO's competence for matters of human rights are precisely defined. The Office of International Standards and Legal Affairs, when confirming the receipt of a communication, informed the authors in a 'standard letter'.[8]

In this letter a list of guarantees falling within UNESCO's competence is quoted, using the wording in the Universal Declaration of Human Rights of 1948. In the first part, the list contains four rights which fall essentially in its spheres of competence – namely, the rights to education (Article 26 of the Universal Declaration), the right to share in scientific advancement and to participate freely in cultural life (both from Article 27), and the right to information, including freedom of opinion and expression (from Article 19).

The second part also contains four rights, whose exercise may be implied in the rights of the first category. Only the most noteworthy are set out, contained in Articles 18, 19, 20 and 27 of the Universal Declaration.

For both categories of rights the same method is used – namely, to select from the articles of the Declaration only certain issues and to assign them either to the first or second category.

The problem has also been discussed between the Secretariats of UN and UNESCO about the exchange of certain documents, according to Article 40(3) of the International Covenant on Civil and Political Rights. The UN Secretary-General took a very restrictive position and proposed to include in this exchange only documents concerning the rights regarded by UNESCO as essential, but not those which only might help to exercise the rights of the first category. The UNESCO representative went further and wanted to include not only this last category of rights but, in addition, the right to freedom of association, including the right to form and join trade unions, and the rights of children and of minorities.[9] This discussion was continued in the Human Rights Committee without clear results.[10]

It seems problematic to define the competence of UNESCO in the field of human rights only by referring to legislative guarantees, since the character of the persons affected by an alleged violation is also important. Teachers, scientists, intellectuals, artists and journalists are active in this field, working both within and outside their professions. Moreover, the manual worker who, in his free time, edits a journal or carries out a similar activity falls within the competence of UNESCO (although, of course, only for this activity). On the other hand, a person exercising an educational or cultural profession cannot claim to fall within UNESCO's fields of competence if he or she commits an act punishable by common law. According to the practice of the UNESCO Committee on Conventions and Recommendations (CR), all acts of violence are excluded.

Certainly there are cases for doubt, an example being the activities of teachers' unions to improve the conditions of education, which do fall within UNESCO's competence. However, if the union is acting apparently in order to increase teachers' salaries, there may be doubt.

When it has to be decided, in a procedure before the CR, whether a communication falls within the competence of UNESCO, it is certainly important to know whether the victim belongs to the cultural sphere and which of his/her human rights has been violated. In addition, it must be ascertained whether such violations were motivated by his/her activities in the fields of education, science, culture or information/communication.

DEVELOPMENT UP TO 1977–1978

In the United Nations

A remarkable development in the UN can be observed in the field of human rights and their protection: that is, from a period of promotion and of furthering their respect towards their effective protection. It may be recalled that several decades passed after the adoption of the Universal Declaration in 1948 before victims of violations were able to introduce procedures before the Human Rights Committee under the International Covenant on Civil and Political Rights and its Optional Protocol which entered into force in 1976. During the first two decades of its existence the UN Commission on Human Rights had to limit its activities mainly to drafting instruments in this field. For many years the opinion prevailed that the Commission was not entitled to take any effective concrete measure when violations of human rights were brought to its knowledge. When this opinion was revised in 1967 and 1970,[11] the Commission was only authorized to deal with communications concerning flagrant and systematic violations, whereas an activity in favour of mere individual and specific cases would constitute a prohibited intervention. It could only be used as a source of information on the existence of large-scale violations.

In UNESCO

The development in UNESCO was very similar. The basic provisions in its Constitution are nearly identical to those in the Charter. There also existed a sub-organ of the Executive Board with specific competence in the field of human rights – namely, with the task of examining the periodic reports of member states of the Convention against Discrimination in Education of 14 December 1960. When some individual complaints concerning human rights in UNESCO's field were received, the Executive Board decided to bring them to the notice of the above-mentioned Committee (CR) in order to be handled in the same manner as stipulated in ECOSOC Resolution 728 F (XXIII) of 30 July 1957. On this occasion, the Board recalled expressly that UNESCO was not authorized to take any measure in connection with such complaints.[12] This meant that the Committee was only entitled to draft a list of these communications, to inform the member states concerned and to ask them for comments. The authors of these communications had to be informed that the Committee had no competence to take any steps. Total harmony between UNESCO and the UN was thus assured.

Between 1968 and 1976, no less that 73 communications of this kind were placed before the CR under the terms of document 77EX/Decision 8.3. When they were discussed, a large number of problems were raised concerning the procedure to be followed, mainly with regard to the respect of the principle of confidentiality and the relationship between the Executive Board and its Committee. But the difficult problem could not be avoided:

how could a more effective system of protection can be established without committing a prohibited intervention?

The 19th Session of the UNESCO General Conference (Nairobi, 1976)

The 19th session of the General Conference in Nairobi constituted the turning point in this development.[13] The highest governing body of UNESCO agreed to the task of reforming the procedures for the protection of the victims of human rights violations. The Director-General and the Executive Board were entrusted to study comparable procedures applied in the United Nations, by specialized agencies and also by regional organizations, with a view to elaborating a new system for a more effective protection of victims of violations in the Organization's field of competence. Already, at this time, a distinction was being made between individual and specific cases, on the one hand, and systematic or flagrant 'situations', on the other.

It was an issue of controversy, at the General Conference, whether the model of the UN Commission on Human Rights should be followed to authorize the competent organ to take measures only with respect to systematic and flagrant violations, regarded as 'questions', or whether authorization should be extended to include specific and individual cases submitted in communications. A compromise was found to include both categories of violations, without, however, deciding whether different procedures would be adequate for these two kinds of violation.

Problems for a Revised System

In a reformed system the following problems had to be solved in order to make it more effective:

- how to avoid interference in domestic affairs of member states, mainly when dealing with specific and individual cases
- how rules for appropriate procedures could be now brought into force and by which organs
- which sources of international law could serve as a basis for promoting human rights
- who should be able to present communications concerning violations of human rights
- which governments would have to respond to such communications
- how the procedure for examining the admissibility of communications should be structured
- how, and on the basis of which sources, should cases be examined on their merits.

THE ORIGINS OF THE NEW PROCEDURE

Participating Organs

Quite a number of organs of UNESCO's ad hoc bodies participated in preparing a draft for the rules of procedure.

- The CR was asked by the Executive Board to review its current procedures for handling communications on the basis of 77 EX/Decision 8.3.[14] In view of the very limited competence of the CR for examining individual cases, it was not able to make any valuable contribution to the realization of the programme adopted at Nairobi.
- In 1977 the Director-General presented to the Executive Board the 'Study of the procedures which should be followed in the examination of cases and questions which might be submitted to UNESCO concerning the exercise of all human rights in the spheres of its competence, in order to make its action more effective'.[15] This study contains vast material on the procedures of the various organs in the United Nations, its specialized agencies and also in regional organizations for the promotion and protection of human rights. Considerations are added as to how this material may be used for the work of a new system.[16]
- The Executive Board established an Ad Hoc Working Party comprising 13 of its members, with the assistance of some experts partly participating as deputies for members, including T. Buergenthal (USA) and V. Kartashkin (USSR). Some members of the Board also submitted written comments.[17] The Working Party met first from 1 to 5 August 1977. Its report[18] showed that no common agreement had been reached on a great number of problems. A general consensus existed only on two of them: that the Organization's competence in the field of human rights '… did not authorize it to take enforcement measures' (para. 14) and, second, that the competent body, instead of accusation and confrontation, should seek a dialogue with the state concerned (para. 44).

Under these circumstances the Executive Board felt the need to invite the Working Party to meet again in January 1978 in order to adopt a final report. Instead of a report, the Working Party drafted a decision containing detailed rules of procedure for dealing with specific or individual cases and some principles for dealing with 'situations'. It explained the reasons for its action in a preamble of no less than 12 paragraphs. This draft was adopted by consensus on 26 April 1978 by the Executive Board without any changes (104 EX/Decision 3.3).[19] The decision was adopted, formally by the Executive Board and brought to the attention of the 20th session of the General Conference. It does not have the character of a conventional instrument.

THE MAIN CHARACTERISTICS OF THE UNESCO PROCEDURE

Access to the CR

Most systems of monitoring the respect for human rights in the United Nations are rather restrictive in determining, which persons, groups or organizations shall be authorized to present claims concerning alleged violations of human rights committed by member states. In general, this competence is only recognized for the victims of such violations and, eventually, also to close relatives and lawyers acting on behalf of victims. It was regarded as a remarkable exception when, in the UN Commission on Human Rights and its organs, any person, group of persons, as well as non-governmental organizations, were admitted if they had at least a direct and reliable knowledge of such violations.[20]

The Executive Board proposed in its study to follow this model and suggested, referring to 'common sense', that the possibility of submitting communications should be open also to non-governmental organizations under the condition, however, that they had shown a legitimate interest in so acting. Such interest would exist when the alleged victim was a member of the organization in question or when this organization was effectively working to defend the human rights allegedly violated.[21] This suggestion was taken up by the Working Party on 11 January 1978, without, however, requesting a legitimate interest of the non-governmental organization.[22]

This generous rule has certain advantages. Non-governmental organizations may be better informed on the task of defending human rights than the victims of violations themselves; many of them have experience in drafting the text of a communication, thus supporting the preparatory work of a Secretariat; and, finally and more importantly, they can act on behalf of victims from countries which would not allow their residents to approach an international organization working in the field of human rights. Of course, it may be doubtful whether UNESCO should in fact welcome all kinds of non-governmental organization as partners in the work '... in the spirit of international co-operation, conciliation and mutual understanding'. Also non-governmental organizations should carefully avoid an aggressive or offensive attitude.[23]

Some additional remarks may be made in this connection: in the doctrine the question has been raised whether member states of UNESCO, regarded as groups of persons, are entitled to use this procedure and to present communications concerning alleged violations of human rights committed by other states.[24] This possibility exists in other systems with a special procedure, but not under 104 EX/Decision/3.3. Member states of UNESCO have direct access to the main organs (the Executive Board and General Conferences) and do not need to use a procedure before a sub-organ such as the CR. To date, it seems that no such communication has been received.

The States Concerned

The communications presented to the CR concern violations of human rights committed by states. The problem whether the member states of UNESCO are legally bound to collaborate with the CR has already been discussed and answered in the affirmative. The legal basis is the internal law of UNESCO.

Can a communication concerning a non-member state be presented when it may be the object of a violation committed not by the state concerned or its authorities, but by another authority or a private person?

Communications concerning non-member states are not expressly excluded. Although at least some rules of procedure are based on the internal law of the Organization, the CR is not obliged to declare such communication inadmissible *ab initio*:[25] it depends on the state concerned whether it is willing to cooperate with UNESCO and to accept the conditions provided for in 104 EX/Decision 3.3. In a case already referred to the CR, it acted accordingly.

If the alleged violation has not been committed by an authority of the state concerned or one that is under its control, it is possible that the state is obliged to prohibit this violation. Referring to periods of disturbances in which the government concerned was not able to control a situation, the Committee has considered that '... without taking any decision having the force of a rule ... a government is normally responsible for the safety of its citizens and of those under its jurisdiction.[26]

THE STRUCTURE OF THE COMPETENT ORGANS

The Executive Board and the CR

The structure of the Executive Board also determines to a large extent the structure of its subsidiary body, the Committee on Conventions and Recommendations (CR). Both have been changed. Up until 1991 the General Conference elected members of the Executive Board from individuals and representatives of member states. Since 1991, member states themselves have been candidates for election and are entitled to appoint a representative and eventually, after a consultation with their governments, alternates.[27] They do not need confirmation by the General Conference.

It is evident that there exists a difference between the election of a state for a certain function and that of a person. For the election of a state, political considerations are primarily decisive. However, when an individual runs for a seat on the Executive Board, such political considerations are not excluded. The personal merits of the candidate, his/her dignity and reputation are, nevertheless, considered in addition by the electoral body and may be decisive for the outcome.

When UNESCO was founded in 1945 at the London Conference, its Constitution, in its original version,[28] defined the function of the then 18 members of the Executive Board in Article V(11):

... the members of the Executive Board shall exercise the powers delegated to them by the General Conference on behalf of the Conference as a whole and not as representatives of their respective Governments.

In 1954 the General Conference amended this provision at its eighth session to read:

12. Although the members of the Executive Board are representatives of their respective governments, they shall exercise the powers delegated to them by the General Conference on behalf of the Conference as a whole.[29]

This provision was in force from 1954 until 1991 and charged the Board member with two tasks: at the same time, to represent his/her government and also to comply with the decisions of the General Conference. It was not determined whether one of these duties had priority. If the representative found no way to obey both of them, an *impasse* existed. This was the situation until the last recent reform.

Since this last reform, 51 member states and then (in 1995) 58 are elected to the Executive Board by the General Conference – not individual persons. 'Each member [state] shall appoint one representative ...' states the revised Article V.1 and 2(a) of the Constitution.

A problem concerning the status of the members of the CR was on its Agenda for several years.[30] When a communication is discussed in the CR, representatives of the state concerned may attend meetings in order to provide additional information and to answer questions from CR members (104 Decision/3.3, paragraph 14(e)).[31] If these representatives are sent ad hoc, they leave the room after having fulfilled their functions, without participating in the deliberations of the Committee. If, however, the state concerned has a member on the Committee, this task is fulfilled by this member in order to save time. Objections were, however, raised when this member remained in his/her place at the committee table after fulfilling his/her functions in the exercise of his right to participate in the Committee's work. All states – and their representatives – had to be treated equally. They should not, at the same time, be judges and be judged. These arguments were finally accepted by the Committee which decided that '... members of the Committee should not be present for the private discussions leading to a decision or recommendation when a communication concerning their own country is considered' in order to ensure equal treatment of all states.[32]

It is remarkable that the institution of ad hoc judges appointed by the parties in arbitration and procedures before international courts has apparently not been considered.

The present situation can therefore be characterized in the following way. The CR consists – since 1994–1995 – of 30 members appointed by member states who do not serve as experts in their personal capacity. According to Weissbrodt and Farley, in practice not all of them usually attend: 'Moreover, members may be motivated to attend meetings only if communications relating to their governments or allies of their governments are being considered'.[33]

The Name of the CR

The name of the Committee has been frequently changed in the past, together with changes of its functions. When it was founded in 1965 it was called the 'Special Committee to examine the reports of Member States on the implementation of the Convention and Recommendation against Discrimination in Education'. Two years later, this overlong name was abbreviated to 'Special Committee on Discrimination in Education' and in 1968 to 'Committee on Conventions and Recommendations in Education' as a permanent body with 12 to 16 members. Only in 1978 did it receive its present name 'Committee on Conventions and Recommendations' by 104 EX/Decision 3.3, together with its foregoing reform. Also, the abbreviation changed from 'CRE' to 'CR'.

This name apparently does not indicate clearly the present functions of the CR. Various attempts have been made in recent years to change this name again in order to reflect its functions in the field of human rights, the last time being during the 141st session of the Executive Board in 1993.[34] The proposal made by the Chairperson of 'UNESCO Committee for Human Rights and Conventions' was not adopted by the Board.

EXAMINATION OF ADMISSIBILITY AND MERITS

Distribution of Functions

In the present study some elements and characteristics of the procedures have already been analysed. They have the scope to promote the respect for human rights in the relations between states and persons affected by their actions.

Five different tasks have to be accomplished by various organs of UNESCO:

- the preparation of the text of a communication fulfilling all the necessary conditions
- the examination of the admissibility of such a communication
- the examination of its merits
- the decision whether it refers to an individual and specific case and warrants further action in order to bring about a friendly solution
- whether the existence of a 'question' is confirmed and if it should be transmitted to the Executive Board and/or the General Conference for further examination and decision.

These substantive tasks are fulfilled by different organs of UNESCO. The Secretariat has preparatory functions which include the selection of communications outside the competence of the Organization. If it is manifestly outside this competence, it can be excluded. If it is manifestly ill-founded or if its author is apparently mentally unbalanced, the Secretariat needs the agreement of the Chairperson of the Committee before striking it from the list.[35]

The Committee itself decides on the admissibility of all communications in accordance with the conditions mentioned in para. 14(a)(i) to (x) of 104 EX/Decision 3.3. These conditions also have to be examined if the Committee has the impression that the case submitted might constitute a 'question' of massive, systematic or flagrant violations of human rights and should therefore be submitted to the Executive Board for its final examination. Before taking this decision, the Committee should make an attempt to reach a friendly solution. This cannot be undertaken without a rather complete knowledge of the situation in question.

The Secretariat

Communications can be presented in very different forms. In order to start procedures in the Secretariat it is sufficient that an identified author expresses the intention to have examined his case by an organ of UNESCO. The receipt of his desire is acknowledged by the Director of the Office of International Standards and Legal Affairs with a standard letter together with a copy of the text of the 104 EX/Decision 3.3 containing the conditions governing admissibility of communications and a 'form for communications concerning human rights' with the invitation to answer the questions raised and to return it to UNESCO, duly signed, as soon as possible. Already, on this occasion, the author is asked whether he/she agrees that his/her communication shall be examined in accordance with the procedure laid down in these documents and, in particular, whether he/she is willing for his/her name to be divulged and for the communication to be transmitted to the government concerned and brought to the notice of CR. This ample information on the author, together with the questions put to him/her, have been recently criticized as being extremely time-consuming and superfluous.[36]

It is true that this first contact between the author and the Secretariat has frequently led to ample correspondences, mainly when the author had not filled in the 'form letter' with precision. On the other hand, such extensive information of petitioners seemed necessary after the experiences of former times. This is also the reason why it was found necessary to insert paras 14(b)(i) and (ii) into 104 EX/Decision 3.3.

During the discussions between 1983 and 1985, the problem was extensively discussed as to whether it would be advisable to entrust the examination of the admissibility of communications to a small Working Group of three to five members of the CR. As models, the experience in the UN Commission on Human Rights and also in the Human Rights Committee are quoted. The functions of this Working Group for ECOSOC organs are entirely different, as are the functions of ECOSOC machinery in general.

In the Human Rights Committee, under the International Covenant on Civil and Political Rights, only a first screening of a purely procedural order was delegated to the Working Group or a Rapporteur. They are limited to examine only the fulfilment of Articles 1, 2, 3 and 5(2) of the Optional Protocol.[37] In addition, the admission of alternates for members of the Executive Board creates practical difficulties.

Conditions of Admissibility

Communications are only admissible if they meet with not less than ten conditions listed in para. 14(a)(i) to (x) of 104 EX/Decision 3.3. Not all of them are of a procedural character; some concern substance.

Under the UNESCO system, it is regarded as essential that the author of a communication does this under his name, assuming full responsibility for his allegations. For this reason anonymous complaints are not admitted.[38]

A person, a group of persons or organizations, who are not victims of an alleged violation, may submit a case concerning such violations if she, he or it has reliable knowledge of the case.[39] In the Model Rule[40] a 'direct and reliable knowledge' is even required; secondhand information, however, is admitted if the communication contains clear evidence. In addition, claims exclusively based on information from the mass media are not admitted.[41] It does not seem necessary to eliminate a weakness of 104 EX/Decision 3.3, as required by a Board member.[42]

Conditions (iii) and (iv), taken together, indicate the legal sources for a claim. The following principles are applied:

- A human right allegedly violated must be legally binding for all participants of a procedure.
- The alleged violation must have been already committed and not only expected or feared.
- The human right must fall within the competence of UNESCO. 104 EX/Decision 3.3 apparently supposes that not only human rights guaranteed in such instruments as the two Covenants are legally binding but, in addition, those based on customary law such as the Universal Declaration of Human Rights. Should a member state not have ratified the two Covenants, it would still be sufficient, if the petitioner refers in his/her communication to the corresponding provision in the Universal Declaration.

'Potential violations' are, according to the practice of the CR, not sufficient.[43] The problem of which human rights fall within the competence of UNESCO is treated above.

It can be regarded as an open question whether all 'other international instruments' accepted as recommendations can be regarded as 'standard-setting'.

The provision of para. 14(a)(v) covers two issues: the communication must not be ill-founded and must appear to contain relevant evidence. This evidence should be presented, or at least be offered, by the author from the beginning of the procedure in order to justify the assertion that a state has failed to respect human rights. Whether, during the examination of the admissibility of a claim, it is already appropriate to raise the question concerning the merits of a claim can be doubted. A clear separation of the procedural examination from the consideration of the merits may be an advantage for both of them. Otherwise, the danger exists that a case is hastily declared admissible because it seems to be ill-founded without giving sufficient attention to the evidence presented.[44]

The condition that communications should not be offensive or abusive to submit them[45] raises a delicate question. If a victim has been cruelly tortured, it cannot be expected that he/she reports on his/her experiences in polite terms. Certain states already regard it as an abuse to assert that they have failed to respect human rights. In practice, the Committee has shown some understanding if either the victim himself or his family informed the author of the communication with some virulence, but has regarded it as offensive if the author declared the behaviour of the authorities as typical for the country concerned, as shown in other cases reported to him. 104 EX/Decision 3.3 indicates how the author can avoid his/her communication being declared inadmissible – that is, by the exclusion of the offensive or abusive parts. This has been done in several cases.

The presentation of a large number of communications by the same author is not regarded as abusive.[46] Once non-governmental organizations were admitted to table complaints, such limitations could hardly be justified. In such an open system, even querulous persons have to be tolerated. As already mentioned, an exception is valid only for mentally unbalanced persons and also for authors who do not respect the confidentiality of the procedure.

It is requested that the communication be submitted within a reasonable time following the facts which constitute its subject-matter or after these facts have been made known.[47] This knowledge alone would not yet enable the author to table a communication. He/she would need some time in order to collect the necessary information concerning the victim's present situation and the necessary evidence and also to fulfil other conditions required for an admissible communication, mainly the attempt to exhaust internal remedies which would, under any circumstances, need some time.[48]

In certain human rights instruments, a stronger rule concerning the exhaustion of internal remedies exists. A well-documented study found, however, that a kind of customary rule in this respect only exists for judicial procedures which lead to a judgement or other enforcement measures but not for humanitarian actions as here.[49]

If, in a case examined by the CR, not all available judicial instances have been exhausted, it is not declared inadmissible but left on the agenda for the next session in order to receive additional information.[50]

In view of the great number of monitoring systems existing on the universal and regional level, it is difficult to avoid the same matter being examined by various systems at the same time. In the Optional Protocol to the International Covenant on Civil and Political Rights, Article 5(2) therefore provides that no communication shall be considered until it is ascertained whether the same matter is being examined under another procedure of international investigation or settlement. However, because of the very specific characteristics of UNESCO's procedure, no provision of this kind has been inserted in 104 EX/Decision 3.3. If, however, the case has already been settled by the state concerned, according to the international standard of human rights, the CR shall not consider the communication as having been transferred to it.[51]

It is remarkable that, in this situation, the petitioner is not only informed about the settlement, but his/her attention is also drawn to the possibility of using local remedies, before the decision is taken to strike the communication from the list.[52]

The CR's Procedure

The communications transmitted to the CR are examined by the Committee in private session in order to decide first on their admissibility and later on their merits. The examination begins with the report of the Legal Adviser on the communication, its content, on the reply of the government concerned and also on eventual further information received by the author. Representatives of the government concerned are entitled to attend such meetings in order to provide additional information or to answer questions from Committee members. Although they are not formally obliged to appear, the Committee is very interested in their collaboration and usually asks for the good offices of the Director-General, if it is not sure whether the 'invitation' will be accepted. Recent experience has shown that 'an increasing number of the governments concerned by the communications send representatives to the Committee and co-operate with it'.[53] It has been objected, however, that the participation of the petitioners is not provided for in this dialogue and that they are informed of the position taken by the government only after the case has been decided by the CR.[54] This problem should certainly be considered when the agenda for a future reform of the procedures is drafted.

An Examination of Merits

An examination of the merits of the case should take place in the third phase of the procedure. It has to be taken into account that one of the conditions of admissibility of a communication is that it is 'not to be manifestly ill-founded'.[55] Representatives of governments concerned are therefore expected to answer questions concerning the merits of a communication.[56] Information only testifying that the communication is 'manifestly' ill-founded is insufficient; during the examination on its merits a more profound and intensive verification of its substance is required. The Committee would certainly appreciate it if the government representative would provide such additional information as the Committee 'may consider necessary for the disposition of the matter'.[57]

During this phase an inequality again exists between the government representative and the petitioner. Whereas the government representative is entitled to attend the meetings,[58] the Committee would need, 'in exceptional circumstances', special authorization by the Board for the authors of communications or witnesses to be permitted to be present at such private meetings and to take the floor.

The Report of CR and its Examination

After each session, the CR sends a report on the results achieved to the Board. This contains summaries of the facts, presented by the Secretariat to the CR, of the declarations of the parties and of the discussions in the Committee, whereas its decisions are only verbally transmitted as are the recommendations '… which the Committee may wish to make either generally or regarding the disposition of a communication under consideration'.[59]

The Executive Board examines this report in private session. If it takes a decision there, this shall be the object of a summary report at a later public session. The Board may also decide to publish a release on its work during a private session. In this way, a communication can be made public in a more or less detailed form.

The Board takes note of the report and decides on the recommendations of the Committee. It may, for instance, demand that the Director-General follow the suggestions made[60] or entrust a member of the Board with a mission of investigation or negotiations with a government.

'CASES' AND 'QUESTIONS'

The Two Categories

When, with the adoption of ECOSOC Resolutions 1235 (XLII) and 1503 (XLVIII), a new system of promotion and protection of human rights was developed and the two categories of violations were treated differently. Only those which revealed a 'consistent pattern of gross and reliably attested violations' could be examined in detail by the organs of the UN Commission on Human Rights in order to decide on what action should be taken. It did not seem necessary or appropriate to do the same with 'specific or individual cases'; they just served as material in order to discover cases of the first category.

Another solution was found at UNESCO, although some delegations initially recommended closely following the model of the UN Commission on Human Rights.

Different Procedures

As a compromise between delegations which recommended including only either procedures for 'questions' or for mere 'cases', it was decided to include both of them.[61] Procedures should, however, differ. For 'cases', the CR should be competent in all phases of their examination; for 'questions', however, only during an initial phase, their final examination being reserved for the Executive Board and the General Conference. Different rules were also adopted for publicizing the sessions of these bodies.

Definitions

'Questions' have been defined as referring to:

> ... massive, systematic or flagrant violations of human rights which result either from a policy contrary to human rights applied *de jure* or *de facto* by a State or from an accumulation of individual cases forming a consistent pattern.[62]

A more detailed definition is given in para. 18:

> [The Executive Board] considers that questions of massive, systematic or flagrant violations of human rights and fundamental freedoms – including, for example, those perpetrated as a result of policies of aggression, interference in the internal affairs of States, occupation of foreign territory and implementation of a policy of colonialism, genocide, apartheid, racialism, or national and social oppression – falling within UNESCO's field of competence should be considered by the Executive Board and the General Conference in public meetings.

During the whole time a communication is being handled by the CR, precisely from its receipt until its transmittal to the Board, all the rules enacted in 104 EX/Decision 3.3 are applicable to it. This is valid for the rules concerning the right to table communications. A state, as a group of persons, is not entitled to do it nor is the Director-General, although the Committee may use information delivered by him.[63]

It is also valid for the application of all the conditions mentioned in para. 14(a)(i) to (x), including the necessary attempt to exhaust available internal remedies. The phases to be covered by the CR have been precisely indicated: declaration as admissible, examination on merit and, in addition, an attempt to bring about a friendly solution.[64]

Procedures for 'Questions'

The procedures of the Executive Board and of the General Conference have been defined in para. 18 of 104 EX/Decision 3.3 in a rather summary manner. According to the text of this paragraph, a question '... should be considered by the Executive Board and the General Conference in public meetings'. It neither determines how the competence between the Board and the Conference is distributed, nor which organ decides on the publicity of meetings. In view of the CR's status as a sub-organ of the Board, it can hardly be accepted that the Committee is authorized to bind its superior organs by a decision. In general, the results of its examination concerning admissibility and substance are also not binding for its superior organs. It is therefore preferable for the Committee to follow the opinion of the Board than to decide for itself whether or not all 'questions' transmitted to it shall be examined and decided in public session.[65]

FURTHER REVISIONS?

UNESCO's work for an effective promotion of human rights has been highly praised; it was called 'one of the most beautiful ornaments of the Organization' by a Board member. A former Chairperson, the Belgian historian, George-Henri Dumont, expressed his praise in a more concrete form. He emphasized, in a number of articles (see the Bibliography (p.131)) the concrete action in an effective dialogue led with the member states in full confidentiality, sometimes resulting in 'a combat in the shadows'. In these terms, he mentioned two important elements characterizing the procedures: first, dialogue in order to find a friendly solution in conciliation; second, the full respect for confidentiality and absolute renunciation of publicity as far as individual and specific cases are concerned. Without these two elements the astonishing results of the Committee's work can hardly be explained. Mr Dumont stated that about half of the cases have been concluded successfully.

Of course, there is no absence of critical voices. Already in 1984, the Executive Board delegations of Yugoslavia, India and Algeria had proposed a revision of the procedures adopted in 1978 by 104 EX/Decision 3.3. The admissibility of communications should be examined by a working group of five members of the Committee; the rule of a prior exhaustion of internal remedies should be stricter; and the competence of UNESCO in the field of human rights defined more precisely. Also, the Committee should pay more attention to massive, flagrant and systematic violations of human rights instead of losing precious time by examining mere individual complaints which frequently lead to avoidable political discussions.[66]

Already a clear majority existed in the Committee in favour of maintaining the procedures actually in force. Although they might be improved in future, no urgent need was felt to act immediately. It was felt that further experience should be gained. The Executive Board and the General Conference agreed on this.

During recent years, the Committee has frequently examined questions of its procedure. Apparently, there is still an active idea of improving them. In order to create a basis for such deliberations, the Secretariat has analysed the methods of work of the CR and, separately, its own 'procedural practice'.[67]

Two interesting problems have been treated in this document which could lead to revisions of the present rules. First is the participation of authors of communications in the dialogue, which actually takes place between the CR and the governments concerned alone. Authors are informed on governments' position on their claims after the Committee has discussed them. This, in general, is confirmed in the document 146 EX/7.[68] Only in the exceptional case where a communication is struck from the list because it appears to be settled by the state concerned,[69] the Secretariat needs a confirmation of the facts (possibly by the author of the claim).[70] Second, the provision that an attempt to exhaust already domestic remedies is sufficient[71] has frequently been criticized. Now, according to the practice of the CR, the author of a communication who fails to seek such redress is 'punished' by striking his/her case off the list *ipso facto*.[72]

At its 154th session in spring 1998, the Executive Board considered it necessary to evaluate the methods of work of the CR in the light of past experiences. The Board asked the Director-General to seek the views and comments of the member states on this subject. Only 13 letters were received in reply, of which ten contained proposals and comments.

At the 155th session in autumn 1998, the Executive Board agreed to ask the Director-General to mail a second circular letter to invite member states to contribute on a larger scale. Finally, 21 proposals were examined on 25 February 1999 by a Working Group set up by the CR in order 'to draw up proposals … which would lead to an improvement in the situation of alleged victims of human rights violations'. The CR then decided to specify its procedural practice as follows:

- The CR stresses that in declaring a communication admissible it is in no way implying any condemnation of the government concerned; it is simply recognizing that the communication meets the admissibility criteria set out in 104 EX/Decision 3.3 and that it may be examined as to its substance;
- The CR is determined to speed up its decision-making on the admissibility of communications; any government concerned by a communication is required to make its position known within the time-limit of three months after the Secretariat has transmitted a new communication to it; if the government does not react in time, the CR would proceed without further delay to examine the admissibility of the communication;
- If the government concerned fails to cooperate, the CR may, in its report to the Executive Board, draw the Board's attention to such a case and suggest a debate by the Executive Board in private meeting;
- The CR will consider under which circumstances each of its annual reports drafted by the Secretariat may be made public.[73]

It is interesting to note that, during the debate in the CR, most members did not wish to change the Committee's practice; stressing the special character of UNESCO's procedure as compared with United Nations procedures, those procedures were interpreted as not incompatible but, rather, complementary. The CR did not feel it necessary to undertake a comparative analysis, thereby examining the procedures developed by the United Nations treaty bodies.[74]

CONCLUDING REMARKS

This chapter has concentrated on the UNESCO procedures concerning individual communications although the Committee on Conventions and Recommendations, as its very name indicates, has been created in order to periodically consider the member states' reports on UNESCO conventions in detail.

Today, the CR only receives summary reports prepared by the UNESCO Secretariat which do not offer further details about the performance of individual member states. This procedure has led to extremely low response rates from member states; in addition, the quality of the individual reports has deteriorated. In other words, the mechanisms in the meantime developed by the United Nations treaty bodies clearly indicate that the CR will have to examine its states' reporting system in the light of the experiences of the other treaty bodies. At its 158th session in November 1999 the Executive Board decided 'that the Committee will also consider all questions entrusted to it by the Executive Board concerning the implementation of UNESCO's standard-setting instruments'.[75]

NOTES

* Karl Josef Partsch died on 30 December 1996; the present Chapter is an updated version prepared by Klaus Hüfner.
1 The main UNESCO documents have been published by the Organization in the booklet UNESCO (2000).
2 Alston (1992). It contains monographs by various authors of seven United Nations Charter-based organs, five organs monitoring treaty compliance and four contributions concerning general issues, including a chapter on ILO. There is no chapter on UNESCO.
3 Doc. 19C/Res. 12.1, para. II/10, 1976.
4 Alston, 'The Commission on Human Rights' in Alston (2000, note 2, p.127).
5 Article IV, para. 11 of the Constitution (General Conference) and Article V, para. 6(b) in less precise terms (Executive Board).
6 Adopted by the General Conference on 14 December 1960; in force since 1962.
7 Doc. 70/EX/Decision 5.2.1, 1964.
8 UNESCO (2000, Annex II, p.69).
9 Alston (1980, p.674 *et seq.*).
10 The 78th and 82nd sessions on 12–14 July 1978. See United Nations (1986, pp.274–77 and 280–86).

11   By ECOSOC Res. 1235 (XLII) of 6 July 1967 and 1503 (XLVIII) of 27 May 1970.
12   Doc. 77 EX/Decision 8.3, 1968, paras 4 and 6; text in Annex I to Doc. 100 EX/CR.2.
13   Doc. 19C/Res. 6.113 and 12.1, 1976; cf. Bastid (1983).
14   Doc. 100 EX/CR.2 of 1976; Doc.102 EX/19, 1977, Annex II.
15   Doc. 102 EX/19 of 7 April 1977.
16   See note 15, Part V, paras 125–62.
17   Doc. 103 EX/WP/HR/Inf.1/Add. 1 and 2.
18   Doc. 103 EX/19 of 19 August 1977.
19   This document is published in UNESCO (2000) but does not appear in the usual collections of human rights instruments in English. It does, however, appear in United Nations (1994, p.322).
20   Resolution 1 (XXIV) of the Sub-Commission on Prevention of Discrimination and Protection of Minorities of 13 August 1971, para. 2(a) requires not only a reliable, but also a direct, knowledge. 104 EX/Decision 3.3, para. 14(a)(vii) at least bans information from the mass media.
21   Doc. 102 EX/19, para. 136 of 7 August 1977.
22   Doc. 104 EX/WG/HR/2(ii), verbally taken over in 104 EX/Decision 3.3, para. 14(a)(ii).
23   104 EX/Decision 3.3, para. 14(a)(vi).
24   Alston, (1980, p.677), referring to doc. 102 EX/19, paras 134–35.
25   Alston (1980, p.678), with reference to the practice of CRE before 1978.
26   Doc. 146 EX/7 of 24 February 1995, Annex III, p.7.
27   Constitution, Article V.A, para. 2(a), text revised by the General Conference at its 26th session (1991).
28   *United Nations Treaty Series*, Vol. 4, 1947, p.247.
29   Doc. 8C/Rec., para. 12.
30   Doc. 146 EX/7 (1995) Annex III, p.5.
31   104 Decision/3.3, para. 14(e).
32   Doc. 140 EX/3 para. 154.
33   Weissbrodt and Farley (1994, p.412).
34   Doc. 141 EX/6 of 19 March 1993, Part V, Conclusions.
35   The very limited functions of the Secretariat result from the discussions in the 33rd and 34th sessions of the Executive Board in June 1985 (Annex III to Doc. 23C/17 with the interventions of Mrs Margan and Mr. Pompei (33rd session, paras 14.1 to 14.9 and 15.1 to 15.7) and the Legal Adviser, followed by the Director-General (34th session, paras 21.1 to 21.3 and 22).
36   Weissbrodt and Farley (1994, pp.393–98).
37   Opsahl (1994, p.434).
38   104 EX/Decision 3.3, para. 14(a)(i).
39   104 EX/Decision 3.3, para. 14(a)(ii).
40   Res.1 (XXXIV) of the Sub-Commission on Prevention of Discrimination and Protection of Minorities of 13 August 1973, paras 1 and 2(a).
41   104 EX/Decision 3.3, para. 14(a) (vii).
42   Cf. note 35 concerning Mrs Margan.
43   Doc. 146 EX/7 Annex III, p.3 to para. 14(a)(vi).
44   104 EX/Decision 3.3, para. 14(a)(vi).
45   Weissbrodt and Farley (1994, pp.398 and 404).
46   104 EX/Decision 3.3, para. 14(a)(viii).
47   As Ermolenko (USSR) meant at the 34th session of the Executive Board; see note 35, para. 5.4.

48   104 EE/Decision 3.3, para. 14(a)(ix). According to para. 5 of Res. 1 (XXXIV), *op. cit.*, note 37, the 'reasonable time-limit' begins only with the exhaustion of internal remedies.
49   Delbrück (1989).
50   See para. 14(h) of 104 EX/Decision 3.3.
51   Doc. 146 EX/7, para. 48.
52   104 EX/Decision 3.3, para. 14(a)(x); Annex III to Doc. 146 EX/7, p.4.
53   Doc. 146 EX/7, para. 55.
54   Weissbrodt and Farley (1994, p.401).
55   104 EX/Decision 3.3, para. 14(a)(v).
56   104 EX/Decision 3.3, para. 14(b) and (c).
57   104 EX/Decision 3.3, para. 14(h).
58   104 EX/Decision 3.3, para. 14(e).
59   104 EX/Decision 3.3, para. 15, sentences 2 and 3.
60   An example is mentioned by Alston (1980, p.682).
61   Bastid (1983, p.47).
62   104 EX/Decision 3.3, para. 10(b).
63   Doc. 120 EX/17, para. 25(i).
64   Ibid., para. 25(ii).
65   See report of the Board, Doc. 120 EX/17 of September 1984, para. 25(iii); also Alston (1980, p.692).
66   Doc. 23C/17 of 8 October 1985 contains in its Annexes I–III documents from all three levels, including the summary Records of the 33rd and 34th sessions of the Board in June 1985.
67   Doc. 146 EX/7 of 24 February 1995 with 56 paragraphs and Annex III with seven pages reflecting the Procedural Practice of CR. This non-confidential paper has already been used in this Chapter.
68   Para. 45 and Annex III p. 3, concerning para. 14(a)(V).
69   104 EX/Decision 3.3, para. 14(a)(x).
70   Annex III, p.4.
71   104 EX/Decision 3.3, para. 14(a)(ix).
72   See above under VIII/3 (g) with note 4.
73   Doc. 156 EX/52
74   According to Weissbrodt and Farley (1994), the UNESCO has not progressively evolved in the way that other United Nations procedures have.
75   Doc. 158/Doc 2.

BIBLIOGRAPHY

Alston, Philip (1980), 'UNESCO's procedure for dealing with human rights violations', *Santa Clara Law Review*, **20**(3), pp.665–96.
Alston, Philip (ed.) (1992), *The United Nations and Human Rights – A Critical Appraisal*, Oxford: Clarendon Press.
Bastid, Suzanne (1983), 'La mise en oeuvre d'un recours concernant les droits de l'homme dans le domaine relevant de la compétence de l'UNESCO', *Festschrift (Mélanges) H. Mosler*, pp.45–57.
Delbrück, Jost (1989), 'The exhaustion of the local remedies rule and the international protection of human rights. A plea for a contextual approach', *Mélanges (Festschrift) K. J. Partsch*, pp.213–31.

Dumont, Georges-Henri (1989), 'Une action concrète de l'UNESCO en matière des droits de l'homme', *Revue internationale des sciences sociales*, **122**, pp.651–60.

Dumont, Georges-Henri (1990), 'Droits de l'homme: le combat dans l'ombre', *Le Courrier de l'UNESCO*, June, pp.43–4.

Dumont, Georges-Henri (1990), 'UNESCO, the quest for Human Rights: UNESCO's ultimate goal', *UNESCO Sources*, **16**(1), June.

Marks, Stephen (1977–78), 'UNESCO and human rights: the implementation of rights relating to education, science, culture and information', *Texas International Law Journal*, **13**, pp.35–67.

Marks, Stephen (1992), 'The complaint procedure of UNESCO', in H. Hannum (ed.), *Guide to International Human Rights Practice*, 2nd edn, London: Macmillan Press, pp.86–98.

Opsahl, T. (1992), 'The Human Rights Committee', in P. Alston (ed.), *The United Nations and Human Rights – A Critical Appraisal*, Oxford: Clarendon Press.

Partsch, K.J. (1992), 'La mise en oeuvre des droits de l'homme par l'UNESCO – remarques sur un système particulier', *Annuaire français de droit international*, **XXXVI**, pp.482–506.

Rolland, P. (1980), 'La nouvelle procédure d'examen des communications concernant la violation des droits de l'homme à l'UNESCO', *Revue internationale des sciences administratives*, **46** (3), pp.266–74.

Saba, Hanna (1982), 'UNESCO and human rights', in Karel Vasak and Philip Alston (eds), *The International Dimensions of Human Rights*, Vol. 2, Paris, UNESCO; Westport, CT: Greenwood Press, pp.401–26.

Symonides, Janusz and Volodin, Vladimir (eds) (1999), *UNESCO and Human Rights. Standard-Setting Instruments, Major Meetings, Publications*, 2nd edn, Paris: UNESCO.

UNESCO (2000), *The Executive Board of UNESCO*, 10th edn, Paris: UNESCO.

United Nations (1986), *Yearbook of the Human Rights Committee 1977–1978*, Geneva: United Nations.

United Nations (1994), *United Nations Action in the Field of Human Rights*, Geneva: UN Centre for Human Rights.

Weissbrodt, David and Farley, Rose (1994), 'The UNESCO human rights procedures – an evaluation', *Human Rights Quarterly*, **16** (2), May, pp.391–414.

PART II
REGIONAL SYSTEMS

4 The European Systems for the Protection of Human Rights

MAXIME TARDU

INTRODUCTION

The concept of human rights expressed in contemporary international law flows from many cultural horizons. Nevertheless, it is true that the European philosophical and institutional trends of the last three centuries have had a significant impact on the progressive development of this concept. Furthermore, since the end of the First World War, several important mechanisms for the international protection of human rights have been established and tested to a large extent within Europe.

Among the early attempts at international implementation was the minorities system which was created at the end of the First World War by the victorious states and was developed by the League of Nations. Although it invoked universal concepts, this procedure was in fact applied essentially to minorities living within the defeated states of Austria, Hungary, Bulgaria and Turkey or within new states which had come into being in Central and Eastern Europe, and the Balkans.

After the atrocities of the Second World War, human rights aspirations initially focused on the United Nations. The recognition of human rights in the United Nations Charter seemed to justify hopes for the creation of effective implementation mechanisms at the universal level. These hopes met with early frustration as the Cold War immobilized human rights at the United Nations for a long time.

The Council of Europe was founded in 1949 as a statement of the Western European federationist tendencies and ideological identity in the Cold War. In 1950, under the aegis of the Council of Europe, the European Convention for the Protection of Human Rights and Fundamental Freedoms, commonly called the European Convention on Human Rights, defined a number of civil and political rights to be enjoyed without discrimination, including: the right to life; protection against torture; the prohibition of slavery and forced labour; the liberty and security of persons; the right to a fair trial; freedom of expression and association; and the right to marry and found a family. The Convention further established a state and individual complaints procedure to an independent Commission, the European Commission on Human Rights, which could lead to binding judgments and compensatory awards by the European Court of Human Rights. The case-law under the European Convention on Human Rights had a strong impact, not only within Europe but also in many other parts of the world.

In 1998 the European Convention on Human Rights was restructured after the entry into force of Protocol No. 11. Individual plaintiffs may now present their complaints to the renovated European Court of Human Rights directly and the European Commission has been abolished, as well as the 'judgment' function of an intergovernmental organ, the Committee of Ministers. The European Convention has also expanded geographically through the admission of most Central and Eastern European states to the Council of Europe.

Within the framework of the Council of Europe, economic, social and cultural rights are protected in other normative instruments, in particular the European Social Charter of 1961 and its three Additional Protocols of 1988, 1991 and 1995; the European Social Charter was then revised in 1996.

For a long time, the European Convention focused essentially on *post facto* action, based on complaints by victims of human rights violations. Lately, however, the Council of Europe has paid increasing attention to preventive techniques, notably through the establishment of a Commissioner for Human Rights, a post created in May 1999.

The European Community, built over the years since the Treaty of Rome of 1957, at first differed markedly from the Council of Europe in its goals, membership and procedures. Whereas the Council of Europe is an intergovernmental entity, the Community's goal was the integration of its member states on a federal or quasi-federal model. *Ratione materiae*, the European Community system initially covered only economic affairs and, later, also some social, judicial and political matters. However, the Treaty of Maastricht (1992) and the Treaty of Amsterdam (1997), which created the European Union, make respect for human rights another explicit concern.

On this normative basis – restating its earlier case-law – the European Communities' Court of Justice asserts its power to apply international human rights instruments – particularly the European Convention on Human Rights – in Community matters having human rights aspects, such as freedom of movement and residence.

European countries also belong to a third system of human rights protection created by the Organization for the Security and Cooperation in Europe (OSCE). This Organization was born at the 'East–West' Helsinki Conference of 1975 and covers a wide geographical range, from the USA to the Russian Federation and the Commonwealth of Independent States (CIS). Since the Helsinki Final Act of 1975, the Conference for Security and Cooperation in Europe (CSCE), an intergovernmental body, has adopted by consensus some far-reaching documents on the 'Human Dimension', including human rights, notably in Vienna (1989), Paris (1989), Copenhagen (1990) and Moscow (1991). The Helsinki Final Act concentrated essentially on freedom of thought, belief and expression, and on freedom of movement and contacts across frontiers as essential factors in the strengthening of peace. The 'Human Dimension' commitments proclaimed after the fall of the Berlin Wall from 1989 expanded these concerns considerably.[1] They stress, in particular, the importance of building democratic institutions, including systems of free periodic elections, and of promoting support for elected democratic governments against attempted overthrow. They also play a leading role among international bodies in highlighting minority problems and in proclaiming the need to protect the human rights involved therein, in close relationship with European security and peace. These four conferences also expressed their concern for a number of specific human rights such as: the right to peaceful assembly and demonstration; the right to enjoy one's property peacefully; the rights of the child; the struggle against aggressive nationalism, racism and xenophobia; and the role of media in democratic societies.

These 'Human Dimension' commitments are not legally binding on states, but these proclamations, formulated unanimously at the highest level and politically binding, have a considerable impact on peoples and leaders. Furthermore, the Moscow Summit Conference of 1991 stated that the content of the 'Human Dimension' commitments did not apply only to internal affairs but were issues of legitimate concern to all OSCE member states – a principle that was constantly reiterated at subsequent conferences. Consequently, a dynamic of accountability was developed within the framework of the Organization for Security and Cooperation in Europe (OSCE),[2] the CSCE having been renamed the OSCE on 1 January 1995. Several mechanisms have been instituted within the OSCE to assist in, and monitor, the implementation of 'Human Dimension' commitments, including, in particular, the Office for Democratic Institutions and Human Rights (ODIHR) and the High Commissioner on National Minorities. The OSCE action appears to be largely, but not exclusively, preventive.

In addition, a fourth, sub-regional, human rights system, open to the members of the CIS, was established by the Minsk Convention of 1995. This allows individual and collective complaints to be brought before an intergovernmental body, raising issues of harmonization with the Council of Europe system and, possibly in the future, with the European Union.

Finally, these regional systems coexist with the universal procedures of the United Nations, the International Labour Organization (ILO) and UNESCO. All – or nearly all – European states have accepted these universal procedures, such as those provided for in the United Nations International Covenants on Human Rights. However, some United Nations human rights institutions, in particular the International Criminal Court for the Former Yugoslavia, are only concerned with European problems.

Thus, while Asia has no regional human rights mechanisms, Europe appears to have an abundance. Hence, issues concerning European intersystem relationships should receive increased attention.

This chapter seeks to provide a broad survey of existing European mechanisms for implementation of human rights. Due to the complexity of the European processes and institutions, it is structured on the basis of the widely accepted distinction between 'prevention' and '*post facto* techniques' – investigation, redress and sanctions. This distinction should not be viewed as rigid; most if not all implementation mechanisms, in Europe as elsewhere, have a dual role to some degree – preventive and repressive. No human rights implementation system can be fully effective without including both functions and acknowledging their close interrelationship.

Taking these functional links into consideration, some 'multipurpose' human rights mechanisms have been created. Under broadly worded mandates, the same organ may play alternatively, in the same situation, the preventive roles of educator, observer, mediator or conciliator, and the roles of *post facto* investigator and prosecutor.

A number of such varied activities are covered under the frequently used term 'monitoring'. This is essentially an ambivalent concept, being potentially either preventive or repressive, and close examination of the practice is required in order to elucidate the prevailing function.

Multipurpose mechanisms may have positive aspects, possibly facilitating a broader perception of complex issues, as well as achieving institutional streamlining and swiftness of intervention. However, if the mandates are too loosely worded and decision-making organs do not exercise adequate guidance, such mechanisms may be fraught with dangerous ambiguities. In particular, human rights exigencies may be blurred or sacrificed for the sake of reaching a preventive settlement. Peoples would then denounce what appears to them as impunity. Conversely, public condemnation, if too strong and too rapid, may increase tensions and the risk of mass atrocities.

Recent human rights problems of this kind, especially in the Balkans, have brought to light the need for a clear statement of the differing, though interrelated, functions of prevention and repression. These differences should be affirmed with sufficient clarity, both at the legislative and at the operational levels, whatever the scope of international mandates may be. European organizations now seem to be more fully aware of this need for a minimum of procedural clarity. In fact, multipurpose organs are to be found mostly in the OSCE; other systems, including those of the Council of Europe and the European Union, generally maintain preventive organs as distinct from repressive mechanisms.

Taking all these developments and considerations into account, this broad functional division between 'preventive techniques' and '*post facto* procedures' provides a meaningful structure for the analysis of the complex European institutions.

PREVENTIVE TECHNIQUES AND MECHANISMS

The concern for preventive mechanisms emerged only recently among European diplomats, jurists and intergovernmental organizations. Even the

Northern Ireland crisis did not induce much awareness in this regard. The real catalysts were the Bosnian and Kosovo atrocities. Possibly the strong European tradition of the rule of law and faith in the judiciary had the perverse effect of inhibiting the search for 'upstream', less formal action.

At present, there is a great diversity of European processes, formal or informal, well-defined or inchoate, which aim at strengthening human rights in order to prevent other Bosnias. Many of these processes, where legal institutional aspects are minimal, may be said to belong to the broad category of 'human rights technical cooperation'. This is true, notably, of increasing awareness of human rights and of education for human rights, human rights training of key professionals, national institution-building, and the strengthening of civil society and non-governmental organizations.

These so-called technical cooperation programmes, which seek long-term prevention, are of fundamental importance and must be strengthened. At the universal level, the United Nations, UNESCO and the ILO, in particular, carry out such programmes. At the European level, the OSCE, and perhaps to a lesser degree the Council of Europe and the European Union, are now similarly engaged. The OSCE technical assistance work is carried out mostly through the ODIHR, applying the 'Human Dimension' clauses of the Charter of Paris for a New Europe of 1990. Within the Council of Europe, various bodies and offices pursue educational and training activities, which are among the missions of the Council's Commissioner for Human Rights.

Notwithstanding their crucial importance, such technical cooperation activities will not be studied here, due to lack of space. Institutionalized mechanisms under which European organs of a permanent or long-standing character, rather than technical assistance field missions, play a major role, in accordance with established procedural rules or guidelines will be analysed. Some of these mechanisms place the emphasis on long- and medium-term prevention, while others appear to be more specifically mandated to apply preventive efforts at the ultimate stages of crisis development and impending violations of human rights.

Monitoring

Periodic reports

This is the most widely used technique of international supervision. It is provided for, *inter alia*, in: the European Social Charter of 1961 (Articles 21 to 29); the European Framework Convention on Minorities of 1994 (Articles 24 to 26); the Convention for the Protection of Human Rights and Dignity of the Human Being with regard to the Application of Biology and Medicine; and the Convention on Human Rights and Biomedicine of 1997, all adopted by the Council of Europe. The European Union also requests its member states to report periodically on their implementation of various directives with human rights implications.

Surprisingly, the European Convention on Human Rights has not established a periodic reporting system. Its Article 57 merely provides that the Secretary-General may request any State Party 'to furnish an explanation of the manner in which its internal law ensure the effective implementation of any of the provisions of the Convention'. This clause was intended apparently to target states which had not accepted the optional procedure of individual petition of Article 25. In this regard, its usefulness is now reduced because of the wide acceptance of the petition procedure. Article 57 might still provide a legal basis for a periodic reporting system, should the need be felt. Meanwhile, the European states, which are all Parties to the International Covenant on Civil and Political Rights, report to the Human Rights Committee under that instrument.

To sum up, under the periodic reporting system, states are under an obligation to inform the European organ concerned at certain intervals – usually two or three years – of the legal and factual human rights situation within their territories. The outcome of the review is the adoption of recommendations which aim at guiding the future policy of states and/or at condemning them for actual violations. Thus this mechanism has inherently a dual nature, preventive and repressive. Its preventive role appears especially significant in this system: long- and medium-term guidance to states may greatly benefit from country-to-country comparisons over substantial periods of time.

The nature and composition of the examining bodies vary according to the normative instrument in question. The Framework Convention on Minorities entrusts the supreme intergovernmental organ, the Committee of Ministers of the Council of Europe, with the task of evaluating the reports. The Committee must, however, seek the assistance of a Consultative Committee of Experts (Article 26). Under Article 17 of the European Charter for Regional and Minority Languages, this mission is incumbent on a Committee of Experts composed of one member per State Party, appointed by the Committee of Ministers from a list of individuals who shall be nominated by them. This body of experts draws up a report, although the power to make recommendations belongs to the Committee of Ministers. As in most other intergovernmental organizations (for example, the United Nations as regards the International Covenant on Economic, Social and Cultural Rights), the political organs of European institutions wish to retain this power for themselves as provided for in the texts of their normative instruments. However, international practice often tends to increase *de facto* the recommending power of the 'expert' examining body. For many of these European bodies, it is too early to see tangible proof of such an evolution.

One important aspect is the degree of involvement of non-governmental organizations. In this regard, European instruments may appear to be more forward-looking than the International Covenants and other United Nations normative instruments. The possibility of comments by non-governmental organizations is mentioned, for instance, in Articles 23, para. 1, and 27, para. 2, of the European Social Charter and in Article 16, para. 2, of the European Charter for Regional or Minority Languages. There are, however, restrictions as to numbers (European Social Charter) and geographical representation (European Charter for Regional or Minority Languages). Here also, much depends on the practice of organs and the eagerness of non-governmental organizations.

The coexistence of so many reporting procedures, even within Europe, creates risks of contradictions and overlapping. In this regard, the European Social Charter, in Article 26, contains a pioneering clause which obliges the Review Committee to invite the ILO to participate in deliberations in a consultative capacity. A similar provision in the International Covenant on Economic, Social and Cultural Rights is only optional. Interagency harmonization, however, remains a serious problem.

Finally, two issues of significance are not clarified in the European instruments: the public or private character of the meetings of the Review Committee, and the stage at which its reports and the recommendations are published. It would appear that these meetings are usually held in private as in most other intergovernmental organizations, the United Nations being an outstanding exception where public debates on state reports are the norm under the International Covenants. The extent and timing of publication vary from instrument to instrument.

The European Committee for the Prevention of Torture and Inhuman or Degrading Treatment or Punishment

The European Convention for the Prevention of Torture and Inhuman or Degrading Treatment or Punishment, adopted in 1987 under the aegis of the Council of Europe, provides for periodic visits to all places of detention by the independent European Committee for the Prevention of Torture and Inhuman or Degrading Treatment or Punishment, assisted by medical and penitentiary experts of its own choosing.

The Committee is guaranteed free and confidential contacts with detained persons, as well as with public officials. It writes a report and may make confidential recommendations to the state concerned. Follow-up inquiries may ensue. States may publish the Committee's reports and their own responses. Only in cases of serious and lasting suspicion of torture does the Council of Europe publish these reports. The matter may then be taken up by the Consultative Assembly and/or by the Committee of Ministers.

In addition to periodic visits, the Committee may conduct ad hoc extraordinary visits as would seem required under serious circumstances, as in the case of Turkey.

The sponsors of the Convention have stressed its preventive character. Inspired by the experience of the International Committee of the Red Cross (ICRC), its aim is to guide states towards more enlightened detention practices through confidential exchanges, without loss of face if at all possible.

The Convention has been widely ratified, and the Committee has been active in carrying out its tasks. Many reports and states' replies have been published.

The Council of Europe Commissioner for Human Rights

This institution was created on 7 May 1999 by resolution 99(50) of the Committee of Ministers as a non-judicial entity mandated to promote education in, awareness of, and respect for, human rights.

Part of its mission certainly has the character of technical cooperation and will not be discussed here. However, Article 3(e) of the resolution empowers the Commissioner to identify possible shortcomings, promote the effective implementation of standards and assist member states, with their agreement, in their efforts to remedy such shortcomings. It also appears to provide the basis for preventive activities of the 'quiet diplomacy' type, in the medium or short term.

The Commissioner may act on any information relevant to his/her functions (Article 5, para. 1), including those from individual sources. States must facilitate his/her task, including inquiries *in situ* (Article 6). Furthermore, the Commissioner may act in a more sanction-like fashion, as will be seen later.

Gil Robles of Spain was elected as the first Commissioner. It is far too early to assess the impact of this new institution. The similarity and harmonization of problems with the United Nations High Commissioner for Human Rights are obvious. Article 3 of the resolution directs the Commissioner to cooperate with other international institutions while avoiding unnecessary duplication.

One of the very first actions of the Commissioner, publicized by the media, was to contact the government of the Russian Federation regarding the human rights situation in Chechnya, and it was agreed by that government that he could visit Chechnya under certain conditions.

Preventive Mechanisms in Cases of the Threat of Violations

Many recently developed European processes have the dual mandate of de-escalating human rights tensions and providing early warning to the international community, whenever there is a clear and growing threat of violations.

Some of the organs described below are of a permanent character. Others operate mostly in the field and have a temporary, though renewable, mandate.

The Council of Europe Commissioner for Human Rights

This new institution, mentioned above, carries out conciliation, tension-reducing and early warning activities. In addition to the clauses already cited, its broad mandate authorizes the Commissioner to address, whenever deemed appropriate, a report concerning a specific matter to the Committee of Ministers or to the Parliamentary Assembly and the Committee of Ministers (Article 3f), and it is stressed that he may directly contact

the governments of member states (Article 7). The Commissioner may provide advice and information on the protection of human rights and the
prevention of human rights violations.

The OSCE High Commissioner on National Minorities[3]

Ethnic conflict is one of the main sources of large-scale human rights violations in Europe today. In 1992, in response to this challenge, the CSCE,[4] in
1992, decided to establish the post of High Commissioner on National
Minorities. The Minister of State of The Netherlands, Max van der Stoel,
was appointed as the first High Commissioner in December 1992, his mandate terminating on 30 June 2001. Rolf Ekéus (Sweden) was appointed High
Commissioner on 28 November 2000 for a three-year term beginning on 1
July 2001.

The High Commissioner's mandate is to provide early warning and, as
appropriate, early action as soon as possible with regard to tensions involving national minority issues which have not yet developed beyond an early
warning stage but, in the judgment of the High Commissioner, have the
potential to develop into a conflict within the OSCE area. While this mandate of conflict prevention has important political implications, the human
rights aspects of minority problems are always present and are fully borne
in mind by the High Commissioner. His mission is, first, to contain and de-
escalate tensions and, second, to act as a 'tripwire', meaning that he is
responsible for alerting the OSCE whenever such tensions threaten to rise
to a level at which he cannot contain them with the means at his disposal.

The High Commissioner has a wide measure of discretion as to procedures. He is empowered to conduct missions *in situ*. He acts essentially
through a confidential dialogue with the governments and parties involved.

Even though his mandate places the High Commissioner's work first and
foremost in the category of short-term conflict prevention, he cannot overlook the important long-term aspects of the situations confronting him if he
wishes to be effective. His goal is to start, sustain and develop a process
involving an exchange of views and cooperation between the parties, leading to concrete steps to reduce tensions and, if possible, resolve underlying
issues. At the initiative of the High Commissioner, projects have been
launched in several countries to contribute to the solution of interethnic
tensions – for instance, pedagogical institutions and legal aid.

Individual cases concerning persons belonging to national minorities are
excluded from the High Commissioner's mandate. It does not permit either
considering national minority issues in situations involving organized acts
of terrorism or to communicate with, or acknowledge communications from,
any person or organization that practises or publicly condones terrorism or
violence.

The High Commissioner has been involved in minority issues in many
OSCE participating states, including Albania, Croatia, Estonia, Hungary,
Kazakhstan, Kyrgyzstan, Latvia, Romania, Slovakia and the former Yugo-
slav Republic of Macedonia. In 1993, at the request of the CSCE member

states, the High Commissioner undertook a special CSCE study of the general situation of the Roma and Sinti.

The OSCE Representative on Freedom of the Media[5]

This post was formally established by a decision of the OSCE Permanent Council on 5 November 1997 and confirmed at the meeting of the Copenhagen Ministerial Council in December 1997. Freimut Duve of Germany was appointed to the post in January 1998 for a period of three years. His basic task is to cooperate with, and assist, the participating states in furthering free, independent and pluralistic media, which are crucial to a free and open society and to an accountable system of government. The Office of the Representative is in Vienna, Austria.

When faced with growing threats of infringements of freedom of expression, the Representative must pursue confidential contacts with governments and the parties concerned in order to promote solutions. Should this fail, he should report to the Chairman-in-Office and to the Permanent Council of the OSCE and recommend further action.

The Representative may collect and receive information on the situation of the media from all *bona fide* sources. In particular, he is to draw on information and assessments provided by the ODIHR. His mandate precludes, as does that of the High Commissioner on National Minorities, acting in a judicial capacity on receipt of individual complaints and from communicating with persons or entities involved in terrorism or violence.

OSCE Office for Democratic Institutions and Human Rights (ODIHR)[6]

The OSCE Office for Democratic Institutions and Human Rights was established in 1990 and expanded in 1992 and 1994 to assist member states globally in the implementation of their 'Human Dimension' commitments which focus essentially on human rights,[7] starting from the 1975 Helsinki Final Act. This supervision is undertaken, as are many other OSCE field activities, under the broad concept of monitoring. This term, and its practice, is highly ambivalent, being potentially both preventive and repressive in meaning. Close examination is required to discern the prevailing objective behind this term.

The ODIHR holds periodic Human Dimension Implementation Meetings, which examine information gathered in respect of the implementation of human rights commitments.[8] In 1998 the ODIHR increased its emphasis on such monitoring.

The goal is to influence states to improve their human rights policies and behaviour, according to a cooperative approach which aims at assisting, rather than isolating, states.[9] This flexible, consensus-seeking policy is characteristic of the OSCE, although it affirms that this approach in no way implies appeasement.

Field missions

A growing number of human rights field missions are undertaken by the OSCE, the Council of Europe and the European Union. A large proportion of these activities is devoted to education, training, institution-building and other technical assistance projects. Increasingly, however, a human rights monitoring component is also included in these missions.

The interethnic crises in the Balkans in recent years have raised awareness in this regard and, indeed, this new policy can be dated roughly from the Bosnian conflict. Thus the OSCE mission to that area, established on 8 December 1995 to implement the Dayton Peace Agreements, aims, *inter alia*, at prevention. It does so through a complex network of institutions created by the Dayton Agreements, including ombudspersons. The mission is a major undertaking, with antennae in various areas employing over 200 international staff. Other related aspects of its mandate concern elections, democracy-building and reform of the judiciary.

To a lesser extent, but nevertheless present, are human rights prevention components in the mandates of the OSCE Kosovo Verification Mission, established on 16 October 1998, and in well over 20 other field missions of the OSCE.

Concluding Remarks on Preventive Techniques and Mechanisms

This chapter shows the great complexity of the European preventive network, much of which has only emerged since 1992 in response to major intergroup conflicts, whether ongoing or impending. Goodwill has flown in from all directions – from the Council of Europe, the European Union, the Organization for Security and Cooperation in Europe and the United Nations system – low priority being granted at first to institutional coordination.

Furthermore, there is often an ambivalence of goals within each mandate. Thus, the stated objectives of political stability and the prevention of armed conflicts are frequently mixed with those of the prevention of human rights violation. This is the case, for example, as regards the OSCE 'Human Dimension' implementation mechanism and the work of the High Commissioner on National Minorities.

Far from being contradictory, these two sets of goals are closely interconnected. The wording of the United Nations Charter, the Universal Declaration of Human Rights and the UNESCO Constitution hold that the recognition of the inherent dignity and of the equal and inalienable rights of all members of the human family are the foundation of freedom, justice and *peace* in the world. Conversely, but perhaps in a less consensual manner among states, peace is affirmed in certain instruments as a prerequisite for the full enjoyment of human rights. On the normative level, therefore, this interrelationship is clear.

Unfortunately, this is not always the case in the world of diplomacy: various actors at the state level and in intergovernmental organizations still view respect for human rights as, at least, an irritant, if not as a major obstacle to peace. The danger is of confusing peace with appeasement and maintaining an unjust status quo. The mandates of some European preventive mechanisms, worded in very broad terms, may perhaps unwittingly be misinterpreted as a permission to practise appeasement.

On the other hand, broadly worded mandates are justified in order to target the largest possible variety of threats to respect for human rights. A certain degree of generality in drafting is also inevitable as the price of European consensus. It is all a matter of skilful legal wording and of setting the right balance between freedom of negotiation, on the one hand, and adequate supervision of the negotiator by European decision-making organs comprising representatives of democratic states on the other hand. Above all, it is a matter of selecting carefully persons of sufficient experience, statesmanship and devotion to the cause of human rights.

Some mandates grant discretion, so that the same organ may play different human rights roles: education and other technical cooperation activities; supervision for long- or medium-term prevention; action in cases of impending crises; and even some *post facto* investigation and reporting with sanction-like undertones. Illustrations include the Council of Europe Commissioner for Human Rights, as well as the many OSCE organs and field missions.

The positive aspects and possible risks of such multipurpose mandates were dealt with in the introduction to this section. However, there is a need for the aims of the various procedures to be clearly defined and understood by the general public, or else a great deal of confusion may ensue. For example, the High Commissioner on National Minorities reported that he had received, and continues to receive, a large number of individual complaints from members of minorities seeking individual redress. However, that post is not a judicial or quasi-judicial *post facto* organ like the European Court of Human Rights, but a preventive actor seeking justice and peace between ethnic groups. As he himself acknowledges, the very title of the Office may be misleading to the general public.[10] An analogous problem occurs at the United Nations where thousands of persons each year seek redress of individual grievances through the '1503 procedure', although this mechanism is purely an information process regarding complaints. The resulting loss of faith in international procedures and human rights values is considerable.

The plurality of competing European institutions raises serious problems of coordination. Jurisdictional overlapping and the risk of contradictory action and confusion are apparent between, for instance, the Council of Europe Commissioner for Human Rights, the ODIHR and, to some extent, the High Commissioner on National Minorities. The problem is compounded as it concerns not only the European agencies, but also universal preventive institutions acting in the European theatre, such as the United Nations High Commissioner for Human Rights. Furthermore, there are many foundations and non-governmental organizations which deploy various forms of preventive action through information-gathering and field observation.

Only within recent years have these difficulties appeared to be acknowledged seriously. The lessons of interagency competition in Bosnia (first phase), and in Ethiopia and Rwanda are being understood. For example, cooperation between the ODIHR and other international institutions was a priority for 1998.[11] The ODIHR is now working with the Council of Europe, the United Nations High Commissioner for Refugees, the United Nations Development Programme and the European Union, among others, in a number of different fields. Mary Robinson, United Nations High Commissioner for Human Rights, and Ambassador Gerard Stoudmann, Director of the ODIHR, signed an agreement on cooperation between their two institutions on 19 June 1998. An exchange of letters on cooperation has also taken place between the ODIHR and the Office of the United Nations High Commissioner for Refugees.

However, true cooperation involves more than an exchange of letters; it requires a genuine team spirit overcoming competition on all levels, including day-to-day work.

POST FACTO PROCEDURES, INVESTIGATION, REDRESS AND SANCTIONS

Various European mechanisms which operate after human rights have been violated will now be analysed. Their common goals are to end violations and to apply a measure of dissuasion and sanction as far as is possible. The sanctions are of different types, from mere exposure to formal condemnations, exclusions and even penal sanctions, such as those before the International Penal Tribunal for the former Yugoslavia. Some procedures, like those before the European Court of Human Rights and the Court of Justice of the European Communities, also provide for compensation to victims.

The mechanisms leading to such sanctions differ from one instrument to another. At one end of the spectrum they include flexible monitoring procedures and, at the other, formal judicial processes.

Taking into account the nature and degree of gravity of sanctions as well as a typology of procedures, it is necessary to survey monitoring processes leading to *post facto* action, and formal investigation procedures based upon initial complaints, including judicial procedures and *ex officio* punitive measures, without initial complaints.

Monitoring Processes Leading to *Post Facto* Action

There are various European organs whose mandates, often broadly worded as 'monitoring', allow them to carry out, *inter alia*, *post facto* fact-finding and to initiate some form of dissuasive action.

Under Articles 3(f) and 8 of the Statute of the Council of Europe Commissioner for Human Rights, in addition to his/her preventive functions, he/

she may possibly act *post facto* by addressing a report on a specific matter to the Committee of Ministers (Article 3(f)) and issuing recommendations, opinions and reports which the Committee may publish (Article 8).

At the OSCE, the Personal Representatives of the Chairmen-in-Office are high-level personalities with ad hoc mandates in 'hot areas' of Europe. They may act in various fields, including human rights, examples being the Felipe Gonzalez Mission to Yugoslavia in December 1996 and the Vranitsky Mission to Albania from March to November 1997. Although their terms of reference aim essentially at short-term prevention, they are worded so as to encompass sanction-like measures through recommendations and exposure or the threat thereof. As an illustration, the Felipe Gonzalez report made recommendations which became the basis for bringing pressure to bear on the Belgrade authorities to overturn their decision to cancel municipal elections.[12]

The ODIHR general monitoring mechanisms concerning the 'Human Dimension' may also be used for *post facto* exposure, or the threat thereof, in the case of alleged non-compliance. This aspect was apparently strengthened at the 1998 implementation meeting which, in contrast to previous meetings, was characterized by the substantial participation of non-governmental organizations and their integration into the list of speakers.[13]

The special OSCE Field Mission to Bosnia, founded upon the Dayton Peace Agreements, is more explicitly empowered to investigate and intervene in cases of human rights violations throughout the country.[14] The focus is mainly on property questions and the return of refugees and displaced persons. *Post facto* action may also be one of the aspects of other OSCE field missions.

All these mechanisms share certain traits: flexible procedures; gathering of data from all sources to be used as 'complaint-information' only; high-level publicity of the mission's existence and goals; confidential contacts with officials and others involved; and exposure and the threat of possible further action by superior organs as a sanction for continuous violations of human rights.

This technique has proved itself to a considerable extent in other fora, notably in the United Nations with its array of country and thematic Special Rapporteurs, and the ILO. The statesmanlike qualities of the heads of mission are often a decisive factor.

Formal Investigation Procedures Based upon Initial Individual Complaints, Including Judicial Procedures

The European Convention on the Protection of Human Rights and Fundamental Freedoms, commonly known as the European Convention on Human Rights (1950)

This is by far the most famous instrument for the protection of human rights in Europe. The rights guaranteed by the Convention include: the right to life; protection against torture and other inhuman or degrading treatment or punishment; prohibition of slavery, servitude and forced labour; protection against arbitrary arrest and detention; the right to a fair trial; non-retroactivity of penal law; protection of privacy, family life, home and correspondence; freedom of thought, conscience and religion; freedom of expression; freedom of peaceful assembly and association, including trade union rights; the right to marry and to found a family; the right to an effective remedy; and prohibition of discrimination.

Additional rights are guaranteed by various protocols: protection of property; the right to education; the right to free elections; the prohibition of imprisonment for debt; freedom of movement; the prohibition of exile; the prohibition of collective expulsion of aliens; the abolition of the death penalty; procedural safeguards regarding the expulsion of aliens; the right to appeal in criminal matters; compensation for wrongful conviction; the right not to be tried or punished twice for the same offence; and equality between spouses.

As in the International Covenant on Civil and Political Rights, these rights may be subject to limitations. They may be derogated from in time of public emergency, except for the right to life, protection against torture, the prohibition of slavery and servitude, and the non-retroactivity of penal law.

The case-law of the implementation organs established by the European Convention on Human Rights – the European Commission and European Court of Human Rights – has developed the meaning of the Convention in an innovative manner concerning freedom of expression, fair trial, the duration of pre-trial detention, the internment of mental patients, torture and ill-treatment. The Convention has finally succeeded in being regarded as a genuine source of law – and of supreme law – in several European countries. The legal literature on the subject is highly specialized, thorough and abundant.

Originally, the system laid down in the European Convention was only partly judicial. The first stages of the procedures took place before a commission of independent persons which did not have the power to issue binding judgments. Furthermore, as an alternative to the intervention of the European Court, a political organ, the Committee of Ministers of the Council of Europe, had the final responsibility. On 1 November 1998, in accordance with Protocol No. 11 to the European Convention, this mixed system was replaced by an entirely judicial one:[15] a permanent European Court of Human Rights, which could be seized directly by all plaintiffs, now has sole jurisdiction. The Commission has been eliminated and the Committee of Ministers no longer plays a role in the procedure. However, it is likely that both the substantive and procedural case-law developed under the former system will be maintained and developed under the new mechanism.

From 1950 until 1998, the procedures can be summarized as follows. The international organ which first intervened was the European Commission on Human Rights, composed of independent experts elected for six years by an absolute majority of the Committee of Ministers from a list of names drawn up by the Bureau of the Consultative Assembly of the Council of Europe.

Complaints could be submitted to it by States Parties or by any person, non-governmental organization or group of individuals (Articles 24–25). Individual and group petitions, however, were receivable only if the accused state had declared its acceptance of the system and if at least six states had so declared (Article 25).

The conditions and procedures of admissibility played a most important role. Conditions were minimal for states which were plaintiffs. It was only required that all domestic remedies had been exhausted, according to the generally recognized rules of international law, and that the recourse be made within a period of six months from the date on which the final decision was taken (Article 26). These requirements were also applied to individual and group claimants. Furthermore, other stringent conditions had to be met.

The prior exhaustion of domestic remedies is a classical rule of international adjudication. It has always been understood that patently illusory recourses need not be exercised. The case-law of the Convention went somewhat further in excluding, *inter alia*, domestic procedures which prove devoid of reasonable chances of success,[16] as well as situations where administrative practices of human rights violations and of disregard for court decisions nullify *de facto* all recourses.[17]

The European Court, however, has carefully defined certain criteria for applying its concept of administrative practices.[18] First, the violations must be of minimum gravity. Second, they must be repeated in identical or similar situations so as to indicate a pattern. Last, there must be a pattern of toleration by the competent state authorities, manifested by an absence of significant sanctions and prosecutions over a period of time. A few occasional 'token' sanctions do not suffice to exonerate the state. Most interestingly, the Court has rejected claims regarding lack of knowledge or lack of power by superior state authorities. Such rulings are in harmony, *mutatis mutandis*, with the case-law of the Nuremberg and Tokyo International Military Tribunals after the Second World War.

Individual petitions are not receivable unless they show the author to be the victim of a violation (Article 25, para. 1). This is not an *actio popularis*, but a recourse seeking redress of an individual grievance. This condition, which appears stringent, has become a little more flexible in practice.

In certain exceptional circumstances, petitions have been admitted when laws complained against were judged in themselves to be capable of victimizing plaintiffs. Thus, at the admissibility stage, the law of the Federal Republic of Germany on abortion, in view of its requirements, was considered in itself to affect the right to privacy of a female plaintiff, even though she was not pregnant at the time.[19] The law was also judged to affect the plaintiff directly when its measures of implementation were to remain secret, as in the field of wiretapping under national security legislation.[20] The Court also accepted petitions in circumstances of imminent violations, mostly regarding the expulsion of aliens when already ordered but not yet executed.[21]

It is firmly established that petitions are admissible when submitted on behalf of the victim by another person, if the victim is clearly unable to act by him/herself or through a representative – for instance, through being held *incommunicado*.[22] This rule has been applied essentially to the benefit of close relatives of the victim.

Finally, the Court recognized the concept of the 'indirect victim' whenever a breach of the Convention has second-degree repercussions on another person because of his/her specific relationship with the victim (such as a spouse or blood relative).[23]

The exclusion of anonymous complaints (Article 27, para. 1(a)) does not raise many difficulties. The rule-barring claims, which are substantially the same as those which have already been examined by the Commission (Article 27, para. 1(b)), have been elaborated upon by the Court rather liberally: the prohibition applies only when there is strictly identity *ratione personae* as to the facts and the object of the petition. The Commission and the Court have exercised some discretion in appreciation of the criterion of identity. Thus, a petition first rejected on the grounds that domestic remedies had not been exhausted was later ruled admissible – though the facts and objects remained the same – after recourses had been exercised at the national level.[24]

The Convention further excludes 'any petition ... which ... b) is substantially the same as a matter which has already been submitted to another procedure of international investigation or settlement' (Article 27, para. 1(b)).

The Council of Europe, in substantial agreement with the United Nations, the ILO, UNESCO and the inter-American system, has elaborated criteria of comparability between international procedures. It is now widely agreed that the mechanisms in question must be implemented at least partially by independent – not intergovernmental – bodies; that they must clearly define the grounds and procedures of admissibility; and that the procedures and rules of evidence must present genuine adversarial characteristics, affording broadly equal rights to plaintiffs and defendants. It is further agreed that restrictions of coexistence operate only between individual grievance procedures and not to complaint information processes, such as those of ECOSOC resolution 1503 and the United Nations Declaration on the Granting of Independence to Colonial Countries and Peoples of 1960, both of which deal with global human rights problems.

Even after such clarifications, Article 27, para. 1(b), of the European Convention raises major problems of coexistence with other international procedures at the global and regional levels. The European Convention excludes all petitions if they have been first submitted to a parallel mechanism, even if they are later rejected there on grounds of admissibility or withdrawn by the plaintiffs. This is a very restrictive system, strictly applying the principle *una via electa*.

However, other international instruments do not impose similar limits to their jurisdiction. Thus, various complaint procedures of the ILO have no restrictions of coexistence at all, thus allowing its bodies to deal in principle with complaints despite their competing examination by the European system. The Human Rights Committee, under Article 5, para. 2(a), of the Optional Protocol to the International Covenant on Civil and Political Rights, is only barred from considering individual communications if they are being examined under a parallel international procedure. This means that the Committee may deal with a complaint as soon as its consideration has ended under the European Convention on Human Rights, either by withdrawal or by the issuance of a final decision on admissibility or merit. In effect, this may be tantamount to allowing the Human Rights Committee to play the role of an appeals court vis-à-vis the Council of Europe. The European instances concerned with this situation have recommended that the States Parties to the European Convention enter a reservation or declaration to the Optional Protocol prohibiting the Human Rights Committee to deal with any complaint already submitted to the Council of Europe. Most of the States Parties made such a reservation.

At present, coexistence problems arise between the Council of Europe system, the European Union and the Minsk Convention of the Commonwealth of Independent States (CIS).

Article 27, para. 2, of the European Convention raises serious difficulties. It excludes individual petitions which are incompatible with the provision of the present Convention, manifestly ill-founded, or an abuse of the right of petition. These loosely defined terms are inherited from discretionary petition arrangements of the nineteenth and early twentieth centuries then viewed not as the rights of victims but as 'the pleasure of the King'. They are not in harmony with the judicial spirit of the European Convention. This chapter calls for a preliminary consideration of merits already at the admissibility stage, even though no investigation has taken place. Yet, despite these negative aspects, the Commission and the Court have often invoked these grounds. In fact, most decisions of inadmissibility have been based on Article 27, para. 2.[25]

Furthermore, it appears that, in various cases, complaints were rejected as manifestly ill-founded, although the superficial or implausible character of the claims was far from clear.[26] This impression was strengthened by the fact that, in several instances, decisions on that ground were taken with a majority of only one vote. This case-law is almost unanimously criticized by specialists.[27]

The principal or only reason invoked in defence of such decisions stressed the growing backlog of the Commission and Court and the need to weed out frivolous claims. In this respect, the reformed system of Protocol No. 11, creating a Permanent Court instead of a two-tier part-time structure, aims precisely at speeding up the procedures. It would, therefore, have been expected that the discretionary grounds of incompatibility and manifestly ill-founded character would be restricted or eliminated altogether. Nevertheless they still appear in Article 35, paras 2 and 3, of the Protocol. It is to be hoped that the new Court will apply these provisions much more sparingly and coherently than its predecessor.

The procedure of admissibility included many hurdles for individuals who could not easily enjoy a complete feeling of legal security concerning the admissibility of their petitions. Decisions of non-admissibility had to be taken, albeit unanimously, by subsidiary committees of the Commission, composed of only three members (Article 20, para. 3), and petitions first accepted could be later rejected at any time by a majority of two-thirds of the Commission on newly-discovered grounds of inadmissibility (Article 29). These provisions were criticized as being too severe, it being noted that they were not applied to complaining states.

Once they were declared admissible, complaints were subjected to investigation and, at the same time, to attempts at friendly settlements by the Commission (Article 28). The authors of the Convention placed a strong emphasis on conciliation, partly out of a desire to prevent the growing of tensions, partly also as a strategy to reassure states and invite ratification of the petition clause.

Settlements could also be effected between the petitioner and the state at any stage without the open intervention of the Commission. In such cases, the Commission would strike a case off the list, if it considered that the matter has been resolved (Article 30).

The inherent danger was that of the abusive influence of the state to induce an unjust settlement. In this regard, restating the doctrine of the Commission in the first Cyprus case, Article 30, para. 1, as amended, demonstrates that, notwithstanding a friendly settlement, the Commission could continue the examination of a petition if respect for human rights as defined in the Convention so required, and that it could decide to restore a petition to the list if it considered that the circumstances justified such a course.

The formal procedure of friendly settlement before the Commission was seldom resorted to during the first 20 years of the European Convention on Human Rights. Possibly, states feared that such a decision might be construed to some extent as a tacit admission of guilt and therefore preferred to engage in direct and less publicized negotiations with the plaintiffs. The growing control exercised by the Council of Europe organs, under Article 30, over the *bona fide* character of direct settlements probably convinced states that they might as well involve the Commission formally into their negotiations. Thus, since 1965, the number of formal friendly settlements involving the Commission grew as follows: three between 1965 and 1970; six between 1971 and 1975; ten between 1976 and 1980; 22 between 1981 and 1985; 55 between 1986 and 1990; and 47 between 1991 and 1992.[28]

If there was no conciliation, direct friendly settlement or withdrawal of the complaint for other causes, Article 31 directed the Commission to draw up a report and state its opinion as to whether the facts found disclosed a breach by the state concerned of its obligations under the Convention. The report was transmitted to the Committee of Ministers and to the states concerned. In transmitting the report, the Commission could make such proposals as it thought fit.

In accordance with the former procedure, now replaced by Protocol No. 11, if the case was not referred to the European Court of Human Rights within three months, it was incumbent upon the Committee of Ministers of the Council of Europe to decide in a binding manner, by a two-thirds majority, whether there had been a violation (Article 32). If the state concerned had not complied within a period prescribed by the Committee, this body decided by the same majority what effect should be given to its original decision and, only then, published the report.

The practice of the Committee of Ministers gave rise to criticism.[29] In various cases, the required two-thirds majority could not be reached and the cases were left hanging, the legal meaning of such non-decisions being highly ambiguous. Worse, in some instances, disregarding its duty under Article 32, the Committee abstained from voting on the issue of violation. It was patent that political factors strongly interfered with the judicial consideration of such cases. In this system, the jurisdiction of the Court was optional (former Article 46 of the Convention). The Court members were elected by the Consultative Assembly of the Council of Europe from a list of persons nominated by the member states.

Former Article 48, as amended by Protocol No. 9, provided that a case might be brought before the Court by: the Commission; the State Party whose national is the alleged victim; the State Party which referred the case to the Commission; the State Party against which the complaint had been lodged; and the person, non-governmental organization or group of individuals having lodged the complaint with the Commission.

Under the terms of Article 50, if the Court found that a decision taken by a legal authority or any other authority of a High Contracting Party was completely or partially in conflict with the obligations arising from the present Convention, and if the internal law of the said Party allowed only partial reparation to be made for the consequences of this decision, the Court could, if necessary, afford just satisfaction to the injured party. Most of the time just satisfaction took the form of financial compensation, but other forms of reparation were not excluded.

The reform by Protocol No. 11 replaces this two-tier structure – the Commission and Court or the Committee of Ministers – by a single Court. All States Parties to the Convention have ratified Protocol No. 11.

Individuals and groups, as well as states, now have direct access to the Court. As mentioned earlier, Protocol No. 9, in force since 1 October 1994, already allowed individuals to present their complaints to the renovated Court. However, a three-member panel of the Court, including one judge, elected in respect of the state against which the complaint had been lodged, could, by unanimous vote, bar access of the individual to the Court if the case did not raise a serious question affecting the interpretation or application of the Convention or did not for any other reason warrant consideration by the Court (Article 5, para. 2, of Protocol No. 9). Nowadays, there is no such hurdle regarding access to the three-member Committees and the seven-member Chambers of the new Court. However, final appeals to the Grand Chamber may be allowed only in exceptional cases and only if a five-member panel of the Grand Chamber finds that the case raises a serious question affecting the interpretation or application of the Convention or a serious issue of general importance (new Article 43 of the European Convention).

In accordance with the new system, the Court comprises a number of judges equal to that of the States Parties. This means a considerable expansion in view of the admission of Central and Eastern European countries. As in the past, the judges are elected by the Parliamentary Assembly of the Council of Europe with respect to each State Party by a majority of votes cast from a list of three candidates nominated by the State Party.

A significant and novel provision requires that judges abstain from all activities incompatible not only with their independence and impartiality but also with the demands of a full-time office (Article 21, para. 3). Equally important are the new rules setting an age-limit of 70 (Article 22, para. 6). Questions have been raised concerning these limitations on the grounds that they might deprive the Court of some helpful expertise.

A further major change in Protocol No. 11 consists in eliminating the alternative jurisdiction of the Committee of Ministers. This reform is generally approved of, as the political character of the Committee, composed of state representatives, was not in harmony with the judicial model.

Otherwise, the procedure remains essentially the same as that of 1950, with the admissibility stage and the conciliation and merit stage described above. It is hoped that the procedural simplification and the requirement that the judges be available full-time may speed up proceedings, as there were considerable delays in the former system, which the huge expansion of the Convention's scope of *ratione loci* (all Eastern Europe adhering) would have indeed compounded.

Collective complaints under the Additional Protocol to the European Social Charter[30]

For a long time, periodic state reports were the only system of international supervision under the European Social Charter. The Additional Protocol to the European Social Charter Providing for a System of Collective Complaints was adopted in 1995 and, as of November 2001, had been ratified by nine states. It permits certain kinds of organizations to submit complaints alleging unsatisfactory application of the Charter. The complaints may relate to the obligations undertaken by a party in respect of any right in the Charter. It remains to be established whether a competent organization may take up an alleged breach of the Charter in respect of a particular person (for example, a complaint that an individual was refused public employment on grounds of race contrary to Article 1, para. 2). Complaints may be submitted by three categories of organization (Article 1):

- the international organizations of employers and trade unions invited to participate as observers in the work of a governmental committee
- other international non-governmental organizations having consultative status with the Council of Europe and inscribed on a list established for this purpose by the governmental committee

- representative national organizations of employers and trade unions within the jurisdiction of the party against which they have lodged a complaint.

All Contracting Parties to the Protocol recognize the right of an organization falling within any of the above categories to bring a complaint. In addition, a Contracting Party may choose to declare that it recognizes the right of any other representative national non-governmental organization within its jurisdiction, which has particular competence in the matters governed by the Charter, to lodge complaints against it. In all of the above cases, complaints may be submitted by organizations only in respect of those matters regarding which they have been recognized as having particular competence (Article 3).

A collective complaint is considered by the Committee of Independent Experts. Provision is made for the Committee first to make a decision as to admissibility.

Having considered arguments on the merits of an admitted application, the Committee of Independent Experts draws up a report in which it presents its conclusions as to whether the Charter has been satisfactorily applied. The report is transmitted to the Committee of Ministers, whose competence is laid down in Article 9 as follows:

1   On the basis of the report of the Committee of Independent Experts, the Committee of Ministers shall adopt a resolution by a majority of those voting. If the Committee of Independent Experts finds that the Charter has not been applied in a satisfactory manner, the Committee of Ministers shall adopt, by a majority of two-thirds of those voting, a recommendation addressed to the Contracting Party concerned. In both cases, entitlement to voting shall be limited to the Contracting Parties to the Charter.
2   At the request of the Contracting Party concerned, the Committee of Ministers may decide, where the report of the Committee of Independent Experts raises new issues, by a two-thirds majority of the Contracting Parties to the Charter, to consult the Governmental Committee.

The state concerned must provide information on its follow-up measures in its next periodic report.

The European Union Court of Justice

As pointed out in the introduction to this chapter, the system of the European Communities and the European Union did not initially display an explicit concern for the international protection of human rights.

However, since the late 1960s, the Court of Justice of the European Communities (also called the European Union Court of Justice) has gradually built up a remarkable case-law on human rights. It started by affirming, in the *Handelgesellschaft* judgment of 17 December 1970, that respect for fundamental rights is an integral part of the general principles of law which the Court of Justice must protect, and that in this mission the Court takes into account the constitutional traditions common to all member states.[31]

In the *Nold* case of 14 May 1974,[32] the Court referred, in addition, to international instruments on human rights ratified by member states as an indication to determine the contents of the general principles of Community law. The European Convention on Human Rights was explicitly mentioned first in the *Rutili* judgment of 28 October 1975 concerning freedom of movement.[33]

This case-law was enshrined in conventional form, first in the Treaty of Maastricht on the European Union, and then in the Treaty of Amsterdam. As it stands, Article 6, para. 2 (former Article F, para. 2) of the Treaty of Maastricht proclaims that the European Union respects the fundamental rights as guaranteed in the European Convention on Human Rights and as embodied in the constitutional traditions common to all member states, as general principles of community law.[34]

This subtle formula apparently bestows a high status on the European Convention (while ignoring references to other normative instruments, such as the International Covenants on Human Rights, conventions adopted by UNESCO and the ILO, and the European Social Charter). However, it places the common constitutional traditions at par, or almost at par, with the Convention. It is clear that the Convention is respected, inasmuch as it is an expression of the general principles of Community law.

This provision clearly falls short of accepting the European Convention as legally binding on the European Union and its organs. Indeed, even in its latest judgments, the Court apparently continues to apply the principles of the European Convention only through the concept of general principles of Community law. As an extreme scenario, if a majority of European states, or even a large minority of them, cease to apply the European Convention, could the European Court and other organs of the European Union feel free to disregard the Convention as no longer being part of the common traditions and principles of community law?

This note of caution does not detract from the positive and sometimes innovative case-law of the European Court of Human Rights. Thus, the Court has, over the years, affirmed as binding notably the following principles and rights: the right to self-defence; the principle of legal security; the non-retroactivity of penal law; the principle of equality before the law; the right of defence in all procedures, including administrative; the principle of proportionality as binding on the state; the right to be judged; respect for private and family life, home and correspondence; and freedom of expression.

The Convention on Human Rights of the Commonwealth of Independent States (CIS), commonly known as the 'Minsk Convention'[35]

In Minsk on 26 May 1995, seven of the 12 states of the CIS (ex-USSR, *grosso modo*) signed a new convention on human rights open to all country members of the CIS. The Minsk Convention, composed of representatives of all States Parties, will be implemented by a Human Rights Commission, already foreseen in the Charter of the CIS.

Three member states of the CIS – the Russian Federation, Moldova and Ukraine – are also members of the Council of Europe. Ukraine, which is not a signatory of the Minsk Convention, has ratified the European Convention on Human Rights. Moldova, which is only a signatory to the Minsk Convention, has ratified the European Convention. The Russian Federation has ratified the Minsk Convention and signed the European Convention with a promise to ratify it in the near future. It is not known at present whether the three required ratifications for the entry into force of the Minsk Convention have been received.

The Minsk Convention recognizes, in a rather detailed manner, a wide array of civil and political rights: the right to life; protection against torture and ill-treatment; prohibition of slavery, servitude and forced labour; the right of liberty and security of person; protection against arbitrary arrest and detention; the right to a fair trial; the non-retroactivity of penal law; the prohibition of imprisonment for non-fulfilment of contractual obligations; respect for privacy, family life, home and correspondence; freedom of thought, conscience and religion; freedom of expression; freedom of peaceful assembly and association, including trade union rights; the right to marry and to found a family; the right to an effective remedy; equality before the law; the rights of members of national minorities; freedom of movement and residence; the right to the recognition of one's own juridical personality; the right to a nationality; the prohibition of exile; the right to enter one's own country; protection against arbitrary expulsion of aliens; and the right to take part in government.

In addition, the following economic, social and cultural rights are recognized: the right to work; the right to just conditions of work and protection against unemployment; the right to health protection, the right to social security; special protection for children; the rights of disabled persons; the right to own property; the right to education; and the right to professional education and training. The Convention proclaims the right to equality before the law and prohibits discrimination in the exercise of the rights recognized within it.

As in the International Covenants on Human Rights and the European Convention on Human Rights, these rights are subject to various limitations. Except for the right to life, the prohibition of torture, slavery and servitude and the non-retroactivity of penal law, these rights may be derogated from in time of war or in other emergency situations.

The Human Rights Commission mentioned above may consider both interstate complaints and petitions from individuals and non-governmental organizations. Interstate complaints are receivable if prior discussions between the two governments concerned prove unsuccessful within six months. The Commission verifies that domestic remedies are exhausted, and it may hear the parties concerned. If the matter is not settled after such hearings, the Commission may set up a Special Conciliation Sub-Commission, with the agreement of the parties concerned. This Sub-Commission comprises representatives of other States Parties and presents its conclusions to the parties concerned through the Commission. It hears reports at each session on the measures taken to implement these conclusions. This procedure appears to be more a procedure of diplomatic settlement than a quasi-judicial mechanism.

Petitions from individuals and non-governmental organizations, according to the Convention, may appear admissible even if they do not claim that the authors were victims of the alleged violation. The Convention itself merely provides that the petitions must not be anonymous, that domestic remedies be exhausted, that the petition is lodged within a six-month time limit, and that the subject of the petition is not under consideration within the framework of another procedure of international investigation or settlement. This latter clause raises, of course, problems of coexistence and harmonization with the Council of Europe system and other procedures.

Complaint procedures: coexistence issues

The jurisdiction *ratione materiae* and *ratione loci* of the European Convention on Human Rights, the European Union system and the Minsk Convention, which all include petition clauses, overlap either fully or partly. Overlapping instruments, such as the International Covenant on Civil and Political Rights and many other United Nations and the ILO instruments providing for complaint systems have been ratified by all or nearly all European states. In such situations, and in the absence of appropriate rules, nothing prevents claimants from petitioning the largest number of international fora on the same specific matter.

It is true that the coexistence of different international complaint procedures tends to create confusing legal situations and interagency tensions. There is an inherent risk of contradictory decisions on substance. Equally, or more seriously, is the risk of the denial of justice: both competing organs may decline to judge on the same complaint out of overscrupulous respect for jurisdictional divisions and for the rule *una via electa*. The underlying motive is sometimes embarrassment due to a political 'hot potato'. This is possibly the most serious danger. Everyone should be guaranteed a judgment at the European level. The present texts do not appear to fully guarantee this basic right on the international plane.

On the other hand, the coexistence of competing petition procedures offers important advantages for the victims. Having to cope with the formidable hurdles of admissibility and being the weakest party against the whole state apparatus, under ideal conditions a victim must have more than one chance of obtaining international redress. As in the old *habeas corpus* rules, he/she should be allowed to approach 'all judges in the Realm'. Invoking the criminal law rule of *non bis in indem* is rather inappropriate here, as the victim cannot be equated to a powerful prosecutor or the state to a helpless indicted individual.

That procedural coexistence could be accepted, provided that it takes place between fully comparable organs satisfying the criteria of the rule of law and fair trial. In particular, there should be sufficient guarantees of independence and impartiality, as well as sufficient clarity of the substantive legal basis. How far are these conditions met in the procedural relationships between the Council of Europe and European Union systems, on the one hand, and between the Council of Europe and the Minsk systems, on the other?

One solution, promoted by the European Parliament, would have been for the European Union to become a party to the European Convention on Human Rights. This was rejected by an Advisory Opinion of the Court of Justice of the European Communities on 28 March 1996.[36] It ruled, not too convincingly, that the Communities had no basis in the Treaty of Rome and the Treaty of Amsterdam to allow them to adhere to the Council of Europe system.

An alternative would be to include a declaration of human rights in the constituting treaties.[37] This has been left in abeyance for many years. The only basis remains the case-law of the European Court of Human Rights and its restatement in the Treaties of Maastricht and Amsterdam, concerning the general principles of Community law. This might perhaps not be perceived by the victims as a fully secure foundation. At any rate, there is no doubt that both the Council of Europe and the European Union systems offer comparable, high-level, fair trial guarantees.

Substantive divergences between the two case-laws have been relatively few.[38] One – the *Hoechst* case of 1989 – concerns the interpretation of Article 8 of the European Convention on Human Rights on the right to privacy. Here, the European Union Court of Justice affirmed that this protection did not extend to commercial places, while the European Court of Human Rights took the opposite view on a similar case. There have been some other cases where competition between the two Courts has apparently resulted in broader protection for individuals. The potential competition between the European Convention on Human Rights and the Minsk Convention, on the other hand, would raise problems,[39] the main difficulty stemming from the intergovernmental character of the Minsk Commission, in contrast to the independent status of the European judges. The different wordings of the coexistence clauses in the European Convention on Human Rights (Article 35, para. 2(b) neo) and in the Statute of the CIS Commission (third part, para. 2(a)) compound the problem. Their combined effects might be, on the one hand, to prevent a victim from seizing the elaborate system of the European Court after an unsuccessful first claim before the Minsk Convention, and, on the other, to allow him/her to lodge a complaint before the Minsk Convention after failure at the European Court. This is an unsatisfactory situation which preoccupies the Council of Europe.

A similar situation of coexistence exists between the European Convention on Human Rights and the Optional Protocol to the International Covenant on Civil and Political Rights.[40] However, the problems raised here (also addressed by the Council of Europe) are not at all comparable to those of the coexistence between the European Convention and the Minsk

Convention. The Human Rights Committee presents guarantees of independence similar to those of the European Court. Each organ has recognized the other as an acceptable parallel procedure.

Ex-officio **Punitive Measures**

These are sanctions pronounced by an European organ against a state for gross violations of human rights, without a need for an initial complaint by the victims.

One example is the Statute of the Council of Europe which provides for the expulsion by the Committee of Ministers of states guilty of the most serious and repeated breaches of the principles upon which the Council is based, including the protection of human rights. The Greek junta was just about to be expelled when it withdrew from the Council of Europe. The desired effect was obtained to marginalize, at best, the culprit within the community of nations.

Article 7 (ex-F.1) of the Treaty of Amsterdam on the European Union introduces a similar procedure in two stages: a declaration that grave and persistent violations of the principles of Article 6 (including respect for human rights) have taken place, and a decision to suspend the exercise of certain membership rights. This appears to be a more flexible procedure than that of the Council of Europe.

Finally, the operations of the United Nations International Penal Tribunal for the former Yugoslavia, sitting in The Hague, deals with the most atrocious violations of human rights which occurred recently in Europe.

CONCLUSIONS

This chapter has surveyed the most imposing network of institutions, of which there is indeed a large number. Many display innovative features as to accuracy of detection and swiftness of reaction. Nevertheless, Kosovo still occurred recently, as well as other situations with a human rights crisis potential, such as in the Basque country, Corsica, Northern Ireland and elsewhere. However, there is absolutely no reason for cynicism or discouragement; the situation would certainly be worse without the present institutions.

However, efforts must be intensified along carefully selected paths. Increased funding is essential and the existence of political will remains fundamental.

Another vital need is adequate training in human rights monitoring for a greater number of persons, intergovernmental organizations staff, non-governmental organizations personnel and so on. Such training is currently minimal in the European organizations and in educational institutions.

It is also necessary to ensure much more effective coordination between organizations, as well as between sectors (education, training, early warning, *post facto* action) in each organization. Too often, these efforts remain dispersed, and intersectoral opacity and rivalry still exist.

However, all these efforts will have little impact unless there is a much stronger, more systematic, better funded European and world policy of human rights education and consciousness-raising, and unless there is a true resolve to build a culture of peace in the minds of men.

These are politically difficult undertakings. In a dangerous world, where violence and tensions exist at all levels, the search for collective identities will increase; no alternative has yet appeared between such a crusade and a new Dark Age.

NOTES

1   OSCE *Handbook* (1999, pp.103–105).
2   Hanski and Suksi (1997, pp.275–76).
3   *OSCE Handbook* (1999, pp.93–100); *Annual Report* (1998, Section 3).
4   OSCE since 1995.
5   *OSCE Handbook* (1999, pp.111–13); *Annual Report* (1998, Section 5).
6   *OSCE Handbook* (1999, pp.101–10); *Annual Report* (1998, Section 4).
7   The other components of the 'Human Dimension' programme are the promotion of the rule of law and democratic institution-building. The three components are clearly interdependent. See *OSCE Handbook* (1999, p.101).
8   Ibid., p.111.
9   Ibid., p.101. This unique OSCE approach is also analysed in Bloed *et al.* (1993).
10   *OSCE Handbook* (1999, p.93).
11   *Annual Report* (1998, para. 4.2).
12   *OSCE Handbook* (1999, p.83).
13   *Annual Report* (1998, para. 4.5).
14   Ibid., para. 21.9, p.15.
15   On this subject, see, for instance: Drzemczewski (1997); Tavernier (1998); and Wachsmann *et al.* (1995).
16   See, for example, the *Van Droogenbroek* case, Court judgement of 24 June 1982, Ser. A, No. 78, paras 54–55. See also the analysis in Petitti *et al.* (1995, p.605).
17   See the Greek case, D. No. 3 321–67 and 3 344–67, 5 November 1969, *Yearbook of the European Convention*, 2 (1), p.13.
18   See Petitti *et al.* (1995, p.609).
19   *Brüggemann* v. *Federal Republic of Germany*, decision of the European Commission on human rights of 19 May 1976, application no. 6.
20   *Klass* v. *Federal Republic of Germany*, judgment of 6 September 1978, Ser. A, no. 28, paras 34 and 36.
21   *Soering* v. *United Kingdom*, judgment of 7 July 1989, Ser. A, no. 161.
22   See, for instance, decision of the Commission of 16 December 1957, application 282/57, *Yearbook*, 1, p.164.
23   See for instance decision of the Commission of 30 May 1956, application 113/55, *Yearbook*, 1, p.161.
24   *X* v. *Belgium*, decision of 30 August 1959, application 347/58, *Yearbook*, 2, p.407.
25   Petitti *et al.* (1995, p.634).
26   *Inersen* v. *Norway*, decision of 17 December 1963, Application 468/62, *Yearbook*, 6, p.329.

27   Petitti *et al.* (1995, p.635).
28   Ibid., p.662.
29   Ibid., pp.706–7 and cases cited.
30   See, for example, Gomien *et al.* (1996, pp.426–29).
31   Case No. 11/70, *Recueil de la Jurisprudence de la Cour de Justice et du Tribunal de Première Instance*, p.1125.
32   Ibid., Case 4/73, p.491.
33   Ibid., Case 36/75, p.1219.
34   *Consolidated Treaties of the European Union*, Luxembourg: European Communities Publishing Office, 1997.
35   See English text in document H (95) 7, Directorate of Human Rights, Council of Europe, 1995.
36   Advisory Opinion C-2/94.
37   See, for example, the resolution of the European Parliament of 18 January 1994, *Official Journal of the European Community*, No. C 44 of 14 February 1994.
38   Tavernier (1998b, pp.98–99).
39   Malinverni (1998).
40   See, for example, M. Tardu (1971).

BIBLIOGRAPHY

Akandji-Kombe, J.F. and Leclerc, S. (eds) (1998), *L'Union européenne et les droits fondamentaux*, Brussels: Bruylant.
Annual Report on OSCE Activities (1998), Vienna: OSCE, Sections 2.1, 3, 4 and 5.
Berger, V. (1989), *Case Law of the European Court of Human Rights*, Vol. I (1960–1987), Dublin: The Round Hall Press.
Berger, V. (1992) *Case Law of the European Court of Human Rights*, Vol. II (1988–1990), Dublin: The Round Hall Press.
Betten, L. and Macdewitt, D. (1996), *The Protection of Fundamental Social Rights in the European Union*, Amsterdam: Kluwer.
Bloed, A., Leicht, L., Nowak M. and Rosas, A. (eds) (1993), *Monitoring Human Rights in Europe*, Dordrecht: Nijhoff.
Brett, R. (1996), 'Human rights and the OSCE', *Human Rights Quarterly*, **18**, pp.668–93.
Buergenthal, T. and Kiss, A. (1991), *La Protection internationale des droits de l'homme*, Strasbourg: Engel.
Cohen-Jonathan, G. (1990), 'La Convention européenne des droits de l'homme', in *Jurisclasseur Europe*, Fascicule 6500: Caractères généraux, Paris: Editions techniques.
Cohen-Jonathan, G. (1991), 'La Convention européenne des droits de l'homme', in *Jurisclasseur Europe*, Fascicule 6510: Système international de contrôle, Paris: Editions techniques.
Cohen-Jonathan, G. (1992), 'La Convention européenne des droits de l'homme', in *Jurisclasseur Europe*, fascicule 6520, 6521, 6522: Droits garantis, Paris: Editions techniques.
Cohen-Jonathan, G. (1995), 'L'adhésion de la Communauté européenne à la Convention européenne des droits de l'homme', *Journal des Tribunaux*, Droit européen, March.
Convention on Human Rights of the Commonwealth of Independent States of 26 May 1995 and Statute of the Commonwealth of Independent States Convention

on Human Rights, 1995. Translated from Russian. Doc. H (95) 7, Strasbourg: Council of Europe.

Decaux, E. and Sicilianos, L-A. (1993), *La CSCE: Dimension humaine et règlement des différends*, Paris: Montchrestien.

Drzemczewski, A. (1997), 'A major overhaul of the European Human Rights Convention control mechanism: Protocol No. 11', *Recueil des cours de l'Académie de droit européen'*, **VI** (2), pp.121–244.

Frowein, J.A. (1990), 'The European Convention on Human Rights as the Public Order of Europe', *Recueil des cours de l'Académie de droit européen de Florence*, Vol. 1–2, Dordrecht, Nijhoff.

Gomien, D. (1991), *Vade-mecum de la Convention européenne des droits de l'homme*, Series 'Documents européens', Strasbourg: Editions du Conseil de l'Europe.

Gomien, D., Harris D. and Zwaak, L. (1996), *Law and Practice of the European Convention on Human Rights and the European Social Charter*, Strasbourg: Council of Europe Publishing.

Hanski, R. and Suksi, M. (eds), *An Introduction to the International Protection of Human Rights*, Turku/Abo: Institute for Human Rights, Abo Akademi University.

Iliopoulos-Strangas, J. (ed.) (1993), *La Protection des droits de l'homme dans le cadre européen*, Fondation Marangopoulos pour les droits de l'homme, Baden-Baden: Nomos Verlag.

MacDonald, R. St. J., F. Matscher and H. Petzold (1993), *The European System for the Protection of Human Rights*, Dordrecht: Nijhoff.

Malinverni, G. (1998), *Report to the European Commission for Democracy through Law ('Venice Commission') on the legal problems arising from the co-existence of the CIS Convention and the European Convention on Human Rights*. Doc. CDL-INF (98) 8, Strasbourg, 26 March.

OSCE Handbook, (1999), Vienna: OSCE,Chapters 3, 5, 6 and 7.

Petitti, L-E., Decaux, A. and Imbert, P.H. (1995), *La Convention européenne des droits de l'homme, Commentaire article par article*, Paris: Economica.

Tardu, M. (1971), 'Quelques questions relatives à la coexistence des procédures universelles et régionales de plainte individuelle dans le domaine des droits de l'homme, *Revue des droits de l'homme*.

Tavernier, P. (1996), *Quelle Europe pour les droits de l'homme?*, Brussels: Bruylant.

Tavernier, P. (1998a), 'Coexistence des systèmes de protection des droits de l'homme en Europe', in *La Coexistence, enjeu européen, Actes du Colloque du CRUCE d'Amiens*, Paris: Presses universitaires de France.

Tavernier, P. (1998b), 'L'entrée en fonction de la nouvelle Carde Strasbourg', *Actes de Collogne Europe*, Paris: Université Paris-Sud.

van Dijk, P. (1991), 'The relation between the European Convention on Human Rights and Fundamental Freedoms and the Human Dimension of the CSCE', *Helsinki Monitor*, **2** (4), pp.5–14.

Van Dijk, P. and Van Hoff, G.J.H. (1990), *Theory and Practice of the European Convention on Human Rights*, Deventer: Kluwer.

Velu, J. and Ergec, R. (1990), *La Convention européenne des droits de l'homme*, Brussels: Bruylant.

Wachsmann, P. (1997), 'Les droits de l'homme', *Revue trimestrielle de droit européen*, 33 (4), October–December.

Wachsmann, P. *et al.* (1995), *Le Protocole No. 11 à la Convention européenne des droits de l'homme*, Brussels: Bruylant.

5 The Inter-American System for the Protection of Human Rights

HUGO CAMINOS

INTRODUCTION

The Inter-American system for the protection of human rights is based and, has evolved from, the premise that the defence of the rights of the individual and the effective exercise of representative democracy are closely interrelated. This basic notion is inscribed in the Charter of the Organization of American States (OAS), the American Declaration of the Rights and Duties of Man, the American Convention on Human Rights and its Additional Protocol in the Area of Economic, Social and Cultural Rights, 'Protocol of San Salvador'.[1]

The Inter-American Court of Human Rights has supported that premise. It stated that: 'The just demands of democracy must consequently guide the interpretation of the Convention and, in particular, the interpretation of those provisions that bear a critical relationship to the preservation and functioning of democratic institutions'.[2]

In a subsequent opinion, the Court confirmed this view when it declared that the intention of all the American states, as expressed in the Preamble of the Convention, is '... to consolidate in the hemisphere within the framework of democratic institutions a system of personal liberty and social justice based on respect for the essential rights of man'.[3] It added: 'Representative democracy is the determining factor throughout the system of which the Convention is a part. It is a "principle" reaffirmed by the American States in the OAS Charter, the basic instrument of the Inter-American system.'[4]

In the Inter-American system for the protection of human rights, two different legal regimes coexist. One is the original regime based on the Charter of the OAS; the other was established by the 1969 American

165

Convention on Human Rights. The former regime applies to OAS member states which are not parties to the American Convention, while the latter applies to OAS member states which are parties to it. The Inter-American Commission on Human Rights is, in both cases, the organ entrusted with the functions of promoting respect for, and defence of, human rights. For this purpose, in relation to non-parties to the American Convention, human rights 'are understood to be' the rights proclaimed in the American Declaration of the Rights and Duties of Man; and in relation to States Parties to the Convention, human rights 'are understood to be' the rights set forth in it.[5] The functions of the Commission differ in accordance with the applicable regime. Thus, the competence of the Commission vis-à-vis states not parties to the Convention is considerably more limited than its competence vis-à-vis States Parties to the Convention. For instance, the right of the Commission to submit cases to the Inter-American Court of Human Rights can only be exercised with respect to States Parties to the Convention which have accepted the adjudicatory jurisdiction of the Court and are involved in an alleged violation of any of the rights protected under the Convention. American states not parties to the Convention are not subject to the contentious jurisdiction of the Court. Like all member states of the Organization, they are entitled to request advisory opinions from the Court.[6]

The first legal instruments for the promotion and protection of human rights in the Inter-American system were adopted at the Ninth International Conference of American States (Bogotá, 1948). The Conference established the OAS as a regional agency within the United Nations. The OAS Charter proclaims '... the fundamental rights of the individual without distinction as to race, nationality, creed, or sex' as one of its basic principles.[7] In April 1948 the Conference also approved a resolution containing the American Declaration of the Rights and Duties of Man.[8] The American Declaration preceded the Universal Declaration of Human Rights and, even though it was not adopted in the form of a treaty, the Inter-American Court has declared that this does not '... lead to the conclusion that it does not have legal effect...'.[9]

The next step forward in the development of an Inter-American system for the protection of human rights appeared through a resolution adopted at the Fifth Meeting of Consultation of Ministers of Foreign Affairs, one of the OAS organs, in Santiago, Chile in 1959.[10] The resolution created an Inter-American Commission on Human Rights, composed of seven members elected in their individual capacity by the OAS Council. The latter was entrusted with the task of organizing the future Commission which would have the specific functions assigned to it by the Council and would be charged with 'furthering respect' for human rights. In May 1960 the Council approved the Statute of the Commission which was described as an 'autonomous entity' of the OAS and, once its members were elected, the new body began its work in that year. For the purpose of the Statute, human rights were '... understood to be those set forth in the American Declaration'. Despite the fact that the legal authority conferred on the Commission was minimal, it accomplished a remarkable task. As Buergenthal explains, the Commission, at its first session, adopted a formal interpretation of the Statute, according to which it was empowered '... to make general recommendations to each individual Member State, as well as to all of them'. Relying on this interpretation, the Commission embarked upon studies investigating 'situations relating to human rights' in various OAS member states; it began to address recommendations to governments found to be engaged in large-scale violations of human rights; and it started to issue reports documenting violations of human rights in specific countries.[11]

The Second Special Inter-American Conference (Rio de Janeiro, 1965) approved a resolution strengthening the legal authority of the Commission. Through this resolution, which was incorporated in 1966 to the Statute, the Commission developed a new area of competence: that of acting on individual petitions for alleged violations of some of the human rights enumerated in the American Convention.[12] These were the right to life, liberty and personal security, equality before the law, freedom of religion, freedom of expression, freedom from arbitrary arrest and due process of law. Since then, the examination of individual complaints has become one of the Commission's main activities.

A decisive step in the evolution toward the protection of human rights in the region was the result of the 1967 Protocol of Amendment to the Charter of the OAS 'Protocol of Buenos Aires' which entered into force in 1970. Under the amended Charter, the Inter-American Commission on Human Rights became an organ of the OAS.[13] The responsibilities of the new organ were described in another provision of the amended Charter which prescribes that its '... principal function shall be to promote the observance and protection of human rights and to serve as a consultative organ of the Organization in these matters'. This provision further stated that '... an Inter-American convention on human rights shall determine the structure, competence, and procedure of this Commission, as well as those of other organs responsible for these matters'.[14] Finally, a transitory provision reads as follows: 'Until the Inter-American Convention on Human Rights, referred to in Chapter XVI, enters into force, the present Inter-American Commission on Human Rights shall keep vigilance over the observance of human rights.'[15] Thus, the constitutional foundation for a more developed system for the protection of human rights in the region was laid down.

The American Convention on Human Rights, 'Pact of San José, Costa Rica' was opened for signature on 22 November 1969 and entered into force on 18 July 1978, after 11 states deposited their instruments of ratification (Article 74, para. 2).[16] It created an additional legal regime for the protection of human rights in the hemisphere which draws upon the American Declaration, the European Convention on Human Rights and the International Covenant on Civil and Political Rights.

Only member states of the OAS are entitled to ratify or adhere to the Convention (Article 74, para. 1). Until now, 25 states out of the 35 member states are parties to the Convention. All the Latin American countries, except for Cuba, became parties. The United States signed the Convention in

1977. Soon afterwards it was passed to the Senate by the President of the United States for its advice and consent, but no further action was taken.[17]

The Convention has been supplemented by two additional protocols. The first is the Additional Protocol to the American Convention on Human Rights in the Area of Economic, Social and Cultural Rights or 'Protocol of San Salvador' adopted in 1988, which entered into force in 1999. The second Additional Protocol to the American Convention on Human Rights to Abolish the Death Penalty, adopted in 1990, has not yet entered into force.

Finally, three other conventions have been adopted concerning human rights in the region. One is the Inter-American Convention to Prevent and Punish Torture, which was approved by the General Assembly of the OAS in 1985 and entered into force in 1987. The second is the Inter-American Convention on Forced Disappearance of Persons, adopted by the General Assembly of the OAS in 1994 and entered into force in 1996. The latest one is the Inter-American Convention on the Prevention, Punishment and Eradication of Violence Against Women, 'Convention of Belem do Para', also approved by the General Assembly of the OAS in 1994; it entered into force in 1995.

THE AMERICAN CONVENTION AND STATE OBLIGATIONS

Article 1, para. 1, of the Convention reads as follows:

> The States Parties to this Convention undertake to respect the rights and freedoms recognized herein and to ensure to all persons subject to their jurisdiction the free and full exercise of those rights and freedoms, without any discrimination for reasons of race, colour, sex, language, religion, political or other opinion, national or social origin, economic status, birth, or any other social condition.

The Inter-American Court has declared that this provision '... specifies the obligation assumed by the States Parties in relation to each of the rights protected' and that '... each claim alleging that one of those rights has been infringed necessarily implies that Article 1, para. 1, of the Convention has also been violated'.[18] The Court also stated that this provision '... constitutes the generic basis of the protection of the rights recognized by the Convention'.[19] This judgement clearly distinguishes between the two concepts contained in Article 1, para. 1: namely, the duty to 'respect' and the duty 'to ensure'. Regarding the former, the Court declared that it is '... the first obligation assumed by the States Parties'.[20] On the latter, the tribunal observed:

> ... the second obligation of the States Parties is to 'ensure' the free and full exercise of the rights recognized by the Convention ... . This obligation implies the duty of the States Parties to organize the governmental apparatus and, in general, all the structures, through which public power is exercised so that they are capable of juridically ensuring the free and full enjoyment of human rights. As a consequence of this obligation, the States must prevent, investigate and

punish any violation of the rights recognized by the Convention and, moreover, if possible attempt to restore the right violated and provide compensation as warranted for damages resulting from the violation.[21]

The Court referred further to the meaning of this obligation, in quite realistic terms:

> The obligation to ensure the free and full exercise of human rights is not fulfilled by the existence of a legal system designed to make it possible to comply with this obligation – it also requires the government to conduct itself so as to effectively ensure the free and full exercise of human rights.[22]

Article 2 of the Convention is taken almost verbatim from Article 2, para. 2, of the International Covenant on Civil and Political Rights. It reads as follows:

> Where the exercise of any of the rights or freedoms referred to in Article 1 is not already insured by legislative or other provisions, the States Parties undertake to adopt, in accordance with their constitutional processes and the provisions of this Convention, such legislative or other measures as may be necessary to give effect to those rights or freedoms.

In the opinion of the Inter-American Court, this provision codifies a basic rule of international law that a State Party to a treaty has a legal duty to take whatever legislative or other steps as may be necessary to enable it to comply with its treaty obligations. The Court added that '... this conclusion is in line with Article 43' which obliges States Parties '... to provide the Commission with such information as it may request ... as to the manner in which their domestic law ensures the effective application of any provision' of the Convention.[23]

THE RIGHTS AND FREEDOMS PROTECTED UNDER THE AMERICAN CONVENTION

Civil and Political Rights

Chapter II of Part I of the Convention entitled 'Civil and Political Rights' regulates the rights and freedoms protected under its regime (Articles 3–25).

The right to juridical personality

Article 3 guarantees to every person 'the right to recognition as a person before the law'. Since para. 2 of Article 1 states that, for the purposes of the Convention, 'person' means every human being, human beings are recognized as subjects of the law – that is, capable of having rights and being subject to legal duties and liabilities. In other words, Article 3 places the individual at the very centre of the regime established by the Convention. As an author has said, the purpose is to reaffirm the 'basic political philosophy' of the Convention '… and in this regard, to prevent possible negative consequences of an eventual push of totalitarian barbarity'.[24]

The right to life

Article 4 is proclaimed '… as the right of every person to have his life respected' and '… protected by law and, in general, from the moment of conception' (para. 1).

On the basis of the legislative history of this paragraph, the Inter-American Commission has interpreted the expression 'in general from the moment of conception', explaining that the words 'in general' were introduced while the Commission was preparing its final draft Convention, in order '… to accommodate the views that insisted on the concept "from the moment of conception" with the objection raised since the Bogotá Conference based on the legislation of American States that permitted abortion, *inter alia*, to save the mother's life, and in case of rape …'. The Commission concluded that '… the legal implications of the clause "in general" are substantially different from the shorter clause "from the moment of conception" …'.[25]

While Article 4 does not abolish the death penalty, it restricts its scope. Thus, it prohibits those countries which have not abolished the death penalty to extend its application 'to crimes to which it does not presently apply' (para. 2); to inflict capital punishment 'for political offences or related common crimes' (para. 4); to impose capital punishment 'upon persons who at the time the crime was committed, were under 18 years of age or over 70 years of age', or to apply it to pregnant women (para. 5). In states which have abolished the death penalty it shall not be re-established (para. 3).

The Inter-American Court of Human Rights rendered an advisory opinion on this matter.[26] Following a request made after the *de facto* military government of Guatemala established in 1982 courts of special jurisdiction which imposed the death penalty for crimes which, when Guatemala became a party to the American Convention on Human Rights, were not so punishable. Guatemala argued that, at the time of ratification of the Convention, it had entered a reservation with regard to Article 4, para. 4, inasmuch as the Constitution of Guatemala only excludes political crimes from the application of the death penalty, but not common crimes related to political crimes. The Court was unanimously of the opinion that the application of the death penalty would constitute a violation of Article 4, para. 2, which prohibits the application of capital punishment '… to crimes to which such a penalty was not previously provided for under its domestic law'. Regarding the reservation, the Court stated '… that a reservation restricted by its own wording to Article 4, para. 4, of the Convention does not allow the Government of a State Party to extend by subsequent legislation the application of the death penalty to crimes for which this penalty was not previously provided for'.[27]

The Inter-American Court considers the practice of disappearances as a violation of the right to life. It declared that this practice '… often involves secret execution without trial, followed by concealment of the body to eliminate any material evidence of the crime and to ensure the impunity of those responsible. This is a flagrant violation of the right to life, recognized in Article 4 of the Convention.'[28]

The right to humane treatment

Article 5 recognizes the right of every person '… to have his physical, mental, and moral integrity respected' (para. 1). Torture or cruel, inhuman, or degrading punishment or treatment are prohibited (para. 2). This provision provides further that accused persons shall, save in exceptional circumstances, be segregated from convicted persons and shall be subject to appropriate separate treatment (para. 4) and that minors, while subject to criminal proceedings, shall be separated from adults (para. 5).

In the opinion of the Inter-American Court, the forced disappearance of human beings constitutes '… a multiple and continuous violation of many rights under the Convention'.[29] Among the obligations which are violated through this practice the Court mentions those under Article 5. In this respect, the Court declared that:

> … prolonged isolation and deprivation of communication are in themselves cruel and inhuman treatment, harmful to the psychological and moral integrity of the person and a violation of the right of any detainee to respect for his inherent dignity as a human being. Such treatment, therefore, violates Article 5 of the Convention … . In addition, investigations into the practice of disappearances and the testimony of victims who have regained their liberty show that those who have disappeared are often subjected to merciless treatment, including all types of indignities, torture and other cruel, inhuman and degrading treatment, in violation of the right to physical integrity recognized in Article 5 of the Convention.[30]

In December 1985 the OAS General Assembly adopted the Inter-American Convention to Prevent and Punish Torture.[31] Under this instrument, the States Parties '… shall prevent and punish torture in accordance with the terms of this Convention' (Article 1). 'Torture shall be understood to be any act intentionally performed whereby physical or mental pain or suffering is inflicted on a person for purposes of criminal investigation, as a means of intimidation, as personal punishment, as a preventive measure, as a penalty, or for any other purpose.' The 'use of methods upon a person intended to obliterate the personality of the victim or to diminish his physical or mental capacities' shall also be understood to be torture '… even if they do not cause physical or mental pain or mental anguish' (Article 2). Public servants or employees or a person acting at the instigation of any of them, shall be held guilty of the crime of torture (Article 3). The fact of having acted under superior orders '… shall not provide exemption from criminal liability' (Article 4). The crime of torture shall not be justified or admitted by invoking the existence of circumstances such as a state of war, state of siege or of emergency, domestic disturbance or strike or other public emergencies or disasters (Article 5). States Parties shall take effective measures to prevent and punish torture within their jurisdiction (Article 6). Torture shall be deemed to be included among the extraditable crimes in every extradition treaty between States Parties (Article 13). The Inter-American Commission of Human Rights is given some competence to supervise the working of the Convention. Thus, States Parties shall inform the Commission '... of any legislative, judicial, administrative or other measures they adopt in application of this Convention' and the Commission '... will endeavour in its annual report to analyse the existing situation in the Member States of the OAS in regard to the prevention and elimination of torture' (Article 17).

Freedom from slavery

Article 6 states that slavery and involuntary servitude are prohibited '... in all their forms, as are the slave trade and traffic in women' (para. 1). 'No one shall be required to perform forced or compulsory labour', but this '... shall not be interpreted to mean that in those countries in which the penalty established for certain crimes is deprivation of liberty or forced labour, the carrying out of such sentence imposed by a competent court is prohibited' (para. 2). Finally, this provision enumerates four instances which do not constitute forced or compulsory labour. These are related to persons imprisoned, national services in lieu of military service for conscientious objectors, services in time of danger or calamity and normal civic obligations (para. 3).

The right to personal liberty

Article 7 recognizes the right to personal liberty and security of every person (para. 1). It provides further that '... no one shall be deprived of his physical liberty except for the reasons and under the conditions established beforehand by the Constitution of the State Party concerned or by a law established pursuant thereto' (para. 2).[32] No person '... shall be subject to arbitrary arrest or imprisonment' (para. 3). Any person detained 'shall be brought promptly before a judge or other officer authorized by law to exercise judicial power and shall be entitled to trial within a reasonable time or to be released without prejudice to the continuation of the proceedings' (para. 5). Article 7 also recognizes the right to demand a writ of *habeas corpus* – that is, the entitlement of any individual who is deprived of his/ her liberty '... to recourse to a competent court, in order that the court may decide without delay on the lawfulness of his arrest or detention and order his release if the arrest or detention is unlawful' (para. 6). Finally, no one shall be imprisoned for debt (para. 7).

The Inter-American Court of Human Rights has declared that '... *habeas corpus* performs a vital role in ensuring that a person's life and physical integrity are respected, in preventing his disappearance or the keeping of his whereabouts secret and in protecting him against torture or other cruel, inhumane, or degrading punishment or treatment'.[33]

The right to a fair trial

The rights included under Article 8 are related to those proclaimed in Article 7. In particular, the right to be tried within a reasonable time or to be released and the right of *habeas corpus* are judicial guarantees in criminal procedures.

Article 8 proclaims a general principle consisting in the right of every person to a hearing '... within a reasonable time, by a competent, independent, and impartial tribunal, previously established by law' for the substantiation of civil, labour, fiscal or matters of any other nature (para. 1).

The Inter-American Court has underlined the importance of the relationship between rights and guarantees:

> Guarantees are designed to protect, to ensure or to assert the entitlement to a right or the exercise thereof. The State Parties not only have the obligation to recognize and to respect the rights and freedoms of all the persons, they also have the obligation to protect and ensure the exercise of such rights and freedoms by means of the respective guarantees (Article 1, para. 1), that is, through suitable measures that will in all circumstances ensure the effectiveness of these rights and freedoms.[34]

After setting the general principle on judicial remedies, Article 8, para. 2, recognizes the right of every person accused of a criminal offence '... to be presumed innocent so long as his guilt has not been proven according to law'. This paragraph enumerates the minimum guarantees to which an accused person is entitled. These are, *inter alia*: adequate time and means for the preparation of his defence; the right to defend himself personally or to be assisted by a legal counsel of his own choice; the right not to be compelled to be a witness against himself or to plead guilty; and the right to appeal to a higher court against the judgment.

Article 8 also establishes that: '... a confession of guilt by the accused shall be valid only if it is made without coercion of any kind' (para. 3.); that '... an accused person acquitted by a non-appealable judgement shall not be subjected to a new trial for the same cause' *non bis in idem*, a basic principle of criminal procedure (para. 4); and that '... criminal proceedings shall be public, except insofar as may be necessary to protect the interests of justice' (para. 5).

Freedom from ex post facto *laws*

It has been observed that the title of Article 9 is '... equivocal and partly wrong because it establishes the general principle of non-retroactivity of the penal laws except of a law providing for the imposition of a lighter punishment'.[35] In fact, this provision proclaims the fundamental principle of criminal law: *nullum crimen nulla poena sine lege.*

The right to compensation

Article 10 recognizes the right of every person '... to be compensated in accordance with the law in the event he has been sentenced by a final judgement through a miscarriage of justice'.

The right to privacy

Article 11 establishes the right of every person '... to have his honour respected and his dignity recognized' (para. 1). It also provides that nobody '... may be the object of arbitrary or abusive interference with his private life, his family, his home or his correspondence, or of unlawful attacks on his honour or reputation' (para. 2) and, finally, declares 'the right to the protection of the law against such interferences or attacks' (para. 3).

Freedom of conscience and religion

After recognizing this right to every person, the Convention states, in Article 12, that this right '... includes freedom to maintain or to change one's religion or beliefs, and freedom to profess or disseminate one's religion or beliefs, either individually or together with others, in public or in private' (para. 1). This freedom may only be subject '... to the limitations prescribed by law that are necessary to protect public safety, order, health, or morals, or the rights on freedom of others' (para. 3). Lastly, parents or guardians '... have the right to provide for the religious and moral education of their children or wards that is in accord with their own convictions' (para. 4).

The Inter-American Commission analysed some aspects of the freedom of religion in dealing with a complaint from the religious associations known as the Jehovah's Witnesses and the Watch Tower Bible and Tract Society.[36] In their complaint, these religious groups denounced a Decree issued by the Argentinian government in August 1976 which prohibited their activities in all the territory of the nation. After examining the case and receiving additional information during its on-site observation, the Commission adopted a resolution stating that Argentina had violated several rights enumerated in the American Declaration of the Rights and Duties of Man, including the right of freedom of religion proclaimed in Article V of this Declaration. It recommended that the Argentinian government: (a) re-establish the observance of religious freedom; (b) repeal the Decree in question; (c) adopt the necessary measures to put an end to the prosecution of the congregation of Jehovah's Witnesses; (d) inform the Commission within 60 days as to the measures taken to put into practice these recommendations.[37]

Freedom of thought and expression

Article 13 proclaims that every person '... has the right to freedom of thought and expression', which includes freedom to seek, receive, and impart information and ideas of all kinds, regardless of frontiers, either orally, in writing, in print, in the form of art, or through any other medium of one's choice (para. 1). This right '... shall not be subject to prior censorship but shall be subject to subsequent imposition of liability, which shall be expressly established by law to the extent necessary to ensure: (a) respect for the rights or reputations of others; or (b) the protection of national security, public order, or public health or morals' (para. 2). This right '... may not be restricted by indirect methods or means' (para. 3). As an exception to the latter rule, '... public entertainments may be subject by law to prior censorship for the sole purpose of regulating access to them for moral protection of childhood and adolescence' (para. 4). Finally, Article 13 provides that 'Any propaganda for war and any advocacy of national, racial, or religious hatred that constitute incitements to lawless violence or to any similar action against any person or group of persons on any grounds including those of race, colour, religion, language, or national origin shall be considered as offences punishable by law' (para. 5).

In an advisory opinion, the Inter-American Court of Human Rights dealt with some aspects of the freedom of expression in the American Convention. The Court declared:

> ... when an individual's freedom of expression is unlawfully restricted, it is not only the right of that individual that is being violated, but also the right of all others to 'receive' information and ideas. The right protected by Article 13 consequently has a special scope and character, which are evidenced by the dual aspect of freedom of expression. It requires, on the one hand, that no one be arbitrarily limited or impeded in expressing his own thoughts. In that sense, it is a right that belongs to each individual. Its second aspect, on the other hand, implies a collective right to receive any information whatsoever and to have access to the thoughts expressed by others.[38]

With regard to possible restrictions on freedom of thought and expression, the Court said:

> The Convention itself recognizes that freedom of thought and expression allows the imposition of certain restrictions whose legitimacy must be measured by reference to the requirements of Article 13, para. 2. Just as the right to express and to disseminate ideas is indivisible as a concept, so too must it be recognized that the only restrictions that may be placed on the mass media are those that apply to freedom of expression. It results therefore that in determining the legitimacy of restrictions and, hence, in judging whether the Convention has been violated, it is necessary in each case to decide whether the terms of Article 13, para. 2, have been respected (para. 36).
> Article 13, para. 2, of the Convention defines the means by which permissible limitations to freedom of expression may be established. It stipulates, in the first place, that prior censorship is always incompatible with the full enjoyment of

the rights listed in Article 13, but for the exception provided for in subparagraph 4 dealing with public entertainment, even if the alleged purpose of such prior censorship is to prevent abuses of freedom of expression. In this area any preventive measure inevitably amounts to an infringement of the freedom guaranteed by the Convention (para. 38).

Abuse of freedom of information thus cannot be controlled by preventive measures but only through the subsequent imposition of sanctions on those who are guilty of the abuses. But even here, in order for the imposition of such liability to be valid under the Convention, the following requirements must be met: (a) the existence of previously established grounds for liability; (b) the express and precise definition of these grounds by law; (c) the legitimacy of the ends sought to be achieved; (d) a showing that these grounds of liability are 'necessary to ensure' the aforementioned ends. All of these requirements must be complied with in order to give effect to Article 13, para. 2 (para. 39).

The Court also acknowledged the close relationship between these restrictions and the requirements of democracy. After quoting Article 29, para. (c) and (d), and Article 32, para. 2, of the Convention, and the paragraph in the Preamble of the OAS Charter on the consolidation of democratic institutions, the Court declared:

These articles define the context within which the restrictions permitted under Article 13, para. 2, must be interpreted. It follows from the repeated reference to 'democratic institutions', 'representative democracy' and 'democratic society' that the question whether a restriction on freedom of expression imposed by a State is 'necessary to ensure' one of the objectives listed in subparagraphs (a) or (b) must be judged by reference to the legitimate needs of democratic societies and institutions (para. 42).

The Court summarized this by stating that '… freedom of expression is a cornerstone upon which the very existence of a democratic society rests' (para. 70).

The right of reply

Article 14 recognizes that any individual '… injured by inaccurate or offensive statements or ideas disseminated to the public by a legally regulated medium of communication … has the right to reply … using the same communications outlet, under such conditions as the law may establish' (para. 1).

This right is related to those embodied in the concept of freedom of thought and expression – that is, of seeking, receiving and imparting information as provided for in Article 13, para. 1 of the Convention. In interpreting Article 14, para. 1, in relation to Articles 1, para. 1, and 2, of the Convention, the Inter-American Court has declared:

A: That Article 14, para. 1, of the Convention recognizes an internationally enforceable right to reply or to make a correction which, under Article 1, para. 1, the State Parties have the obligation to respect and to ensure the free and full exercise thereof to all persons subject to their jurisdiction.

B: That when the right guaranteed by Article 14, para. 1, is not enforceable under the domestic law of a State Party, that State has the obligation, under Article 2 of the Convention, to adopt, in accordance with its constitutional processes and the provisions of the Convention, the legislative or other measures that may be necessary to give effect to this right.[39]

The Court emphasized that:

> ... the fact that the State Parties may fix the manner in which the right of reply is to be exercised does not impair the enforceability, on the international plane, of the obligations they have assumed under Article 1, para. 1 ... . If for any reason, therefore, the right of reply or connection could not be exercised by 'anyone' who is subject to the jurisdiction of a State Party, a violation of the Convention would result which could be denounced to the organs of protection provided by the Convention.[40]

The right of assembly

Article 5 proclaims '... the right of peaceful assembly, without arms'. The exercise of this right cannot be subject to restrictions '... other than those imposed in conformity with the law and necessary in a democratic society in the interest of national security, public safety or public order, or to protect public health or morals or the rights or freedoms of others'.

Regarding these requirements for the imposition of restrictions, the Inter-American Court, based on Article 29 which prohibits any interpretation of Convention '... precluding other rights or guarantees ... derived from representative democracy as a form of government', has stated: 'The just demands of democracy must consequently guide the interpretation of the Convention and, in particular, the interpretation of those provisions that bear a critical relationship to the preservation and functioning of democratic institutions'.[41]

Freedom of association

In Article 16 the Convention recognizes the right of every person '... to associate freely for ideological, religious, political, economic, labour, social, cultural, sports, or other purposes' (para. 1). The exercise of this right is also subject to similar restrictions as those mentioned in connection with the right of assembly (para. 2). Finally, these provisions '... do not bar the imposition of legal restrictions, including even deprivation of the exercise of the right of association, on members of the armed forces and the police' (para. 3).

The absence of an express reference to the right of 'non-association' has been criticized, particularly in view of the existence, in some Latin American countries, of laws establishing an obligation to be affiliated with certain professional associations.[42] On this subject, in his separate opinion to the advisory opinion of the Inter-American Court on the question of 'Compulsory Membership in an Association prescribed by law for the Practice of Journalism', Judge Nieto Navia, stated:

The text of Article 16, para. 1, deals with, at the same time, both a right and a freedom, that is to say, with the right to form associations, which cannot be restricted except in the case and for the purposes contemplated in paragraphs 2 and 3 of Article 16, and with a freedom in the sense that nobody can be compelled or obligated to join an association. It is necessary to understand that both extremes are protected by the Convention, although the Convention does not mention the negative freedom – the right not to join an association – which disappeared from the original draft of the Convention without any indication of the reason for the decision ... but it is expressly contemplated in Article 20 *in fine* of the Universal Declaration of Human Rights. ... Under the doctrine of this Court human rights must be interpreted in favour of the individual ... and it would be against all reason and an aberration to interpret the word 'freedom' as a 'right' only and not as 'the inherent power that man has to work in one way or another, or not to work' according to his free will.[43]

He concluded that:

... freedom of association is violated if the law compels individuals to join associations, if the proposed aims of that association are such that they could be achieved by associations created by individuals using their freedom, that is if such associations are those that are referred to in Article 16.[44]

Rights of the family

Article 17 declares that 'The family is the natural and fundamental group unit of society and is entitled to protection by society and the State' (para. 1)[45] and that '... the right of men and women of marriageable age to get married shall be recognized, if they meet the conditions required by domestic laws insofar as such conditions do not affect the principle of non-discrimination established in the Convention' (para. 2). Marriage cannot be effected '... without the free and full consent of the intending spouses' (para. 3). A specific obligation of States Parties is to '... take appropriate steps to ensure the equality of rights and the adequate balancing of responsibilities of the spouses as to marriage, during marriage, and in the event of its dissolution'. In the latter case, provision should be made for the necessary protection of any children (para. 4). Finally, States Parties shall recognize in their laws '... equal rights for children born out of wedlock and those born in wedlock' (para. 5).

The right to a name

Article 18 recognizes the right of every person '... to a given name and to the surname of his parents or that of one of them'. The manner in which this right shall be ensured for all shall be regulated by law.

The rights of the child

Article 19 of the American Convention affirms the right of every child '... to the measures of protection required by his condition as a minor on the part of his family, society, and the State'. The implementation of this right requires State Parties to enact appropriate domestic legislation.

The right to nationality

Article 20 para. 1, states 'Every person has the right to a nationality.' In granting recognition to the rule of *jus soli*, this article provides that 'Every person has a right to the nationality of the State in whose territory he is born if he does not have the right to any other nationality' (para. 2). Arbitrary deprivation of nationality or of the right to change it is prohibited (para. 13).

The Inter-American Court has declared:

> ... that in order to arrive at a satisfactory interpretation of the right to nationality, as embodied in Article 20 of the Convention, it will be necessary to reconcile the principle that the conferral and regulation of nationality fall within the jurisdiction of the State, that is they are matters to be determined by the domestic law of the State, with the further principle that international law imposes certain limits on the State's power, which limits are linked to the demands imposed by the international system for the protection of human rights.[46]

The right to property

Article 21 recognizes for everyone '... the right to the use and enjoyment of his property'. Such use and enjoyment may be subordinated by law '... to the interest of society' (para. 1). Deprivation of property is prohibited '... except upon payment of just compensation, for reasons of public utility or a social interest, and in the cases and according to the forms established by law' (para. 2). Finally, 'Usury and any other form of exploitation of man by man shall be prohibited by law' (para. 3). In compliance with this paragraph, States Parties have to enact appropriate domestic legislation. Under Article 21, the right to property is recognized for everyone – that is, for every person – and, since the Convention defines 'person' in Article 1, para. 2, as 'every human being', corporations and other legal persons would not be protected by this provision.[47]

Freedom of movement and residence

Article 22 enumerates a number of rights dealing with freedom of movement and residence. First, 'Every person lawfully in the territory of a State Party, has the right to move about in it, and to reside in it subject to the provisions of the law' (para. 1) and the right '... to leave any country freely, including his own' (para. 2). These rights '... may be restricted only pursuant to a law to the extent necessary in a democratic society to prevent crime or to protect national security, public safety, public order, public morals, public health or the rights or freedoms of others' (para. 3) or '... in designated zones for reasons of public interest' (para. 4). No one may be expelled from the state of which he/she is a national or be deprived of the right to enter it (para. 5) and 'An alien lawfully in the territory of a State Party ... may be expelled from it only pursuant to a decision reached in accordance with law' (para. 6).[48] The right of asylum in a foreign territory – territorial asylum – is also recognized in the event that a person '... is being pursued for political offences or related common crimes' (para. 7). 'In no case may an alien be deported or returned to a country, regardless of whether or not it is his country of origin, if in that country his right to life or personal freedom is in danger or being violated because of his race, nationality, religion, social status, or political opinions' (para. 8). 'The collective expulsion of aliens is prohibited' (para. 9).

The right to participate in government

The political 'rights and opportunities' of every citizen, listed in Article 23 are: '(a) to take part in the conduct of public affairs, directly or through freely chosen representatives; (b) to vote and to be elected in genuine periodic elections ... by universal and equal suffrage and by secret ballot; (c) to have access, under general conditions of equality, to the public service of his country.' The exercise of these rights and opportunities may be regulated by law '... only on the basis of age, nationality, residence, language, education, civil and mental capacity, or sentencing by a competent court in criminal proceedings' (para. 2).

The Inter-American Court has declared that: 'The Convention itself expressly recognizes political rights (Article 23) which are included among those rights that cannot be suspended under Article 27. This is indicative of their importance in the system'.[49]

The right to equal protection

Article 24 declares the equality of all persons before the law and their entitlement, without discrimination, to equal protection of the law. The Court quoted the European Court of Human rights in support of its view that '... because equality and non-discrimination are inherent in the idea of oneness in dignity and worth of all human beings, it follows that not all differences in legal treatment are in themselves offensive to human dignity'.[50]

The right to judicial protection

Under Article 25, every person '... has the right to simple and prompt recourse, or any other effective recourse, to a competent court or tribunal for protection against acts that violate his fundamental rights recognized by the Constitution or laws of the State concerned or by this Convention, even though such violation may have been committed by persons acting in the course of their official duties' (para. 1).

In order to guarantee this right, States Parties to the Convention undertake: '(a) to ensure that any person claiming such remedy shall have his rights determined by the competent authority provided by the legal system of the State; (b) to develop the possibilities of judicial remedy; and (c) to ensure that the competent authorities shall enforce such remedies when granted' (para. 2).

The Inter-American Court has declared that Article 25, para. 1:

> ... is a general provision that gives expression to the procedural institution known as *amparo*, which is a simple and prompt remedy designed for the protection of all of the rights recognized by the constitutions and laws of the States Parties and by the Convention. Since *amparo* can be applied to all rights, it is clear that it can also be applied to those that are expressly mentioned in Article 27, para. 2, as rights that are non-derogable in emergency situations.[51]

In comparing *amparo* and *habeas corpus*, the Court stated:

> If the two remedies are examined together, it is possible to conclude that *amparo* comprises a whole series of remedies and that *habeas corpus* is but one of its components. An examination of the essential aspects of both guarantees, as embodied in the Convention and, in their different forms, in the legal systems of the States Parties, indicates that in some instances *habeas corpus* functions as an independent remedy. Here its primary purpose is to protect the general freedom of those who have been detained or who have been threatened with detention. In other circumstances, however, *habeas corpus* is viewed either as the *amparo* of freedom or as an integral part of *amparo*.[52]

In another Advisory Opinion the Court stated that:

> Article 25, para. 1, incorporates the principle recognized in international law of human rights of the effectiveness of the procedural instruments or means designed to guarantee such rights ... . According to this principle, the absence of an effective remedy to violations of the rights recognized by the Convention is itself a violation of the Convention by the State Party in which remedy is lacking.[53]

Economic, Social and Cultural Rights

Chapter III of the American Convention deals with economic, social and cultural rights in one single provision entitled 'Progressive Development' (Article 26). This is a pragmatic norm providing that States Parties '... undertake to adopt measures, both internally and through international co-operation ... with a view to achieving progressively ... the full realization of the rights implicit in the economic, social, educational, scientific, and cultural standards set forth in the Charter of the OAS'. In relation to this provision, Article 42 of the Convention stipulates that States Parties shall transmit to the Inter-American Commission of Human Rights a copy of each of the reports and studies which they submit annually to the Executive Committees of the Inter-American Economic and Social Council and the Inter-American Council for Education, Science and

Culture, so that the Commission may watch over the promotion of the above-mentioned rights.

A significant step in the evolution towards the protection of those rights in the Inter-American system was the adoption by the OAS General Assembly at its Eighteenth Regular Session in 1988 of an Additional Protocol to the American Convention on Human Rights in the Area of Economic, Social and Cultural Rights, entitled the 'Protocol of San Salvador'.[54] Article 1 of this Protocol reiterates the basic idea contained in Article 26 of the American Convention. The States Parties to the Protocol '… undertake to adopt the necessary measures … to the extent allowed by their available resources, and taking into account their degree of development, for the purpose of achieving progressively and pursuant to their internal legislations, the full observance of the rights recognized in this Protocol'. The reference to the rights implicit in the OAS Charter, which appears in Article 26 of the American Convention, has been eliminated in the Protocol.

Regarding the obligation to enact domestic legislation, the obligations of non-discrimination, the inadmissibility of restrictions and the scope of restrictions and limitations (Articles 2, 3, 4 and 5 respectively), the Additional Protocol establishes similar rules to those contained in Articles 2, 29, and 30 of the American Convention. The Protocol also deals with the right to work (Article 6); under just, equitable and satisfactory conditions (Article 7); trade union rights (Article 8); the right to social security (Article 9); the right to health (Article 10); the right to a healthy environment (Article 11); the right to food (Article 12); the right to education (Article 13); the right to the benefits of culture (Article 14); the right to the formation and the protection of families (Article 15); the rights of children (Article 16); protection of the elderly (Article 17); and protection of the handicapped (Article 18).

As to means of protection (Article 19), State Parties '… undertake to submit periodic reports on the progressive measures they have taken to ensure due respect for the rights set forth in this Protocol', which are transmitted to the Inter-American Economic and Social Council and the Inter-American Council for Education, Science and Culture. A copy is sent to the Inter-American Commission on Human Rights. The annual reports of both OAS Councils contain a summary of the information received and the recommendations they consider appropriate. Violations of the right to organize trade unions or workers, or of the rights to education attributable to State Parties, may give rise, through participation of the Inter-American Commission and, when applicable, of the Inter-American Court, to the application of the system of individual petitions under the American Convention. The Commission may formulate such observations and recommendations concerning the status of the economic, social and cultural rights established in the Protocol in all or some of the State Parties which may be included in the Commission's Annual Report to the General Assembly or in a special report.

There is a close linkage between the real existence of the rights proclaimed in the Protocol of San Salvador and the social and economic development of the countries involved, particularly those in Latin America and the Caribbean. In this connection, the Inter-American Court observed that any extension of the rights protected under the Convention should be placed under the protection of the Commission and the Court – otherwise, it would have no sense to call the new instrument an 'Additional Protocol'. Some economic, social and cultural rights could be the subject of jurisdictional complaints but others, which are also fundamental human rights, depend heavily on the economic and social development of each country. In the opinion of the Court, the latter rights could be included in an Inter-American Convention independent of the Pact of San José and with similar guarantees to those established in the International Covenant of Economic, Social and Cultural Rights.[55]

SUSPENSION OF GUARANTEES, INTERPRETATION AND APPLICATION

Chapter IV of the Convention (Articles 27–31) covers the following questions: the suspension of guarantees; the federal clause; the restrictions regarding interpretation; the scope of restrictions and the recognition of other rights.

Article 27, para 1, states the exceptional circumstances under which State Parties may resort to the suspension of some of the rights protected in the Convention. It provides as follows:

> In time of war, public danger, or other emergency that threatens the independence or security of a State Party, it may take measures derogating from its obligations under the present Convention to the extent and for the period of time strictly required by the exigencies of the situation, provided that such measures are not inconsistent with its other obligations under international law and do not involve discrimination on the ground of race, colour, sex, language, religion, or social origin.

Paragraph 2 enumerates the non-derogable rights and freedoms. These are: the right to judicial personality; the right to life; the right to humane treatment; freedom from slavery; freedom from *ex post facto* laws; freedom of conscience and religion; the rights of the family; the right to a name; the rights of the child; the right to nationality; and the right to participate in government or in the judicial guarantees essential for the protection of such rights. Paragraph 3 establishes the formal procedure for the exercise of the right of suspension: State Parties shall immediately inform the other State Parties, through the OAS Secretary-General, '… of the provisions the application of which it has suspended, the reasons that gave rise to the suspension, and the date set for the termination of such suspension'.

In comparing Article 27 of the American Convention with the derogation clauses in the European Convention and the International Covenant on Civil and Political Rights, Buergenthal observes that the texts in both latter instruments '… appear to be more stringent than that of the American Convention, which suggests that the emergency need merely threaten the "independence or security of a State Party" to justify the derogation'. However, as he indicates, '... the catalogue of rights from which no derogation is permitted is much longer under Article 27'. To the extent that '... the American Convention permits derogation in emergencies much less serious than those envisaged by the other instruments', this author concludes: '... an expanded list of non-derogable rights is more justified.'[56]

The Inter-American Commission has declared that:

> ... respect for the rule of law does not preclude, under certain circumstances, the adoption of extraordinary measures. When the emergency situation is truly serious, certain restrictions may be imposed, for example on the freedom of information, or limitations on the right of association, within the framework established in the constitution. In more extreme cases, persons may be detained for short periods without it being necessary to bring specific charges against them. It is true such measures can ultimately pose the risk that the rule of law will be lost, but that is not inevitable provided that governments act responsibly, if they register arrests and inform the families of the detainees of the detention; if they issue strict orders prohibiting torture; if they carefully recruit and train security forces, weeding out sadists and psychopaths; and, lastly, if there is an independent judiciary to swiftly correct any abuse of authority.[57]

In interpreting Article 27, the Inter-American Court has reached some important conclusions which can be summarized as follows:[58]

> (a) We are not here dealing with a 'suspension of guarantees' in an absolute sense, nor with the 'suspension of ... rights', for the rights protected by these provisions are inherent to man. It follows therefrom that what may be only suspended or limited is their full and effective exercise. (b) ... it is a provision for exceptional situations only ... ; (c) ... under certain circumstances the suspension of guarantees may be the only way to deal with emergency situations and, thereby, to preserve the highest values of a democratic society. The Court cannot, however, ignore the fact that abuses may result from the application of emergency measures ... . This has in fact been the experience in our hemisphere. Therefore, given the principles upon which the Inter-American system is founded, the Court must emphasize that the suspension of guarantees cannot be disassociated from the 'effective exercise of representative democracy' referred to in Article 3 of the OAS Charter ... . The suspension of guarantees lacks all legitimacy whenever it is resorted to for the purpose of undermining the democratic system ... rather than adopting a philosophy that favours the suspension of rights, the Convention establishes the contrary principle, namely, that all rights are to be guaranteed and enforced unless very special circumstances justify the suspension of some, and that some rights might be never suspended, however serious the emergency; (d) The lawfulness of the measures taken to deal with each of the special situations referred to in Article 27, para. 1, will depend ... upon the character, intensity, persuasiveness, and particular context of the emergency and upon the corresponding proportionality and reasonableness of the measures; (e) The suspension of guarantees does not imply a temporary suspension of the rule of law, nor does it authorize those in power to act in disregard of the principle of legality by which they are bound at all times ... . The Court has already noted ... that there exists an inseparable bond between the principle of

legality, democratic institutions and the rule of law; (f) ... the judicial remedies that must be considered to be essential within the meaning of Article 27, para. 2, are those that ordinarily will effectively guarantee the full exercise of the rights and freedoms protected by that provision and whose denial or restriction would endanger their full enjoyment; (g) ... writs of *habeas corpus* and *amparo* are among those judicial remedies that are essential for the protection of various rights whose derogation is prohibited by Article 27, para. 2, and that serve, moreover, to preserve legality in a democratic society;[59] (h) ... the Constitutions and legal systems of the State Parties that authorize, expressly or by implication, the suspension of the legal remedies of *habeas corpus* or *amparo* in emergency situations cannot be deemed to be compatible with the international obligations imposed on the States by the Convention.

Finally, '... in response to the question posed by the Inter-American Commission relating to the interpretation of Article 27, para. 2, Article 25, para. 1 and Article 7, para. 6, of the Convention', the Court unanimously was of the opinion '... that, given the provisions of Article 27, para. 2 ... may not be suspended because they are judicial guarantees essential for the protection of the rights and freedoms whose suspension Article 27, para. 2, prohibits'.[60]

Article 28, entitled 'Federal Clause', deals with the implementation of the Convention in those State Parties constituted as a federal state. In this case, '... the national government of such a State Party shall implement all the provisions of the Convention over whose subject matter it exercises legislative and judicial jurisdiction' (para. 1). With respect to '... the provisions over whose subject matter the constituent units of the federal State have jurisdiction, the national government shall immediately take suitable measures, in accordance with its constitution and its laws, to the end that the competent authorities of the constituent units may adopt appropriate provisions for the fulfilment of this Convention' (para. 2). When two or more States Parties form a federation or some kind of association, '... they shall take care that the resulting federal or other compact contains the provisions necessary for continuing and rendering effective the standards of this Convention in the new State ...' (para. 3).

Buergenthal affirms that Article 28 is '... an anachronism which harks back to the days of the League of Nations'. He asserts that:

> ... few modern international human rights instruments contain comparable clauses. The International Covenant on Civil and Political Rights adopts precisely the opposite principle by declaring in Article 50 that its provisions shall extend to all parts of the federal States without any limitations or exceptions. The European Convention, the Genocide Convention, and the UN Racial Convention contain no federal clause; they apply with equal force in unitary as in federal States. Moreover, many States which have a strong federal tradition, including Canada and the Federal Republic of Germany, have been able to adhere to these instruments without federal-State reservations.[61]

Obviously, Article 28 has the potential to create a number of problems for the implementation of the Convention in the territory of federal States Parties.

Article 29, entitled 'Restrictions regarding Interpretation', enumerates some rules for the interpretation of the Convention. This provision '... is drafted in the negative and contains principles which purposes are consistent with those of the Convention in general, that is, the protection or rather the extension of the protection of human rights as a criterion'.[62] It provides that no provision of the Convention shall be interpreted as: (a) permitting any State Party, group or person to suppress the enjoyment of the rights recognized in the Convention or to restrict them to a greater extent than is provided for in the Convention; (b) restricting the enjoyment of the rights recognized by the laws of any State Party or by another convention to which one of the said States is a Party;[63] (c) '... precluding other rights or guarantees that are inherent in the human personality or derived from representative democracy as a form of government'; (d) excluding or limiting the effect that the American Declaration of the Rights and Duties of Man and other similar international acts may have.

Article 30, 'Scope of Restrictions', provides that restrictions '... may not be applied except in accordance with laws enacted for reasons of general interest and in accordance with the purpose for which such restrictions have been established'. The American Court declared that:

> ... the meaning of the word 'laws' in Article 30 cannot be disassociated from the intention of all the American States, as expressed in the Preamble to the Convention, 'to consolidate in the hemisphere within the framework of democratic institutions a system of personal liberty and social justice based on respect for the essential rights of man' ... Representative democracy is the determining factor throughout the system of which the Convention is a part. It is a 'principle' reaffirmed by the American States in the OAS Charter, the basic instrument of the Inter-American system. The Convention itself expressly recognizes political rights (Article 23) that are included among those rights which cannot be suspended under Article 27. This is indicative of their importance in the system.[64]

On this basis, the Court stated that the laws referred to in Article 30 are '... normative acts directed towards the general welfare, passed by a democratically elected legislature and promulgated by the Executive Branch. This meaning is fully consistent with the general context of the Convention, in line with the philosophy of the Inter-American system'.[65] The Court concluded '... that, for purposes of the interpretation of this Article, the concepts of legality and legitimacy coincide, inasmuch as only a law that has been passed by democratically elected and constitutionally legitimate bodies and is tied to the general welfare may restrict enjoyment or exercise of the rights or freedoms of the individual'.[66]

DUTIES AND RIGHTS: A MUTUAL RELATIONSHIP

Chapter V of the Convention, entitled 'Personal Responsibilities', contains one provision (Article 32), dealing with the 'Relationship between Duties and Rights'. After declaring that 'Every person has responsibilities to his family, his community, and mankind' (para. 1), it provides that '… the rights of each person are limited by the rights of others, by the security of all, and by the just demands of the general welfare, in a democratic society' (para. 2).

Referring to the meaning of 'general welfare' in Article 32 , para. 2, the Inter-American Court stated that it is possible to understand this concept:

> … as referring to the conditions of social life that allow members of society to reach the highest level of personal development and the optimum achievement of democratic values. In that sense it is possible to conceive of the organization of society in a manner that strengthens the functioning of democratic institutions and preserves and promotes the full realization of the rights of the individual as an imperative of the general welfare.[67]

The Court recognized that the concept of general welfare, as that of public order:

> … can be used as much to affirm the rights of the individual against the exercise of government power as to justify the imposition of limitations on the exercise of those rights in the name of collective interests. In this respect, the Court wishes to emphasize that 'public order' or 'general welfare' may under no circumstances be invoked as a means of denying a right guaranteed by the Convention or to impair or deprive it of its true content.[68]

THE COMPETENT ORGANS

Part II of the Convention, 'Means of Protection', is divided into three chapters: Chapter VI – Competent Organs (Article 37); Chapter VII – Inter-American Court of Human Rights (Articles 34–51); and Chapter VIII – Inter-American Court of Human Rights (Articles 52–69).

The Inter-American Commission of Human Rights

Article 33 establishes the two organs that '… shall have competence with respect to matters relating to the fulfilment of the commitments made by the State Parties': the Inter-American Commission of Human Rights and the Inter-American Court of Human Rights.

The Inter-American Commission, which is an organ of the OAS (Articles 52 and 112 of the OAS Charter), was created in 1959 at the Meeting of Consultation of the OAS Ministers of Foreign Affairs, and its first statute was approved by the then OAS Council in 1960.[69] The Commission fulfilled its mandate '… to promote respect for human rights' as an 'autonomous entity' and accomplished an important pioneer task, particularly in Latin America.

As stated earlier, the Commission has a dual competence: as an OAS organ, with regard to all the Organization's member states, and as one of the organs of the American Convention, with regard to the State Parties to this treaty. The first competence is exercised in relation to the rights proclaimed in the 1948 American Declaration of the Rights and Duties of Man; the second is exercised on the basis of its powers under the Convention. This dual regime is clearly stated in the OAS Charter. The second paragraph of Article 150, introduced by the 1967 Protocol of Amendments to the OAS Charter, reads as follows:

> Until the Inter-American Convention on Human Rights, referred to in Chapter XVI, enters into force, the present Inter-American Commission on Human Rights shall keep vigilance over the observance of human rights.[70]

The Commission comprises seven members '... who shall be persons of high moral character and recognized competence in the field of human rights' (Article 34), elected in their individual capacities by the OAS General Assembly, from a list of candidates proposed by the governments of the member states, whether or not they are parties to the Convention. Each government may propose up to three candidates, who may be nationals of the state proposing them or of any other OAS member state (Article 36). The members of the Commission shall be elected for a term of four years and may be re-elected only once (Article 37). The Commission shall represent all the OAS member states (Article 35).

The main function of the Commission is characterized as being '... to promote respect for and defence of human rights' (Article 41). This provision enumerates the Commission's functions and powers in the exercise of its mandate. These are:

(a)   to develop an awareness of human rights among the peoples of America;

(b)   to make recommendations to the governments of the Member States, when it considers such action advisable, for the adoption of progressive measures in favour of human rights within the framework of their domestic law and constitutional provisions as well as appropriate measures to further the observance of those rights;

(c)   to prepare such studies or reports as it considers advisable in the performance of its duties;

(d)   to request the governments of the Member States to supply it with information on the measures adopted by them in matters of human rights;

(e)   to respond, through the General Secretariat of the OAS, to inquiries made by the Member States on matters related to human rights and, within the limits of its possibilities, to provide these States with the advisory services they request;

(f)   to take action on petitions and other communications pursuant to its authority under the provisions of Articles 44 through 51 of the Convention; and

(g)   to submit an annual report to the General Assembly of the OAS.

Except for subparagraph (f), which applies to State Parties to the Convention, the rest of the functions and powers assigned to the Commission under Article 41 are applicable to all the OAS members.[71]

Article 42, which we have mentioned in dealing with Article 26 of the Convention, refers to the functions of the Commission regarding '… the promotion of the rights implicit in the economic, social, educational, scientific, and cultural standards set forth' in the OAS Charter.

The State Parties '… undertake to provide the Commission with such information as it may request of them as to the manner in which their domestic law ensures the effective application of any provisions' of the Convention (Article 43). The Inter-American Court of Human Rights has stated that the '… basic rule of international law that a State Party to a treaty has a legal duty to take whatever legislative or other steps as may be necessary to make it to comply with its treaty obligations', codified in Article 2 of the Convention, is in line with Article 43.[72]

Section 3 (Articles 44–51) of Chapter VII of the Convention refers to the Commission's competence to examine petitions containing denunciations or complaints of violations of the Pact of San José. Regarding individual complaints, Article 44 provides: 'Any person or group of persons, or any non-governmental entity legally recognized in one or more Member States of the Organization, may lodge petitions with the Commission containing denunciations or complaints of violation of this Convention by a State Party.' Thus, according to this norm, any State Party to the Convention accepts *ipso facto* the competence of the Commission to deal with private complaints against that state.[73] This is one of the most progressive achievements of the Inter-American system for the protection of human rights.

Conversely, the Commission's competence to deal with interstate complaints is subject to a voluntary declaration by any State Party that it recognizes the competence of that organ '… to receive and examine communications in which a State Party alleges that another State Party has committed a violation of a human right set forth' in the Convention (Article 45, para. 1).[74] Such communications may be admitted and examined only if they are presented by a State Party which has made a declaration recognizing the competence of the Commission under Article 45. Any communication against a state which has not recognized this competence shall not be admitted by the Commission (para. 2).

The Inter-American Court declared that a fundamental aspect of the role of the Commission in the Inter-American system is that it is:

> … the body which is authorized to receive individual complaints, that is the entity to which victims of violations of human rights and other persons referred to in Article 44 can resort directly to present their complaints and allegations. The Convention is unique among international human rights instruments in making the right of private petition applicable against State Parties as soon as they ratify the Convention; no special declaration to that effect is required for individual petitions, although it must be made for inter-State communications.[75]

The admission of both private and interstate petitions or communications is subject to certain requirements enumerated in Article 46, para. 1. The substantive requirements are the following: (a) the exhaustion of the remedies under domestic law '… in accordance with general recognized principles of international law'; (b) the submission of the petition or com-munication to the Commission within six months from the date on which the party alleging violation of his rights was notified of the final decision; (c) '... that the subject of the petition or communication is not pending in another international proceeding for settlement'. However, Article 46, para. 2, provides that these requirements shall not apply when:

> (a) the domestic legislation of the State concerned does not afford due process of law for the protection of the right or rights that have allegedly been violated; (b) the party alleging violation of his rights has been denied access to the remedies under domestic law or has been prevented from exhausting them; or (c) there has been unwarranted delay in reaching a final judgement under the aforemen-tioned remedies.

Based on the reference to generally recognized principles of international law in Article 46, para. 1, the Court stated, that, in respect of the norm requiring the prior exhaustion of domestic remedies:

> ... first, that this is a rule that can be waived, either expressly or by implication, by the State having the right to invoke it, as this Court has already recognized (see Viviana Gallardo *et al.*, Judgment of 13 November 1981, No. 6 101/81. Series A, para. 26). Second, the objection asserting the non-exhaustion of domestic remedies, to be timely, must be made at an early stage of the proceedings by the State entitled to make it, lest a waiver of the requirement be presumed. Third, the State claiming non-exhaustion has an obligation to prove that domestic remedies remain to be exhausted and that they are effective.[76]

The Court has also affirmed that:

> ... although the exhaustion of domestic remedies is a requirement for admissi-bility before the Commission, the determination of whether such remedies have been pursued and exhausted or whether one is dealing with one of the exceptions to such requirement is a matter involving the interpretation or application of the Convention. As such, it falls within the contentious jurisdic-tion of the Court pursuant to the provisions of Article 62, para. 1, of the Convention. The proper moment for the Court on an objection concerning the failure to exhaust domestic remedies will depend on the special circumstances of each case.[77]

On the question of the burden of proof, the Court has declared that:

> ... once a State Party has shown the existence of domestic remedies for the enforcement of a particular right guaranteed by the Convention, the burden of proof shifts to the complainant who must then demonstrate that the exceptions provided for in Article 46, para. 2, are applicable, whether as a result of indi-gence or because of a generalized fear to take the case among the legal community or any other applicable circumstance. Of course, it must also be shown that the rights in question are guaranteed in the Convention and that legal representa-tion is necessary to assert or enjoy these rights.[78]

In connection with the requirement that the petition be lodged within the six-month period following the date on which the party whose rights have allegedly been violated, Article 38, para. 2, of the Regulations of the Commission allows for the relaxation of this deadline in serious or urgent cases or when the life, personal integrity or health of a person is in danger. In these instances, the deadline '… shall be within a reasonable period of time, in the Commission's judgement, as from the date in which the alleged violation of rights has occurred considering the circumstances of each specific case'.

The requirement in Article 46, para. 1(c), intended to eliminate duplication of international procedures is closely linked to the provision in Article 47, para. D, which provides that a petition or communication which is '… substantially the same as one previously studied by the Commission or by another international organization', shall be considered inadmissible. Gros Espiell observes that the application of the exception of *lis pendens* in this case '… poses serious and difficult problems of co-existence and co-ordination with other international systems of protection, in particular with the Optional Protocol to the International Covenant of Civil and Political Rights and with procedures in the ILO system'.[79]

Article 47 makes it compulsory for the Commission to declare expressly and formally when a petition or communication is found inadmissible. The Court has stated that '… no such requirement is demanded for admissibility. The foregoing holds provided that a State does not raise the issue of admissibility, whereupon the Commission must make a Statement one way or the other.'[80]

Section 4 of Chapter VII of the Convention deals with the procedure before the Commission (Articles 48–51). The Court stated that the procedures contained in these provisions have a broader objective as regards the international protection of human rights: compliance by the states to their obligations and, more specifically, with their legal obligation to cooperate in the investigation and resolution of the violations of which they 'have been accused'.[81] When receiving a petition or communication alleging violation of any of the rights protected under the Convention, the Commission shall request information from the government concerned and shall furnish it with a transcript of the pertinent portions of the complaint (Article 48, para. 1(a)). After the information has been received, or the period for its submission has elapsed, the Commission shall ascertain whether the grounds for the petition still exist. If not, it shall order the record to be closed (Article 48, para. 1(b)). The Commission may also declare the petition inadmissible or out of order (Article 48, para. 1(c)). If the record is not closed, the Commission shall investigate the facts and, if it requests the state concerned to furnish any information, it shall hold hearings or receive written statements from the parties (Article 48, para. 1(d) and (e)). The Court has stated that '… a preliminary hearing is a procedural requirement only when the Commission considers it necessary to complete the information or when the parties expressly request a hearing'.[82]

In this stage of the procedure, '… the Commission shall place itself at the disposal of the parties … with a view to reaching a friendly settlement of the matter, on the basis of respect for the human rights recognized' in the Convention (Article 48, para. 1(f)). The friendly settlement procedure, in which the Commission acts '... as an organ of conciliation',[83] is not, as the Court has declared, a compulsory procedure: 'It is clear that the Commission shall attempt such friendly settlement only when the circumstances of the controversy make that option suitable or necessary, at the Commission's sole discretion.'[84] If a friendly settlement is reached, the Commission shall prepare a report, containing a description of the facts and of the solution attained, which shall be transmitted to all States Parties and communicated to the OAS Secretary-General for publication (Article 49). The Commission's exercise of its functions as an organ of conciliation has been minimal.[85]

The procedure to be followed if the parties cannot reach a friendly settlement is established in Articles 50 and 51 of the Convention. This procedure has been described as 'very cumbersome and ambiguous'.[86]

Article 50 provides that, when no settlement in the matter is attained, the Commission shall draw up 'a report setting forth the facts and stating its conclusions', that may include proposals and recommendations, which shall be transmitted to the parties concerned. These latter shall not be authorized to publish it. If, within three months from the date the report was transmitted to the state concerned, the matter has not either been settled or submitted to the Court by the Commission or by the state concerned, the Commission '... may by the vote of an absolute majority of its members, set forth its opinion and conclusions' concerning the case (Article 57, para. 1). This second report, unlike the one referred to in Article 50, is not mandatory. If the Commission adopts this report, 'where appropriate', it '... shall make pertinent recommendations and shall prescribe a period within which the State is to take the measures that are incumbent upon it to remedy the situation examined' (para. 2). Finally, at the expiration of the prescribed period, the Commission shall decide by a majority vote '... whether the State has taken adequate measures and whether to publish its report' (para. 3).[87]

The Commission's resolutions are contained in its Annual Report. For those State Parties which have not accepted the jurisdiction of the Court, the publication of a condemnatory resolution adopted by the Commission marks the conclusion of the case.

Since its creation over 40 years ago, the Commission has accomplished important work in the promotion of human rights in the region and, particularly, in condemning massive violations by dictatorial regimes in Latin America. Its principal tasks have been the handling of thousands of individual complaints, the preparation of reports on the human rights conditions in a number of OAS member states (country studies) and the conduct of on-site observations. The Commission also has a leading role in proposing to the political organs of the OAS the adoption of legal instruments in the field of human rights as, for instance, the prevention and punishment of torture, the forced disappearance of persons and the protocol on economic, social and cultural rights, as well as in preparing draft articles on these matters.[88]

The Inter-American Court of Human Rights

Chapter VIII of the Convention deals with the Inter-American Court of Human Rights. As the Court itself has stated:

> ... [it] is, first and foremost, an autonomous judicial institution with jurisdiction both to decide any contentious case concerning the interpretation and application of the Convention as well as to ensure to the victim of a violation of the rights or freedoms guaranteed by the Convention the protection of those rights. (Convention, Article 62 and Statute of the Court, Article 1). Because of the binding character of its decisions in contentious cases (Convention, Article 68), the Court also is the Convention organ having the broadest enforcement powers designed to ensure the effective application of the Convention.[89]

The norms on the organization of the Court are contained in Section 1 of Chapter VIII (Articles 52–60). Article 52 prescribes that the Court shall consist of seven judges, nationals of the OAS member states, elected in an individual capacity among jurists of the highest moral authority and of recognized competence in the field of human rights, who possess the qualifications required for the exercise of the highest judicial functions in their respective countries or in the state proposing them as candidates (para. 1). No two judges may be nationals of the same state (para. 2).

The judges are elected by the States Parties to the Convention, in the OAS General Assembly, from a list of candidates proposed by those States (Article 53, para. 1). Each State Party may nominate up to three candidates, nationals of the state which proposes them or of any other OAS Member State (para. 2). The term of office of the judges is six years and they may be re-elected only once (Article 54, para. 1). A judge elected to replace a judge whose term has not expired shall complete the term of the latter (para. 2). The judges shall continue in office until the expiration of their term. Though replaced, they shall finish any pending cases they have begun to hear (para. 3).

If a judge is a national of any of the States Parties to a case before the Court, he shall retain his right to hear it (Article 55, para. 1). If one of the judges called upon to hear a case is a national of one of the States Parties to the case, any other State Party in the case may appoint an ad hoc judge (para. 2). If none of the judges is a national of any of the States Parties to the case, each of the latter may appoint an ad hoc judge (para. 3). Ad hoc judges shall possess the same qualifications as the elected judges (para. 4). If several States Parties have the same interest in a case, they shall be considered a single party for the purposes of the above provisions (para. 5).[90] Five judges shall constitute a quorum (Article 56).

Article 57 provides that 'The Commission shall appear in all cases before the Court'. In accordance with this norm, Article 28 of the Rules of Procedure of the Court prescribes that the Commission shall appear 'as a party' before the Court in all cases within its adjudicatory jurisdiction. As the Court itself stated, the Convention has given the Commission '... in proceedings before the Court a quasi-judicial role, like that assigned to the

"Ministerio Público" of the Inter-American system, obligated to appear in all cases ...'.[91] As a matter of fact, as the Court has consistently applied the procedure prescribed for the contentious jurisdiction to the advisory opinions, the Commission has appeared before the Court in both of these proceedings.

In conformity with Article 58, the States Parties established the seat of the Court in San José, Costa Rica. However, the Court may convene in the territory of any OAS member state (para. 1). The Court shall appoint its own Secretary (para. 2). The staff of the Court's Secretariat shall be appointed by the OAS Secretary-General (Article 59). The Court, as provided in Article 60, drafted its statute and adopted its Rules of Procedure.[92]

Section 2 of Chapter VIII (Articles 61–65) is entitled 'Jurisdiction and Functions'. The contentious jurisdiction of the Court is not compulsory for States Parties which are not subject to it unless they make a declaration to this effect. Article 62, para. 1, prescribes:

> A State Party may, upon depositing its instrument of ratification or adherence to this Convention, or at any subsequent time, declare that it recognizes as binding, *ipso facto*, and not requiring special agreement, the jurisdiction of the Court on all matters relating to the interpretation or application of the Convention.[93]

The declaration '... may be made unconditionally, on the condition of reciprocity, for a special period, or for specific cases' (para. 2). The Court's jurisdiction '... shall comprise all cases concerning the interpretation and application of the provisions of the Convention that are submitted to it, provided that the States Parties to the case recognize or have recognized such jurisdiction, whether by special declaration pursuant to the preceding paragraphs, or by a special agreement' (para. 3).[94]

The right to submit a case to the Court is limited to States Parties and the Commission (Article 61, para. 1). Individuals do not have such a right. 'In order for the Court to hear a case, it is necessary that the procedures set forth in Articles 48 to 50 shall have been completed' (para. 2). These articles, as mentioned above, govern the procedure for the Commission's treatment of complaints – whether individual or interstate. One of the questions raised by Article 61, para. 2, is whether the Commission's proceedings can be avoided by the unilateral waiver of the state concerned. This question was examined by the Court in its first decision in 1981. The Government of Costa Rica had requested the Court to hear a case of a woman who was killed in prison by a member of the Civil Guard. In its application, the government asked the Court to decide whether this act constituted a violation of the Convention, and declared that it formally waived the requirement of the prior completion of the Commission's procedures. The Court stated that those procedures had not been created only for the benefit of the states, but also to allow '... for the exercise of important individual rights, especially those of the victims' and decided, unanimously, not to admit the government's application and granted its subsidiary plea to refer the matter to the Commission.[95]

Article 63, para. 1, prescribes that, in case the Court finds that a violation of a right or freedom protected by the Convention has been committed, it '... shall rule that the injured party be ensured the enjoyment of his right or freedom that was violated. It shall also rule, if appropriate, that the consequences of the measure or situation that constituted the breach of such rights or freedoms be remedied and that fair compensation be paid to the injured party'. On this provision, the Court has declared '... that in order to fix the corresponding indemnity, the Court must rely upon the American Convention and the applicable principles of international law'.[96]

The Court is empowered to adopt provisional measures '... in cases of extreme gravity and urgency, and when necessary to avoid irreparable damage to persons' (Article 63, para. 2). Those measures can be indicated in cases before the Court, as well as on petitions submitted to the Commission and pending. However, it would seem '... that this jurisdiction would be limited to those States Parties which have accepted the Court's jurisdiction'.[97] The Court has exercised its powers under this provision in the Honduran cases to '... protect the basic rights of those who have appeared or have been summoned to do so'.[98]

Section 3 of Chapter VIII of the Convention, under the title of 'Procedure', contains certain rules on the Court's judgment: the Court is obliged to state reasons for the judgment (Article 66, para. 1); judges are entitled to attach separate or dissenting opinions (Article 66, para. 2); the judgement '... shall be final and not subject to appeal' and shall be interpreted by the Court if requested by any of the parties (Article 67); states which are parties to the case must undertake to comply with the judgment (Article 68, para. 1); '... the part of a judgement that stipulates compensatory damages may be executed in the country concerned in accordance with domestic procedure governing the execution of judgement against the State' (Article 68, para. 2); '... the parties to the case shall be notified of the judgement' and it shall be also '... transmitted to the States Parties to the Convention' (Article 69).[99]

There is no mechanism in the Convention for the enforcement of judgments or preliminary measures ordered by the Court. However, Article 65 provides that the Court, in its Annual Report to the General Assembly, the supreme organ of the OAS, '... shall specify, in particular, the cases in which a State has not complied with its judgement, making any pertinent recommendations'. Thus, the OAS political organs – the General Assembly or the Permanent Council when the Assembly is not in session – could be in a position to adopt any resolution on the question within their spheres of competence under the OAS Charter.

Article 64 of the Convention deals with the advisory jurisdiction of the Inter-American Court. It prescribes that OAS member states '... may consult the Court regarding the interpretation of this Convention or of other treaties concerning the protection of human rights in American States'. Also, all the OAS organs within their areas of competence have the right to consult the Court in like manner (para. 1). Furthermore, at the request of an OAS member state, the Court '... may provide that State with opinions regarding the compatibility of any of its domestic laws' with the Convention or other treaties on the protection of human rights in American states (para. 2). As has been rightly observed, the jurisdiction of the Court '… to render advisory opinions is more extensive than that of any other international tribunal in existence today'.[100] The Court has declared that '… the advisory jurisdiction conferred on the Court by Article 64 of the Convention is unique in contemporary international law'[101] and has also pointed out that '… the evolution of the text that ultimately became Article 64 indicates a marked desire to expand the advisory jurisdiction of the Court'.[102] This explains the importance of the consultative competence of the Court in the American regional system for the protection of human rights. The Court has rendered various opinions – most of them on the interpretation of several provisions of the Convention at the request of states and the Commission. Reference is made to a number of these opinions in this chapter. They constitute a remarkable *corpus juris* which has contributed not only to the consolidation of the system as a whole but also to its credibility and prestige.

Which are the procedural norms to be applied by the Court in the exercise of its consultative functions? Article 55 of the Rules of Procedure, entitled 'Application by Analogy', prescribes that its provisions dealing with the procedure in contentious cases shall apply to advisory proceedings to the extent that the Court '… deems them to be compatible'. It has stated that, in contentious cases, '… the exercise of the Court's jurisdiction ordinarily depends upon a preliminary and basic question involving the State's acceptance of or consent to such jurisdiction'. If the consent has been given, the states which participate in the proceedings become, technically speaking, parties to the proceedings, and are bound to comply with the resulting decision of the Court (Convention, Article 68, para. 1). By the same token, the Court cannot exercise its jurisdiction where such consent has not been given. It would make no sense, therefore, to examine the merits of the case without first establishing whether the parties involved have accepted the Court's jurisdiction. The Court concluded that '… there is nothing in the Convention that would justify the extension of the jurisdictional preconditions applicable to the Court's contentious jurisdiction to the exercise of its advisory functions'. On the contrary, it is quite clear that the exercise of the Court's advisory jurisdiction is subject to its own prerequisites which relate to the identity and legal capacity of the entities having standing to seek the opinion – that is, OAS member states and OAS organs acting within their 'spheres of competence'.[103]

The Court has acknowledged the fact that an interpretation rendered in an advisory opinion might affect a state's interest in one way or another and that, for example, '… its legal position in a current or future controversy might be either weakened or strengthened'. However, it stated that the legitimate interests of a state are properly protected since it has the right to participate fully in the advisory opinion proceedings and make its views known to the Court.[104]

As the Court declared, unanimously, in its first opinion, its advisory jurisdiction:

... can be exercised in general, with regard to any provision dealing with the protection of human rights set forth in any international treaty applicable in the American States, regardless of whether it be bilateral or multilateral, whatever be the principal purpose of such a treaty, and whether or not non-Member States of the Inter-American system are or have the right to become parties thereto.[105]

On the question which the Court has referred to as 'the line which divides the advisory jurisdiction from the contentious jurisdiction', the Court made reference to the most recent instances in which the International Court of Justice – notwithstanding the objections to the exercise of its advisory jurisdiction on the ground that it served as a method of evading the application of the principle requiring the consent of all States Parties involved in a legal dispute before it could be adjudicated – decided to render the opinion. The Inter-American Court pointed out that its advisory jurisdiction is closely related to the purposes of the Convention: 'This jurisdiction is intended to assist the American States in fulfilling their international human rights obligations and to assist the different organs of the Inter-American System to carry out the functions assigned to them in this field.' It held that, consistent with the jurisprudence of the World Court, '... its advisory jurisdiction is permissive in character in the sense that it empowers the Court to decide whether the circumstances of a request for an advisory opinion justify a decision rejecting the request'.[106]

As regards opinions requested by an OAS member state under Article 64, para. 2, on the compatibility of any of its domestic laws with the Convention or other treaties concerning the protection of human rights in the American States, the Court has declared that a restrictive reading of that provision which would permit such requests '... only in relation to laws already in force, would unduly limit the advisory function of the Court'.[107] Consequently, it concluded that '... the mere fact that a legislative proposal is not as yet in force does not *ipso facto* deprive the Court of jurisdiction to deal with a request for an advisory opinion related to it'.[108]

Chapter IX of the Convention entitled 'Common Provisions' contains four articles applicable to the privileges and immunities of the judges and the members of the Commission (Article 70); incompatibilities of their positions with other activities which might affect their independence or impartiality (Article 71); emoluments and travel allowances (Article 72); and sanctions (Article 73).

The final clauses of the Convention are embodied in Part III entitled 'General Transitory Provisions'. Chapter IX (Articles 74–78) deals with 'Signature, Ratification, Reservations, Amendments, Protocols and Denunciation'. The Convention is open for signature, ratification or adherence by any OAS member state and requires the deposit of 11 instruments of ratification or adherence for its entry into force. For those states ratifying or adhering thereafter, the Convention shall enter into force on the date of the deposit of the corresponding instrument (Article 74, paras 1 and 2). Article 75 prescribes that the Convention '... shall be subject to reservations only in conformity with the Vienna Convention on the Law of Treaties.[109] Proposal of amendments to the Convention may be submitted to the OAS General Assembly and shall come into force when ratified by two-thirds of the States Parties to the Convention (Article 76). Article 77 refers to the submission by States Parties of proposed protocols to the Convention, in accordance with Article 31, '... with a view to gradually including other rights and freedoms within its system of protection'. States Parties may denounce the Convention with one-year notice (Article 78).

FINAL REMARKS

The important work of the Inter-American system for the protection of human rights during more than 30 years shows that regional institutions in this area cannot only coexist with the UN universal system but also that their interaction can improve the efficacy of the protection.

On this subject, the Inter-American Court stated that '... a certain tendency to integrate the regional and universal systems for the protection of human rights can be perceived in the Convention'. The Preamble recognizes that the principles on which the treaty is based are also proclaimed in the Universal Declaration on Human Rights and that '... they have been reaffirmed and refined in other international instruments, world wide as well as regional in scope'.[110] The Court especially mentioned Article 29 containing the rules governing the interpretation of the Convention '... which clearly indicates an intention not to restrict the protection of human rights to determinations that depend on the source of the obligations'. Article 29, para. (b), is an example of this 'integrated' approach. It prescribes that no provision of the Convention may be interpreted as '... restricting the enjoyment or exercise of any right or freedom recognized by virtue of the laws of any State Party or by virtue of another convention to which one of the said States is a party'.

One of the main achievements of the OAS has been the creation of a system for the promotion and protection of human rights. In this respect, the Inter-American Commission – a pioneer of the system – accomplished a commendable job despite the limited powers with which it had to confront massive and individual violations of human rights. With the entry into force of the American Convention, the Commission acquired a new status within the system which was further improved with the establishment of a judicial organ: the Inter-American Court.

In the opinion of Gros Espiell, the lack of coordination in the work of these two bodies is '... the principal defect in the present functioning of the system of the Convention'. Regarding contentious matters, he continues, '... there is no normal flux of cases from the Commission to the Court' and a number of unresolved complaints '... do not get to the Court as they should'.[111] This is particularly relevant today for, as Buergenthal anticipated some years ago, the OAS Charter-based regime for the protection of human rights has become less important as a result of the increasing number of American states which are parties to the Convention.[112]

The return to democracy in several Latin American countries, which until recently were under military rule or dictatorial regimes, has considerably improved the human rights situation in the region. As a result of this development, the number of ratifications to the Convention and declarations of acceptance of the jurisdiction of the Inter-American Court has increased, and new legal instruments, such as the Protocol of San Salvador, the Convention to prevent and punish torture, the Protocol to abolish the death penalty and the Convention on the forced disappearance of persons, have been adopted.

However encouraging, the current state of affairs cannot guarantee the efficacy of the system. Economic, social and educational progress in the countries of the region are also essential requirements for the full and free exercise of human rights and freedoms. The future of the Inter-American system for the protection of human rights is closely linked to the fulfilment of these requirements.

NOTES

1 See Preamble, para. 4 and Articles 3(d) and (k) of the OAS Charter; Article XXVIII of the American Declaration; Preamble, para. 1 and Articles 29(d) and 32(r) of the American Convention and Preamble, para. 1 of the 'Protocol of San Salvador'.

2 Inter-American Court of Human Rights (I/A Court HR) Compulsory Membership in an Association Prescribed by Law for the Practice of Journalism (Articles 13 and 29, American Convention on Human Rights), Advisory Opinion OC-5/85 of 13 November 1985. Series A No. 5, para. 44.

3 Preamble to the American Convention on Human Rights, para. 1.

4 I/A Court HR, The word 'laws' in Article 30 of the American Convention on Human Rights, Advisory Opinion OC-6/86 of 9 May 1986. Series A No. 6, para. 34. The Court has corroborated these views in two other opinions in which it declared that '… in a democratic society, the rights and freedoms inherent in the human person, the guarantees applicable to them and the rule of law form a triad. Each component defines itself, complements and depends on the others for its meaning.' I/A Court of HR, Habeas Corpus in Emergency Situations (Articles 27, paras 2, 25, paras 1 and 7, para. 6), American Convention on Human Rights), Advisory Opinion OC 8/87 of 30 January 1987. Series A No. 8, para. 26 and I/A Court HR, Judicial Guarantees in States of Emergency (Articles 27, para. 2, 25 and 8, American Convention on Human Rights), Advisory Opinion OC-9/87 of 6 October 1987. Series A No. 9, para. 35.

5 Article 1, para. 2, of the Statute of the Inter-American Commission on Human Rights.

6 Thomas Buergenthal observes that the two regimes '… overlap to a certain extent and share various institutions … . At times both regimes are applicable to one and the same case, strengthening the institutional pressures that can be brought to bear on governments charged with violating human rights' (Buergenthal, 1981, p.80). The Inter-American Court of Human Rights has confirmed this view when it stated that '… for Member States of the Organization, the Declaration is the text that defines the human rights referred to in the Charter … . For the State Parties to the Convention, the specific source of

their obligations with respect to the protection of human rights is, in principle, the Convention itself. It must be remembered, however, that given the provisions of Article 29(d), these States cannot escape the obligations they have as members of the OAS under the Declaration, notwithstanding the fact that the Convention is the governing instrument for the States Parties thereto'. I/A Court HR, Interpretation of the American Declaration of the Rights and Duties of Man Within the Framework of Article 64 of the American Convention on Human Rights, Advisory Opinion OC-10/89 of 14 July 1989. Series A No. 10, paras 45 and 46.

7   Article 5(j) of the 1948 text, now Article 3(k) of the OAS Charter as amended by the Protocols of Buenos Aires (1967) and Cartagena de Indias (1985).

8   Resolution XXX, Final Act of the Ninth International Conference of American States, Bogotá, Colombia, 30 March–2 May 1948 in *International Conferences of American States*, Second Supplement, 1942–1954, Washington, DC, Pan American Union, 1958, p.260. The evolution towards the adoption of the American Declaration had begun at the Inter-American Conference on Problems of War and Peace (Mexico, 1945) which requested the Inter-American Juridical Committee to draft such a declaration.

9   See note 6, para. 47.

10   Resolution VII, Fifth Meeting of Consultation of Ministers of Foreign Affairs, Santiago, Chile, 12–18 August 1959, Final Act, OAS Official Records, OEA/ Ser. C/II. 5, pp.10–11.

11   Buergenthal (1981, pp.106–107) (footnote omitted): This author indicates that preparing country reports, making general recommendations and the authorization to move to the territory of any American states with the consent of the government concerned, '... provided the Commission with the legislative authority to develop the system of country studies and "on-site" observations' (ibid., p.113).

12   Resolution XXII, Second Special Inter-American Conference, Rio de Janeiro, Brazil, 17–30 November 1965, Final Act, OAS Official Records, OEA/Ser. C/I, pp.32–34.

13   Article 51(e), now Article 52(e) after the 1985 Protocol of Amendment to the Charter of the Organization of American States, 'Protocol of Cartagena de Indias', entered into force in 1988.

14   Article 112, now Article 111 of the OAS Charter, after the 1985 Protocol of Amendment.

15   OAS Charter, Article 150.

16   The American Convention on Human Rights (hereinafter American Convention or Convention) was adopted at an Inter-American Specialized Conference held in San José, Costa Rica. For the *travaux préparatoires*, see Conferencia Especializada Interamericana Sobre Derechos Humanos, San José, Costa Rica, 7–22 November 1969, *Actas y Documentos*, OEA/Ser. KXVI 1.2 (1973). See also OAS (1973); Gros Espiell (1975, pp.23 *et seq.*).

17   The American states that are not parties to the Convention are: Antigua and Barbuda, Bahamas, Belize, Canada, Cuba, Guyana, St Kitts and Nevis, St Lucia, St Vincent and the Grenadines.

18   I/A Court HR, *Velásquez Rodriguez Case*, Judgment of 29 July 1988. Series C, No. 4, para. 162. See also I/A Court HR, *Godinez Cruz Case*, Judgment of 20 January 1989. Series C, No. 5, paras 171–78.

19   Ibid., para. 163.

20   Ibid., para. 165.

21 Ibid., para. 166.
22 Ibid., para. 167.
23 I/A Court HR, Enforceability of the Right to Reply or Correction (Articles 14, para. 1, 1, para. 1, and 2 of the American Convention on Human Rights), Advisory Opinion OC-7/86 of 29 August 1986. Series A, No. 7, paras 28–30. In its separate opinion, Judge Gros Espiell declared that '... the obligation that results from Article 2 ... complements, but in no way substitutes or replaces, the general unconditional obligation imposed by Article 1' (para. 6). In its judgments in the *Velásquez Rodriguez* and *Godinez Cruz* cases (see *supra*, note 18) the Court said that the obligations of the states under Article 1, para. 1: '... is much more direct than that contained in Article 2 ...' (paras 168 and 177, respectively). At the San José Conference, where Article 2 was adopted following a proposal by Chile, the United States delegation stated that this provision gives states the choice between making the rights protected directly effective as domestic law or to implement the treaty consistent with the domestic practice and that '... is not the intention of the United States to interpret the articles of the treaty in Part I as being self-executing'.
24 Gros Espiell (1989, p.249).
25 IACHR, 'Resolution No. 23/81, Case 2141 (US), 6 March 1981, Annual Report 1980–1981, OEA/Ser. L/V/II, 54, doc. 9, rev. 1, 16 October 1981. Following the Commission's interpretation, Gros Espiell states that a law introducing a clause '... for reasons of general interest' with the idea of 'common good' (Article 30 of the Convention), which permits the interruption of life, after the conception and before birth, in very special cases – for example, to save the mother's life, serious deformation of the foetus causing an incurable physical or psychical injury and rape of the mother – would not be contrary to the Convention (Gros Espiell, 1989, p.250).
26 I/A Court HR, Restrictions to the Death Penalty (Articles 4, para. 2, and 4, para. 4 of the American Convention on Human Rights), Advisory Opinion OC-3/83 of 8 September 1983. Series A, No. 3.
27 Ibid., para. 76.
28 I/A Court HR, *Velásquez Rodriguez Case*, *supra*, note 18, para. 157. The Court said: 'Disappearances are not new in the history of human rights violations. However, their systematic and repeated nature and their use not only for causing certain individuals to disappear, either briefly or permanently, but also as a means of creating a general state of anguish, insecurity and fear, is a recent phenomenon. Although this practice exists world-wide, it has occurred with exceptional intensity in Latin America in the last few years' (para. 149). Similar considerations were stated by the Court in I/A HR, *Godinez Cruz Case*, *supra*, note 18, paras 157 and 198. As mentioned earlier, the OAS General Assembly approved the Inter-American Convention on the Forced Disappearance of Persons in 1994 on the basis of a draft prepared by the Inter-American Commission on Human Rights.
29 *Supra*, note 18, *Velásquez Rodriguez Case*, para 155, and *Godinez Cruz Case*, para. 167.
30 *Godinez Cruz Case*, para. 164. See also *Velásquez Rodriguez Case*, para. 156.
31 Adopted at the Fifteenth Regular Session on 9 December 1985. OAS Treaty Series No. 67. In accordance with Article 22, the Convention entered into force on the 30th day following the date on which the second instrument of ratification was deposited – that is on 28 February 1987. As of May 2001, these American states are parties to the Convention: Argentina, Brazil, Chile,

Colombia, Costa Rica, Dominican Republic, El Salvador, Guatemala, Mexico, Panamá, Paraguay, Peru, Suriname, Uruguay and Venezuela.

32   In criticizing the reference to the domestic law, Gros Espiell states that '... it is dangerous and deprived of any sense', although he admits that the problem could be overcome by the prohibition of arbitrary arrest or imprisonment established in Article 7, para. 3 (Gros Espiell, 1989, p.257).

33   I/A Court HR, Habeas Corpus in Emergency Situations (Articles 27, para. 2, 25, para. 1, and 7, para. 6 of the American Convention on Human Rights), Advisory Opinion OC-8/87 of 30 January 1987. Series A, No. 8, para. 35.

34   Ibid., para. 25.

35   Gros Espiell (1989, p.266).

36   This analysis, together with the Commission's resolution is included in the Report on Human Rights in Argentina, OAS Doc., OEA/Ser. L/V/II, 49, doc. 19, corr.1, 11 April 1980, pp.251–54.

37   Resolution 02/79 of 5 March 1979. At the time Argentina was not a State Party to the American Convention on Human Rights. In its reply to the Commission, the Argentinian government stated that, under the Constitution, both nationals and foreigners were guaranteed the rights to profess their religion. It expressed that the registration of the group of Jehovah's Witnesses in the Registry of Non-Catholic Sects of the Ministry of Foreign Affairs and Worship had been denied on the ground that the group acted against principles of the Constitution.

38   I/A Court HR, see *supra*, note 2, Advisory Opinion OC-5/85, para. 30. Following this reasoning the Court stated: 'In its individual dimension, freedom of expression goes further than the theoretical recognition of the right to speak or to write. It also includes and cannot be separated from the right to use whatever medium is deemed appropriate to impart ideas and to have them reach as wide an audience as possible. When the Convention proclaims that freedom of thought and expression includes the right to impart information and ideas through "any ... medium", it emphasizes the fact that the expression and dissemination of ideas and information are indivisible concepts. This means that restrictions that are imposed on dissemination represent, in equal measure, a direct limitation on the right to express oneself freely. The importance of the legal rules applicable to the press and to the status of those who dedicate themselves professionally to it derives from this concept' (para. 31). This advisory opinion, requested by the Government of Costa Rica, related to the interpretation of Articles 13 and 29 of the American Convention.

39   I/A Court HR, Enforceability of the Right to Reply or Correction (Articles 14, para. 1, 1, para. 1, and 2 of the American Convention on Human Rights), Advisory Opinion OC-7/86 of 29 August 1986. Series A, No. 7, para. 35, para. 2.

40   Ibid., para. 30.

41   I/A Court HR, OC-5/85, *supra*, note 2, para. 44.

42   Gros Espiell (1989, pp.278–79). This author recalls that the right of non-association had been included in most of the drafts submitted to the Specialized Inter-American Conference which adopted the American Convention in 1969. However, it did not appear in the final text.

43   I/A Court HR, OC-5/85, *supra*, note 2, Separate Opinion Judge Nieto, para. 4.

44   Ibid., para. 8.

45   A similar principle is proclaimed in Article 15, entitled 'Right to the formation and the protection of families', of the Additional Protocol to the American

Convention on Human Rights in the Area of Economic, Social and Cultural Rights, 'Protocol of San Salvador'. Taking into account the protection extended to children out of wedlock Article 17, para. 5, of the Convention, Gros Espiell is of the opinion that paragraph 1 of this provision refers to the legitimate family, based on marriage, without prejudice to the protection of natural children in the last paragraph of Article 17. Furthermore, paragraphs 2, 3 and 4 are a direct consequence of paragraph 1 and they make reference to marriage and spouses (Gros Espiell, 1989, p.280).

46   I/A Court HR, Proposed Amendments to the Naturalization Provisions of the Constitution of Costa Rica, Advisory Opinion OC-4/84 of 19 January 1984, para. 56.

47   Buergenthal observes, however, that '… to the extent that an injury to a corporation or association does violate an individual's rights under the Convention, it can be assumed to give rise to a cause of action under it' (Buergenthal, 1981, p.82).

48   Gros Espiell recalls that this paragraph was adopted at the Inter-American Conference in San José, Costa Rica, in 1969, by a small majority and marks '… the acceptance of a quite less liberal position regarding foreigners than the one contained in all the previous drafts'. He says that the application of this norm should be made taking into account the UN Convention on the Status of Refugees and respecting the principle of *non-refoulement*. However, he concludes that paragraph 8 limits the possibilities of expulsion under paragraph 6 (Gros Espiell, 1975, p.285).

49   I/A Court HR, Advisory Opinion OC-6/86, *supra*, note 3, para. 34.

50   I/A Court HR, Advisory Opinion OC-4/84, *supra*, note 46, para. 38.

51   I/A Court HR, Advisory Opinion OC-8/87, *supra*, note 33, para. 32. The Court then refers to the writ of *habeas corpus* which it describes as '… a judicial remedy designed to protect personal freedom or physical integrity against arbitrary detentions by means of a judicial decree ordering the appropriate authorities to bring the detained person before a judge so that the lawfulness of the detention may be determined and, if appropriate, the release of the detainee be ordered' (ibid., para. 33). This right, as we have seen, is provided for in Article 7, para. 6.

52   Ibid., para. 34.

53   I/A Court HR, Judicial Guarantees in States of Emergency (Articles 27, para. 2, 25 and 8 of the American Convention on Human Rights), Advisory Opinion OC-9/87 of 6 October 1987. Series A, No. 9, para. 2. On the principle of effectiveness, the Court stated further: '… it should be emphasized that for such a remedy to exist, it is not sufficient that it be provided for by the Constitution or by law or that it be formally recognized, but rather it must be truly effective in establishing whether there has been a violation of human rights and in providing redress. A remedy which proves illusory because of the general conditions prevailing in the country, or even in the particular circumstances of a given case, cannot be considered effective. That could be the case, for example, when practice has shown its ineffectiveness: when the Judicial Power lacks the necessary independence to render impartial decisions or the means to carry out its judgements; or in any other situation that constitutes a denial of justice and when there is an unjustified delay in the decision; or when, for any reason, the alleged victim is denied access to a judicial remedy.'

54   OAS Treaty Series No. 69. The Protocol, signed at San Salvador, on 17 November

1988, entered into force on 16 November 1999. As of mid-2001, it had been ratified by 12 states.

55   Annual Report of the Inter-American Court of Human Rights, 1985. OEA/ Ser. L./V/III.12, doc. 13. 15 August 1985. Annex III.

56   Buergenthal (1981, p.88). This author rightly observes that, given the political realities of the Western hemisphere with its frequent national emergencies and states of siege, it is probably less unreasonable than it appears on first glance to prohibit derogation from rights, such as the right to participate in government, whose suspensions for long periods of time have tended to make it easier for dictatorial regimes to remain in power (footnote omitted).

57   Report on the Situation of Human Rights in Argentina (OEA/Ser. L/V/II 49, dv. 19 con. 1, 11 April 1980) p.177, quoted in OAS (1982, p.342).

58   I/A Court HR, Advisory Opinion OC-8/87, *supra*, note 33, paras. 18–43.

59   In a subsequent opinion, the Court confirmed this conclusion mentioning among the 'essential' judicial guarantees which are not subject to derogation '... any other effective remedy before judges or competent tribunals (Article 25, para. 1), which is designed to guarantee the respect of the rights and freedoms whose suspension is not authorized by the Convention. The Court also declared that these judicial guarantees should be exercised within the framework and the principles of due process of law, expressed in Article 8 of the Convention.' See I/A Court HR, Advisory Opinion OC-9/87, *supra*, note 53 paras 41, paras 1 and 3.

60   Advisory Opinion OC-8/87, *supra*, note 33, para. 44.

61   Buergenthal (1981, p.86). This author explains that Article 28 '... found its way into the treaty because of US insistence'. In explaining the meaning of this provision, the US delegation to San José Conference reported to the Secretary of State that '... the present Convention ... does not obligate the US Government to exercise jurisdiction over subject matter over which it would not exercise authority in the absence of the Convention. The US is merely obligated to take suitable measures to the end that state and local authorities may adopt provisions for the fulfillment of this Convention. The determination of what measures are suitable is a matter of internal decision. The Convention does not require enactment of legislation bringing new subject matter within the federal ambit' (footnotes omitted). Notwithstanding this interpretation, the United States has not ratified the American Convention.

62   Nieto Navia (1993, p.108). As this author observes, these rules do not modify or alter the ones embodied in the Vienna Convention.

63   A similar provision appears in Article 4, 'Inadmissibility of restrictions', of the Additional Protocol to the American Convention on Human Rights, 'Protocol of San Salvador'.

64   Advisory Opinion OC-6/1986, *supra*, note 3, para. 34.

65   Ibid., para. 35.

66   Ibid., para. 37.

67   Advisory Opinion OC-5/85, *supra*, note 2, para. 66.

68   Ibid., para. 67. In its Advisory Opinion of 9 May 1986 (see *supra*, note 3 para. 39), the Court reaffirmed this interpretation emphasizing the importance of the idea of democracy in the context of the Inter-American regional system. The Court declared that general welfare and public order '... are terms of the Convention that must be interpreted with reference to the treaty, which has its own philosophy under which the American States "require the political organization of these States on the basis of the effective exercise of representative

democracy"' (Charter of the OAS, Article 3(d)); and the rights of man, which '... are based upon attributes of his human personality', must be afforded international protection (American Declaration, Second Introductory Clause; American Convention, Preamble, para. 2).

69 The Commission was created by resolution III at that Meeting. After the 1967 Protocol of Amendment to the Charter of the Organization of American States 'Protocol of Buenos Aires', which entered into force in 1970, prior to the adoption of the American Convention, the Commission became an organ of the OAS. The Protocol introduced into the OAS Charter a new chapter XVI entitled 'The Inter-American Commission on Human Rights', which in Article III states that the Commission's principal function '... shall be to promote the observance and protection of human rights and to serve as a consultative organ of the Organization in these matters' and further declares that '... an Inter-American Convention on Human Rights shall determine this structure, competence, and procedure of this Commission, as well as those of other organs responsible for those matters'.

70 In conformity with this provision, the present statute of the Commission, adopted by the OAS General Assembly in 1979, provides that for its purposes, human rights are understood to be: (a) the rights set forth in the American Convention in relation to the States Parties thereto; and (b) the rights set forth in the American Declaration, in relation to the other Member States (Article 1, para. 2). The Statute also distinguishes between the powers of the Commission vis-à-vis States Parties to the Convention (Article 19); vis-à-vis OAS member states which are not parties to the Convention (Article 20), and its powers with respect to all OAS member states. The Commission adopted its Regulations in 1980, which it modified in 1987.

71 Regarding OAS member states which are not parties to the Convention, Article 20(b) of the Statute of the Commission empowers it '... to examine communications submitted to it and any other available information, to address the government of any Member State not a Party to the Convention for information deemed pertinent by this Commission, and to make recommendations to it, when it finds this appropriate, in order to bring about more effective observance of fundamental human rights'.

72 I/A Court HR, Enforceability of the Right to Reply or Correction (Articles 14, para. 1, 1, para. 1, and 2 of the American Convention on Human Rights, Advisory Opinion OC-7/ 86 of 29 August 1986. Series A, No. 7, para. 30.

73 Buergenthal (1981, p.92). This author observes that '... the right of private petition makes the enforcement of human rights less dependent on the extraneous political considerations that tend to motivate governmental action and inaction'. According with Article 26, para. 2 of its Regulations, the Commission, '... also may *motu proprio* take into consideration any available information that it consider pertinent and which might include the necessary factors to begin processing a case which in its opinion fulfills the requirements for the purpose'.

74 The following States Parties have made a declaration recognizing the competence of the Commission under Article 45, para. 1: Argentina, Chile, Costa Rica, Ecuador, Jamaica, Perú, Uruguay and Venezuela. So far no interstate complaints have been received by the Commission.

75 I/A Court HR, *Viviana Gallardo et al.*, Case No. G 101/81, 13 November 1981, Series A, 22. The Court further stated that 'The Commission thus is the channel through which the Convention gives the individual *qua* individual the

possibility to activate the international system for the protection of human rights' (ibid., para. 23).

76   I/A Court HR, *Velásquez Rodriguez Case*, Preliminary Objections, Judgment of 26 June 1987. Series C No. 1 para. 88. These same conclusions were stated by the Court in the *Godínez Cruz Case*, Preliminary Objections, Judgment of 26 June 1987. Series C, No. 3, para. 90 and in the *Fairen Garbi and Solís Corrales Case*, Preliminary Objections, Judgment of 26 June 1987. Series C, No. 2 para. 87.

77   Ibid., para. 84. Similar considerations were also stated by the Court in the *Godinez Cruz Case*, Preliminary Objections, Judgment of 26 June 1987, para. 86 and in the *Fairen Garbi and Solís Corrales Case*, Preliminary Objections, Judgment of 26 June 1987, para. 83. *In Viviana Gallardo et al.*, No. G 101/81 13 November 1981, para. 26, the Court stated that the admissibility requirements of a complaint or application before the Commission '… is in principle for the Commission in the first place to pass on the matter. If, thereafter, in the course of the judicial proceedings, there is a dispute relating to the question whether the admissibility requirements before the Commission have been complied with, it will be for the Court to decide, which for that purpose it has the power to accept or reject the views of the Commission in the manner analogous to its power to accept or reject the Commission's final report'.

78   I/A Court HR, Exceptions to the Exhaustion of Domestic Remedies (Article 46, para. 1, 46, para. 2(a) and 46, para. 2(b) of the American Convention on Human Rights, Advisory Opinion OC-11/90 of 10 August 1990. Series A, No. 11, para. 41.

79   Gros Espiell (1989, p.326) (footnotes omitted). Article 39 of the Regulations of the Commission puts limits to the application of this restriction. It states that the Commission shall not refrain from taking up a petition when: '(a) the procedure followed in the other organization is limited to an examination of the general situation on human rights in the State in question and there has been no decision on the specific facts which are the subject of the petition submitted to the Commission, or is one that will not lead to an effective settlement of the violation denounced; (b) the petitioner before the Commission or a family Member is the alleged victim of the violation denounced and the petitioner before the organizations in reference is a third party or a non governmental entity having no mandate from the former'.

80   I/A Court HR, *Godinez Cruz Case*, Preliminary Objections, *supra*, note 76, para. 43. Similar statements were made by the Court in the *Velásquez Rodriguez Case*, Preliminary Objections and *Fairen Garbi and Solís Corrales Case*, Preliminary Objections, *supra*, note 76, paras 40 and 45, respectively.

81   *Godinez Cruz Case*, Preliminary Objections, *supra*, note 76, para. 62.

82   Ibid., para. 56.

83   Article 45 of the Regulations of the Commission.

84   *Velásquez Rodriguez Case*, Preliminary Objections, *supra*, note 76, para. 44. The Court stated that friendly settlement is one of the mechanisms included in the Convention '… whose operation and effectiveness will depend on the circumstances of each case, and most specially, on the nature of the rights affected, the characteristics of the acts denounced, and the willingness of the government to cooperate in the investigation and to take the necessary steps to resolve it (ibid., para. 60).

85   Gros Espiell characterizes the handling by the Commission of communications and petitions, as irregular and atypic, and too distant from the strict

procedure established in the Convention. He affirms that '... the friendly settlement procedure is an institution which, with some exceptions, is not normally applied' (1989, p.332).

86 Buergenthal (1981, p.95). Gros Espiell (1989, p.333) affirms that the procedure is 'complicated and contradictory'. This author believes that Articles 50 and 51 '... are an incomplete and bad copy of Articles 31 and 32 of the European Convention and that it is indispensable to modify them, in order to be adapted to the reality and to organize an effective procedure that may make it clearly possible a settlement of the case or its jurisdictional solution by the Court' (ibid., p.335).

87 The Court has stated that once an application is filed with the Court, the provisions of Article 51 regarding the Commission's drafting of a new report cease to apply. Such a report is in order '... only after three months have elapsed since transmittal of the communication mentioned in Article 50'. Under Article 51, it is the drafting of the report that is conditional on the failure to file a case with the Court and not the filing of a case that is conditional on the report not having being prepared or published. Consequently, if the Commission were to draft or publish the report mentioned in Article 51 after having filed the application to the Court, it would be misapplying the Convention. Such action would affect the juridical value of the report but not the admissibility of the application (*Velásquez Rodriguez Case, supra*, note 76, para. 76).

88 While praising the important accomplishments of the Commission, specially prior to the adoption and subsequent entry into force of the Convention and with regard to states not parties to it, Gros Espiell observes that the Commission '... has not acted with the required rigour and precision towards State Parties in facing petitions or communications under Article 44'. He states that the Commission '... has not completely understood that the system of the Inter-American Convention requires the simultaneous operation of the Commission and the Court in co-ordination and concert, and that to refer contentious cases to the Court is not the expression of a residual competence of an exceptional character ... but, on the contrary, the manifestations of a competence that must be exercised within the legal frame of the Convention, which foresees a gradual procedure which objective is the solution of the case; if the latter is not resolved in a proper manner, it must result in a judgement of the Inter-American Court, the only jurisdictional legal organ of the system entitled to adopt a definite decision' (Gros Espiell, 1989, pp.335–36).

89 I/A Court HR, 'Other Treaties'. Subject to the Advisory Jurisdiction of the Court (Article 64 of the American Convention on Human Rights), Advisory Opinion OC-1/82 of 24 September 1982. Series A, No. 1 para. 22.

90 The Statute of the Court provides for the appointment of interim judges by the States Parties, in a meeting of the OAS Permanent Council, at the request of the President of the Court, in order to preserve the quorum of the Court (Article 6, para. 3) and to replace one or more judges who have been disqualified to take part in a given matter (Article 19, para. 4). While acknowledging '... its practical usefulness', Nieto Navia wonders whether these provisions do not exceed the power of the Court to draw up its Statute under Article 60 of the Convention considering that the Statute was approved by the OAS General Assembly. See Nieto Navia (1993, p.77).

91 *Viviana Gallardo et al. Case, supra*, note 75, para. 22.

92 The Statute of the Court was approved by the OAS General Assembly at its Ninth Regular Session, held in La Paz, Bolivia, in October 1979. The present Rules of Procedure were adopted by the Court at its 23rd Regular Session held 9–18 January 1991.

93 Until March 1995, the following States Parties had made declarations of acceptance: Argentina, Bolivia, Colombia, Costa Rica, Chile, Ecuador, Guatemala, Honduras, Nicaragua, Panamá, Paraguay, Perú, Suriname, Uruguay, Venezuela, and Trinidad and Tobago.

94 Furthermore, the Commission may call upon a State Party which has not accepted the jurisdiction of the Court to make use of the option under Article 62, para. 2, to recognize the jurisdiction of the tribunal in the specific case that is the subject of the report of the Commission (Article 50, para. 3, of the Rules and Procedure of the Commission).

95 *Viviana Gallardo et al.*, *supra*, note 75, para. 25. The Court declared that the procedures before the Commission '... cannot be dispensed with in this kind of case without impairing the institutional integrity of the protective system guaranteed by the Convention'. Those procedures could not be waived or excused '... unless it were to be clearly established that their omission, in specific case, would not impair the functions which the Convention assigns to the Commission, as might be the case against another State and not by an individual against a State'. The Court also declared that the requirement of the prior exhaustion of local remedies (Article 46, para.1(a)) could be waived by a state, since it is designed for its own benefit (para. 26).

96 *Velásquez Rodriguez Case*, Compensatory Damages, Judgment of 21 July 1989 (Article 63, para.1, of the American Convention on Human Rights). Series C, No. 7 para. 30. In this case, as well as in the *Godinez Cruz Case*, the Court awarded compensatory damages to the family of the victim to be paid by the State of Honduras. In these two judgments rendered on the same day, the Inter-American Court, for the first time, imposed the payment of a pecuniary compensation for the consequences resulting from a violation of human rights.

97 Shelton (1983, p.251).

98 Annual Report of the Inter-American Court of Human Rights, 1988, OAS/ Ser. L/V/III. 19, doc. 13, 31 August 1988, paras 25–26 and 27–28. The Court issued two orders, on 15 and 19 January 1988 addressed to the government of Honduras after the assassination of three of the witnesses submitted by the Commission and the threats against other individuals who had appeared before the Court or who had been summoned to appear in the *Velásquez Rodriguez, Faiven Garbi and Solís Corrales* and *Godinez Cruz* cases. The Court has recently ordered the adoption of provisional measures in several other cases, at the request of the Commission, in relation to petitions pending in the Commission which had not been referred to the Court for adjudication.

99 The rules regulating the examination of the cases by the Inter-American Court are basically found in the Statute of the Court and, particularly, in its Rules of Procedure. They are inspired in the procedure before the International Court of Justice. The procedure consists of two parts: written – consisting of memorials and counter-memorials – and oral – consisting of the hearing by the Court of witnesses and expert witnesses. The official languages of the Court are those of the OAS (English, French, Portuguese and Spanish). The working languages shall be those agreed by the Court, taking into account the language spoken by the judges.

100 Buergenthal (1981, p.102); Shelton (1983, p.253); and Gros Espiell (1989, p.348) share this view.

101 I/A Court HR, Advisory Opinion OC-3/83 of 8 September 1983, *supra*, note 26, para. 43. The Court stated further that '... neither the International Court of Justice nor the European Court of Human Rights has been granted the extensive advisory jurisdiction which the Convention confers on the Inter-American Court ... . Here it is relevant to emphasize that the Convention, by permitting Member States and OAS organs to seek advisory opinions, creates a parallel system to that provided for under Article 62 and offers an alternate judicial method of a consultative nature, which is designed to assist States and organs to comply with and to apply human rights treaties without subjecting them to the formalism and the sanctions associated with the contentious judicial process. It would therefore be inconsistent with the object and purpose of the Convention and the relevant individual provisions, to adopt an interpretation of Article 64 that would apply to it the jurisdictional requirements of Article 62 and thus rob it of its intended utility merely because of the possible existence of a dispute regarding the meaning of the provision at issue in the request.'

102 Advisory Opinion OC-1/82 of 24 September 1982, 'Other Treaties', subject to the Advisory Jurisdiction of the Court (Article 64 American Convention on Human Rights), para. 46. The Court stated that the very fact that Article 64 '... was drafted at a time when the narrowly drawn Article 1 of Protocol No. 2 of the European Convention had already been adopted demonstrates that the drafters of the Convention intended to confer on the Court the most extensive advisory jurisdiction, intentionally departing from the limitations imposed upon the European system'.

103 Advisory Opinion OC-3/ 83, *supra*, note 26, paras 21 and 23.

104 Ibid., para. 24.

105 Advisory Opinion OC-1/82, *supra*, note 89, para. 52. In reference to a number of submissions addressed to the Court contending that a broad interpretation of Article 64 '... would authorize the Court to render opinions affecting States which have nothing to do with the Convention or the Court, and which cannot even be represented before it', the Court stated that '... if a request for an advisory opinion has as its principal purpose the determination of the scope of, or compliance with, international commitments assumed by States outside the Inter-American system, the Court is authorized to render a motivated opinion refraining to pass on the issues submitted to it' (para. 49).

106 Ibid., paras 23, 25 and 28.

107 Advisory Opinion OC-4/84 of 19 January 1984, proposed amendments to the Naturalization Provision of the Political Constitution of Costa Rica, para. 28.

108 Ibid., para. 29. The Court stated further that '... in deciding whether to admit or reject advisory opinion requests relating to legislative proposals as distinguished from laws in force, the Court must carefully scrutinize the request to determine, *inter alia*, whether its purpose is to assist the requesting State to better comply with its international human rights obligations' (para. 30).

109 The Court has interpreted that '... the reference in Article 75 to the Vienna Convention makes sense only if it is understood as an express authorization designed to enable States to make whatever reservations they deem appropriate, provided the reservations are not incompatible with the object and purpose of the treaty'. The Court considered that '... reservations compatible with the object and purpose of the Convention do not require acceptance by the States

Parties' and that the instruments of ratification or adherence containing them enter into force, pursuant to Article 74 of the Convention, as of the moment of their deposit.

110   Advisory Opinion OC-1/82, see *supra*, note 89, para. 41.
111   Gros Espiell (1989, p.407). He observes that '… the Commission, that as Janus, is acting with two faces, one turned toward the States that are not parties to the Convention, and the other toward those which are already States Parties, continues to work, in fact and in general terms, as if the Convention would not exist. Its work is essentially carried on outside the framework of the Convention, on the basis of procedures, methods and working systems anterior to the entry into force of the Convention'.
112   Buergenthal (1981, p.120).

BIBLIOGRAPHY

Aguilar, Andrés (1984), 'Organización y Funcionamiento de la Comisión Interamericana de Derechos Humanos', *Anuario Jurídico Interamericano*, pp.164–91.

Buergenthal, Thomas (1981), 'The Inter-American system for the protection of human rights', *Anuario Jurídico Interamericano*, pp.80–120.

Buergenthal, Thomas, Norris, Robert E. and Shelton, Dinah (1990), *Protecting Human Rights in the Americas. Selected Problems*, 3rd edn, Arlington: Engel.

Cançado Trindade, A.A. (1983), *The Application of the Rule of Exhaustion of Local Remedies in International Law*, Cambridge: Cambridge University Press.

Cançado Trindade, A.A. (1982), 'The evolution of the Organization of American States (OAS) system of human rights protection: an appraisal', *German Yearbook of International Law* (25), pp.498–514.

Fix-Zamudio, Héctor (1986), 'El sistema americano de protección de los derechos humanos', *Cuadernos del Instituto de Investigaciones Jurídicas (UNAM)*, **1** (1), January–April, pp.47–80.

García Bauer, Carlos (1987), *Los Derechos Humanos en América*, Guatemala: CA.

Goldman, Robert K. (1972), 'The protection of human rights in the Americas: past, present and future', *International Studies Policy Papers*, **5** (2), New York: New York University Center for International Studies.

Gros Espiell, Héctor (1975), 'Le système interaméricaine comme régime régional de protection international des droits de l' homme', *Collected Courses at The Hague Academy of International Law*, **145** (VI).

Gros Espiell, Héctor (1989), 'La Convention américaine et la Convention européenne des droits de l'homme: analyse comparative', *Collected Courses at The Hague Academy of International Law*, **218** (VI), pp.167–412.

Inter-American Commission on Human Rights (1984), *Human Rights in the Americas. Homage to the Memory of Carlos A. Dunshee de Abranches*, Washington, DC: OAS.

Jimenez de Aréchaga, Eduardo (1988), 'La Convención Americana de Derechos Humanos como Derecho Interno' in *Normas Vigentes en Materia de Derechos Humanos en el Sistema Interamericano*, Montevideo: Boletin da Sociedade Brasileira de Direito Internacional.

Nieto Navia, Rafael (1993), *Introducción al sistema interamericano de protección a los derechos humanos*, Instituto Interamericano de Derechos Humanos, Bogotá: Editorial Temis SA. Corte Interamericano de Derectos Humanos.

Nieto Navia, Rafael (ed.) (1994), *La Corte y el Sistema Interamericano de Derechos Humanos*, San José, Costa Rica.

Nikken, Pedro (1987), *La Protección Internacional de los Derechos Humanos, su Desarrollo Progresivo*, Instituto Interamericano de Derechos Humanos, Madrid: Editorial Civitas.

Organization of American States (OAS) (1973), *Inter-American Yearbook of Human Rights, 1968*, Washington DC: OAS.

Organization of American States (OAS) (1982), *Inter-American Commission on Human Rights. Ten Years of Activities, 1971–1981*, Washington DC: OAS.

Padilla, David J. (1983), 'The Inter-American Commission on Human Rights of the Organization of American States: a case study', *The American University Journal of International Law and Policy*, **9** (1), Fall, pp.95–115.

Piza, Rodolfo E. and Trejos, Gerardo (1989), *Derecho Internacional de los Derechos Humanos. La Convención Americana*. San José, Editorial Juricentro.

Shelton, Dinah (1983), 'Implementation procedures of the American Convention on Human Rights', *German Yearbook of International Law*, **26**, pp.238–68.

Shelton, Dinah (1980), 'Symposium on the American Convention on Human Rights', *American University Law Review* (30), pp.1–187.

Vasak, Karel (1968), *La Commission interaméricaine des droits de l'homme*, Paris: Revue des droits de l'homme, pp.109–17.

Zovatto, Daniel (1990), *Los estados de excepción y los derechos humanos en América Latina*, Instituto Interamericano de Derechos Humanos, Caracas/San José: Editorial Jurídica Venezolana.

The American Convention and other instruments on human rights of the Organization of American States are included in: *Basic Documents Pertaining to Human Rights in the Inter-American System*, published and annually updated by the OAS General Secretariat. Additional materials appear in the *Inter-American Yearbook of Human Rights* also published by the OAS General Secretariat and in the Annual Reports of the Inter-American Commission of Human Rights and the Inter-American Court of Human Rights to the General Assembly of the Organization of American States. The Commission's reports on countries are published as OAS official documents. The Court's judgments and Advisory Opinions are published by the Secretariat of the Court in San José, Costa Rica.

6 The Protection of Human Rights in Africa: The African Charter on Human and Peoples' Rights

DANIEL D.C. DON NANJIRA

THE PROTECTION OF HUMAN RIGHTS: MEANING AND APPLICATION IN THE AFRICAN CONTEXT

The protection of human values means that human rights must be freed from ad hoc, periodic or constant denial, curtailing, deprivation and other abuses and violations. They are rights and freedoms to which the individual and his/her community are entitled by virtue of the stipulations of the moral, natural, and international law of civilized nations. The individual and his/her society are entitled to a dignified status of life which demands and comprises universal recognition and unqualified protection of the welfare of humankind. The protection of human rights thus means unqualified and universal protection of the dignity of the human person in a just manner.

The value and significance of the international law of human rights lies in the extent of its protection of human and individual rights. This is because human rights, which protect the values of the individual in his/her local, national and global society therefore has, as their ultimate goal, the protection of the dignity of the human person. The protection of human rights through legislation, such as constitutions and laws, should be expected to provide the most effective and reliable normative framework for the observance of human rights. Unfortunately, this is not always the case. Among other forms of human rights protection, four are particularly noteworthy. One is political, to be provided mainly by the executive branch of government and other political authorities: presidents, prime ministers,

213

members of parliament and local authorities. Another is administrative, to be provided mainly by the civil service of a country. Yet another is societal, to be provided by the people and community associations, groups or individuals, non-governmental organizations and so on. Human rights protection can also be provided by the individual. Every human person has the duty to protect his rights and duties, and those of other people. This is because domestic and international law impose an obligation on governments and peoples alike, not only to acknowledge and defend, but also to promote and protect, the rights and corresponding duties of the individual against the abuses, excesses and arrogance of power which may be, and is quite often, committed by organs of the state, and to create conditions appropriate for a multifaceted development of the individual.

For all practical purposes, however, the conditions of humanity in Africa can be divided into three periods of its history: the pre-colonial period; the colonial period; and the post-colonial period. Prior to the arrival of foreigners (Arabs, Europeans, Americans and Asians) and the imposition of their rule on Africans, the latter had lived traditional lives celebrating their ancestors, major events, traditions and sociopolitical, cultural and economic arrangements and associations.[1] The 'Spirit of Africa' had reigned – fairness, justice, honesty, discipline, obedience, collaboration, collective responsibility, African virtues and values, and extended family codes had been shared and enjoyed from time immemorial. That was the essence of African socialism until European colonial rule began to dismantle it. Complete ownership of environs and possessions – the common heritage of *homo africanus* – had existed. Thus, the status of Africa as *terra africana*, the property of *homo africanus* excluded every condition of *terra nullius*.

Alas, things changed after 1492 which introduced a new 'period of discovery' by Europeans. Contacts with Africa and other foreign lands – that is, non-European countries – were formalized. This period thus started the end of pure African human rights observances and deprived Africa of its status of *terra africana* because foreigners made it their land (*terra peregrina*). The arrival of *homo alienus* in Africa therefore marked the beginning of a period in which the rights of the African peoples would not only be disregarded but would also be systematically suppressed and even abolished by foreign interests. *Homines alieni* were mainly interested in exploiting and subjugating Africa through commercial enterprises such as the slave trade, through the quest for fame, and through greed and gratification in terms of territorial aggrandisements, wealth and adventure. Those concerned – that is, American and European explorers, geographers and missionaries who were interested in the 'conversion of souls and their civilization', rebels and the exiled who fled Europe to avoid persecution, poverty and other forms of social and religious injustices – deprived Africa of its identity. They were interested in exploiting Africans, taking over their possessions and perpetuating African dependency on foreigners and administrators who were determined to subjugate them to Europeans rule and ways of living. They deprived Africans of their ways of thinking, living and political processes and procedures. African values were described as 'primitive' by Europeans.

The latter's colonial policies and practices, by depriving Africans of their culture and the traditional human values inherent in the African person from time immemorial, carried out some of the worst human rights violations ever recorded in history. Those policies and practices were institutionalized in the late nineteenth century, following the Berlin Congress of 1884–85 on the 'Scramble for Africa'.

The Berlin Conference was convened by six European powers – Belgium, France, Germany, Italy, Spain and the United Kingdom – which decided to divide Africa into their 'spheres of influence' by fixing artificial borders on arbitrary, geographical lines on the map of Africa, without considering or respecting ethnic or tribal possessions, backgrounds, cultures, traditions or customs.

These geographical divisions either disintegrated nations and peoples who should have been together or united those who should have remained separate. However, in 1964 the Organization of African Unity (OAU), in one of its resolutions provided, *inter alia*, that 'All Member States pledge themselves to respect the frontiers existing on the achievement of national independence'.[2] That decision of the OAU summit to uphold the colonial divisions was historic but has since been questioned. Should African leaders have redefined and redrawn borders, taking into account national entities and tribal demarcations, in order to correct the colonial errors of the Berlin Conference? The answer to this question must be negative, because any attempt to reposition African boundaries would have caused immense conflicts, disagreement and bloodshed and would have proved impossible among the newly liberated African nations. This fear was realized in subsequent years whenever groups of individuals and/or 'liberation' movements demanded self-determination or secession, and/or independence.

The colonial masters implicitly, and often explicitly, encouraged and even supported such secessionist activities and tendencies. The colonial policy of 'divide and rule' not only set the various African tribes and ethnic groups against each other, it also introduced a class system in African society which valued people according to the colour of their skin: the whites were at the top of the ladder; the Asians followed; then came the Arabs; and the Africans were at the bottom.[3] Africans had their lands confiscated by European colonialists and they became squatters or servants on their ancestral lands. Such racial stratification blatantly violated the rights of the African peoples and led in subsequent years to bloody African resistance to racial injustice and discrimination whose repercussions are still felt today.

Despite independence, the remnants of European colonial policies and practices have haunted Africa in the form of tribal wars and conflicts which threaten the disintegration of African countries. The genocides among the Tutsi and Hutu of Rwanda and Burundi are good examples in point. Unfortunately for Africa, the violation of human rights is quite often believed to be more pronounced in post-colonial Africa. Indeed, the behaviour of some African leaders has been far worse in terms of human rights than that of the colonial rulers in pre-independence Africa. Furthermore, Africa's political and economic immaturity at independence not only caused tensions and led to corrupt practices among the first post-independence African leaders, but also led to a series of *coups d'état* against those leaders by military officers whose regimes turned out to be even more corrupt, brutal and dictatorial, overthrowing democratically elected governments and mercilessly slaughtering or imprisoning the first African political leaders as well as innocent African people who became victims of the excessive and arrogant exercise of power on the continent.

WHY A HUMAN RIGHTS PROTECTION REGIME IN AFRICA?

Political independence clearly failed to restore to Africa the status of *terra africana* as might have been expected. Some African leaders were more dictatorial than the European imperialists had been, and set out to demonstrate their superiority in brutal action against the people they ruled. Thus, President Jean Bedel Bokassa of the Central African Republic proclaimed himself Emperor, comparable to, if not more glorious than, Napoleon. Bokassa was prepared to personally torture children and prisoners. President Idi Amin of Uganda is believed to personally have shot and killed opponents. Other African dictators who grossly violated human rights in their respective countries, and thereby prevented the restoration of a *terra africana*, were many and notorious.

The massive human rights violations in post-colonial Africa became embarrassing to some of the African elite and leaders, such as President Leopold Senghor of Senegal, who had great respect for genuine African socialism and moral values and were cognizant of the requirements of international law as well as the stipulations of the existing international instruments on the basic standards of universal behaviour. They were ashamed of the uncivilized and primitive behaviour of some African rulers who denied the continent not only the dignity it deserved in the eyes of the world but also the necessary adjustment to the changing times and circumstances of the universal moral order of the post-Second World War era. Consequently, they felt they had to do something to ensure respect of the rule of law and to protect Africa's image by restoring African liberties and rights in the post-colonial period. They regretted the breakdown of the African code of the extended family and African values. However, this situation continues to decline, as African values are disregarded in theory and practice. Even though practically all African states refer to the Universal Declaration of Human Rights of 1948 in their Constitutions and even include human rights protection clauses in them, in reality, the International Covenants on Human Rights of 1966 and other instruments on human rights and fundamental freedoms are subjected to constant abuse and disregard. All these violations have negative implications for Africa's socioeconomic development. Economic embargos, reductions in, or removals of, overseas development aid (ODA) and so on have been stepped up by the donor community and, though aimed at removing leaders who violate human rights in developing countries, these punitive measures have generally victimized ordinary, innocent Africans rather than the politicians who, personally, are hurt neither economically nor financially.

In recent years, following the collapse of the Berlin Wall and the end of the ideological divide in Europe in November 1989, the close interdependence, especially after the World Conference on Human Rights (Vienna, June 1993), between human rights, development, democracy and good governance has been stressed. It is at present unclear as to how far the current lines of discussion and action on human rights observance worldwide will bring about change to human rights protection in Africa.

One thing is clear, however. As was the case in the late 1960s, 1970s and 1980s, Africans themselves must be responsible for improvements in the human rights conditions on their continent. They must reformulate a human rights protection regime patterned on the spirit of two decades ago, but with stronger enforcement mechanisms. The African Charter on Human and Peoples' Rights, the so-called Banjul Charter (ACHPR), was the best hope for such arrangements, but it did not deliver. Nevertheless, its origins and developments are noteworthy.

PRECURSORS OF THE AFRICAN CHARTER ON HUMAN AND PEOPLES' RIGHTS: FROM LAGOS (1961) TO NAIROBI (1981)

The African Charter on Human and Peoples' Rights, otherwise known as the ACHPR or the Banjul Charter, because its final draft was endorsed in Banjul, the capital of the Gambia, did not spring full-blown from the Charter which established the Organization of African Unity (OAU), the first and most important political organization in post-independence Africa. The OAU Charter was adopted by African heads of state or government on 25 May 1963 in Addis Ababa, Ethiopia, where the seat of the OAU has remained ever since.

The events preceding the adoption of a legal instrument to protect human rights in Africa occurred over a 20-year period:

- In 1961 the International Commission of Jurists (ICJ) organized an African Conference on the Rule of Law in Lagos, Nigeria, which produced the so-called 'Law of Lagos' containing the origins of the idea of a legal instrument on human rights protection in Africa: '… in order to give full effect to the Universal Declaration of Human Rights, this Conference invites the African Governments to study the possibility of adopting an African Convention on Human Rights …'.
- In March 1967 the United Nations Commission on Human Rights decided to study the possibility of establishing regional commissions on human rights where they did not already exist.[4]
- On 2–15 September 1969 a seminar was cosponsored by the government of Egypt and the United Nations and attended by representatives of 20 African states, the League of Arab States and the Council of Europe. They agreed to create a Commission on Human Rights in

Africa, which would promote greater respect for human rights, and also serve as a weapon with which to attack political opponents of governments and disseminate propaganda for African governments.

- In 1978 the Assembly of the Heads of State and Government of the OAU adopted Decision 115 (XVI) Rev. 1 on the preparation of a draft of an African Charter of Human Rights and Rights of Peoples.[5]
- In July 1979 a highly qualified group of experts was commissioned to draft the Charter.
- On 10–21 September 1979 a United Nations Seminar on the Establishment of Regional Commissions on Human Rights with Special Reference to Africa was held in Monrovia, Liberia.[6] The Seminar, attended by representatives of 30 African states, the OAU, non-governmental organizations and international organizations, posed a direct challenge to, and modification of, the sacrosanct principle of territorial integrity and sovereignty of African states. It adopted three important conclusions:
  - In cases of human rights violations in a particular African state, the principle of non-interference in the internal affairs of a sovereign state could not, and should not, exclude or prevent international action.
  - It was essential that a commission be created to protect human rights in Africa.
  - The commission, once created, must perform four basic functions:
    - study the causes and manifestations of human rights violations in Africa
    - offer good offices to member states, individually or collectively, in cases of human rights violations – for example, through acts of reconciliation, arbitration for settlement of disputes, payments of compensation for loss or damage, deprivation of rights and so on
    - make recommendations to the OAU on courses of action to be taken
    - serve as the agent of governments for propaganda and other promotional activities for African states.

  Here, it was already clear that African governments, though desirous of having a human rights protection regime, did not wish it to be independent of their influence;
- In November 1979 a ministerial conference, held in Dakar, Senegal, adopted the so-called Dakar Draft Articles comprising the first draft of the proposed African Charter,[7] following discussion there of the report of the Monrovia Seminar. In that same year, Bokassa, Idi Amin and Macias Nguema, among Africa's most notorious despots, were ousted from power.
- June 1980 and January 1981 African governments met in Banjul to discuss the Dakar Draft Articles.
- In June 1981 the Plenary Session of the OAU Council of Ministers in Nairobi, Kenya, received and discussed the draft Charter, which was

finally approved without amendment by the 18th OAU Assembly of Heads of State and Government in Nairobi on 16 June 1981.[8]

THE HISTORICAL SIGNIFICANCE OF THE AFRICAN CHARTER ON HUMAN AND PEOPLES' RIGHTS (ACHPR)

General Observations: The *Sui Generis* Character of the Charter

It took 20 years to agree on the creation of a legal instrument for human rights in Africa. The ACHPR became effective on 21 October 1986, after the deposit of the 26th instrument of ratification, as required by Article 63, para. 3. By then, however, 30 countries had deposited their instruments of ratification. By the end of 2001, 52 states had ratified the Charter.

The Charter possesses a *sui generis* character and is a unique and innovative concept not just in Africa but also in other contexts. It departed from the traditional and contemporary provisions and stipulations in multilateral instruments on human rights in that the ACHPR, *expressis verbis*, introduced the concept of 'people' and 'peoples' rights' and 'man's duties' in the theory and reality of public international law and international human rights. The African drafters of the Charter were fully aware that no institutional arrangement(s) to promote and/or protect human rights had existed in Africa before the adoption of the ACHPR. They were convinced, and rightly so, that the conditions of human rights in Africa could not, cannot and should not be judged or determined solely on the basis of the Western concept of human rights patterned on Western civilizations and cultures. Also, and as indicated above, human values in pre-colonial times in Africa were indeed recognized and observed according to African socialism, African family values, and customs and traditions.

Human rights codes in African societies were granted to groups, not individuals, and the rights, privileges and duties corresponding to the codes were not for individuals but for communities and groups. The rights granted included the right to life, property, privacy and security of family life, family and community property, and the duty to care for the family and maintain the corporate spirit of the African community.

Unlike the normal preambles to international instruments, the Preamble to the ACHPR stands on its own as a project on human rights, calling for the recognition of the existence of the African people in their own right, and for the eradication of any policies or practices that would deny the rights and duties of Africans. Among the policies to be abolished were all forms of colonialism, which must be replaced by international cooperation to promote the application, across the board and globally, of the principles and purposes of the United Nations Charter and of the Universal Declaration on Human Rights.

Apart from the Preamble, the ACHPR comprises 68 articles divided into three sections. The first section is on 'Rights and Duties' and comprises Articles 1–29. The second section, comprising Articles 30–63, deals with

'Measures of Safeguard' of human rights, and the third section is on 'General Provisions' which relates to measures concerning the signature and ratification of the Charter and so on. The section on 'Measures of Safeguard' can be considered too long, as it merely deals with the African Commission on Human and Peoples' Rights, its composition, competence, principles, procedures and so on. This was supposed to be the enforcement machinery for human rights protection in Africa but it was unfortunately denied the empowerment of independent action by the member states.

Article 30 opens the section on 'Measures of Safeguard' by stating that the purpose of the Charter is '... to promote human and peoples' rights and ensure their protection in Africa'. This concept is elaborated in Article 12 of the Charter which prohibits the expulsion of any foreigner legally present or resident in a territory of a State Party to the Charter, although the same provision allows expulsion if a decision is taken to demand it in accordance with the law. Mass expulsions – that is, those aimed at national, racial, ethnic or religious groups – are, however, totally prohibited.

Thus the overall message of the ACHPR, though fraught with short-comings, was most encouraging. The very fact that African regimes, led at that time by many leaders whose despotic characters and unwillingness to respect the Universal Declaration of Human Rights and to protect human rights, had agreed to endorse such a Charter, was an important milestone in the development of new legal concepts which would, in turn, renovate international law and challenge the dictatorial rejections of, and practices against, genuine democracy and the supremacy of individual rights. The distinct stress on, and enumeration of, individual duties to preserve the harmonious development of the family and work for the cohesion and respect of the family by the individual, who must 'respect his parents at all times, to maintain them in case of need', were novel and innovative in international law, as was the demand on African citizens (that is, peoples) 'to preserve African values and traditions and civilizations'. Here, the Charter follows in the footsteps of African customs and tradition which bestow duties and protect the rights of the individual – the African person. African communal traditions emphasize the responsibility of every individual citizen to the family, local collectivities and the national community.

The ACHPR also departs from the normal practice of despotic and autocratic regimes by allowing to individual and collective African citizens fundamental freedoms and accepting some obligations vis-à-vis African citizens, as stated in Article 47. But perhaps the most important concession to the African leaders at that time was its acceptance of the legal basis for foreign intervention in support of anybody fighting for the democratization process in Africa. This was a major departure from the sacrosanct principle of non-interference in the internal affairs of states. The Charter in effect gives African states the right to intervene in domestic affairs of other African nations if human rights are, or are believed to be, violated.

The Charter also required member states to guarantee the independence of the courts and the judiciary – another unusual and quite novel occurrence in African legislation.

CONCEPTUAL CONFLICTS IN 'POPULAR', 'INDIVIDUAL', 'STATE' AND 'MINORITY' RIGHTS

Duties in the African Charter on Human and Peoples' Rights

Definitions

As explained above, the reference to 'duties' in the ACHPR is one of the novel characteristics of this international instrument. Thus, the term 'human rights' in the Charter refers not only to human rights and freedoms but also to the duties corresponding to those rights and to the kinds of right enumerated by the Charter – that is, 'popular', 'individual', 'state', 'universal' rights and so on. Moreover, it is not always easy to distinguish between these rights.

Thus, the authors of the Charter had clear reasons for differentiating 'peoples'' from 'human' rights. Whose rights does the Charter cover – 'popular', 'state' or 'individual' rights, liberties and duties? Perhaps it is in these differentiations and definitions that the Charter differs completely from any other instrument of international law that we know of today.

The expression 'popular' or 'peoples'' has a quite different meaning in the African context, as described in the ACHPR, from the one it carries in contemporary international instruments on human rights. The American Declaration of Independence of 1776, the French Declaration of 1789, the Charter of the United Nations of 1945 and its Preamble, many resolutions of the United Nations, the Universal Declaration of Human Rights of 1948, the Algiers Declaration on the Rights of Peoples of July 1976 and many other international legal instruments have referred to the 'rights of man and rights of peoples' in one way or another, whether they have described in terms of 'We, the people', 'the self-determination of peoples' or 'the rights of peoples to self-determination'. Why 'popular' or 'peoples'' in a charter on human rights? This is a fair question. However, it is this concept that adds a unique meaning and importance to the ACHPR. Under normal circumstances, the notion of peoplehood has at least four characteristics: a group identity; distinctiveness; a communality of interests; and some territorial linkage. Thus, any homogenous group having a common language, common culture, common history, common customs and traditions, and the like, is a people.

'Peoples' can also mean all peoples or persons, not a state, but within a state or country and as a separate community and source of rights and corresponding duties, with their own legitimacy and identity.

'Peoples' may also mean the state in which control over the natural resources of a nation is exercised by the state on behalf of the people. This definition implies the right to development as a human right, and self-determination in economic terms.

'Peoples' can further mean oppressed or colonized people in politico-economic terms, within specific geographic limits. The stress here is on political self-determination and a demand and desire to have the right to political freedom and self-determination. Furthermore, 'peoples' can be used to refer to different minorities with rights and characteristics quite different from general human rights. Minority rights – for example religion, custom and tradition – are often unique to the people in question. The first exhaustive international treatment of the question of minority rights took place within the system of the League of Nations. The League's Principles on Protection of Minorities and Their Rights are still applicable under international law.

Finally, a 'people' may mean all the different communities or peoples – that is, all the persons within the boundaries of a country or geographical entity that is still a dependent territory. Once it attains majority rule or independence, no further independence may be permissible. What becomes necessary is to recognize the rights of the different peoples as minority rights, and protect them as such.

The definition of 'people' or 'peoples' in the Charter is given in the African philosophical concept of 'peoples'. Thus, even though no universally accepted definition of 'people' or 'peoples' exists, the African notion may be the most sensible and original. According to African socialism, a person belongs to a community or society, and he/she is governed by societal rules of existence and behaviour, better known as the extended African family codes. A person is an integral member of a group animated by a spirit of African solidarity. His/her individual rights must conform to community or peoples' rights. Culturally, therefore, group socialism necessarily suppresses individualism. This great African perspective was particularly stressed by Mozambique and Ethiopia at the adoption of the Charter. They insisted on the protection of these African values and virtues by any and every African law which would be made on the protection of human rights.

That argument was particularly valuable, since human rights as defined by Western concepts stress and consist of individual rights. The Charter affirms the conceptual difference between 'peoples'' – that is, collective – rights from 'individual' – that is, human – rights. Thus, civil and political rights include the right to self-determination, the right to development, the right to own property, the right to religion and worship, the right to protection against foreign exploitation of natural resources, freedom of colonized or oppressed peoples from foreign rule and exploitation, the right to protection against corruption, tribalism, nepotism and exploitation by the ruling class, the right to protection against denials of the enjoyment or exercise of the rights of minorities and indigenous populations, the right to existence, and the right to one's religion and culture. All these can best be described as collective or peoples' rights, as defined in Articles 19 and 20 of the Charter.

However, the distinction between individual and collective or peoples' rights is not always clear. Thus the right to life, inheritance and ownership of lands is just as important to an individual as it is to indigenous peoples or to ethnic and racial minorities. The same applies to social, cultural, religious, traditional, civil, economic or customary rights. Similarly, the right to self-determination is just as important to an individual as it is to all colonized or oppressed peoples who wish to resort to any means recognized by the international community, and to the oppressed themselves, so they may be freed from foreign domination, whether it be political, economic, civil or cultural. International law recognizes all these rights and bestows upon individuals, peoples and states corresponding duties to respect and protect them.

Peoples' and/or state rights

For a long time, many African states, especially those which chose to follow the socialist system of government, made no differentiation between peoples' rights and state rights. Planned or centrally controlled economies in such states made the latter the sole owners of property. Therefore, the expression 'peoples' was used interchangeably with 'the state'. No wonder, therefore, that President Michel Samora of socialist Mozambique and Haile Mengistu, Chairman of the Revolutionary Council of socialist Ethiopia, insisted on having 'peoples" rights included in the Charter at its adoption in Nairobi in 1981. Furthermore, even where African countries were described as having adopted 'mixed' and 'free' economies similar to those of the West, sovereignty over natural resources and control of the main means of production and development were always the business of the state. Thus, 'peoples' equals the state where the right to development is concerned. It is also instructive to note that the United Nations Charter of Economic Rights and Duties of States, adopted in 1974 under the umbrella of the New International Economic Order (NIEO), vested these rights not in the people but in states. This contradiction, together with the deliberate inclusion in the ACHPR of 'escape clauses', may help to explain the impotence of the Charter and its lack of effective implementation. So, in talking about the ACHPR, whose rights are at stake: are they 'popular'/'peoples" rights or 'individual', 'minority' or 'state' rights? How can political and civil rights be 'balanced' with economic, social and cultural rights, including the right to development, so much stressed by the peoples of Africa, Asia, Latin America and the Caribbean? These are fundamental questions which, if adequately and positively answered by the ACHPR, would assure this Charter a significant place in the history of human rights legislation in Africa. In any case, the inclusion of 'peoples' in the Charter has already signified, as seen above, economic, social and cultural rights to balance them with political and civil rights in Africa. What we must now look at is how these rights and duties are protected through the Charter.

The determination of African political leaders to bring into existence a human rights regime in Africa which would modernize this continent prompted them to model the Charter on existing international instruments for the protection of human rights, whether they be universal, or regional.

Six international instruments come to mind: the Charter of the United Nations of 1945; the Universal Declaration of Human Rights of 1948; the International Covenant on Civil and Political Rights and the International Covenant on Economic, Social and Cultural Rights of 1966; the European Convention for the Protection of Human Rights and Fundamental Freedoms of 1950; and the American Conventions on Human Rights, 'Pact of San José', of 1969. A comparative analysis of these international instruments and the ACHPR clearly indicates that it was modelled not so much on the European and American Conventions as on the Universal Declaration and the International Covenants.

Protection of Human Rights through the Articles of the African Charter on Human and Peoples' Rights: Duties, Rights, Guarantees and Flaws

Practically every African constitution contains a Bill of Rights based on the International Covenants on Human Rights and the Universal Declaration of Human Rights. The ACHPR contains 27 articles on the rights and duties which require protection. These can be divided into four categories.

- Articles 25–29, on *duties* to respect, promote and protect human rights
- Articles 19–24, on *peoples' rights*
- Articles 15–18, on *economic, social and cultural rights*
- Articles 3–14 on *civil and political rights*.

The significance of many of these rights and duties has already been explained above. Thus, for example, the right to non-discrimination is both a peoples' and a political right. The rights to equal protection of, and equality before, the law (Article 3), life (Article 4), respect for human dignity (Article 5), liberty (Article 6), information (Article 9), religion (Article 7), to seek and be granted asylum and freedom of movement (Article 12), participation in government through democratic means, and access to public service and public property (Article 13) and property ownership (Article 14) are civil and political rights, although the right to property ownership can also be an economic right, as are the rights to work and equal pay for equal work (Article 15), health (Article 16) and education (Article 16), which can also be social and cultural rights. The right to development is an economic right, but it could also be a social or environmental right, if we accept the definition of (sustainable) development as entailing economic growth, social development and protection of the environment.

From the preceding analysis, the following conclusions can be drawn. The distinctions made among the categories of the rights of the ACHPR are similar to those in the International Covenants and the Universal Declaration on which the ACHPR is based. Any guarantees in law remain theoretical until they are translated into practical implementation. This means that, in practice, such distinctions have little or no meaning, since legal guarantees for the protection of rights do not offer automatic enjoyment of these rights in practice – for example, the right to self-determination does not automatically grant self-rule to an individual or group of people. (This dilemma haunts the ACHPR and is one of its fundamental weaknesses.) A complication may arise, however, where a right automatically implicates a corresponding duty to realize that right. Thus, the right to development as a human right may be guaranteed legally – that is, in domestic or international law – but the assurance of its implementation, for example by an African country, may not be guaranteed owing to lack of the means to implement the legally guaranteed right. A poor African country without resources cannot guarantee the economic well-being of all its citizens. However, that country and/or its government can, and should, be held responsible for ill-advised economic/agricultural policies or political instability introduced into the country through corruption and mismanagement of its natural and human resources. Therefore, economic problems caused by natural disasters are beyond the control of governments, but man-made disasters, which result in the weakening and destruction of national economies and lead to poverty, unemployment, ill-health and environmental degradation can and do lead to human rights violations, and the governments concerned must be held responsible for them.

What must, therefore, be done is to ensure that the various categories of human rights are balanced among themselves, so that civil and political rights receive equal, and not lower, status than social, cultural and economic rights, including the right to development. Similarly, duties should correspond to rights, because any demand for rights without the acknowledgement of their corresponding duties is unfair and unrealistic. Furthermore, the concept of peoples' rights in the ACHPR has introduced a new category of human rights which underscores the importance of African values.

This means that whereas so-called distinctions between and among the various categories of human rights appear to be broad in law, the real distinctions among them are narrow in practice, and depend on the extent of their implementation. In summary, guarantees and flaws in the ACHPR depend on whether they occur within or beyond legal protection, whether they are within or beyond the control of states, and whether the enforcement mechanisms, if any, possess an independent character or are mere tools at the whim of governments. This reality should help to explain the inevitable imbalance between the strengths and weaknesses of the ACHPR.

THE STRENGTHS OF THE AFRICAN CHARTER ON HUMAN AND PEOPLES' RIGHTS

Clearly, the weaknesses of the ACHPR far outweigh its strengths. Nevertheless, the Charter introduced the innovative concept of African socialism and its traditional family code system which, in effect, is totally opposed to discrimination of any kind and treats the individual and other peoples in society as equal human beings (Articles 2 and 19). The ACHPR thus grants the state and everybody in it the duty to respect, promote and protect fundamental African traditions and values. This is the unique characteristic of this human rights instrument; it is found in no other convention. Obviously, the ACHPR is modelled on key international human rights instruments, and its drafters were fully aware of existing regional instruments, although they decided to inject the African philosophical concept into the Charter.

Of course, African society does not offer a higher position to women than to men, but nonetheless, in Article 18 of the ACHPR, the drafters allocated to the state the duty and responsibility to provide moral welfare and physical healthcare to the family, to help and protect every family, and to eliminate discrimination against women and children. Another unique characteristic of the ACHPR appears in Articles 27 and 28, which introduce, in the context of a regional convention, the concept of everybody being 'his/her brother's keeper'. In this sense, the Charter grants to every state and every individual the duty and responsibility for the family, the society and community, both national and international, in which the individual lives and works. The state and the individual also have duties and responsibilities toward everybody's relatives and parents, to provide for their needs and development and to preserve their cultural values in their relations with other members of the society. Furthermore, African unity is to be promoted by all as a common duty (Article 29).

Articles, 27, 28 and 29 thus stress the Charter's imposition of a code of good conduct on all African citizens, and that legal rights as individual human rights must be completed or balanced by corresponding legal obligations of the individual to others. The inclusion of 'peoples' in the Charter, as we have seen above, was quite novel in an instrument. The argument by the governments of Ethiopia and Mozambique, led by Chairman Mengistu and President Samora respectively, that the individual had no greater rights than those attributable to his/her society as a whole was wholly innovative. They argued that individual rights must give way to societal/ communal/group rights. This concept of human rights is still unique to Africa and challenges Western concepts of human rights, as stipulated in the Universal Declaration and the International Covenants. African customs, traditions, culture and values are group- or community-oriented in contrast to those of the West.

THE WEAKNESSES OF THE AFRICAN CHARTER ON HUMAN AND PEOPLES' RIGHTS

For Africa and, in particular, for African political leaders, self-determination, self-rule and independence, meaning political independence, have been top priorities in governance. Territorial integrity and national sovereignty, including sovereignty over natural resources, have formed the mainstay of the politico-economic process on the continent. Everything else, including human rights, has been of secondary consideration. This is mainly because of what colonial rule and domination, as well as neo-colonialism and foreign exploitation, have done to Africa.

Against this background, there was no way in which the ACHPR would gain prominence in the African political system. However, there were also other reasons. One was the extremely weak economic situation mainly due to the general economic and political immaturity of many African countries at independence. Another was the straitened fiscal standing of African countries, which has little improved since the attainment of independence. Most of the existing African institutions, including the OAU itself, do not function satisfactorily because of lack of funds. Most member states do not pay their contributions and other dues, and this undermines the effectiveness of the institutions. In the case of the ACHPR, not only does it lack funds to implement its provisions, but it also lacks competent mechanisms to enforce the observance of human rights stipulations. This is especially true for the African Commission on Human and Peoples' Rights.

The African Commission on Human and Peoples' Rights

The treatment of the African Commission on Human and Peoples' Rights is certainly the most elaborate in the entire ACHPR – it takes up 32 Articles (Articles 30–61) and 120 Rules of Procedures – and yet the Commission does not, for all practical purposes, have the power to implement the Charter's provisions. That was precisely what the African political leaders of the day wanted the Commission to be – a tool of African governments. The nature and function of the Commission are explained in the present contribution. It was created at the 23rd OAU summit held in Addis Ababa, Ethiopia, from 27 to 29 July 1987 and became operational in late 1987. Article 30 of the Charter contains two important stipulations: the main purpose of the ACHPR, and the mechanism to implement it – that is, the Commission as the main continental body which would promote and protect human rights in Africa. This mechanism would be intergovernmental and supervise the implementation of the Charter stipulations for member states, but only in an informal manner, because the Commission was not given any jurisdiction or enforcement character of its own.

The mandate of the Commission is contained in Article 45 of the Charter and comprises four basic functions: the promotion of human and peoples' rights; the protection of human and peoples' rights; the interpretation of the Charter provisions; and the performance of any other duties that might be assigned to the Commission by member states.

The most significant weakness of the Charter lies in the following shortcomings:

- The Commission lacks an independent and impartial status with sufficient funds, personnel and powers to enable it to implement the provisions of the articles of the ACHPR. Therefore its mandate is to defend the interests of African governments. As an organ controlled by the African countries, the Commission cannot independently oppose the governments to which it has the duty to report on its work.

- The Commission's positions have no legally binding character; its powers are therefore recommendatory, and it can only implement the decisions of member states.

- The Commission operates completely under the political influence of member states, and suffers from the principle of confidentiality. This lack of transparency is deliberate, for that is how its member states intended the Commission to be and to function. Thus, any human rights violations which governments wish to hide remain hidden from the public, including human rights watches, non-governmental organization activists, academicians and other interested bodies who are denied access to the Commission's deliberations. This denial to the public of access to the Commission's work and its mere advisory role to African presidents and premiers are among its weaknesses. The deliberate subordination of the Commission by the OAU Assembly of Heads of State and Government and the granting to member states of the role of 'enforceable' protection of human rights impede the prompt implementation of the ACHPR and encourage countries to neglect their duty to submit detailed reports to the Commission, which would enhance the enforcement of its mandate.

- The Commission lacks sufficient effective and trained personnel and adequate facilities for the implementation process.

- The Commission lacks independent, Africa-based information sources on violations and abuses of human rights. Non-governmental organizations, whether domestic or foreign and other civil society human rights groups, are excellent sources of grassroots human rights information, and yet they are excluded from participating in the Commission's substantive activities.

Other Weaknesses of the African Charter on Human and Peoples' Rights

Of the other deficiencies in the protection of human rights in Africa, the following are particularly noteworthy:

- The ACHPR fails to provide any guarantee of legal aid to those who cannot afford it. Ordinary Africans are too poor to afford the high fees for legal representation.

- With the exception of Zambia which enacted a law on legal aid in 1967, almost all African Constitutions fail to provide any guaranteed right to legal aid.

- In cases where security and political considerations clash with legal protection of human rights, the former prevail in Africa.

- As presidential or 'premier' appointees in Africa, the judiciary and individual judges lack the independence of judgement and decision on human rights issues in Africa. No enforcement mechanisms of a legally binding nature exist.

- The Charter lacks a judicial system to implement the Commission's work: no courts or other national legal institutions exist to promote and protect human rights under the ACHPR.
- Illiteracy and ignorance of their rights and duties on the part of the overwhelming majority of the African people, together with a lack of reliable transportation systems and undeveloped infrastructures as well as long distances from the nearest law services, deny the African people prompt and adequate access to good and effective administration of justice.
- The 'drawback' or 'safety valve' clauses enumerated in Articles 6, 9 and 10 of the ACHPR make it quite difficult to protect human rights under the Charter. A 'drawback' or 'derogation' clause is a clause included in a law, which temporarily suspends any right or rights guaranteed under the same law in certain specific circumstances. A 'drawback' clause thus permits a violation or breach of an obligation for a specific number of reasons, in order to suit the convenience or discretion of a member state, and excludes any external intervention to prevent such legal breaches in domestic African law. In the ACHPR, for example, the rights to liberty (Article 6), freedom of expression (Article 9) and freedom of association (Article 10) are subject to law and order – that is, they are only guaranteed subject to 'reasons and conditions previously laid down by law'. These provisions allow governments to impose extensive restrictions on fundamental human rights on their own discretion.[9]
- The ACHPR fails to indicate when and if cases exist of non-suspendable – that is, non-derogable – clauses (those which cannot be suspended under any circumstances). The judicial guarantees essential for the protection of such rights are also non-suspendable. In general, in international law, non-derogable rights include the right to a name, to a nationality, to participation in government, to freedom from slavery, torture and so on.
- The right of the accused to be notified in advance of the charges brought against him/her, is missing in the ACHPR.
- The right of the accused to obtain help where there is a language problem is also missing.
- The right to request a witness to attend a trial is likewise missing.
- The lack of education of Africans regarding their right to improve and enhance the protection of their human rights and impartiality is a serious handicap in the Charter.
- Serious problems also exist with regard to political instability accompanied by the excessive arrogance of power in many African countries. Frequent changes of government impose restrictions, and suspend, drastically amend or even abolish constitutions and other legislative instruments in order to suit the political authorities of the day. Such arrogance is usually prompted by greed, undemocratic indecency

and other forms of hunger for power which, in turn, prompt and perpetuate human rights violations.

- In the interests of national security, safety, health, ethics and other rights and freedoms of others, the existing legal mechanisms and instruments in Africa lack independence and impartiality. The constitutions of African States, the OAU Charter and the ACHPR and bills of rights are good cases in point.

RECENT DEVELOPMENTS IN THE PROTECTION OF HUMAN RIGHTS IN AFRICA

Although recorded history indicates that Liberia gained political independence on 26 July 1847, Egypt on 28 February 1922, South Africa on 11 December 1931, Libya on 24 December 1951, Sudan on 1 January 1956, Morocco on 2 March 1956, Tunisia on 20 March 1956 and Guinea on 2 October 1958, and therefore attained their status of independence before 1960, it was only in the 1960s and later that most nations emerged as newly independent African states. In sub-Saharan Africa, Ghana had opened the gate to independence in West Africa when it attained political freedom from the United Kingdom on 6 March 1957.

By signing the United Nations Charter at independence, the African nations adhered to the human rights principles enshrined therein and enacted bills of rights in their constitutions, like those embodied in the Universal Declaration of Human Rights. These constitutions and bills guarantee, at least on paper, the protection of groups and communities, including minorities and other vulnerable groups as well as individuals. The new states also accepted, whether by ratification or practice, the stipulations of the International Covenant on Civil and Political Rights and the International Covenant on Economic, Social and Cultural Rights. Unfortunately, many African states were accused of violating these international instruments, some of which had not even been ratified by them and therefore bore no legally binding force.

The term 'recent' is employed here to refer to the 1990s. This was a paradoxical decade in terms of human rights in Africa in that it witnessed what many have described as a 'New World Order', but which, in fact, marked the beginning of the intensification of a 'New World Disorder' whose dictates have led both to positive and negative consequences in the protection and observance of human rights. The New World Disorder actually began with the collapse of the Berlin Wall in 1989, which in turn, marked the beginning of the end of the ideological division of the North – that is, the developed world – into East and West. As this process advanced, the African nations struggled to integrate themselves continentally through increased sub-regional and regional coalitions and associations.

By losing the benefits of East–West ideological divisions, African countries and their governments not only lost the political and ideological protection they had enjoyed since independence and throughout the Cold

War era, but also became vulnerable as the Western allies turned their backs on those African regimes whose outrageous human rights records had previously been 'overlooked' in the interests of retaining 'African friends' for strategic, economic, political, military reasons and other reasons.

With the end of the Cold War the West applied new conditions and pressures on African regimes and used human rights as a weapon against certain African governments perceived as perpetuating human rights abuses. Pressures appeared in different forms, including political isolation, economic embargos and incitement of political forces to strongly oppose some governments' poor human rights records. Pressures and demands for change also came from within African states themselves, and these pressures were applied by the power of public opinion. Most African governments were thus forced to accept multipartyism and to practise the principles of good governance, democracy and human rights.

Moreover, the dismantling of the Soviet bloc deprived African countries of the protection and tolerance they had enjoyed from their Western allies. Consequently, most African governments were forced to adjust their thinking and behaviour if they were to escape the pressure of domestic public opinion, as well as external demands for democratization, especially from the donor community. Any African government which decided to ignore such pressure risked isolation or removal from power.

Within three years of the fall of the communist system in Eastern and Central Europe, four particularly noteworthy developments occurred. First was the acceptance to succumb to the demands for change: the wishes of the governed people had to be recognized. Second was the decision of African governments to demonstrate to the world that they supported the demands for human rights protection and observance, both in their countries and internationally. Third was the creation of the International Criminal Tribunal for the former Yugoslavia in The Hague, The Netherlands, and of the International Criminal Tribunal for Rwanda in Arusha, Tanzania. Fourth was an intensification of sub-regional and regional interventions for conflict resolution and peaceful settlement of disputes which had long been recognized as being among the top priorities for sustained development in Africa.

THE AFRICAN POSITION REGARDING THE WORLD CONFERENCE ON HUMAN RIGHTS (VIENNA, AUSTRIA, 1993)

Perhaps the greatest demonstration of Africa's determination to improve its human rights situation occurred when the African Ministers of Justice and Attorneys-General met in Tunis in November 1992 to prepare an African position paper for presentation to the World Conference on Human Rights. At the end of this meeting, they had adopted an African Declaration of the Regional Meeting for Africa of the World Conference on Human Rights. In this Declaration – as in the 12 resolutions that the meeting also adopted on the human rights situation in Africa – stress was laid on the need to promote and protect human rights everywhere in Africa by all concerned institutions, groups and individuals, as well as by governments, national institutions, non-governmental organizations and other bodies. These actors must all join forces to combat all kinds of discrimination, xenophobia, religious intolerance and extremism as well as apartheid and extreme poverty. Such social evils and inhuman practices prevent the enjoyment of inherent civil, political, social, cultural and economic rights, including the right to development and to democratic participation by the people in decision-making processes on issues affecting their own daily lives.

The meeting further emphasized the need to improve the human rights situation in Africa through elevating the status of women and children in African society by supporting their rights and defending their democratic participation in and contribution to national development. It also called for African and global measures to enhance the national capacities of the African nations and institutions to enable them to deal competently with their own development challenges and the administration of justice and other complex human rights issues in Africa.

All the above-mentioned resolutions and the above Declaration mentioned the ACHPR, whose stipulations and standards should be reaffirmed and applied appropriately in Africa today. The World Conference on Human Rights marked a new awareness in the arena of human rights by universally endorsing the right to development as a human right. Ironically, the World Conference was followed by probably the worst massacres and mass executions ever seen on the African continent.

The process of establishing a global mechanism to investigate the crimes committed against humanity was thus intensified in the 1990s following the genocide in the former Yugoslavia and the Great Lakes region of Central Africa. This 'ethnic cleansing' resulted in unrivalled massacres and mass executions of civilian populations, many of whom were children, women, the handicapped and the elderly. International public opinion prompted the United Nations, as well as regional organizations such as the North Atlantic Treaty Organization (NATO) and the OAU, to call for the urgent creation of International Criminal Tribunals for both the former Yugoslavia and Rwanda.

The decision to establish such an international mechanism for Rwanda came after long months of discussion at the United Nations and at the request of the Rwandan government. It was agreed that the atrocities lasted from 1 January to 31 December 1994. On 9 November 1994, the Security Council adopted, by consensus, resolution 955 (1994) by which it established the International Criminal Tribunal for Rwanda (ICTR). It also formulated the Tribunal's Statute and annexed to it the resolution. The main mandate of the Tribunal was to prosecute persons responsible for genocide and other serious violations of international humanitarian law committed on the territory of Rwanda, as well as Rwandan citizens responsible for such violations on the territories of neighbouring states between those dates. The ICTR interpreted genocide as defined by the Genocide Convention of 1948.[10] In the case of the massacres in Rwanda, the ICTR concluded that '… there was an intention to wipe out the Tutsi group in its entirety, since even new-born babies were not spared'.

By adopting a resolution on the genocide in Rwanda, the United Nations Security Council sought to halt the massive violations of human rights and to redress them effectively not only in Rwanda but also in the entire region of the Great Lakes, and also to warn other violators in Africa that they would all be severely punished if they continued to violate human rights which are protected in accordance with international human rights instruments and other stipulations of international humanitarian law.

However, as in Rwanda, violations of human rights increased during the 1990s due to the political situations which existed in various parts of Africa, most notably Algeria, Burundi, the Democratic Republic of Congo (formerly Zaire), Liberia, Nigeria, Sierra Leone, South Africa and the Sudan. The root causes of these violations included ethnic and tribal conflicts aggravated by other societal and economic injustices increasing the impoverishment of African families and prompting rebellions especially by the oppressed, victimized and poorest strata of society.

Thus, as an international machine, the ICTR acted commendably by arresting, by the end of 1999, 38 out of the 45 individuals who had been indicted by its own mechanism.

Demands and pressures on African governments to increase their conciliation and mediation efforts to end civil wars and conflicts have increased in recent years. Individually and collectively, African governments have intensified efforts to resolve internal and regional conflicts in order to protect human rights. To this effect, African ministers and the OAU have adopted resolutions and undertaken human rights reconciliation missions to Côte d'Ivoire, Liberia, Niger and Sierra Leone among other countries. The United Nations Security Council and the General Assembly, as well as African regional and sub-regional institutions, have demanded that these missions encourage warring groups in Africa to resolve their differences by peaceful means.

The Lusaka Peace Agreement of 7 July 1999, which ended the 1996–1999 civil war, was initiated by the Democratic Republic of the Congo and supported by the international community. When, in 1999, a military coup replaced an elected government in Sierra Leone, troops of the Economic Community for West Africa (ECOWAS) and the OAU, led by Nigeria and backed by the United Nations Security Council, intervened and restored the civilian government of President Alhaji Ahmad Tejan Kabbah. Prior to that, in 1995, the Nigerian government had signed an agreement with the Armed Resistance Organization, a forceful opposition faction in the country. In the Democratic Republic of the Congo, the regime faced tough opposition on all fronts – domestic, sub-regional and regional, as well as international opposition from the United Nations.

Subsequently, the African Heads of State or Government met at the Security Council in New York from 24 to 28 January 2000 to discuss ways of assuring peaceful settlement of the continent's political problems and violations of human rights. Concrete and practical proposals for tackling African conflicts had been made by Kofi Annan, the United Nations Secretary-General, in early 1999, which the United Nations endorsed fully. In the case of the Democratic Republic of the Congo, a special meeting of the Security Council urged the implementation of the stipulations of the International Covenant on Civil and Political Rights, including those contained in its Article 14.

In Nigeria, profound changes have occurred since the new government came to power in 1999 and initiated actions and other measures to promote human rights.

CONCLUSION: AFRICA AND THE QUESTION OF HUMAN RIGHTS IN THE TWENTY-FIRST CENTURY – CHALLENGES, CHOICES AND CHANCES

The probability of human rights being top priority on the international agenda of the twenty-first century is much greater now than it was before, or even at, the collapse of communism in 1989. Ten years earlier, in 1979, three ruthless dictators were removed from power in Africa: Idi Dada Amin of Uganda, Jean-Bedel Bokassa of the Central African Republic and Macias Nguema of Equatorial Guinea. It is highly improbable that Africa will allow itself to be ruled by such despots in the twenty-first century.

Similarly, it is doubtful that the practice of instituting powerless institutions and ineffective political mechanisms will continue in Africa. Demands to create more efficient and effective mechanisms and adopt stronger constitutions, charters and other legal instruments to replace the Charter of the OAU, the ACHPR, the African Commission on Human and Peoples' Rights and others already in existence but almost impotent are likely to grow in the coming decades.

The above scenario is suggested by a number of events which point to major changes, challenges and choices for Africa and Africans. The process of democratization and multi-partyism, for instance, has marked a significant watershed in the African human rights debate. The new era, which began with the fall of the Berlin Wall in November 1989, not only marked the end of the Cold War but also signalled the beginning of the North's use of human rights as a serious foreign policy and foreign aid tool towards the South, including Africa. It has brought about an awareness and need to create and develop national debates and institutions, both in Africa and elsewhere, to promote and protect the rights and freedoms of the individual and society.

The oversensitivity of African nations and their leaders regarding self-determination, self-rule, territorial integrity and sovereignty over natural resources may persist into the twenty-first century, and it is evident that lamentations over colonialism and neo-colonialism will continue to prevail. Political sanctioning of human rights violations and abuses will be seriously challenged, as will be the 'safety valve' clause in national legislations. Constant efforts to suppress the silent majority and to deny them public access to government will themselves be suppressed by the power of public opinion and the popular vote.

The curtailing or qualifying of the protection of human and peoples' rights through domestic legislation by the authorities to fit their whims, as is the case today and as it was during the period of one-party political systems in Africa, is unlikely to survive in the third millennium.

The future protection of human rights in Africa will thus only be effective if launched from within. The best and most effective measures and actions to protect human rights cannot come from external sources. Protection is best guaranteed and is most effective when undertaken from national sources. This primarily implies the implementation of legislation, decisions and recommendations by states and internal enforcement mechanisms.

The African Commission on Human and Peoples' Rights, though extremely weak, nonetheless still has the duty to interpret the ACHPR and offer impartial opinions on how best to protect human rights in Africa.[11] These shortcomings pose enormous challenges to African political leaders and academics alike. It is no use having mechanisms without effective and enforceable powers. Effective measures and relevant courts should be instituted to deal with abuses and violations of human rights. Governmental support and enhancement of these mechanisms and their performance standards are inevitable.

The OAU cannot, and will not, guarantee or ensure the protection of human rights unless individual African states do so themselves. Mere references to international human rights instruments and their inscriptions in national constitutions and laws will not ensure their implementation. Improvement of human rights protection calls for the targeting of human rights education on economic, political, social, legal and cultural actors for the better administration of justice, and the inclusion of human rights advocates from the grassroots to the highest levels of society, including local and national organizations, international non-governmental organizations, government leaders, parliamentarians, senior government officials, administrators, the judiciary, teachers, journalists, students, diplomats, doctors, the military, and leaders in public opinion and education. Their involvement in human rights protection is crucial to the effectiveness of mechanisms to protect and promote human rights in Africa. Non-governmental organizations and other actors of civil society should be allowed to intervene on human rights violations whenever and wherever they occur. International organizations, including the United Nations, should also be enabled to perform their mandates to promote and protect the observance of human rights across the board. African governments should tolerate criticism of methods, processes and procedures that run counter to human rights, especially if it is constructive and offered in good faith.

One of the weakest features of the ACHPR is its neglect of the role of women, children, youth, the elderly and handicapped in the human rights field. The Charter is surprisingly and completely silent on protecting these most vulnerable sections of society, and this is one of the reasons why it should be revised.

Thus, the challenge of human rights protection in Africa lies not so much in the ACHPR *per se*, in the inclusion of human rights in African constitutions, in democratization or multi-partyism *per se*, or indeed in increasing the transparency of the ACHPR, but in instituting the mechanisms and political commitment which will effectively implement its provisions at the national level.

In short, the national and international road to the promotion and protection of human rights in Africa is long, tortuous, erratic and rough, but it must be traversed. The challenges, choices and chances will be most difficult to elucidate and fulfil, but this must be done and taken into account for the twenty-first century.

NOTES

1   See Don Nanjira (1976).
2   See resolution AHG/16/(1)(1964), adopted at the Ordinary Session of the Assembly Heads of State and Government (of the OAU), 17–21 July 1964.
3   Don Nanjira (1976).
4   See UN Document ST/TAO/HR/38, 1969.
5   See OAU Document AHG/115/(XVI), 1978.
6   See UN Document ST/HR/Ser.A/4 NY 1979.
7   See OAU Document CAB/LEG/67/3/Rev.1, 1979.
8   For a full text of the ACHPR, see *International Materials*, **21** (1982), p.58. The Charter was adopted on 27 June 1981 in Nairobi by the OAU summit. It took effect on 21 October 1986. By October 1991, 38 African states had ratified the Charter.
9   For an exhaustive analysis of this matter, see Gittleman (1981, p.692).
10   The 1948 Convention on the Prevention and Punishment of the Crime of Genocide defined 'genocide' as 'the act of committing certain acts, including the killing of members of the groups with the intent to destroy, in whole or in part, a national racial or religious group, as such'.
11   For a fascinating exposé on this question, consult Umozurike (1988).

BIBLIOGRAPHY

Badawi-El-Sheikh, Ibrahim Ali (1989), 'The African Commission on Human and Peoples' Rights: prospects and problems', *Netherlands Quarterly of Human Rights*, 7(3), pp.272–83.
Benedek, Wolfgang (1993), 'The African Charter and Commission on Human and Peoples' Rights: how to make it more effective', *Netherlands Quarterly of Human Rights*, **II**(i), pp.25–40.
De Zayas, Alfred M. (1993), 'The international judicial protection of peoples and minorities' in *Peoples and Minorities in International Law*, Dordrecht/Boston, Martinus Nijhoff Publishers, pp.253–87.
Don Nanjina, D.P.C. (1976), *The Status of Aliens in East Africa. Asians and Europeans in Tanzania, Uganda and Kenya*, New York: Praeger Special Publishers.
Gittleman, R.G. (1981), 'The African Charter on Human and Peoples' Rights: a legal analysis', *Virginia Journal of International Law*, **22**(4), pp.152–76.

Kodjo, Edem (1990), 'The African Charter on Human and Peoples' Rights', *Human Rights Law Journal*, **11**(3/4), pp.271–83.

Kunig, Philip (1985), 'Regional protection of human rights by international law: the emerging African system', Documents and three introduction essays by P. Kunig, Wolfgang Benedek and Costa R. Mahalu, *Nomos Verlagsgesellschaft*, Baden-Baden, p.ix.

Magnarella, Paul S. (1993), 'Preventing interethnic conflict and promoting human rights through more effective legal, political and in structures focus on Africa', *Georgia Journal of International and Comparative Law*, **23**(2) Summer, pp.327–45.

Parpart, Jane L. (1986), 'Women's rights and the Lagos Plan of Action', *Human Rights Quarterly*, **8**(2) May, pp.180–96.

Umozurike, U.O. (1988), 'The protection of human rights under the Banjul (African) Charter on Human and Peoples' Rights', *African Journal of International Law*, **1**(1), Summer, pp.65–83.

Wanda, B.P. (1991), 'The one-party State and the protection of human rights in Africa, with particular reference to political rights', *African Journal of International and Comparative Law*, **3**(4), December, pp.756–70.

Wean, Deborah A. (1988), 'Real protection for women? The African Charter on Human and Peoples' Rights', *Emory Journal of International Dispute Resolution*, **2**(2) Spring, pp.425–58.

Welch Jr, Claude E. (1991), 'The Organization of African Unity and the promotion of human rights', *Journal of Modern African Studies*, **29**(4) December, pp.535–55.

Welch Jr, Claude E. (1993), 'Human rights and African women: a comparison of protection under two major treaties', *Human Rights Quarterly*, **15**(3) August, pp.549–74.

Winston, S. (1987), 'The rights of women, the African Charter, and the economic development of Africa', *Boston College Third World Law Journal*, **7**(2) Spring, pp.215–21.

7 Regional Protection of Human Rights in the Arab States *In Statu Nascendi*

BAHEY EL DIN HASSAN

INTRODUCTION

Geographically, the Arab states do not constitute a separate region. However, historical, linguistic, religious, cultural and political factors have contributed, throughout history, to endowing them with common traits. Those traits have obliged the world to look upon the Arab states as a separate region, although they are located in both Asia and Africa. Nevertheless, the links between Arab states are much stronger than the links between each of them and the part of the world to which they belong.

The Arab states comprise 22 states. Asia includes Bahrain, Iraq, Jordan, Kuwait, Lebanon, Oman, Palestine, Qatar, Saudi Arabia, Syria, United Arab Emirates and Yemen. Africa includes Algeria, Egypt, Libyan Arab Jamahiriya, Mauritania, Morocco, the Sudan and Tunisia. Recently, new states have acceded to the League of Arab States, among them Comoros, Djibouti and Somalia, although these states are less attached to the Arab world.

The Arab region is characterized by various fundamental aspects that make it unique among other regions in the world. This is generally reflected in the situation of human rights there, and in the question of their regional protection. The first and most prominent of these characteristics is the issue of collective rights which gains exceptional pertinence for the following reasons:

- It is the only region in the world where some states – for example, Palestine and Syria – are still subject to colonial occupation.
- It is a region that has witnessed permanent suffering of refugees (53 years for Palestinian refugees, in addition to the tragedies of Kurdish, Somali and Sudanese, as well as Sahraoui, refugees).

239

- It is a region that has witnessed brutal wars for over half a century (Arab–Israeli wars, civil wars; the Sudan for 30 years and Yemen in 1994), in addition to acts of armed terrorism (Algeria and Egypt).
- It is a region that has witnessed chronic violent struggles with national, religious or sectarian minorities (Iraq, Lebanon and Algeria) and other unarmed tensions (Bahrain, Egypt, Morocco and Saudi Arabia).

Second, the Arab region is less affected, if affected at all, by the waves of democratic transition that have pervaded the world since the late 1980s, the majority of Arab states having been under the domination of totalitarian or despotic regimes for decades. Furthermore, the era of change – that is, the 1990s – witnessed regression. This is explained by the following:

- Many states applied restricted political plurality with respect to their open policies towards diverse political currents in the 1990s. They opted in favour of further restrictions that have led them back to one-party regimes.
- Some republican presidents tend to assure succession as Head of State to their sons. Such a tradition was unknown previously, except in the Democratic People's Republic of Korea.

Third, the region is facing a great cultural challenge regarding the universality of human rights. This challenge hinges upon the conservative nature of the prevalent religious culture, be it Islam or Eastern Christianity.

Fourth, the region is also facing a significant political challenge regarding the universality of human rights as a result of the Arab peoples' established belief that international protection mechanisms and the work of international organizations are totally ineffective when it comes to holding Israel accountable for its human rights violations during the last 50 years. These Israeli violations include the perpetration of crimes of genocide, the establishment of an apartheid regime on the West Bank and in Gaza, extrajudicial killings, the confiscation of land and property and changing the geographical boundaries of the Occupied Territories. Another basis for this lack of belief in the universality of human rights is founded on the Arab states' long history of subordination to European colonization, which discredits the very concept of human rights, the current form of which has developed under the cloak of Western culture and European legal thinking. Thus, the Arab region may be the only region where the political expression 'double standards' is known and used by lay people.

Fifth, the region is hostile towards human rights organizations. Among the 26 states that expressed reservations on the United Nations Declaration on the Right and Responsibility of Individuals, Groups and Organs of Society to Promote and Protect Universally Recognized Human Rights and Fundamental Freedoms, commonly known as the Declaration on Human Rights Defenders, of 10 December 1998, 14 were members of the League.[1] Previously, Arab Ministers of the Interior had taken a collective position at their regular meeting on 5 December 1996 considering human rights organizations a source of sabotage and danger to national security.[2]

TOWARDS AN ARAB REGIONAL MECHANISM FOR THE PROTECTION OF HUMAN RIGHTS

In 1945 a regional organization for the Arab states was established – the League of Arab States. This can be considered as the first regional organization, since it was established before the other regional organizations for Europe, Africa or America, and even before the United Nations.[3] However, the League's Charter includes no reference to human rights, nor to the right of self-determination. It does not use the term 'people' or 'peoples', but addresses governments and states.

More than 20 years later, in 1968, the League began to pay attention to the issue when the United Nations organized the International Conference on Human Rights in Tehran (Iran) to mark the 20th anniversary of the adoption of the Universal Declaration of Human Rights. At this time, the United Nations called upon states and regional and international organizations to cooperate in the field of human rights. In the same year, the League responded by convening a conference in Beirut, Lebanon, dedicated to the disclosure of Israeli violations of the human rights of Palestinians and Arabs.[4]

Subsequently in 1968 the League established the so-called Standing Committee on Human Rights (SCHR), thus becoming the first regional organization to respond to a suggestion by the United Nations. The SCHR's mandate can be summarized as follows:

- supporting joint Arab action in the field of human rights
- working on protecting the rights of the Arab human being and presenting the humanitarian dimension of the Arab cause
- developing and raising awareness of human rights in the Arab states.[5]

The wording of the second item is obscure as 'protecting the rights of the Arab human being' is linked in the same phrase to the 'Arab cause', this being equivalent to the 'Palestinian cause'. It is therefore clear that the intended object of protection is the Palestinian people with regard to Israeli violations of their rights. It is worth mentioning that the SCHR made 20 recommendations on the rights of the Palestinian people in the first two years of its mandate.[6] However, despite the fact the SCHR's mandate includes receiving reports by Arab states on their human rights situation, it has never received a single report.[7]

The SCHR has dedicated all its efforts to denouncing Israeli violations of human rights but has remained silent about violations of human rights by Arab governments.[8] In addition, the League Council did not adopt any resolutions pertaining to human rights between 1971 and 1981, except those concerning the appointment of the President of the Standing Committee, the renewal of his mandate, and on the postponement of his appointment.[9]

The former Director of the Human Rights Department of the League attributes the SCHR's silence about human rights violations to the sensitivity of the subject and the differences it might cause between these states. The reason might also be attributed to accepting the investigations by the United Nations Commission on Human Rights and its reports on the subject.

The paralysis of the SCHR can be traced to the nature of its composition, its internal system and dependency. It comprises representatives of League member states, rather than independent experts. This makes the League unique among the other regional organizations on account of its having a governmental committee for human rights.[10] A specialist has described the League as a trade union of Arab governments.[11]

In addition, the SCHR has no statute of its own and applies the internal statutes of the League's technical committees. Furthermore, not only does it hold its meetings *in camera*, it also has no right to enforce decisions unless they are ratified by the Council of the League.[12] Although it has a Standing Committee, no one appears aware of its existence.[13] Nevertheless, its establishment has had some positive results. On reviewing the dates of Arab states' ratification of the International Covenant on Civil and Political Rights and the International Covenant on Economic, Social and Cultural Rights, it can be seen that ratification only began after 1969 – that is, after the establishment of the SCHR.[14] An additional factor, or perhaps the main factor, for ratification (Tunisia and Syrian Arab Republic in 1969, Libyan Arab Jamahiriya in 1970 and Iraq in 1971) was the commemoration by the United Nations in 1968 of the 20th anniversary of the Universal Declaration of Human Rights and the organization of the International Conference on Human Rights.

By the beginning of the 1970s, initiatives were being taken by Arab non-governmental organizations to activate the role of the League in the field of human rights and to issue an Arab instrument on this subject.

THE DECLARATION OF THE CITIZEN'S RIGHTS IN ARAB STATES AND COUNTRIES

In 1970 the Human Rights Association in Iraq proposed the adoption of an Arab Declaration on Human Rights. In 1971 the SCHR prepared the draft Declaration of the Citizen's Rights in Arab States and Countries which was, however, never adopted because of the indifference of the majority of governments. Only nine Arab states commented on the Declaration: Egypt, Iraq, Jordan, Kuwait, Lebanon, Libyan Arab Jamahiriya, Palestine, Saudi Arabia and the Syrian Arab Republic. Some states denounced the Declaration in letter and spirit, despite the fact that it is only morally, rather than legally, binding.

The Preamble of the draft Declaration repeated the principles laid down in the Universal Declaration of Human Rights. Under political and civil rights (Article 22), it enumerated the right to equality, the right to life, freedom, physical integrity, nationality, private life and property, personality and equality before the law, as well as the right of litigation and freedom of belief, exercise of religious rituals, the freedom of opinion and the rights of assembly and participation in public life. It prohibits slavery, forced labour and banishment, and the prohibition of leaving or returning to one's own country.

As far as economic, social and cultural rights are concerned (8 articles), the draft Declaration lists: the right to work; the right to form trade unions; the right to an appropriate standard of living; the right to free education; the right to participation in cultural life; the right to found a family; and the protection of mothers and children.[15] The Declaration comprises 31 articles. However, Article 31 invalidates all the rights included in the other articles, because it grants governments the possibility of derogating from securing all the rights included in the Declaration, including the right to life in cases of emergency. This flaw can be found in all subsequent projects proposed by the League with regard to an Arab Charter on Human Rights.[16]

THE CHARTER ON HUMAN AND PEOPLES' RIGHTS IN THE ARAB WORLD

This Charter was initiated by the International Institute of Higher Studies in Criminal Sciences, Syracusa, Sicily, presided over by Sherif Bassiouni, a well-known international Egyptian expert, in addition to a number of legal experts and human rights advocates from 13 Arab states. A conference was convened for this purpose in December 1986. The most prominent features of this Charter[17] include:

- a consistent democratic position clearly reflected in articles relating to political rights and freedoms
- the total prohibition of the extradition of political refugees, this being considered as the most serious human rights violation by Arab governments
- a respect for the right to life which cannot be violated during emergencies – in distinction from all previous draft Arab declarations and instruments
- an adherence to the United Nations Standard Minimum Rules for the Treatment of Prisoners of 1955 in tackling the problem of physical punishment (although some regard its abandonment as non-Islamic)
- a respect for social and economic rights by their inclusion after civil rights but before political rights
- the inclusion of many rights that deal with the Arab states geographically as one unit – for example, the enjoyment by all citizens of the right to accede to political parties and civil societies in any Arab state and the right of any political party to exercise its activities in all Arab states
- the inclusion of a special section on the collective rights of the Arab people

- the laying down of clear procedures for a mechanism of protection of human rights, monitored by two institutions: an Arab Commission on Human Rights and an Arab Court of Human Rights. The Charter provides the Commission with the relevant independence for exercising its activities, including its composition of independent experts. The Charter also makes the rulings of the Court enforceable over the final rulings in each state.

In short, the Charter is generally consistent with international human rights standards and avoids the chronic flaw in the other draft human rights instruments drawn up by the League – namely, the violation of the right to life in emergencies. However, this may be the reason why it did not come to fruition or was even included in the League's deliberations, and why it was not discussed publicly by the intellectual elite in the Arab world. In fact, the reasons for this can be summarized as follows:

- The Charter was ahead of its time in terms of the readiness of Arab governments to adopt a human rights instrument, even a minimal one such as the Declaration of the Citizen's Rights in Arab States and Countries.
- The Charter was dominated by the political pan-Arab discourse which seemed to be directed towards one political current – that is, the pan-Arab national current which does not place human rights and democracy issues as a top priority. Indeed, this current position on these issues is one of its chronic flaws. The domination of the pan-Arab discourse concerning the Charter is reflected in its title which refers to one Arab people in the Arab states, ignoring the existence of various Arab peoples and significant non-Arab national minorities in many Arab states.
- The Charter also ignored women's issues. It dealt with them in the framework of the state's care of mothers and children.
- The human rights movement in the Arab states was new at the time the Charter was drawn up and discussed. Later, the movement was occupied with defending its own legitimacy. By the time it became relatively strong, it had discarded this Charter and adopted a new one – the Arab Charter on Human Rights.[18]

THE ARAB CHARTER ON HUMAN RIGHTS (ACHR)

In 1979 the Union of Arab Lawyers prepared a draft instrument on human rights which was referred to the League and the SCHR for study. The League referred to two experts who prepared a draft of the Arab Charter on Human Rights in 1983, which was frozen for nine years. However, in preparation for its participation in the World Conference on Human Rights (Vienna, Austria, June 1993), the League presented the draft for deliberation by the Arab states. However, the League's attempts to adopt the Charter before the World Conference were in vain. It was a year later, on 15 September 1994, before it was adopted by the League.

The Arab Charter on Human Rights comprises 43 articles[19] and is divided into a preamble and four parts. Part I comprises only one article, its paragraph (a) covering the peoples' right of self-determination and control over natural resources and wealth. Article 1(b) denounces racism, Zionism, occupation and foreign domination as obstacles to peoples' enjoyment of their basic rights.

Part II covers civil, political, economic, social and cultural rights, including the right to enjoy all the rights and freedoms, without any distinction on grounds of race, colour, sex, language, religion, political opinion, national or social origin, property, birth or other status and without any discrimination between men and women. It also includes: the right to life; freedom and personal integrity; the right to recognition as a person before the law and fair prosecution; the right to equality before the judiciary; the right to a private life; freedom of belief, opinion and thought; the right to practise religious observances; freedom of peaceful assembly and association; the right to form trade unions and the right to strike; the right to work, to a fair wage and to equal remuneration for work of equal value; the right of access to public office in one's own country; the right to education; the right to live in an intellectual and cultural environment in which racial, religious and other forms of discrimination are rejected; protection for the family as the basic unit of society; protection for the family, mothers, children and the aged; and the right to mental and physical development.

The ACHR prohibits the death penalty for political crimes for persons below the age of 18 and pregnant or nursing women. It also prohibits torture and the conduct of medical or scientific experimentation on any person without his/her free consent, prevention from leaving one's own country, exile and depriving minorities of their right to enjoy their cultures and practise their religion.

Part III tackles, in two articles (Articles 40 and 41), mechanisms for implementation of the Charter. The Council of the League shall elect a Committee of Experts on Human Rights comprising seven members nominated by the States Parties to the Charter. The Committee shall elect a Chairman and draw up rules of procedure specifying its method of operation. It shall receive periodic reports every three years for consideration. The Committee shall submit a report, together with the views and comments of the states, to the SCHR.

Part IV tackles the mechanism of the entry into force of the ACHR in two articles: 'The present Charter shall enter into effect two months after the date of deposit of the seventh instrument of ratification or accession with the Secretariat of the League of Arab States' (Article 42(b)). Following its entry into force, the present Charter shall become binding on each state two months after the date of the deposit of its instrument of ratification or accession with the Secretariat (Article 43). As of the end of 2001, no document of ratification or accession had been deposited.

Although the wording of the ACHR is generally better than that of previous draft instruments discussed by the League during the 11 years from 1983 to 1994, it still retains a serious and repeated flaw – the derogation from protecting the right to life in emergencies.[20] The situation is further aggravated by the fact that many Arab states have been living under conditions of semi-permanent emergency for decades.[21] The ACHR has added a general stipulation giving Arab legislators in all Arab states the freedom to enact laws restricting stipulated rights, if deemed necessary, to protect national security and the economy, public order, health or morals or the rights and freedoms of others. This makes the ACHR a dead letter. Its entry into force is meaningless as long as the states can enact laws invalidating all the principles on which they have agreed, without even having to take emergency situations as a pretext.[22]

Although the African Charter on Human and Peoples' Rights suffers from the same problems, the restriction by national law of the rights mentioned therein is only made through a 'general stipulation'.[23]

The ACHR goes further than the Declaration of the Citizen's Rights in Arab States and Countries in prohibiting derogation from some rights (prohibition of torture, return to the homeland, political asylum and fair trials) in cases of emergency. However, it is regressive in comparison with the Declaration in two instances.[24] First, it does not demand the formal announcement of emergency cases so that the state is not obliged to declare which articles are suspended in emergencies. Second, Article 4 not only provides for the derogation of the states from their obligations laid down in the ACHR as an exception in emergency cases, it also includes the right of the legislator in every state to enact laws restricting rights stipulated in the ACHR.

The ACHR and the Declaration both allow the violation of the right to life in states of emergency. Although the ACHR specifies the rights from which no derogation is possible in emergency cases, these rights do not embrace the right to life, the legal personality or religious freedom[25] whose suspension and violation is prohibited by the International Covenant on Civil and Political Rights, even in emergency cases.

In addition, the ACHR has retained some of the most negative elements of previous draft instruments. In particular, a number of important safeguards mentioned in regional and international instruments are omitted, and it also includes further restrictions on rights.[26] In this sense, the ACHR lags behind in the international development of human rights, including the African Charter on Human and Peoples' Rights.[27]

The ACHR also lacks a real mechanism for the protection of human rights. The role of the Committee of Experts on Human Rights is restricted to receiving governmental reports and making recommendations to the SHCR. It cannot receive complaints from individuals or non-governmental organizations;[28] the Committee of Experts can only refer the report to the Secretariat of the League. Moreover, the ACHR does not assign the Committee a role concerning the implementation and application of the Charter's provisions.[29] In the framework of this fragile mechanism, the system of reports is the only tool available for supervising the enforcement of the Charter's provisions. However, this system is extremely weak for the following reasons:

- Reports are submitted every three years which is a very long interval[30] in comparison with the American Convention on Human Rights (annual reports) and the African Charter on Human and Peoples' Rights (every two years).
- The Committee of Experts, an independent body comprising representatives of States Parties to the Charter, has no jurisdictions or competence other than discussing reports. In addition, the SCHR's President and members are appointed by the League's member states. Furthermore, the SCHR cannot make recommendations directly to member states; it has to refer matters to the Council of the League for action.[31]
- The ACHR is ambiguous in many respects – for instance, regarding procedures for discussing reports. Is it obligatory for the concerned state to attend the discussions on its report? Can information be requested from independent sources? What should these reports cover?[32]

To sum up, the mechanism for monitoring the implementation of the provisions of the ACHR is very weak and primitive.[33] It lags behind that of other international and regional instruments.[34]

In terms of its effectiveness at the national level, the ACHR is the weakest[35] of all other regional human rights instruments. It gives precedence to national laws and does not contain any obligation by States Parties to enact legislative measures to protect the rights mentioned therein.[36] This means that states cannot be held accountable if they do not amend national laws to be in line with the ACHR;[37] on the contrary, States Parties can invoke the ACHR to derogate from their obligations thereunder.[38] Similarly, if a national judge wishes to base his rulings on the provisions of the ACHR, he may argue that the Charter itself gives a higher priority over domestic law.[39]

First and foremost, it is a matter of the state's political will and general orientation whether it adheres to or derogates from the provisions of the ACHR. Similarly, if a national judge wishes to base his rulings on the provisions of the ACHR, he may argue that the Charter itself gives higher priority over domestic law.[40]

THE ARAB CHARTER ON HUMAN RIGHTS IN THE CULTURAL AND POLITICAL DEBATE IN THE ARAB STATES

Even before its adoption, Amnesty International welcomed the ACHR as the first regional instrument on human rights that includes all Arab states, and as the first whose State Parties are mostly Muslims. It was therefore very important that the ACHR recognized the universal nature of human rights through asserting the principles of the Universal Declaration of Human Rights and other international human rights instruments.[41]

The ACHR contained a conciliatory formula that met the aspirations of Amnesty International. In its Preamble, it mentions both the Universal Declaration of Human Rights and the Cairo Declaration on Human Rights in Islam, adopted in 1990. However, does this contribute to addressing the debate in the Arab states on the universality of human rights? The answer is 'no'. The reason is not that the ACHR ignores women's rights, except those concerning mothers and children, nor that it restricts the freedom of religion, nor that it does not prohibit slavery; the reason is that the struggle on the universality of human rights in the Arab states and in other regions of the world is mainly political. Many Arab and non-Arab observers now acknowledge that, after the terrorist aggression against the United States on 11 September 2001, arriving at a fair settlement which respects the rights of the Palestinian people could contribute towards the debate on the universality of human rights more positively than the best possible wording of the Arab Charter on Human Rights.[42]

In 2000 Saudi Arabia surprised the world by ratifying the International Convention on the Elimination of All Forms of Discrimination against Women (CEDAW). The issue of the universality of human rights in the Arab states thus took a big step forward. However, it has also taken ten steps backwards because of the apathy of the international community towards the suffering of the Palestinian people and their exemption from international protection as well as the impunity of Israel's stance.

This raised an important question from a late Arab expert in human rights, Monzer Anbatawy: the ACHR is only a more succinct compilation of principles pertaining to some rights laid down in the Universal Declaration of Human Rights. In addition, the ACHR omits many important rights, as well as a mechanism to monitor its implementation and safeguard the rights mentioned therein. Was this for the purpose of external propaganda as some have said? Or is it because the Arab states had not acceded to some of instruments that were an obstacle before drafting the text of the ACHR?[43]

To answer this latter question, we have to go back to decision-making on the ACHR. The testimony of Ambassador Noaman Galal, Permanent Representative of Egypt to the League at the time the Charter was adopted, is very interesting not only because he took part in the drafting procedure but because of the extreme frankness of his testimony. Ambassador Galal, an academic and an expert in human rights, answers the first possibility in the affirmative:

> Egypt's delegation to the League's Legal Committee clearly defended the necessity to adopt the ACHR. The League is the oldest regional organization and other regional organizations had already adopted relevant human rights instruments. The proposed Charter was considered as a 'protective regional fence' to alleviate the pressure of some international circuits on Arab States in the field of human rights.[44]

After the Council of the League had approved the ACHR, states might or might not accede to it in accordance with their circumstances and political will.[45] Those states that do not wish to accede to the ACHR have not signed it.[46] Seven years after the adoption of the ACHR, none of the Arab states has ratified it and only Iraq has signed it. This means that the most enthusiastic states, including Egypt which led a brilliant manoeuvre for its adoption, did not even sign it.[47]

After seven years, the testimony of Ambassador Galal is still credible.[48] The more time that passes, the more it is true. In brief, this was an initiative about 'drawing up' a political document for 'external propaganda' or for use as a 'protective fence' against pressures of the international community.

Other bodies took the matter seriously. Some sectors in the international community started to talk about a regional mechanism for the protection of human rights in the Arab states. Whereas the states which drew up the ACHR forgot all about ratifying it – for them, their mission was accomplished – Amnesty International described the Charter as 'a step towards establishing an effective safeguard of fundamental human rights in the Arab world.'[49]

The position of Amnesty International embodies the realistic viewpoint towards the ACHR. It emanates from considering the ACHR as a substantial positive development consistent with the nature of historical developments and the cultural debate, as well as with relations of political power in the Arab states. Another viewpoint, that may be called 'reformative', considers that it is possible to remedy the shortcomings of the ACHR by preparing, in collaboration with non-governmental organizations, additional protocols, like those drafted for other international mechanisms,[50] based on the text of the Charter on Human and Peoples' Rights in the Arab World. A third viewpoint adopted by the human rights movement in the Arab states calls upon the League to reconsider the ACHR and make it consistent with international human rights standards in preparation for drafting a new Arab human rights instrument in cooperation with Arab human rights organizations.[51]

It is worth mentioning that the First International Conference of the Arab Human Rights Movement, 'Prospects for the Future' (Casablanca, Morocco, April 1999) also arrived at this recommendation instead of a more radical one. It recommended that the ACHR be considered as non-existent, since those which adopted it have not ratified it.

It can be concluded, therefore, that no regional mechanism for the protection of human rights in the Arab states exists because of the extreme weakness of human rights safeguards in the ACHR and the fragility of its mechanisms. Even if it were binding and enforced, it would still suffer from these deficiencies.

Finally, only local or international mechanisms for protecting human rights exist. There is also, of course, the mechanism of the African Charter for Human and Peoples' Rights in respect of Arab states in Africa. Moreover, we cannot, theoretically speaking, rule out the possibility of the emergence of an Euro-Mediterranean mechanism based on Article 2 of the

1995 Barcelona Declaration adopted by the European Union and 12 Mediterranean states.

In any case, it seems likely that the Arab states will continue to depend, for a long time, on the United Nations and African mechanisms of human rights protection. This is due to two seemingly contradictory factors. The first factor is the prevalent negative attitude of the majority of Arab political regimes towards human rights which are merely regarded as a call that aims at 'destabilizing their internal security'.[52]

In this respect it is worth mentioning the position of Arab governments towards the ACHR and the Arab Convention on the Suppression of Terrorism. The latter was adopted four years after the ACHR and was enforced within a few months. By virtue of this Convention, Arab states could extradite refugees accused of being terrorists.

The second factor relates to the acknowledgment of the former Director of the League's Human Rights Department, mentioned above, that governmental pan-Arab relations have a negative impact on the possibility of the League playing an efficient role in protecting human rights. Thus Arab governments tend to be content with the role played by the United Nations in this respect.[53] The most recent indicator of the validity of this opinion is the position of Saudi Arabia which ratified the Convention against Torture and other Cruel, Inhuman or Degrading Treatment or Punishment in 1997 and the CEDAW in 2000, despite the fact that both instruments contradict Saudi concepts of Islam. Nevertheless, Saudi Arabia has expressed reservations regarding the ACHR, as it feels that it is sufficient to adhere to the Cairo Declaration on Human Rights in Islam and the provisions of the Islamic *Shar'ia* (legal opinion).[54]

One factor could radically change all expectations and calculations – namely, the possibility of the international community acknowledging its political and moral responsibility towards the Palestinian people and obliging Israel to implement all previous United Nations General Assembly and Security Council resolutions in order to attain a just and ultimate peace. While this development does not seem to be at all imminent, if it does happen, it will result in many positive consequences – namely:

- The Arab people will again believe in the credibility of the universal principles of human rights.
- Issues of democracy and human rights will no longer be at the bottom of the agenda of the political and cultural elite in the Arab states and will join the forefront currently occupied by the Palestinian issue and confrontations with the West, which exempt Israel from being held accountable for its crimes, as was the case before the events in Bosnia, Kosovo, Eastern Timor and Iraq.
- The present Arab governments would lose the most effective of its weapons – that is, the marginalization of claims concerning democracy and human rights under the pretext that they undermine Arab society and obstruct mobilization against foreign threats.

This development, with its ensuing interactions, could open the door to a historic and qualitative breakthrough regarding human rights in the Arab states in general, and their protection in the region.

NOTES

1 This means that more than 50 per cent of the states expressing reservations were Arab states. In fact, the number of reservations on the Declaration amount to at least 18 states, because two Arab governments known for their animosity towards human rights organizations did not express a reservation.
2 See the newspaper *Al-Hayat*, London, 8 January 1997.
3 See Fateh (1995). In Arabic and English.
4 See Hassan (1995). In Arabic and French.
5 See Zeyada (2000). In Arabic.
6 Fateh (1995).
7 Basel (1987). In Arabic.
8 Nafaa (1982). In Arabic.
9 Basel (1987).
10 Ibid.
11 Ibid.
12 Maydany (2000). In Arabic.
13 Abdel Ghafar (2001). In Arabic.
14 Hassan (1989). In Arabic.
15 See the Declaration in *Al-Haq*, Union of Arab Lawyers, Cairo, Special issue, 1978. In Arabic.
16 Hassan (1995).
17 Hassan (1989).
18 See the Casablanca Declaration, adopted by the First Arab Conference of the Arab Human Rights Movement and Hassan (2001).
19 Galal (1994). In Arabic.
20 Hassan (1995).
21 Abdel Ghafar (2003).
22 Hassan (1989).
23 Abdel Ghafar (2001).
24 Hassan (1989).
25 Ibid.
26 Hassan (1995).
27 Basel (1987).
28 Hassan (1995).
29 Maydany (2000).
30 Abdel Ghafar (2001).
31 Ibid.
32 Ibid.
33 Maydany (2000).
34 Ibid.
35 Abdel Ghafar (2001).
36 Ibid.
37 Ibid.
38 Ibid.
39 Ibid.

40   Ibid.
41   Amnesty International (1993).
42   'On the relation between the problematique of human rights in the Palestinian issue', *Double Standards*, Cairo: Cairo Institute for Human Rights Studies (2001). In Arabic and English.
43   Anbatawy (1991). In Arabic.
44   Galal (1994).
45   Ibid.
46   Ibid.
47   The Egyptian delegation clarified that what was required was to adopt the draft resolution made by the Legal Committee for the adoption of the ACHR while upholding all reservations. The Egyptian delegation requested that the intervention by the Head of the Legal Department would not be lengthy in explaining the opposing viewpoints but would just point out the resolution of the Legal Committee. The Head of the Legal Department was true to his word. The logic behind this was to adopt the resolution quickly without discussion and differences between delegations. The Kuwaiti motion of postponement was not approved. The Chair of the session considered that the draft ACHR was agreed upon and moved to the next item on the agenda. This way the draft ACHR was approved quickly and unexpectedly.
48   Despite the importance of this testimony, it raises an important question which becomes even more pertinent as time passes without Egypt's ratification of the ACHR. Was the Egyptian delegation really enthusiastic about issuing an Arab Charter on Human Rights? Or was it a personal enthusiasm on the part of the head of the Egyptian delegation?
49   Amnesty International (1993).
50   Abdel Ghafar (2001).
51   See the Casablanca Declaration, adopted by the First Arab Conference of the Arab Human Rights Movement, and Hassan (2001).
52   Zeyada (2000).
53   Al Bayaty (1995).
54   For reviewing the reservations of Saudi Arabia and other Arab States on the ACHR, see Galal (1994).

BIBLIOGRAPHY

Abdel Ghafar, Mostafa (2001), 'Safeguards of human rights at the regional level', *Cairo Institute for Human Rights Studies*, pp.1–39.
Abdel Ghafar, Mostafa (2003), 'The right to resort to the judiciary in regional and international human rights conventions', *Rowaq Arabi* (21), Cairo Institute for Human Rights Studies. In Arabic.
Amnesty International (1993), Commentary of Amnesty International on the draft Arab Charter on Human Rights, December.
Anbatwy, Monzer (1991), 'The human being: issues and rights', *Arab Institute for Human Rights*, Tunisia. In Arabic.
Azzam, Fateh (1995), *Safeguards of Political and Civil Rights in Arab Constitutions. A Comparative Study*, Cairo: Cairo Institute for Human Rights Studies. In Arabic and English.
Basel, Yousef (1987), 'Arab joint action and human rights', *Human Rights in the Arab World* (20), Arabic Organization for Human Rights. In Arabic.

Cairo Institute for Human Rights Studies (2001), 'On the relation between the problematique of human rights in the Palestinian issue', *Double Standards*. In Arabic and English.

Galal, Noaman (1994), 'The Arab Charter on Human Rights', in idem (ed.), *League of Arab States: Human Rights,* Cairo: Center for Political Studies and Research, Cairo University. In Arabic.

Hassan, Bahey el Din (1989), 'The rights of the Arab human being', *International Politics*, (96). In Arabic.

Hassan, Bahey el Din (1995), *The Outcome and Prospects of Arab Instruments on Human Rights – Towards a Regional Agreement on Human Rights in the Middle East Starting from Egypt and Lebanon*, Paris/Beirut: University of Catholic Holy Spirit, Human Rights Institute, Lawyers Trade Union. In Arabic and French.

Hassan, Bahey el Din (2001), *The Arab Human Rights Movement: Tasks and Challenges – Arabs Caught between Domestic Oppression and Foreign Injustice*, Cairo: Cairo Institute for Human Rights Studies. In Arabic, French and English.

Maydany, Mohammed Ameen (2000), 'International and regional committees for the protection of human rights', Cairo: Cairo Institute for Human Rights Studies. In Arabic.

Nafaa, Hassan (1982), 'The League of Arab States and human rights', *Arab Affairs* (13), League of Arab States. In Arabic, pp.486–506.

Zeyada, Radwan (2000), *The Human Rights March in the Arab World*, Casablanca: Arab Cultural Center. In Arabic.

PART III
TOWARDS FURTHER
STRENGTHENING OF
HUMAN RIGHTS
PROTECTION

8 National Systems for the Protection of Human Rights

JEAN-BERNARD MARIE

INTRODUCTION

Strangely enough, the unprecedented international expansion of human rights today can have the effect of obscuring the primary requirement to guarantee their protection at the national level, which is the specific responsibility of each state. What seems to be an international code of human rights has been drawn up, and a network of bodies has gradually been installed in both worldwide and regional organizations. This spread of international norms and procedures[1] encourages public opinion and the media, for example, to consider that it is the international community and the bodies it has set up which are mainly and directly responsible for implementing and enforcing human rights throughout the world. One even frequently hears such questions as 'But what is the United Nations doing to guarantee human rights in such and such a country?', as if this worldwide organization were directly responsible for human rights and for their protection in the event of a violation within the frontiers of a given state.

Yet it is the state, with its various institutions, which is primarily responsible for guaranteeing the implementation and enforcement of these rights in respect of its citizens and all those coming under its jurisdiction. This responsibility is explicitly stated in the Charter of the United Nations as follows: 'All Members pledge themselves to take joint and separate action in co-operation with the Organization' for the achievement of 'universal respect for, and observance of, human rights and fundamental freedoms'.[2]

In addition, the many international instruments concerning human rights adopted since then in the context of both the United Nations, with its specialized agencies, and various regional organizations are designed to define specifically each state's undertakings and to set up monitoring mechanisms.

The World Conference on Human Rights in 1993 noted, in the Vienna Declaration and Programme of Action, 'the responsibilities of all States, in conformity with the Charter of the United Nations, to develop and encourage respect for human rights and fundamental freedoms for all, without distinction as to race, sex, language or religion'. The Programme of Action stresses the primary responsibility for human rights by stating that 'their protection and promotion is the first responsibility of governments'.[3] Although this statement seems self-evident, it was no doubt considered useful to recall states' obligations as the protagonists in guaranteeing respect for human rights and as being accountable in the event of their violation.

In addition to being based on the political will of governments, the protection of human rights within each state depends in the first instance on the norms and rules underlying and governing life in society. To quote the Universal Declaration of Human Rights: 'Everyone is entitled to a social and international order in which the rights and freedoms set forth in this Declaration can be fully realized'.[4] This implies the existence of the 'rule of law' and the establishment of the 'democratic society' referred to by the main international human rights instruments.[5]

Second, it is the responsibility of the institutions set up by the state to guarantee respect for human rights. These are the traditional institutions coming under the legislature, judiciary and executive, and also specific institutions for the promotion and protection of human rights which have recently been set up in many countries – for example, ombudspersons and national human rights commissions. In this chapter, we shall briefly note the conditions required for the establishment of a national system of human rights protection, try to situate the place of the institutions traditionally responsible for guaranteeing these rights, and then examine the role of new institutions set up specifically for this purpose.

PREREQUISITES FOR NATIONAL PROTECTION

Any protection system presupposes recognition of human rights in the basic texts which reflect the constitution of each state. When incorporated in the highest-ranking national legal instrument, human rights and the principles governing them enjoy the greatest authority and security in both their definition and their guaranteed observance. They thus become part and parcel of the founding principles of the organization of life in society, since they define the ultimate aim of the political system. In this context, human rights are not only 'objects' which are protected by the highest norm but are, by their very nature, the carriers of meanings and values based on respect for human dignity expressed in the specific array of rights covered.

Today, most national constitutions contain more or less extensive or precise provisions concerning human rights. Some refer to, or include, national declarations of rights;[6] others, in particular those of newly independent countries, refer directly to, or even incorporate, basic international texts such as the Universal Declaration of Human Rights. Generally speaking, the most recent constitutions reflect provisions contained in international instruments, as regards both definitions and the linkage between different categories of rights (civil and political – economic, social and cultural), thus strengthening the indivisible nature of human rights which is recognized by the international community.

In parallel, the establishment of the 'rule of law' is a basic prerequisite for any protection system. This presupposes the existence of a set of rules drawn up in advance to govern the powers of institutions and governments. Failing such rules, arbitrariness prevails, with ensuing widespread violation of human rights. The rule of law must apply to institutions, all the organs of society and every citizen. This means a ranking system of norms characterized by the supremacy of the constitution, the monitoring of the constitutionality of laws and the independence of the judiciary. Not confined to the mere definition or assembly of formal rules, the idea of the rule of law takes on its full significance and scope only when it becomes a working principle which effectively governs all the organs of society and is binding in the exercise of power at all levels.

Yet, in some countries today, it can be seen that, while various theoretical components of the rule of law exist (pre-established rules, a ranking system or hierarchy of norms and so on), this does not really affect the functioning of systems or the organization of society. In this case, the rule of law is purely formal: having no operational character, it does not meet its primary requirements. Further, since the rule of law is a means to an end, it cannot be divorced from the ultimate aim and founding values of a society which recognizes the principles of human rights. A so-called 'rule of law' which reflects only perfunctorily the criteria defining it, regardless of the requirements of justice or the fundamental respect of human dignity, becomes in fact discredited. A genuine rule of law is not an abstract or isolated idea; it must be embodied in social reality.

Taken as a whole, it is the development of a 'democratic society' which makes possible the real exercise of human rights. The basic principles of democracy are set forth in the main international texts on human rights: for example, the Universal Declaration states: 'The will of the people shall be the basis of the authority of government; this will shall be expressed in genuine elections which shall be by universal and equal suffrage'. 'Everyone has the right to take part in the government of his country, directly or through freely chosen representatives.'[7]

The foundations are thus laid, but the organizational methods and operating conditions of the democratic system are relatively vague. For instance, the principle of the separation of powers between the legislature, executive and judiciary, first systematized by Montesquieu, is not stated explicitly in the basic international texts. However, in confirming the requirement of the independence of the courts, these texts implicitly recognize that the judiciary is independent from the other two powers. In addition, where instruments provide for limitations or restrictions to specific rights, some provisions refer to the idea of a 'democratic society'[8] which has gradually been interpreted in the case law of international bodies.[9] In fact, the principle of the separation of powers, first devised and applied in Western democracies, has been gradually extended to the political systems of most countries, though in differing degrees and with varying success.

Yet here again, the issue of democracy arises less in terms of formal criteria – although these retain their importance – than in terms of effectiveness and results. In relatively long-established democracies, instances of malfunctioning and shortcomings can be observed (for example, one speaks of a 'democratic deficit') and even perverse effects, whereas, in countries which have recently embarked on democratization, the introduction and operation of democracy encounter a host of obstacles – and we are not speaking here of regimes in which 'democracy' is only a facade which is systematically violated. Much more than a 'state', democracy is a continuing *process* of development: it proceeds from representative democracy to participative democracy, from majority rule to respect for the rights of the minority (and minorities), from the general will to the recognition of special cases, in particular those of men and women who have been excluded from the system.

These are the conditions, in a pre-established constitutional context of the rule of law and the democratic system, in which the main organs of state, coming under the legislature, judicial and executive powers, are called on to implement and guarantee recognized human rights.

The continuing advance of democracy, as regards both its radical aims and its mode of functioning, as well as its actual achievements, largely condition the extent to which human rights are effectively respected in different countries throughout the world.[10]

LEGISLATIVE, JUDICIAL AND EXECUTIVE POWERS

The Legislature

The legislature is the main institution responsible for the national protection of human rights. To quote the Universal Declaration of Human Rights (Article 21), it represents 'the will of the people' as 'the basis of the authority of government'. The main international legal texts of a binding nature stipulate that States Parties shall undertake in particular to adopt 'legislative measures' to guarantee the exercise of the rights recognized.[11] Thus the organization and guarantee of rights and freedoms are regulated by laws prepared and adopted by an assembly elected by the people whose will it expresses.

As also stipulated in international instruments,[12] when limitations or restrictions on the exercise of certain rights and liberties are necessary, these must be provided for in a law which publicly defines their governing conditions and scope.

While the legislature has a central role in the protection of human rights, and even when it is the result of democratic elections guaranteeing the free expression of the will of the people, it is not immune from violations of human rights. Oppression by the majority, the play of forces, pressure of all kinds, or aberrations or malfunctioning can lead parliaments to overlook or violate basic principles and rights recognized and protected by the constitution. Hence the importance of the monitoring of the constitutionality of laws, which provides the necessary security and is a key guarantee of the respect of human rights. Where monitoring exists, as in many countries, it can be conducted, depending on the system, by the courts or by judicial institutions having their own special competence (constitutional courts, constitutional councils and the like) with specific referral procedures.

There are other limits to the acts of the legislature such as, for example, the principle of non-retroactivity in criminal cases[13] whereby no one can be condemned for actions or omissions which were not a crime at the date when they were committed; this principle debars the legislature from decreeing the retroactivity of a law in this field.

It is nevertheless the case that today, in many countries, the smooth operation of legislative institutions encounters obstacles and difficulties of all kinds. First, it can be seen that, in a variety of situations, the independence of parliaments and their members is seriously compromised by various illegal practices, such as, in certain cases, the arbitrary imprisonment or disappearance of parliamentarians for primarily political reasons.[14] In such cases, parliament becomes merely a hostage to government, and the very principle of the separation of powers is violated.

There are, however, other difficulties which, while not so dramatic, have consequences for the effective role of the legislature and its place in the balance of powers. The complexity and novelty of subjects on which laws have to be passed (for example, bioethics or the new information technologies), the fact that it is difficult for citizens to see and understand how parliaments work (chiefly in committees),[15] the discovery of reprehensible actions perpetrated by individual parliamentarians and many other factors linked to the national and international development of societies may affect the authority and repute of parliaments. If we are to avoid a weakening of this main institution for the protection of human rights, it must be given new scope and increased resources in keeping with present changes and needs.

The Judiciary

Once human rights have been recognized by the constitution and laid down in legislation, their observance and guarantee make it necessary to provide remedies in the event of their violation. As provided for in the Universal Declaration and the relevant main international instruments,[16] it is the judiciary that ensures that 'everyone has the right to an effective remedy … for acts violating the fundamental rights granted him by the Constitution or by law.' The first imperative is the independence of judicial bodies which are also required to meet the requirements of competence, impartiality and legality so that everyone can effectively exercise his/her right to have his/her case heard equitably and in public.

Independence is necessary for all tribunals, whatever the level or category of jurisdiction afforded by the different national systems, whether it be judicial (civil, criminal) or administrative tribunals in countries where these have been set up to deal specifically with disputes between the state and the citizen. The independence of judges also depends on the legal status and guarantees accorded to them (method of appointment, irremovability, career system and so on).

However, it can be seen that, in many countries, the judiciary is not in a position to guarantee the right to a remedy on sufficiently effective and independent lines. Recently, the United Nations Commission on Human Rights re-examined this question and appointed a Special Rapporteur on the independence and impartiality of the judiciary, following a study already carried out by its Sub-Commission on Prevention of Discrimination and Protection of Minorities on this subject.[17]

In addition to extreme situations where a case is not heard or examined, or the court acts under external pressure and instructions, or the legal system has been largely destroyed in conflicts and confrontations, there are other difficulties which arise in most countries. These are related, for example, to the lack of human and physical resources, inadequate training, the malfunctioning or breakdown of systems, the technical complexity of cases, unsuitable procedures and violations of the confidentiality of the examination under media pressure and so on.

Generally speaking, there is a time-lag between developments in modern society and the responses which the legal system can provide. Hence there is a risk of the citizen distancing himself and gradually losing confidence in a system which becomes increasingly inaccessible and incomprehensible, the result being an increase in various forms of violence. Here again, there is an urgent need to respond to new requirements without jeopardizing or violating the principles which are basic to judicial institutions. Otherwise, when the right to a remedy becomes gradually ineffectual, human rights lose a vital prerequisite for their guaranteed observance.

The Executive

Responsibility for ensuring the conditions and specific resources for implementing human rights within each state lies above all with the executive and its organs, which operate in the framework of government and various government departments. The executive has the task of applying, at the national level, the laws adopted by parliament and must act with due respect for constitutional principles and norms; but it is also responsible for fulfilling the human rights commitments undertaken by the state internationally[18] and to report thereon to the appropriate international bodies when the relevant instruments so require.[19] Thus the executive is central to the machinery for the application of human rights: it is required to take the appropriate measures according to the prescribed forms (decree, edict, order, ruling and so on) and within the limits prescribed (in particular by the law) to ensure the effective observance of human rights and guarantee that they are respected; it is therefore subject to supervision by the competent bodies (legal, legislative) and must account for its acts to the various organs of society and to citizens as a whole.

Generally speaking, national systems provide guarantees and remedies for acts and eventual abuses of power by the executive and government departments. Depending on the system, disputes between the state and the citizen are examined either by ordinary courts (judicial) or by special courts such as administrative tribunals which provide a specific remedy and a reinforced guarantee against acts by the administration and government agents. There are also other types of remedy and guarantee provided within the administration itself, under statutes and rules which allow for the examination and eventual rectification of certain situations (for example, an appeal to the hierarchical superior, or even the Head of State, the possibility of appealing to internal bodies, such as committees, commission, offices and so on).

In a growing number of countries, specific institutions such as the ombudsperson, which will be examined below, have been set up to deal with problems arising between government departments and citizens. It is vital that such remedies be effectively accessible to all citizens – in particular those not in close contact or familiar with the system – and that citizens be provided with suitable information and free legal assistance.

In modern societies, government administration is increasingly led to take action in a growing number of sectors of social life which in the past were largely outside its sphere of competence. This is the result, *inter alia*, of the gradual recognition, both nationally and internationally, of specific rights in the economic, social and cultural fields which the state is responsible for implementing in the same way as traditional rights and freedoms – that is, civil and political rights. For example, governments take widespread action at different levels by way of social security, welfare, healthcare, work, education, culture and so on. In so doing, the state – in some cases, described somewhat exaggeratedly as the 'welfare state' – legitimately fulfils functions which meet the present needs of developed societies and also the aspirations of developing societies. The state thus provides a public service in key areas for citizens who are all equally entitled to enjoy it.

However, this considerable expansion of the action, and hence of the power, of the executive and its administration, has resulted in a greater risk of violation of human rights, accentuated in this case again by the complexity of the various fields concerned. Here, it must be possible for the various remedies noted above to be applied effectively but, upstream from this, citizens should also be informed about the acts which concern them and be able to participate, individually or in various bodies or social organizations or groups, in the preparation of choices and decisions in the social, economic, cultural and vocational fields and the various other sectors of state intervention. Specific citizen participation at the various levels of local and national administration will open up the way to 'economic and social democracy' which will supplement and strengthen 'political democracy' and so, to put it briefly, bring about democracy as such.

In the forefront of the scene as a central actor in the implementation and protection of human rights in the national context, the executive, with its bodies and agents, is also, in that capacity, the authority which is likely most frequently and extensively to violate these rights. Violations are manifest in states where there is no real control over the acts of the executive or *effective* remedy against abuses of power. Factual situations in which a government monopolizes all the key powers are particularly serious when, as in certain countries, there exists 'a state of exception' – sometimes virtually permanent – which gives rise to the most flagrant and systematic violations of human rights.[20]

Quite apart from only too frequent situations which require a radical re-establishment of the rule of law and the democratic process, even in so-called 'normal' situations, and whatever the national situation, it is difficult to maintain the balance between the various authorities and institutions responsible for protecting human rights nationally. Generally, it is within the executive, which disposes of the bulk of the government's resources, that there arise the greatest risks of an abuse of power and violation of human rights. Strengthened guarantees are therefore necessary, though without compromising the performance of the key responsibilities entrusted to the bodies and agents of the executive.[21]

In addition to the basic task devolving on each of the three major powers, specific functions are performed by new 'national institutions' specially set up to meet the present-day requirements for the promotion and protection of human rights.

SPECIFIC NATIONAL INSTITUTIONS FOR THE PROMOTION AND PROTECTION OF HUMAN RIGHTS

Far from competing with or taking the place of the traditional institutions which characterize all democratic systems, these 'specialized human rights institutions' perform a complementary function and differ in that they employ specific resources and methods based on their particular status. While their tasks and actions are basically national, they tend gradually to develop relations with the international community. Some of these institutions, set up relatively recently, are nevertheless guided by 'models' first introduced almost two centuries ago at the national level, while others reflect proposals put forward internationally some 50 years ago.

These 'new' institutions, which are constantly developing, consist of different types within which there are also noticeable variations – for example, as regards attributions and functions. However, they have in common the fact that they introduce new approaches and specific modes of action with a view to promoting and protecting human rights at the national level.

We shall begin by singling out institutions headed by an individual on the lines of the relatively familiar model of the ombudsperson, and then consider at greater length collegial-type appeal bodies known generally as national human rights commissions.

Ombudspersons and Similar Institutions

Inaugurated by Sweden in 1809, the institution of the ombudsperson was first taken up by other Scandinavian states and then spread to a growing number of countries in all continents.[22] Originally conceived as being mandated by parliament to monitor the application of laws by legal institutions and the administration, the ombudsperson was gradually led to play the role of defender of citizens' rights in respect of administrative authorities.

However, the ombudsperson's functions and powers may vary greatly depending on the system, and countries have adopted various titles such as: protector of the citizen, mediator, defender of the people or parliamentary commissioner. It should be noted that the term 'ombudsperson' has sometimes been wrongly used in respect of certain methods or initiatives which, while based on some features of this institution, do not meet its basic criteria (public nature, independence, responsibility and so on); examples are 'ombudspersons' who are given this title by the media or private bodies or who in fact simply represent formulae for internal monitoring.

The ombudsperson, who is usually elected by and answerable to parliament,[23] supervises the way in which government departments (and, in some cases, the judicial authorities, as in Sweden) perform their tasks, reports thereon setting out the instances of negligence, maladministration, faults and violations observed, and formulates comments and recommendations. Since he/she is outside the departments he/she has to supervise, his/her institution is entirely independent of them. The ombudsperson is empowered to receive complaints from individuals and may, depending on the case, act on his/her own initiative and examine cases brought to his/her attention by the press or other media. He/she usually has wide powers of investigation, can hear witnesses and is entitled to free access to information, files and official documents of the administration, addressing him/herself directly to the responsible officials.

In some cases, the ombudsperson can act as mediator between individuals who have lodged complaints and the administrative authorities concerned, and try to find solutions and remedies to each situation. The administration is not usually required to comply with requests by the ombudsperson, but the outcome of his/her action depends to a great extent on his/her powers of persuasion combined with the climate of confidence and cooperation established with government departments and civil servants themselves.

Here, the publicity given to the ombudsperson's role and activities is vital for the success of his action as a whole and the influence of his action in special cases. Much of the effectiveness of the institution is based on information, awareness-raising and support of public opinion; in this way public opinion strengthens the powers of the ombudsperson whose acts are usually without binding force. In addition to initiatives taken by the institution to provide information on its action, the role of the media, educational establishments and training facilities is decisive in accrediting and strengthening the action of an institution which, by its very nature, is based on adequate citizen information and support.

In some systems, the ombudsperson is empowered to act as plaintiff by referring a case to the appropriate courts. However, in no case can he/she replace other state institutions – in particular judicial institutions – or encroach on their specific functions. Here the ombudsperson represents a supplementary institution for legal protection – a new form of non-jurisdictional supervision and a new example of the 'right to a hearing' provided to citizens without ignoring or setting aside traditional remedies.

The ombudsperson institution has developed both in countries where the ordinary courts supervise the acts of the administration and in countries which have administrative tribunals (even if, in the latter case, misgivings about the institution are more lively, since specific remedies already exist). Whatever the system, the ombudsperson or similar institutions are seen as providing the citizen with an additional form not only of expression but also of protection against the acts of an administration whose field of action has its tentacles everywhere and whose workings are often impenetrable.

In view of the extent and variety of the fields of competence of administrative authorities and the special problems of society, some countries have instituted 'specialized' ombudspersons to deal with specific sectors or issues. For example, the ombudsperson system has been extended to prisons, the police, the armed forces, race relations, equality of the sexes, consumer protection, official languages among others. Elsewhere, in a number of states with a federal structure, it has developed at the level of constituent units.

In some countries where the institution has developed extensively and the ombudsperson receives many appeals from individuals, a form of distribution and decentralization has been set up to deal more effectively with the many requests. The ombudsperson's function may be shared among several people (as in Sweden since 1968) or be performed in a system at several levels corresponding to the structure of the administration (local, regional and so on). However, these arrangements designed to achieve greater efficiency and be closer to citizens, can sometimes impair the personal nature of the function and its 'visibility' or profile, and also the consistency of approaches adopted. A balance therefore has to be gradually built up between the needs of the ombudsperson's task and the requirements of the institution, whose success depends greatly on the way in which it is perceived by public opinion and the respect that it commands from the administration.

Now spreading in many countries and constantly changing to meet new needs, the ombudsperson and similar institutions provide new resources and a new contribution to the national protection of human rights. But a precondition is that the elementary rules governing the institution – particularly the requirement of independence and impartiality – should be strictly respected; this precludes any possibility of dismissal by the government and presupposes terms of reference with sufficient guarantees. Without these, the so-called ombudsperson might become merely a devious pretence or false front who would not only be unable to perform the true functions of the office but would also compromise the institution's future credibility.

The ombudsperson system provides all citizens with a way of access and a new complementary remedy without depriving them of other traditional remedies, especially jurisdictional ones. Direct accessibility, the provision of services free of charge, flexible procedures and conditions regarding the admissibility of complaints, more rapid examination and settlement are additional resources, often better suited to each specific case, which the system makes available to citizens. While the institution is not primarily designed to decrease the courts' workload, it nevertheless makes an original contribution to the exercise of the 'right to be heard' by an independent body with a view to finding a solution respectful of the law without necessarily having recourse to legal proceedings which are frequently inaccessible, complex, expensive, prolonged and incommensurate with the subject of the dispute.

In addition to these functions in respect of individuals confronting the administration, the ombudsperson presents reports to parliament containing recommendations for proposed improvements or reforms (particularly legislative) when he/she has perceived the need for these in cases referred to him/her or those he/she has examined on his own initiative. This function of making proposals, which does not always enjoy the publicity it deserves, is vital for remedying basic gaps or injustices in systems and preventing the same causes again producing the same effects. It also represents an induced, and far from negligible, role which can be played by the ombudsperson in informing and guiding citizens towards other possible remedies or bodies appropriate to deal with their applications, since the 'man in the street' is often at a loss because of the complexity and burden of the situations with which he/she is faced.

Lastly, the scope and efficiency of the institution are to a great extent bound up with the ombudsperson's personality – that is, his/her authority, command of respect, accessibility to citizens and simplicity of approach, personal impartiality and independence, sense of justice and respect for human rights, and skill at human relations and social communication.

The functions performed by ombudspersons and similar institutions will continue to develop and probably diversify in the future. In order not to lose the key features and specific requirements of the institution, discussions and exchanges of experience must continue to develop between all those responsible for it, as has been done so far especially in the context of the United Nations and the Council of Europe.[24] Comparisons of this kind could provide a surer foundation and consolidate the basic principles underlying these institutions, while encouraging their development in a greater number of states.

Alongside the ombudsperson system, other specific institutions of a collegial nature have recently developed in various countries; these are most frequently known as 'human rights commissions'.

National Human Rights Commissions

The idea that each state should set up bodies specifically concerned with the progress and observance of human rights on its territory is not very recent, since it coincides with the introduction at international level of the early institutions for the promotion and protection of human rights worldwide. In 1946 the United Nations, in its resolution defining the attributions of the Commission on Human Rights created by the Organization, invited member states 'to consider the desirability of establishing information groups or local human rights committees within their respective countries to collaborate with them in furthering the work of the Commission on Human Rights'.[25]

However, this invitation aroused little enthusiasm during the next few years[26] and it was not until the adoption, in 1966, of the two International Covenants on Human Rights that the question of setting up national human rights commissions was again examined in the United Nations.[27] From 1978 onwards more specific proposals for the development of such institutions were formulated in this framework – for example, the preparation of guiding principles for the structure and functioning of national institutions to promote and protect human rights.[28]

Today a growing number of countries[29] have set up specific new human rights institutions which are, in differing degrees, in line with the prospect opened up, and the framework proposed, by the United Nations. Depending on the system, their status varies considerably and their respective attributions reflect a wide range of functions covering the fields of promotion or protection or both at once. While it is sometimes tricky to draw distinctions, given the intermeshing of their structures and functions, tentatively we can identify:

- institutions specially set up as organs for the implementation and monitoring of special legislation on human rights or one aspect thereof
- institutions with a more general and versatile purpose to deal with human rights issues in a national context.

Commissions responsible for specific legislation

This type of body first appeared in the late 1950s in the United States and in the early 1960s in Canada[30] and subsequently developed in certain systems with an Anglo-Saxon tradition. These commissions are mainly responsible for implementing and enforcing specific human rights laws (charters, codes, acts and so on) providing for their creation and defining their terms of reference. In fact, this legislation is mainly concerned with combating discrimination in all its forms, depending on the various alleged grounds and fields involved. Thus most commissions are primarily 'anti-discrimination commissions' which are usually given fairly broad powers which include the conduct of inquiries and the giving of judgments in the cases referred to them.

Their members or 'commissioners' may be appointed by the executive or parliament or by a formula combining both. They are appointed in their personal capacity in the light of their experience in the fields of competence of each commission and usually come from varied sectors of society (in particular from categories or communities which are the most vulnerable to discrimination). Commissioners and the commission itself enjoy independent status in the exercise of their functions.

The legislation to be applied by the commissions concerns the fight against discrimination, particularly in the fields of employment, housing, access to public places, facilities and services, and the publication or posting of notices, symbols or other representations. While some commissions are empowered to act in all of these fields, others have sole competence for a single one (usually employment). As regards the motives for discrimination, alongside a common core of race, colour, sex and religion, there exists a varied list which includes language, ethnic origin, national origin, nationality, descent, whether married or single, family situation, civil status, sexual orientation, social origin, social condition, age, disability, conviction for a crime among others. All these motives are usually added to the initial list each time the legislation is amended to reflect a need to define more precisely, and combat, the factors of discrimination in actual practice.

Under their respective terms of reference, the commissions perform several types of function covering both human rights protection and promotion: they conduct investigation and conciliation procedures, can give advice on recommendations on legislation and current or projected texts, initiate programmes of encouragement and undertake information, awareness-raising and educational activities.

In the first place they are empowered to receive complaints alleging discrimination based on the motives prohibited in the fields covered by the applicable legislation. They can conduct investigations, seek information from the plaintiff and the second party and also from other sources (documents, testimony, on-site inspections and so on). When the investigation establishes that there are grounds for considering that discrimination has taken place, a conciliation procedure is proposed to the parties concerned under the auspices of the commission. The party attacked is invited to put an end to the discriminatory practice and its effects, and make good the damage suffered by the plaintiff, in particular by the payment of compensation or by the institution of programmes for access to equality or any other measure designed to eliminate the practices brought to light. When agreement is reached, the commission is responsible for enforcing its terms, which are legally binding on the parties.

Where conciliation is unsuccessful, under the procedures of some commissions the case may be referred to a board of inquiry or board of adjudication which holds a public hearing in which witnesses are heard under oath and the parties may be assisted by counsel. The board judges whether there has been a violation and decides on the measures to be taken; this judgment can be invoked in law and enforced if the party concerned does not comply.

However, the originality and relevance of the commissions' role in respect of complaints lies primarily in the possibilities afforded by the conciliation or mediation which they propose. This approach and these procedures seem to be more suited to combating the phenomenon of discrimination. First, they usually provide more specific and rapid possibilities of remedying the alleged discrimination than traditional legal proceedings (for example, through swift action, making it possible for an employee to be recruited or restored to his job, to overturn an initial refusal to award housing or to regulate the publication of notices). Conciliation can redress a situation without loss of time, whereas legal proceedings sometimes do no more than compensate damage already suffered, the situation itself often being irreversible. Second, the inquiry and conciliation procedure allows for situating the requirements of proof at a more suitable level. Since the aim is not so much to incriminate as to find a satisfactory settlement, it is enough to establish that there are reasonable grounds for considering that there has been discrimination. It is well known that it is difficult to establish proof of a crime in respect of discriminatory acts however manifest they are. In addition, action by the commission does not, as elsewhere, lay the burden of proof solely on the plaintiff, who is frequently in a situation of aggravated inferiority due to his fear of possible reprisals by the other party.

Again, conciliation may help to raise awareness and educate on the adverse effects of all forms of discrimination, whereas repression can make an insidious contribution to strengthening underlying prejudices. Nevertheless, this is not intended in any way to underestimate, still less to set aside, recourse to the competent judicial bodies which have a decisive role by virtue of the sentences they can pronounce – even if these are still too infrequent in relation to actual instances and practices of discrimination.

Alongside their role of dealing with complaints, commissions are usually empowered, as in the ombudsperson system, to analyse and formulate opinions and recommendations on legislation – particularly on draft legislation and the various texts concerning their fields of competence. They prepare, on request or on their own initiative, studies and reports containing observations and proposals which can be made public. Some studies aim at clarifying the practice of commissions and their interpretation of the applicable legislation with particular reference to the data compiled during investigation procedures. The practical experience gained by commissions makes them specially qualified as agents to analyse the system's deficiencies and suggest necessary modifications.

Lastly, the commissions have a vital function in respect of information, awareness-raising and education. This stems from the approach whereby progress in combating discrimination is more an outcome of awareness of the irrationality and adverse effects of discrimination than of the application of sanctions which might simply shore up prejudices and attitudes. The commissions therefore widely disseminate information on anti-discriminatory principles and legislation, indicating the services and remedies they offer to individuals and also to various groups, communities, institutions and such like. The greatest possible variety of modern communication methods are used to address the widest possible public or target groups; awareness-raising may be conducted with firms (and all categories of staff) and education programmes may be drawn up for the school system.

In addition, in situations which reveal directly or indirectly induced discrimination, some commissions are able to propose – in some cases, even impose – the establishment of affirmative action programmes in order to overcome the obstacles resulting from continuing systematic discriminatory practices. These programmes, developed in particular in firms – even if they have aroused criticism, particularly when they have no underlying fixed policy bases – are a way of breaking with the system and the processes which perpetuate discrimination, making use of both awareness-raising in the community and specific measures (such as the definition of quotas to be gradually achieved).

While the promotional work of commissions initially gave priority to dealing with discrimination, their information, awareness-raising and education activities gradually expanded to include all human rights,[31] thus, in their way, illustrating the principle of the indivisibility of these rights as reaffirmed by the international community. Most of these commissions have thus become bodies which occupy a central place and play a major role in the advancement of all human rights in the countries where they have been set up.

General-purpose commissions

Bodies of this second type, which have a general responsibility for promotion and in some cases also for exercising special functions in the protection of human rights, differ noticeably as regards both their statute and composition and their competence and operation. These differences, which can affect, for example, these institutions' level of independence, has led the United Nations, concurrently with its encouragement for development, to prepare recommendations and principles addressed to them.

Generally known as 'commissions' (in some cases, 'committees' or 'boards'), these institutions have been set up by texts at different levels of municipal legislation. Depending on the country, they have been set up either exceptionally by the constitution,[32] in some cases by a law, or in most cases by an executive text (decree by the head of state or government, or ministerial order). It can be considered that the body's independence and authority is more likely to be ensured where the text setting it up comes from a senior source, although this is not an absolute condition. Generally, these bodies come under the executive power (head of state, government, ministry) or are placed under its authority, and their margin of independence varies depending on the system and in some critical cases also on temporary political circumstances.

Independence also depends on the composition of the bodies, which must reflect social and political pluralism. Generally, members of most commissions represent different sectors of society, in particular those which are the most directly involved in applying human rights: jurists, the medical profession, scientists, teachers, journalists, representatives of non-governmental organizations and trade unions, representative personalities, and representatives of the government, parliament or other institutions. However, the diversity and number of members may vary considerably from one commission to another, some having less than ten members, others more than 50.[33] Members are usually appointed by the executive – that is, by the head of state or government or by a minister (generally the Minister of Justice or of Foreign Affairs); less frequently, they are appointed by parliament. A commission's independence is more reliable when its composition reflects genuine pluralism and the manner of appointing its members protects them from interference and pressure by the executive.

While terms of reference vary markedly from one commission to another, they have common features through the attribution of a general standing advisory function in the form of opinions or recommendations addressed to governments. They are thus chiefly involved in advice and proposals on all questions concerning human rights, taking as a basis the relevant national normative texts (the constitution, laws and so on) and the relevant international instruments, in particular those ratified by the state. At the request of the authorities or on their own initiative – depending on the case and their respective attributions – commissions undertake field studies or inquiries to highlight the legal and factual situations prevailing in the country, and compare them with human rights requirements. Reports addressed to the government (which may be made public), or other forms of communication call attention to the problems encountered and the changes and measures to be adopted to remedy situations. Similarly, commissions may examine legislative or administrative texts in force or in the form of projects, and formulate relevant proposals and recommendations.

Commissions are generally able to carry out various promotional functions simultaneously through developing information and documentation and also through awareness-raising activities and support for human rights education and training programmes. Where their composition is pluralist, they are able to forge links between the representatives of civil society (in particular non-governmental organizations) and state bodies and services, especially those most directly concerned with the implementation and observance of human rights. Such commissions are therefore used to playing a vigilant and critical role regarding the human rights situation in their country, and influencing the decisions and measures to be taken by the authorities. Obviously, however, this role depends closely on the guarantees of independence and authority actually enjoyed by each commission.

In addition to these functions common to most commissions, a more limited number of them have also special attributions enabling them to receive complaints from individuals or to consider cases or situations concerning presumed human rights violations. These commissions can conduct inquiries, establish reports and, in some cases, decide on violations and transmit cases to be settled by the courts. Here again, the scope of their attributions and types of procedure vary depending on the commission, but some perform quasi-jurisdictional functions which require appropriate guarantees for both the plaintiff and the party cited. The role and visibility of commissions' action are strongly reinforced when they are empowered to exercise such functions, and they gain greater authority with both the government and citizens.

Furthermore, the task of a growing number of commissions goes beyond the national framework and concerns the state's international activities and undertakings in the human rights field. Some of them may be informed and consulted on items on the agenda of international bodies (such as the United Nations Commission on Human Rights) or even be represented in their country's delegation on these bodies. Alternatively, they may be directly associated with the monitoring mechanisms of international conventions ratified by their state, by participating in the preparation of periodical reports and, in some cases, their oral presentation to the appropriate bodies. This growing involvement of national commissions in respect of international bodies has recently raised, in the United Nations, the question of recognizing a special status which might be accorded to them at United Nations meetings on human rights.[34] Here again, this poses the issue of the independence of commissions – in this case, in relation to their countries' delegations.

In recent years the United Nations has strongly encouraged the creation of such national institutions worldwide in view of their great value for the progress of human rights in each national framework, and the fact that they can act as intermediaries for action in this field at the international level. Taking into account the basic requirements devolving on such institutions and in the light of the occasionally difficult, or even alarming, experiences of some of them,[35] the United Nations has, in parallel, formulated recommendations and principles concerning the status of commissions, in particular their independence. Without attempting to reduce the diversity which characterizes them and which corresponds to national systems and situations, it has become necessary to set up signposts and define criteria for the appropriate qualification of these institutions.

New principles concerning the status of commissions were adopted in 1991 to take account of changes and new experiments since the preparation, in 1978, of the early guiding principles on their structure and functioning.[36] Adopted at the first international meetings on national institutions for the promotion and protection of human rights organized by the United Nations in Paris from 7 to 9 October 1991,[37] these principles concern the status both of commissions, whose role is mainly advisory, and those which have also virtually jurisdictional functions.

These principles provide as broad terms of reference as possible, clearly defined in a constitutional or legislative text, and list a great variety of attributions including the giving of opinions and the formulation of recommendations and reports on all questions concerning the protection and promotion of human rights. Commissions must be able to: consider '… all legislative and administrative provisions' (in force or planned); examine, on their own initiative, any situation of violation; establish reports on the state of human rights in a country while drawing the government's attention to violations; ensure the state's implementation of international instruments; cooperate in monitoring mechanisms; promote education and training; and inform and sensitize public opinion. The composition of commissions should provide guarantees of independence and pluralism, and, likewise, their operating methods should give them wide independence of action in respect of individuals, non-governmental organizations, public opinion in general and other state institutions. In addition, commissions should be given quasi-jurisdictional responsibilities and initiate procedures for complaints by individuals or groups, aiming at a settlement through conciliation or binding judgments (within the limits fixed by the law).

Such principles concerning different types of commission are especially useful in guiding or reforming existing commissions as necessary, and also serving as a basis for those to be set up in future. A principle recommended will be all the more influential where it forms part of, and develops within, the dynamic framework of regular international meetings for exchanges and comparison of experiences between the representatives of the institutions concerned – as has been the case since 1991 under the auspices of the United Nations.[38] The links and solidarity thus forged between commissions also help defend the independence of each of them, as shown by a number of cases.[39]

CONCLUSION

Human rights protection at the national level depends on the existence of the rule of law and a democratic system which make possible the establishment and effective functioning of the institutions examined above. While traditional institutions – parliamentary, judicial and executive – provide the very foundation of protection, the specific institutions now developing in various countries, such as human rights commissions, are bound to play a decisive part in inaugurating new approaches and methods which correspond to the specific nature of human rights and the need to ensure both their promotion and their protection. These institutions, which are not designed to replace traditional institutions but merely to supplement them, deserve special encouragement combined with care to guarantee their independence strictly at all levels in order to ensure the demonstrable credibility and efficiency of their action. The World Conference on Human Rights (1993) reaffirmed, in its Vienna Programme of Action, 'the important and constructive role' played by national institutions and encouraged their establishment and strengthening on the basis of the principles concerning their status adopted by the United Nations.[40]

However, the institutions examined above are not an exhaustive list of the state bodies called on to play a special human rights role; there are also ad hoc bodies appointed to conduct a one-off study or inquiry, and various permanent bodies specializing in particular rights and freedoms.[41]

In addition, even if, as noted above, it is the state which is chiefly responsible for human rights protection, other 'private' actors in civil society play a vital role nationally. For example, trade unions and professional associations[42] contribute to information on and the defence of human rights in respect of their members and by means of their activities. Likewise, political parties have a special responsibility for awareness-raising and training, not only among their members, but with respect to all citizens in order to develop and strengthen the democratic process and observance of human rights. The media, given the place they occupy and their influence in societies today, are in the forefront and are especially powerful intermediaries. Through the information they transmit and the awareness they can arouse in public opinion, they have heavy responsibilities which have a direct impact on respect for human rights. However, the information of the public at large should not be confined to cases of violation but should go hand-in-hand with information on progress achieved and positive factors to be observed both nationally and internationally.

Non-governmental organizations and associations specializing in human rights, which have developed widely in many countries on all continents, obviously have a vital role in both promotion and protection. They provide traditional institutions with proposals in the legislative field, introduce appeals to judicial bodies where these are provided for statutorily, and intercede with governments. A specially important place belongs to these organizations in connection with the specific institutions of national human rights commissions, either as full members or as preferential partners. Generally these non-governmental organizations, which must themselves meet the requirement of independence, exercise keen vigilance over human rights. While their primary function is usually to alert public opinion and intercede with governments or international organizations on cases or situations of violation, they are increasingly developing awareness-raising and training activities for special categories (professional or other) or a wider population (local or national community). In this way, they participate with their own means and methods in furthering human rights education, which is one of the basic prerequisites for the observance of human rights.

The fact is that, in parallel with the growth of the institutional system, effective protection for human rights in a country depends ultimately on citizens who are informed and aware of their rights and responsibilities. The changes of all kinds necessarily implied by human rights in both individual and collective attitudes and behaviour patterns mean that the necessary education to this end must be furthered in both formal settings (educational establishments at all levels) and informal settings (professional circles, voluntary associations and so on).

It is here we have one of the key missions of institutions such as UNESCO, which in recent years has undertaken programmes to further human rights education in all countries. This is also the purpose of institutes or centres for human rights teaching and research which have been set up not only internationally and regionally, but also nationally.[43]

The UNESCO International Congress held in Montreal in 1993 adopted precisely a World Plan of Action on Education for Human Rights and Democracy[44] which is addressed to all those actively concerned – and in the first instance to states. But considerable efforts remain to be made in all countries if we wish to see, through the development of human rights education for all, the gradual establishment of a culture of human rights, which is the best way of guaranteeing their observance.

NOTES

1   See Marie (1999).
2   The Charter of the United Nations, Articles 55 and 56. For a commentary on Article 55, see Marie and Questiaux (1991).
3   *Vienna Declaration and Programme of Action*, United Nations, A/CONF.157/23, Preamble (5th subparagraph), and Part I, para. 1 (subpara. 3); also para. 1 (subpara. 1).
4   Universal Declaration of Human Rights, Article 28, Resolution 217 A III of the United Nations General Assembly of 10 December 1948.
5   See Universal Declaration of Human Rights, Article 29; International Covenant on Civil and Political Rights, Articles 14, 21, 22; International Covenant on Economic, Social and Cultural Rights, Articles 8, 21, 22; European Convention on Human Rights, Articles 6, 8, 9, 10, 11; American Convention on Human Rights, Articles 15, 16, 22.
6   For example, the French Constitution of 1958 refers in its Preamble to the 1789 Declaration of the Rights of Man and of the Citizen.
7   Article 21 of the Universal Declaration of Human Rights. See also International Covenant on Civil and Political Rights, Article 25; European Convention on Human Rights, First Protocol, Article 3; American Convention on Human Rights, Article 23; African Charter on Human and Peoples' Rights, Article 13.
8   These texts refer to the measures necessary in a democratic society. See, for example: International Covenant on Civil and Political Rights, Articles 21, 22; International Covenant on Economic, Social and Cultural Rights, Article 8; European Convention on Human Rights, Articles 8 to 11 and Protocol 4, Article 2; American Convention on Human Rights, Articles 15, 16, 22.
9   For a brief look at the interpretation by the European Commission and Court of Human Rights, see Council of Europe (1991, p.52 *passim*).
10 On the relations between human rights and democracy, see Marie (1985).
11 See the International Covenant on Civil and Political Rights and International Covenant on Economic, Social and Cultural Rights, Article 2; American Convention on Human Rights, Article 2; African Charter on Human and Peoples' Rights, Article 1.
12 See *supra*, note 5.
13 This principle is set out, for example, in the main international instruments concerning human rights: Universal Declaration of Human Rights, Article 11; International Covenant on Civil and Political Rights, Article 15; European Convention on Human Rights, Article 7; American Convention on Human Rights, Article 9, African Charter on Human and Peoples' Rights, Article 7.
14 On this point, see the reports published by the Interparliamentary Union, an organization comprising 142 national parliaments and five associate members

which, since 1976, has set up a 'Procedure for the examination and treatment of communications concerning violations of the human rights of parliamentarians'. These communications are examined by the Committee on Human Rights of Parliamentarians. During its 84th to 87th sessions in 1999, this Committee examined the situation of 326 parliamentarians in 34 countries.

15   Here the televised rebroadcasting of important parliamentary debates or of question time may be a useful method of awareness-raising which will be both balanced and educational.

16   Universal Declaration, Article 8; International Covenant on Civil and Political Rights, Article 2; European Convention on Human Rights, Article 13; American Convention on Human Rights, Article 25; African Charter on Human and Peoples' Rights, Article 7.

17   See the report of the Special Rapporteur on the question of the independence of judges and lawyers presented in 1999 to the 55th session of the United Nations Commission on Human Rights (doc. E/CN.4/1999/60). In its resolution 1999/ 31 of 26 April 1999 adopted by the Commission on this point, the latter notes 'with concern the increasingly frequent attacks on their independence suffered by judges, lawyers and court officers, and aware of the close link between the weakening of safeguards for judges, lawyers and court officers and the frequency and gravity of violations of human rights'. Previously in the framework of the Sub-Commission on Prevention of Discrimination and Protection of Minorities, a report had been prepared on the independence of the judiciary and the protection of lawyers in the exercise of their profession (doc. E/CN/ Sub.2/1993/25 and Add.1).

18   Depending on the different legal systems, the provisions of international instruments may be self-executing or else be incorporated into national legislation.

19   It is governments which are responsible for preparing the periodical reports required by various international conventions, and it is their representatives who present these reports orally and reply to questions before the expert committees set up for this purpose (as, for example, in the United Nations Human Rights Committee, the Committee on Economic, Social and Cultural Rights, the Committee for the Elimination of Racial Discrimination, the Committee for the Elimination of Discrimination Against Women, the Committee on Torture, the Committee on the Rights of the Child).

20   On this point, see in particular the annual reports of the Special Rapporteur of the United Nations Sub-Commission on Prevention of Discrimination and Protection of Minorities which lists the states which have proclaimed, prorogued or abrogated a state of exception since 1 January 1985 (87 states up to 1995); see also the report of the Office of the United Nations High Commissioner for Human Rights at the 51st session of the Sub-Commission in 1999, regarding the list of states having proclaimed or maintained a state of exception during the period in question (doc. E/CN.4/1999/31).

21   The police are a particularly good example of this 'risky task' of the executive: on the one hand, the police are responsible for maintaining law and order and ensuring citizen security and, on the other hand, they may themselves violate the physical integrity, freedom, private life and so on of citizens; hence the need for effective monitoring of their action and the availability of a practical remedy.

22   To date, more than 90 countries have created a post of ombudsperson at the national, regional or local level (cf. International Ombudsperson Institute, Edmonton, Canada).

23 In some systems, the ombudsperson or mediator is appointed by the executive (government, head of state), which is an infringement of the basic principles of this institution and may jeopardize its independence.

24 Under the aegis of the United Nations, a series of international meetings on national institutions for the promotion and protection of human rights were organized, in which a certain number of ombudspersons and mediators participated (Paris – October 1991; Tunis – December 1993; Manila, Philippines – April 1995; and Merida, Mexico – November 1997). Within the framework of the Council of Europe, five roundtables of European ombudspersons were held (Madrid – June 1985; Strasbourg – June 1988; Florence – November 1991; Lisbon – June 1994; and Riga – June 1997).

25 See resolution 2.9 of the United Nations Economic and Social Council, 21 June 1946.

26 It can, however, be noted that in 1947 France set up an advisory commission for the codification of international law and the *defence* of the rights and duties of states and of *human rights* – our emphasis – a body which was a precursor of the present National Advisory Commission on Human Rights set up by France in 1984.

27 When it adopted the International Covenants, the United Nations General Assembly, in view of the interest of the proposals submitted on the creation of human rights commissions or other appropriate institutions to exercise some of the functions connected with the Covenants, invited the Commission on Human Rights to examine this question from all its aspects; see resolution 2200 (C(XXI) of the General Assembly, 16 December 1966.

28 These guiding principles were prepared at the seminar on national and local institutions for the promotion and protection of human rights organized by the United Nations in Geneva from 18 to 29 September 1978; report by the seminar: United Nations, ST/HR/SER.A/2I, paras 184 *et seq.*; these principles were approved by the Commission on Human Rights in its resolution 24(XXXV) of 14 March 1979, E/CN.4/1347, Chapter XXIV.

29 According to information provided by the Office of the United Nations High Commissioner for Human Rights, nearly 50 countries in different parts of the world have established national institutions such as human rights commissions (or committees or councils), whilst plans exist in other countries in view of creating such institutions. Within certain states, notably federal ones, several institutions of this type have been created at different levels (for example, more than ten in Canada at the federal and provincial levels). This increases considerably the total number of these institutions presently existing throughout the world.

30 In the United States, the US Commission on Civil Rights was set up at federal level by Congress under the Civil Rights Act of 1957. It is independent and reports to both Congress and the President of the United States. Its field of competence includes all civic rights and the implementation of legislation in this field. Other commissions had been set up previously by certain states under their anti-discrimination legislation. In Canada, the first Human Rights Commission was set up at the provincial level by Ontario in 1962; it is responsible mainly for the implementation of anti-discrimination legislation in the Province. At the federal level, the Canadian Commission on individual rights was set up in 1997. For further information, see Marie (1983).

31 From its inception in 1975, the Quebec Commission on Individual Rights was responsible for promoting all the rights contained in the Quebec Charter of

Individual Rights and Freedoms; its role was not confined to anti-discriminatory measures.

32 The Philippines Human Rights Commission was set up under the Constitution and is independent from the President of the Republic, Congress and the judiciary.

33 For example, the French Advisory Human Rights Commission has 70 members (although, as indicated by its title, its status is primarily advisory), while the Philippines Human Rights Commission has five members (although it exercises widespread powers with regard to promotion and protection, as it is empowered to receive and examine complaints).

34 See the report of the Secretary-General on national institutions for the promotion and protection of human rights to the 54th session of the Commission on Human Rights (doc. E/CN.4/1998/55) and resolution 1998/55 of the Commission on Human Rights of 17 April 1998 (doc. E/CN.4/1998/177).

35 To take an extreme example, the President of one national commission was forced to flee abroad; see the resolution adopted at the second international meetings of national institutions for the promotion and protection of human rights, Tunis, 13–17 December 1993, United Nations, E/CN.4/1994/45, para. 81.

36 See *supra*, note 28.

37 Report on the United Nations international meetings, E/CN.4/1992/43, Chapter V. The principles governing the status of commissions were approved by the United Nations Commission on Human Rights in its resolution 1992/54 of 3 March 1992.

38 See *supra*, note 24.

39 See *supra*, note 35.

40 See Vienna Declaration and Programme of Action, United Nations A/CONF.157/23, Part I, para. 36.

41 For example, parliamentary committees to study or investigate a situation or aspect of human rights, organs concerned with on freedom of information in the audiovisual media or on individual freedoms and informatics, medical and scientific ethical committees, bodies specializing in economic, social and cultural rights and so on.

42 For example, associations of jurists which set up internal committees or commissions on human rights and can provide information and assistance (in particular, legal assistance) to victims, and human rights training programmes (bar associations have set up human rights institutes); also associations of doctors, journalists, teachers among others set up nationally or in conjunction with international associations.

43 See *World Directory* (1998).

44 See Final Report of the Congress, UNESCO, SHS-93/CONF.402/4.

BIBLIOGRAPHY

Council of Europe (1983), *Proceedings of the Seminar on Non-Judicial Methods for the Protection and Promotion of Human Rights (Sienna, 28–30 October 1982)*, Strasbourg: Council of Europe.

Council of Europe (1991), *Short Guide to the European Convention on Human Rights*, Strasbourg: Council of Europe.

J.B. Marie (1983), 'Rôle et fonctions des commissions nationales pour la protection et la promotion des droits de l'homme: l'expérience nord-américaine et son application éventuelle dans les pays membres du Conseil de l'Europe', *Proceedings of the Seminar on Non-Judicial Methods for the Protection and Promotion of Human Rights (Sienna, 28–30 October 1982)*, Strasbourg: Council of Europe, pp.69–102.

J.B. Marie (1985), *Human Rights or a Way of Life in a Democracy*, Strasbourg: Council of Europe.

J.B. Marie (1999), 'International instruments relating to human rights: classification and status of ratifications as of 1 January 1999', *Human Rights Law Journal*, **20** (1–3), pp.115–33.

J.B. Marie and N. Questiaux (1991), 'La Charte des Nations Unies. Commentaire article par article', in J.P. Cot and A. Pellet (eds), *Economica*, 2nd edn, Paris: Economica, pp.865–88.

World Directory of Human Rights Research and Training Institution (1998), Paris: UNESCO.

9 Criminal Responsibility for Violations of Human Rights

WILLIAM A. SCHABAS

INTRODUCTION

Prosecution for 'war crimes' became a central theme of human rights discourse during the final decade of the twentieth century, with the creation of ad hoc tribunals for the former Yugoslavia and Rwanda, calls for similar organs to deal with atrocities in Congo, Burundi, Cambodia and East Timor, new-found enthusiasm among domestic prosecutors to pursue erstwhile dictators such as Augusto Pinochet and, ultimately, the creation of the International Criminal Court. Yet the popular term 'war crimes' is quite misleading. The movement has far more to do with prosecution of serious breaches of human rights than with the classical concept of 'war crimes', which were essentially breaches of the norms of fair play among combatants. Today's 'war crimes' prosecutions are principally about the protection of non-combatant civilian populations, generally within the context of internal armed conflicts or in the absence of armed conflict altogether.

The ambiguities of our terminology can be seen in the nomenclature of the ad hoc tribunals, charged by the United Nations Security Council with the enforcement of 'humanitarian law' – a modern formulation of the laws of armed conflict. As the Appeal Chamber of the International Criminal Tribunal for the former Yugoslavia put it in the *Tadic* case, 'the more recent and comprehensive notion of "international humanitarian law" … has emerged as a result of the influence of human rights doctrines on the law of armed conflict'.[1] Yet, several of the crimes within the jurisdiction of the ad hoc tribunals do not concern 'humanitarian' law at all, in that they do not require as one of their elements the existence of an armed conflict. This is so in the case of genocide and, in the case of the Rwanda Tribunal, of crimes against humanity. Indeed, the pattern of prosecution by the ad hoc tribunals shows that their central and overriding concern is with these 'human rights crimes', rather than with the violations of the laws and customs of war in the classic sense, which tend to be on the periphery of their activity.

Three areas of international law converge to provide the framework for the enforcement of human rights by means of criminal prosecution. International humanitarian law, at least as the term is employed by the United Nations Security Council, mandates the prosecution of genocide, war crimes and crimes against humanity. Since its first codifications more than a century ago, its focus has gradually shifted towards civilian victims of armed conflict, both international and non-international. International criminal law provides much of the technical support for such prosecution, including procedural mechanisms such as extradition and a jurisdictional framework. Finally, international human rights law establishes the overarching context, fixing obligations for both individuals and states that have consequences in the area of criminal law. Specifically, Article 29(1) of the Universal Declaration of Human Rights recognizes, albeit rather laconically, that the rights of the individual are accompanied by duties. The major human rights conventions require that states implement the protection of human rights by ensuring prompt and effective repression of violations by means of criminal investigation and prosecution. Some specialized human rights instruments, dealing with such matters as genocide, torture and apartheid, impose quite precise duties upon states in this area.

This chapter will address these issues by focusing on four themes. First, the human rights dimension of the definition of international crimes will be examined. Second, the role of human rights in the creation and operation of international criminal tribunals will be explored. Third, the chapter will consider the international legal obligations in this field from the standpoint of obligations upon states within their own domestic jurisdiction. Finally, it will examine some of the human rights issues involved in the prosecutions themselves.

HUMAN RIGHTS AND INTERNATIONAL CRIMES

The concept of *crimina juris gentium*, or crimes against the international community, has relatively ancient origins. Piracy, the slave trade, narcotic trafficking and prostitution are the classic examples of offences whose prosecution was contemplated by international law at an early stage. Although there are human rights dimensions to all of these areas of criminal conduct, the interest of the international community in prosecution was dictated more by the practical difficulties of domestic repression than by any commitment to the protection of some higher international values. These were crimes committed on the high seas where enforcement was problematic. Their repression dictated a high degree of international cooperation and specialized jurisdictional rules. That states had an exclusive and sovereign right to determine what crimes to repress within their own borders remained relatively sacrosanct until the end of the First World War. The corollary of this was that they could ensure impunity for atrocities, often committed with the support and encouragement at the highest levels of government.

The Treaty of Versailles contemplated the prosecution of German military personnel for breaches of the laws and customs of war.[2] Pursuant to the Hague Convention IV of 1907 and its annexed regulations, such crimes were generally considered to include atrocities committed against civilian populations.[3] The Commission on Responsibilities established by the victorious Allies at the Paris Peace Conference included within its purview such war crimes as rape and 'denationalization', categories of offence that echo our contemporary human rights agenda. The United States claimed that actual prosecution of these crimes would be *ex post facto* justice, and its insistence that this was more an issue of morality than of law ultimately blocked a generous application of the Hague law. The handful of war crimes trials held pursuant to the Treaty of Versailles in Leipzig addressed abuses in submarine warfare and prisoner-of-war camps, staying clear of those directed against civilians.[4]

The Armenian massacres in 1915 had prompted a joint declaration from France, the United Kingdom and Russia denouncing 'new crimes of Turkey against humanity and civilization' and pledging that those responsible would be held personally accountable.[5] This went well beyond the Hague Convention, whose application was clearly limited to occupied territories and could, by no reasonable intepretation, be considered to apply to Armenian victims within the Ottoman Empire. The pledge of prosecution resulted in precise provisions within the Treaty of Sèvres of 1920. The Turkish government undertook to surrender those considered responsible for the massacres and even agreed to the creation of a special tribunal by the League of Nations with jurisdiction over such matters. But the Treaty of Sèvres was never ratified and was in fact superseded by the Treaty of Lausanne, where any reference to accountability was replaced with a disgraceful promise of amnesty.[6]

The argument that war crimes law governed occupied territories but had nothing to contribute to the persecution of a civilian population by its own government resumed in 1943 as the United Nations War Crimes Commission debated the parameters of post-war prosecution. As late as mid-1944, in a letter to the Commission's Chair, the Lord Chancellor of the United Kingdom said that criminalization of anti-Semitic crimes within Germany itself 'raises serious difficulties' for the UK government.[7] Only after insistent lobbying by Jewish organizations in Washington and London did the view that the Nazis might be punished for crimes committed within Germany against German Jews begin to gain some acceptance. The debates came to a head at the London Conference of June–August 1945, which set the groundwork for the Nuremberg Trial of the Major War Criminals. United States negotiator Robert Jackson made it clear that Nazis would be prosecuted for such crimes. He specified that this was an exception, however, because such persecutions were intimatedly bound up with the entire war. '... Ordinarily we do not consider that the acts of a government toward its own citizens warrant our interference. We have some regrettable circum-

stances at times in our own country in which minorities are unfairly treated,'
he admitted in a moment of candour.[8]

The London Charter classified such offences as 'crimes against humanity'
but insisted upon a link or *nexus* with aggressive war.[9] Jackson's unguarded
comment about regrettable circumstances in the United States might well
have been shared by the other delegates, from the Soviet Union, the United
Kingdom and France, all of whom might have felt threatened by some more
general recognition that persecution of minorities within their own territories, or that of their colonies, might incur international criminal liability.
The conservative approach to 'crimes against humanity', which insisted
that they could only be committed in the context of aggressive war, was
entrenched by the judgment of the Nuremberg Tribunal of 30 September to
1 October 1946.[10]

The *nexus* with war also prevailed in the law applicable to the Tokyo
Tribunal. Nevertheless, Control Council Law No. 10, adopted by the victorious powers in December 1945, defined crimes against humanity differently,
with no requirement that they be linked to the armed conflict. Arguably,
this was because the Allies were acting as domestic legislators, making law
for occupied Germany as its *de facto* rulers, rather than developing norms of
international law. In fact, it would take half a century before the concept of
crimes against humanity – a term that is essentially synonymous with
serious violations of human rights – could be thoroughly detached from
this fatal *nexus* with armed conflict. Yet in recognizing that criminal liability
could exist as a question of international law for acts committed under
orders of governments against citizens of that same state, the veil of state
sovereignty had been pierced. The story of international criminal law over
the second half of the century is one of gradual, but inexorable, expansion
of the concept of crimes against humanity. It is inseparable from the parallel
story of the growth of norms and mechanisms for the protection of human
rights.

Within days of the Nuremberg judgment, initiatives at the first General
Assembly of the United Nations sought to chip away at the *nexus* between
crimes against humanity and war. Perhaps not surprisingly, the initiatives
in this regard did not come from the major powers, who had been responsible for drafting the Nuremberg Charter. At the 1946 General Assembly,
Cuba, India and Panama asked that the question of genocide be put on the
agenda, proposing a draft resolution for the body's consideration.[11] Resolution 96(I) on the crime of genocide, adopted in December 1946, stated:

> Genocide is a denial of the right of existence of entire human groups, as homi-
> cide is the denial of the right to live of individual human beings; such denial of
> the right of existence shocks the conscience of mankind, results in great losses to
> humanity in the form of cultural and other contributions represented by these
> human groups, and is contrary to moral law and to the spirit and aims of the
> United Nations.

The resolution mandated the United Nations to prepare a draft treaty and,
two years later, the first major human rights convention of the post-war era,

the Convention for the Prevention and Punishment of the Crime of Genocide, was adopted.[12] René Cassin called the Genocide Convention a specific application of the Universal Declaration of Human Rights.[13] Of course, it is hardly a coincidence that the Genocide Convention was adopted by the General Assembly one day prior to the Universal Declaration, on 9 December 1948. As its title suggests, it melds the preventive dimension of human rights with the punitive. The Convention's drafters consciously eschewed describing genocide as a crime against humanity, precisely to avoid the Nuremberg *nexus* with international armed conflict. Accordingly, Article I specified that genocide was 'a crime under international law whether committed in time of peace or in time of war'.

The crime of genocide, as defined in Article II of the Convention, consists of a norm protecting what were historically referred to as 'national minorities'.[14] The text adopted in 1948 refers to 'national, racial, ethnical and religious groups'. Genocide is now generally acknowledged to be a form of crime against humanity, but precisely because the latter no longer requires a link with armed conflict.[15] What the drafters of the Genocide Convention had done in effect was to carve off a small piece of the concept of crimes against humanity and push it beyond the limitative jurisprudence of the Nuremberg Trial. Henceforth, human rights violations directed against a civilian (or any) population within the boundaries of a sovereign state would incur international criminal liability, provided, of course, that they met the exceedingly narrow definition of the crime found in Article II of the Convention.

Since its adoption in 1948, human rights law has attempted to enhance protection by pushing the Genocide Convention in two directions. First, it has endeavoured to enlarge the scope of genocide to cover widespread or systematic human rights violations even when these could not readily be described as the intentional destruction of a national, racial, ethnic or religious group as such. Examples abound – Cambodia, Lebanon, Vietnam, Tibet, East Timor, Chechnya, to name a few – but exaggerated and unrealistic claims to the Convention's application have only discredited the instrument and tended to trivialize the term 'genocide' itself. Moreover, attempts to expand the definition of genocide to encompass political, economic, social and gender groups have often been welcomed by human rights activists and academic commentators. Yet despite frequent opportunities for revision – in the International Law Commission, the Security Council and the Rome Conference on the International Criminal Court – the original definition has stood the test of time. Article 6 of the Rome Statute of the International Criminal Court repeats the text of Article II of the Genocide Convention without any significant modification.[16] This is perhaps the strongest argument that the Genocide Convention codifies a norm of customary international law. Efforts to enlarge the definition were generally driven by a desire that the term 'genocide' cover all forms of mass killing, rather than those limited to persecution based on ethnic considerations. Of course, broader concepts of mass killing could be addressed within the framework of crimes against humanity, but Nuremberg had saddled crimes against humanity with the *nexus* to international armed conflict. Thus, atrocities that would meet the definition of crimes against humanity, if they were committed in wartime, seemed to escape the international criminal consequences they would have incurred had they taken place in peacetime or in the course of internal armed conflict.

Second, the law has also sought to make further inroads by describing additional sub-categories of crimes against humanity that, like genocide, have been divorced from the *nexus* with armed conflict. The 1973 International Convention on the Suppression and Punishment of the Crime of Apartheid defined as crimes against humanity 'inhuman acts resulting from the policies and practices of apartheid and similar policies and practices of racial segregation and discrimination'.[17] In 1984, conventional obligations were created with respect to a third category of crime against humanity – torture. Nothing in the Convention Against Torture and Other Cruel, Inhuman and Degrading Treatment or Punishment refers to its classification as a crime against humanity, but subsequent instruments consider torture within this category to the extent that it meets the thresholds of being widespread or systematic. Again, there is no *nexus* with armed conflict; indeed, the Torture Convention specifies that armed conflict cannot be a pretext for derogation.[18] In 1992 the General Assembly recognized that the systematic practice of acts of enforced disappearance 'is in the nature of a crime against humanity'.[19] The trend, then, has been to recognize that crimes against humanity, or at least some of them, can be committed in peacetime and without Nuremberg's troubling *nexus* to armed conflict.

The International Law Commission kept alive the debate on the scope of crimes against humanity in the course of its work on the Code of Crimes Against the Peace and Security of Mankind, but no new text defining the concept was finalized until May 1993, when the Security Council adopted the Statute of the International Criminal Tribunal for the former Yugoslavia. There was noticeable progress, because the Statute recognized that crimes against humanity could be committed 'in armed conflict, whether international or internal'.[20] But the *nexus* remained: crimes against humanity were 'war crimes' and did not apply to widespread or systematic gross violations of human rights committed in peacetime. The following year, the Security Council took another stab at the question in the Statute of the International Criminal Tribunal for Rwanda. The references to armed conflict, whether international or internal, were eliminated, although it was not entirely obvious that the silence of the Statute was meant to effect a change in the law.[21] However, in its landmark decision of 2 October 1995, *Prosecutor v. Tadic*, the Appeal Chamber of the ad hoc tribunal for Yugoslavia asserted that the Security Council had defined the category 'more narrowly than necessary under customary international law', because state practice since Nuremberg had made it clear that crimes against humanity did not require a *nexus* with armed conflict.[22]

The Yugoslav Tribunal's bold jurisprudential step was affirmed during the drafting of the Rome Statute of the International Criminal Court. Crimes against humanity, according to Article 7 of the Rome Statute, consist of an enumeration of acts 'committed as part of a widespread or systematic attack directed against any civilian population'. The list of acts develops the previous models and is clearly inspired by the forward march of international human rights law. Among the new criminal acts added since Nuremberg are forcible transfer of population, imprisonment or other severe deprivation of physical liberty, torture, rape and other crimes of sexual violence, persecution against any identifiable group or collectivity on grounds universally recognized as impermissible under international law, enforced disappearance of persons and apartheid.[23]

War crimes as an international offence developed in parallel with crimes against humanity, enriched by evolving codifications of Hague and Geneva law. The Charter of the Nuremberg Tribunal had referred to 'violations of the laws or customs of war', a category that included abuses of civilian population of an occupied territory and that essentially overlapped with that of the protection of human rights. The protection of civilians in occupied territory was further enhanced in the Fourth Geneva Convention of 12 August 1949.[24] Besides establishing an entire catalogue of applicable norms, it defined the more severe violations as 'grave breaches', imposing upon States Parties an obligation to investigate, and prosecute or extradite alleged offenders. But the grave breach provisions did not extend to common Article 3 of the Conventions, which was the 'convention in miniature' applicable to non-international armed conflict. When the Geneva Conventions were updated in 1977, Additional Protocol I, applicable to international armed conflict, expanded the scope of the 'grave breaches' provision and codified the concept of superior or command responsibility.[25] However, the Diplomatic Conference rejected provisions proposed for Additional Protocol II, which is applicable to non-international armed conflict, and refused to recognize that grave breaches could also be committed during internal armed conflict. Indeed, subsequent to 1977, most academic commentators had little doubt that war crimes, as international offences, could only be committed during international armed conflict.

The first suggestion that the law had changed appeared in November 1994, with the adoption by the Security Council of the Statute of the International Criminal Tribunal for Rwanda. Article 4 established criminal jurisdiction over 'serious violations of Article 3 common to the Geneva Conventions of 12 August 1949 for the Protection of War Victims, and of Additional Protocol II', despite the absence of any convention basis for treating them as war crimes. Neither category had ever previously been considered to impose penal liability as 'grave breaches'. The following year, the Appeal Chamber of the Yugoslav Tribunal, in the *Tadic* decision, made it clear that 'violations of the laws and customs of war' extended beyond 'grave breaches' to a wide range of 'serious violations' of the Geneva Conventions and their Additional Protocols, including acts committed during international armed conflict. This ruling was also confirmed by the Rome Diplomatic Conference, which developed detailed codifications of war crimes committed in breach of common Article 3 and Additional Protocol II.

The extension of war crimes to internal armed conflicts, like the removal of the *nexus* between crimes against humanity and armed conflict, reinforces the recognition of individual criminal responsibility, as a matter of international law, for gross violations of human rights. In a practical sense, both paradigms depart from the classic context of international law viewed as an interstate matter to one addressing atrocities committed by a state against its own citizens, whether in civil war or peacetime. This is the direct consequence of the successful inroads made by human rights law into areas of national jurisdiction that had previously been sheltered from international scrutiny.

HUMAN RIGHTS AND INTERNATIONAL CRIMINAL TRIBUNALS

Besides defining the crime of genocide and setting out a variety of obligations relating to its prosecution, Article VI of the Convention for the Prevention and Punishment of the Crime of Genocide stated that trial for genocide was to take place before 'a competent tribunal of the State in the territory of which the act was committed, or by such international penal tribunal as may have jurisdiction with respect to those Contracting Parties which shall have accepted its jurisdiction'. An early version of the convention prepared by the United Nations Secretariat had actually included a model statute for a court, based on the 1937 treaty developed within the League of Nations, but the conservative drafters stopped short of establishing such an institution. Instead, a General Assembly resolution adopted at the same time as the Convention called upon the International Law Commission to prepare the statute of the court promised by Article VI.[26]

The General Assembly had also asked the International Law Commission to prepare what are known as the 'Nuremberg Principles', a task it completed in 1950,[27] and the 'Code of Crimes Against the Peace and Security of Mankind', a job that took considerably longer. Indeed, much of the work on the draft statute of an international criminal court and the draft code of crimes went on within the Commission in parallel. The General Assembly also established a committee charged with drafting the statute of an international criminal court. Composed of 17 states, it submitted its report and draft statute in 1952. A new committee, created by the General Assembly to review the draft statute in the light of comments by member states, reported to the General Assembly in 1954. Meanwhile, the International Law Commission made considerable progress on its draft code and actually submitted a proposal in 1954. Then the General Assembly suspended the mandates, ostensibly pending the sensitive task of defining the crime of aggression. In fact, political tensions associated with the Cold War had made progress on the international criminal tribunal agenda virtually impossible.

The General Assembly eventually adopted a definition of aggression, in 1974,[28] but the work did not immediately resume on the international court. In 1981 the General Assembly asked the International Law Commission to revive the work on its draft code of crimes. Doudou Thiam was designated the Special Rapporteur of the Commission and produced annual reports on various aspects of the draft code for more than a decade. Thiam's work, and the associated debates in the Commission, addressed a range of questions, including definitions of crimes, criminal participation, defences and penalties. A substantially revised version of the 1954 draft code was provisionally adopted by the Commission in 1991, and then sent to member states for their reaction.

But the code addressed substantive criminal law matters and did not necessarily involve an international jurisdiction. That aspect of the work was only launched in 1989, the year of the fall of the Berlin Wall. Trinidad and Tobago, a Caribbean state plagued by narcotics problems, initiated a resolution in the General Assembly directing the International Law Commission to consider the subject within the context of its work on the draft code of crimes. Special Rapporteur Thiam made an initial presentation on the subject in 1992. By 1993 the Commission had prepared a draft statute, this time under the direction of Special Rapporteur James Crawford. The preliminary draft statute was considered by the General Assembly, which encouraged the Commission to complete its work. The following year, in 1994, the Commission submitted the final version of its draft statute for an international criminal court to the General Assembly.[29] Two years later, at its 1996 session, the Commission adopted the final draft of its 'Code of Crimes Against the Peace and Security of Mankind'.[30]

The International Criminal Tribunal for the Former Yugoslavia

While the draft statute of an international criminal court was being considered in the International Law Commission, events compelled the creation of a court on an ad hoc basis in order to address the atrocities being committed in the former Yugoslavia. In late 1992, as war raged in Bosnia, a Commission of Experts established by the Security Council identified a range of 'war crimes' that had been committed and that were continuing. It urged the establishment of an international criminal tribunal, an idea that had originally been recommended by Lord Owen and Cyrus Vance. The proposal was endorsed by the General Assembly in a December 1992 resolution. The Rapporteurs appointed under the Moscow Human Dimension Mechanism of the Conference on Security and Cooperation in Europe, Hans Correll, Gro Hillestad Thune and Helmut Türk, prepared a draft statute. Several governments also submitted proposals or otherwise commented upon the creation of a tribunal.

On 22 February 1993 the Security Council decided upon the establishment of a tribunal mandated to prosecute 'persons responsible for serious violations of international humanitarian law committed in the territory of the former Yugoslavia since 1991'. The Secretary-General's proposal was adopted without modification by the Security Council in Resolution 827 of 8 May 1993. According to the Secretary-General's report, the tribunal was to apply rules of international humanitarian law that are 'beyond any doubt part of the customary law'.[31] The Statute clearly borrowed from the work then underway within the International Law Commission on the statute and the code, in effect combining the two into an instrument that both defined the crimes and established the procedure before the court. The Tribunal's territorial jurisdiction was confined to the territory of the former Yugoslavia. Temporally, it was entitled to prosecute offences beginning in 1991 but no limit was set as to the future.

The International Criminal Tribunal for Rwanda

In November 1994, acting on a request from Rwanda, the Security Council voted to create a second ad hoc tribunal, charged with prosecution of genocide and other serious violations of international humanitarian law committed in Rwanda and in neighbouring countries during 1994. Its Statute closely resembles that of the International Criminal Tribunal for the Former Yugoslavia, although the war crimes provisions reflect the fact that the Rwandan genocide took place within the context of an internal armed conflict. The resolution creating the Tribunal expressed the Council's 'grave concern at the reports indicating that genocide and other systematic, widespread and flagrant violations of international humanitarian law have been committed in Rwanda', and referred to the reports of the Special Rapporteur for Rwanda of the United Nations Commission on Human Rights, as well as the preliminary report of the Commission of Experts, which the Council had established earlier in the year.

The Yugoslav and Rwanda Tribunals are in effect joined at the hip, sharing not only virtually identical statutes but also a number of their structures. The prosecutor was the same for both tribunals, as was the Appeal Chamber. The consequence, at least in theory, is economy of scale as well as uniformity of both prosecutorial policy and appellate jurisprudence. The first major decision by the Appeal Chamber of the Yugoslav Tribunal, *Prosecutor* v. *Tadic* of 2 October 1995, clarified important legal issues relating to the creation of the body. Subsequent rulings on a variety of matters fed the debates on creation of an international criminal court. The ruling in *Tadic* was essentially incorporated in the Statute of the International Criminal Court. Other judgments, such as a controversial holding excluding recourse to a defence of duress,[32] prompted drafters of the Rome Statute to enact a provision ensuring precisely the opposite (Article 31(1)(d)). But the Tribunals did more than simply set legal precedent to guide the drafters. They also provided a reassuring model of what an international criminal court might look like. This was particularly important in debates concerning the role of the prosecutor. The integrity, neutrality and good judgement of Richard Goldstone and his successor, Louise Arbour, answered those who warned of the dangers of a reckless and irresponsible 'Dr Strangelove prosecutor'.

The International Criminal Court

In 1994 the United Nations General Assembly decided to pursue work towards the establishment of an international criminal court, taking the International Law Commission draft statute as a basis. It convened an Ad Hoc Committee, which met twice in 1995. Debates within the Ad Hoc Committee revealed rather profound differences among states about the complexion of the future court, and some delegations continued to contest the overall feasibility of the project, although their voices became more and more subdued as the negotiations progressed. The International Law Commission draft envisaged a court with 'primacy', much like the ad hoc tribunals that had been set up by the Security Council for the former Yugoslavia and Rwanda. If the court's prosecutor chose to proceed with a case, domestic courts could not pre-empt this by offering to do the job themselves. In meetings of the Ad Hoc Committee a new concept reared its head, that of 'complementarity', by which the court could only exercise jurisdiction if domestic courts had failed to prosecute. Another departure of the Ad Hoc Committee from the International Law Commission draft was its insistence that the crimes within the court's jurisdiction be defined in some detail and not simply enumerated. The International Law Commission had contented itself with listing the crimes subject to the court's jurisdiction – war crimes, aggression, crimes against humanity and genocide – presumably because the draft code of crimes, on which it was also working, would provide the more comprehensive definitional aspects. Beginning with the Ad Hoc Committee, the nearly 50-year-old distinction between the 'statute' and the 'code' disappeared. Henceforth, the statute would include detailed definitions of crimes, as well as elaborate provisions dealing with general principles of law and other substantive matters.

Impetuous advocates of the international criminal court had hoped that the Ad Hoc Committee's work would set the stage for a diplomatic conference where the statute could be adopted. But it became evident that this was premature. At its 1995 session, the General Assembly decided to convene a 'Preparatory Committee', inviting participation by member states, non-governmental organizations and international organizations of various sorts. The 'PrepCom', as it became known, held two three-week sessions in 1996, presenting the General Assembly with a voluminous report that comprised a hefty list of proposed amendments to the International Law Commission draft. It met again in 1997, this time holding three sessions. These were punctuated by informal intersessional meetings, of which the most important was surely that held in Zutphen in The Netherlands in January 1998. The 'Zutphen draft' consolidated the various proposals in a more or less coherent text that barely resembled the 1994 draft of the International Law Commission. Few provisions had survived intact. Most of them had a variety of options and alternatives, foreboding difficult negotiations at the Diplomatic Conference.

Pursuant to General Assembly resolutions adopted in 1996 and 1997, the Diplomatic Conference of Plenipotentiaries on the Establishment of an International Criminal Court convened on 15 June 1998 in Rome, at the head-quarters of the Food and Agriculture Organization. More than 160 states sent delegates to the Conference, in addition to a range of international organizations and literally hundreds of non-governmental organizations. The enthusiasm was quite astonishing, with essentially all of the delegations expressing their support for the concept. Driving the dynamism of the Conference were two new constituencies, a geographically heterogenous caucus of states known as the 'like-minded' and a well-organized coalition of non-governmental organizations. The 'like-minded' group had been active since the early stages of the Preparatory Committee, gradually consolidating its positions while at the same time expanding its membership. By the time the Rome Conference began, it included more than 60 of the 160 participating states. The 'like-minded' were committed to a handful of key propositions that were substantially at odds with the premises of the 1994 International Law Commission draft and, as a general rule, in conflict with the conception of the court held by the permanent members of the Security Council. The principles of the like-minded were: an inherent jurisdiction of the court over the 'core crimes' of genocide, crimes against humanity and war crimes (and, perhaps, aggression); the elimination of a Security Council veto on prosecutions; and an independent prosecutor with the power to initiate proceedings *proprio motu*. Although operating relatively informally, the 'like-minded' quickly dominated the structure of the Conference. Strategic positions, including the chairs of most of the Working Groups as well as membership in the Bureau of the Conference, were taken up by its members.

The Conference began with a few days of formal speeches from political figures, United Nations officials and personalities from the growing ranks of those actually involved in international criminal prosecution, including the presidents of the two ad hoc tribunals and their prosecutor. Then the Conference divided into a series of Working Groups with responsibility for matters such as general principles, procedure, state cooperation and penalties. Much of this involved details, unlikely to create insurmountable difficulties since the delegates were committed to the success of the endeavour. But a handful of core issues – jurisdiction, the 'trigger mechanism' for prosecutions, the role of the Security Council – remained under the wing of the Bureau, which was a kind of steering committee. These issues were not publicly debated for much of the Conference.

One by one, the provisions of the statute were adopted 'by general agreement' in the Working Groups – that is, without a vote. The process was tedious, in that it allowed a handful of states, or even one of them, to hold up progress by refusing to join consensus. The chairs of the Working Groups would patiently negotiate compromises, drawing on comments by states which often expressed their views on a provision but then indicated their willingness to be flexible. Within a week of the beginning of the Conference, the Working Groups were forwarding progress reports on their work to the Committee of the Whole, indicating the provisions that had already met with agreement. These were examined by the Drafting Committee for terminological and linguistic coherence in the various official language versions of the statute.

But as the weeks rolled by, key issues still had to be settled. With ten days remaining, the chair of the Committee of the Whole, Philippe Kirsch, issued a draft that set out the options on these difficult questions. The problem, however, was that many states belonged to the majority on one question but dissented on others. Finding a common denominator – that is, a workable statute that could reliably obtain the support of two-thirds of the delegates were the statute ever to come to a vote – remained daunting. Suspense mounted in the final week, with Kirsch promising a final proposal that he in fact only issued on the morning of 17 July, the day the Conference was scheduled to conclude. By then it was too late for any changes. It was a calculated throw of the dice, and it succeeded. Throughout the final day of the Conference delegates expressed their support for the 'package', resisting any attempts to alter or adjust it for fear that the entire compromise might unravel. Hopes that the draft statute might be adopted by consensus at the final session were dashed, however, when the United States exercised its right to demand that a vote be taken. The result was 120 in favour, with 21 abstentions and seven votes against. The vote was not taken by roll call, and only the declarations made by states themselves indicates who voted for what. The United States, Israel and China stated that they had opposed adoption of the statute.

In addition to the Statute of the International Criminal Court, on 17 July 1998 the Diplomatic Conference also adopted a Final Act, providing for the establishment of a Preparatory Commission. The Commission is assigned a variety of tasks, of which the most important are the drafting of the 'Rules of Procedure and Evidence', which are to spell out the procedures of the Court, and the 'Elements of Crimes', intended to elaborate upon the definitions of offences in Articles 6, 7 and 8 of the Statute. The Commission will operate until the Statute comes into force, at which point the Assembly of States Parties will be convened. The Assembly will elect the judges and prosecutor, and presumably endorse the work of the Preparatory Commission.

The Statute requires 60 ratifications before it can enter into force. States are also invited to sign the Statute, which is a preliminary step indicating their intention to ratify. Some delays are to be expected, because most states must undertake significant legislative changes in order to comply with the obligations imposed by the Statute, and they will normally want to resolve these issues before formal ratification. Specifically, they must provide for cooperation with the Court in terms of investigation, arrest and transfer of suspects. Many states now prohibit the extradition of their own nationals – a situation incompatible with the requirements of the Statute. In addition, because the Statute is predicated on 'complementarity', by which states themselves are presumed to be responsible for prosecuting suspects found on their own territory, many must also bring their substantive criminal law into line, enacting the offences of genocide, crimes against humanity and war crimes as defined in the Statute and ensuring that their courts can exercise universal jurisdiction over these crimes.

The influence of the Rome Statute will extend deep into domestic criminal law, enriching jurisprudence of national courts and challenging prosecutors and judges to greater zeal in the repression of serious violations of human rights. The International Criminal Tribunal for the Former Yugoslavia has described the Statute's role as follows:

> ... At present it is still a non-binding international treaty (it has not yet entered into force). It was adopted by an overwhelming majority of the States attending the Rome Diplomatic Conference and was substantially endorsed by the General Assembly's Sixth Committee on 26 November 1998. In many areas the Statute may be regarded as indicative of the legal views, i.e. *opinio juris* of a great number of States. Notwithstanding Article 10 of the Statute, the purpose of which is to ensure that existing or developing law is not 'limited' or 'prejudiced' by the Statute's provisions, resort may be had *com grano salis* to these provisions to help elucidate customary international law. Depending on the matter at issue, the Rome Statute may be taken to restate, reflect or clarify customary rules or crystallise them, whereas in some areas it creates new law or modifies existing law. At any event, the Rome Statute by and large may be taken as constituting an authoritative expression of the legal views of a great number of States.[33]

The International Criminal Court is perhaps the most innovative and exciting development in international law since the creation of the United Nations. Without any doubt, its creation is the result of the human rights agenda that has steadily taken centre-stage within the United Nations since Article 1 of its Charter proclaimed the promotion of human rights to be one of its purposes. From a hesitant commitment in 1945, to an ambitious Universal Declaration of Human Rights in 1948, we have reached a point where individual criminal liability is established for those responsible for serious violations of human rights, and where an institution is created to see that this is more than just some pious wish.

HUMAN RIGHTS, CRIMINAL PROSECUTION AND NATIONAL JURISDICTIONS

The reach of international human rights law into the area of criminal prosecution can be dated to a judgment of the Inter-American Court of Human Rights, in its first contentious case decided under the American Convention on Human Rights. Dealing with disappearances of activists at the hands of a death squad, whose official connections were suspected but unproven, the Court ruled that, in any case, the protection of the right to life required that the state take positive measures 'to prevent human rights violations and to use the means at its disposal to carry out a serious investigation of violations committed within its jurisdiction, to identify those responsible, impose the appropriate punishment and ensure the victim adequate compensation'.[34] The United Nations Human Rights Committee has found the same obligation within the International Covenant on Civil and Political Rights.[35]

More generally, this new orientation of human rights law takes aim at the 'culture of impunity'.[36] The fact that violations of human rights go unpunished is deemed to consist, in and of itself, of a violation of human rights. The Special Rapporteur of the Sub-Commission on the Protection and Promotion of Human Rights, Louis Joinet, has prepared a comprehensive policy statement on this issue, including a 'Set of Principles for the Protection and Promotion of Human Rights Through Action to Combat Impunity'.[37]

Of particular concern are amnesty laws, by which dictators and autocrats secure impunity for themselves. Historically, international human rights law viewed amnesty with favour, as a measure of clemency and a bulwark against oppressive use of penal justice. Thus, reference to amnesty can be found in Article 6 of the International Covenant on Civil and Political Rights and Article 6 of Additional Protocol II. Moreover, one of the pre-eminent human rights non-governmental organizations is named 'Amnesty International'. However, the notorious practice of self-proclaimed amnesties in South and Central America, often a form of blackmail when military rulers reluctantly relinquish control to civilians, has shocked international monitors. The Human Rights Committee has declared that 'amnesties are generally incompatible' with the duties set out in the International Covenant on Civil and Political Rights.[38] Inspired by the *Velasquez Rodriguez* judgment of the Inter-American Court of Human Rights, the Inter-American Commission on Human Rights has ruled that amnesties granted in different South American states violated the American Convention.[39]

But amnesties are often proclaimed in the name of national reconciliation, a measure to accompany and reinforce transitional regimes and to encourage the creation of a democratic culture. While those in Chile and Argentina can be readily dismissed as disingenuous, others, like the amnesties that resulted from the South African Truth and Reconciliation Commission, are viewed as sympathetic initiatives reinforcing the protection of human rights. It is not always easy to distinguish between the two, or to establish precise guidelines. The drafters of the Rome Statute were invited to provide some recognition of 'legitimate' amnesties and other measures of reconciliation within the provisions dealing with the complementarity of the Court. In effect, the International Criminal Court is foreclosed from proceeding against somebody who has already been judged by national courts. But the drafters of the Statute stopped short of extending this protection to individuals who had been amnestied by domestic truth commissions. In the absence of any guidelines within the Statute itself, the future prosecutor and the judges of the Court will have to develop an appropriate practice in this respect that respects the admirable objectives of some truth commissions yet discards sham amnesties with suspect purposes.

If states are now required to prosecute those responsible for committing human rights abuses within their own borders, what of fugitives from other jurisdictions who have sought refuge in order to evade prosecution? As we have seen, an obligation to prosecute those suspected of committing grave breaches of the Geneva Conventions and Additional Protocol I arises as a result of treaty provisions. It applies to offenders found within a state's borders, irrespective of the place where the crime was committed. This is known as the obligation *aut dedere aut judicare* ('extradite or prosecute'). The same obligation is imposed on States Parties by virtue of Article 5(2) of the Convention Against Torture. But within the context of international human rights and humanitarian law, such provisions are relatively rare. The Rome Statute only implies a more general obligation when, in its Preamble, it recalls that 'that it is the duty of every State to exercise its criminal jurisdiction over those responsible for international crimes'.

The obligation to try and extradite is often associated with the principle of universality of jurisdiction, although the latter concept is only permissive and not mandatory. The drafters of the Genocide Convention clearly rejected an extension of universal jurisdiction to genocide, although the courts of Israel, in the *Eichmann* case, claimed that the Convention had not excluded a more general principle drawn from customary law.[40] The reasoning in the *Eichmann* case is hardly convincing as a matter of treaty interpretation and the identification of customary norms, because states had so clearly rejected universal jurisdiction slightly more than a decade earlier. But a recognition that states are entitled to exercise universal jurisdiction over genocide, crimes against humanity and war crimes is rarely disputed today, although, during debates at the Rome Conference in June–July 1998, some states contested its existence. The real problem with defining a customary norm is the absence of state practice. Relatively few states have actually enacted legislation permitting the exercise of universal jurisdiction. Those that have rarely use it.

Spain's efforts to obtain the extradition of Augusto Pinochet suggest that attitudes may be changing.[41] But Spain has historic ties with Chile as well as a significant Chilean population within its own borders. Even if it has no traditional basis of jurisdiction, in the sense of a direct territorial or personal link with the offences or the offender, its ties to the atrocities for which Pinochet is responsible are unquestionable. Yet a few years earlier, when the United States sought a country willing to try Pol Pot and other Khmer Rouge leaders, Spain politely declined. The other historic example of the exercise of universal jurisdiction, the Eichmann trial, shows the same national interest at work. Israel, too, declined to exercise jurisdiction over Pol Pot. In other words, there are few, if any, examples of disinterested and altruistic exercise of universal jurisdiction. To paraphrase Mark Twain, who was speaking of the weather and not universal jurisdiction, everybody talks about it but nobody does anything about it.

CRIMINAL ACCOUNTABILITY AND THE RIGHTS OF THE ACCUSED

Until relatively recently, human rights law and human rights activists have been concerned principally with the rights of the accused and the rights of the detained, and not with seeing that they are convicted and put in prison.

Traditionally, human rights lawyers acted for the defence, not the prosecution. Human rights literature was characterized by appeals for clemency and amnesty, not calls for accountability, prosecution and appropriate punishment. That the highest standards of procedural fairness be respected in prosecutions for human rights abuses is unquestioned. Still, the application of such noble principles in practice is sometimes difficult, particularly when energies are refocused on conviction rather than acquittal. This is especially true in domestic justice systems where problems of poverty and under-development compromise the ability of states to mete out justice to offenders in full respect of the rights of the accused. But even on an international level the difficulties can be serious. On 3 November 1999, the Appeal Chamber of the International Criminal Tribunal for Rwanda discharged Jean-Bosco Barayagwiza.[42] He had been accused of genocide but his trial was aborted after the Tribunal determined that the Office of the Prosecutor was responsible for violations of his human rights, including wrongful detention and denial of the right to *habeas corpus*.

Historically, probably the most significant human rights issue raised in the context of prosecution for genocide, crimes against humanity and war crimes has been the prohibition of retroactive prosecution, known by the Latin phrase *nullum crimen nulla poena sine lege*. The prohibition is set out in Article 11(2) of the Universal Declaration of Human Rights, as well as in all the major human rights treaties. Indeed, its rare status as a non-derogable norm in all of the instruments has led to it being qualified as part of the common denominator of human rights, the *noyau dur*. The issue of retroactivity arises so frequently in this context because courts and tribunals are generally set up after the crimes have been committed. This was the case with Nuremberg and Tokyo, and more recently with the ad hoc Tribunals for the former Yugoslavia and Rwanda.

The plea by the Nazi defendants at Nuremberg that they were being held accountable for crimes that had not previously been recognized in positive law was far from frivolous. Inspired by the writings of Hans Kelsen, the Tribunal dismissed the argument noting that the *nullum crimen* rule was a principle of justice, and that it would be unjust to let the perpetrators of such horrible crimes go free. Yet, since that judgment, international criminal law has been plagued with an obsessive positivism, dictating constantly more exhaustive codifications, allegedly in the interest of protecting the rights of the accused. This is nowhere more obvious than in the Rome Statute whose verbose provisions are still deemed unsatisfactory, and must be completed with the so-called 'Elements of Crimes', an additional instrument to be adopted pursuant to Article 9. In reality, the extensive definitions exist to protect states, not the individual. They will form an obstacle to progressive, innovative judges, inspired by the dynamism of a human rights law that continues to evolve.

In the call for appropriate sentences for offenders, international criminal prosecution may find itself in an implicit conflict with a philosophy of modern human rights that is based on clemency and a desire for rehabilitation. In the only reference to the goals of punishment to be found in the

International Covenant on Civil and Political Rights, Article 10(3) states that the goal of imprisonment shall be 'reformation and social rehabilitation'. However, most references in the case law of the ad hoc tribunals are to the more classic formulations of domestic criminal justice systems – namely, to deterrence and retribution. Infusing criminal sentencing with human rights values when the offenders are human rights abusers seems more difficult than it ought to be. Perhaps the most compelling indicator of the influence of emerging norms of human rights law on traditional approaches to criminal prosecution is the abandonment of capital punishment as an appropriate penalty, even for the most severe crimes. Most of those convicted at Nuremberg were sentenced to death and executed shortly afterwards. But when the Security Council set up the second generation of international tribunals in the early 1990s, there was barely a whimper from states that still imposed capital punishment. Inspired by the debates on the subject in the International Law Commission, the Council set the maximum penalty as a term of imprisonment. This was soon invoked by bodies such as the Commission on Human Rights as a sign of evolving universal norms.[43] There was a fierce battle on the subject during the Rome Conference, but the pro-death penalty states were heavily outnumbered and geographically isolated. The Rome Statute sets the maximum penalty as life imprisonment, and even here only 'when justified by the extreme gravity of the crime and the individual circumstances of the convicted person'. A person sentenced to such an extreme penalty is entitled to mandatory review for the purposes of parole.[44]

CONCLUSION

Criminal prosecution of those responsible for gross human rights violations is now an important part of the international agenda. The most decisive development, without any doubt, is the establishment of the International Criminal Court. Set to come into existence once 60 states have ratified the Rome Statute, it will tighten the net on the future Pinochets and Pol Pots. Pursuant to the doctrine of complementarity, the Statute looks to national courts to assume the primary responsibility for such prosecutions. States are thus expected to reinforce their substantive law in this area, and to plug the gaps created by such anomalies as statutory limitations, deference to superior orders and immunities for heads of state. Where they fall short, the International Criminal Court will take over.

It may yet be too early to assess the contribution of criminal prosecution to the promotion and protection of human rights. Alternative means of accountability, such as truth commissions, also play an important role in appropriate circumstances. At the very least, the development of this area of the law testifies to the increasing willingness of states to sacrifice their precious sovereignty in the interests of international norms and an international machinery. This is the direct and logical result of the process launched in December 1948 by the United Nations General Assembly when it adopted, literally only hours apart as if they were twins, the Universal Declaration of Human Rights and the Convention for the Prevention and Punishment of the Crime of Genocide.

NOTES

1   *Prosecutor* v. *Tadic*, Case No. IT-94-1-AR72, Decision on the Defence Motion for Interlocutory Appeal on Jurisdiction, 2 October 1995, para. 87.
2   *Treaty of Peace between the Allied and Associated Power and Germany* ('Treaty of Versailles'), [1919] TS 4, Articles 228–30. There were similar penal provisions in the related peace treaties: *Treaty of St. Germain-en-Laye*, [1919] TS 11, Article 173; *Treaty of Neuilly-sur-Seine*, [1920] TS 5, Article 118; *Treaty of Trianon*, (1919) 6 LNTS 187, Article 15. The Treaty of Versailles also pledged prosecution of Kaiser Wilhelm II for what would later be called 'crimes against peace'. However, the German Emperor had fled to neutral Holland where he managed to avoid extradition.
3   Convention (IV) Respecting the Laws and Customs of War by Land, [1910] UKTS 9, annex, Article 46.
4   *German War Trials* (1921).
5   English translation quoted in United Nations War Crimes Commission (1948, p.35).
6   Dadrian (1989, p.221).
7   'Correspondence between the War Crimes Commission and H.M. Government in London Regarding the punishment of crimes committed on religious, racial or political grounds', UNWCC Doc. C.78, 15 February 1945.
8   *Report of Robert H. Jackson* (1949, p.333).
9   Agreement for the Prosecution and Punishment of Major War Criminals of the European Axis, and Establishing the Charter of the International Military Tribunal (IMT), annex, (1951) 82 UNTS 279, Article 6(c).
10   *France et al.* v. *Goering et al.*, (1946) 22 IMT 203. The suggestion that the drafters of the Nuremberg Charter contemplated something broader, but that the scope of 'crimes against humanity' was cut back as a result of the Berlin Protocol, cannot be sustained on a reading of the *Travaux Préparatoires*. See Clark (1990).
11   UN Doc. A/BUR.50; UN Doc. A/C.6/SR.22 (Dihigo, Cuba). For a summary of the history of the resolution, see UN Doc. E/621.
12   (1951) 78 UNTS 277. See Schabas (2000).
13   UN Doc. E/CN.4/SR.310, p.5; UN Doc. E/CN.4/SR.311, p.5.
14   See the writings of the man who coined the term: Lemkin (1944).
15   For a discussion of the issue at the time of the drafting of the Genocide Convention, see the annotation to *United States of America* v. *Greifelt et al.* ('RuSHA trial'), (1948) 13 LRTWC 1 (United States Military Tribunal), pp.40–41.
16   UN Doc. A/CONF.183/9 (17 July 1998).
17   It is true, of course, that as early as 1968 there was an expression in treaty law of the view that crimes against humanity could be committed in time of peace as well as in time of war. Article 1(b) of the Convention on the Non-Applicability of Statutory Limitations to War Crimes and Crimes Against Humanity, (1970) 754 UNTS 73, Article I, defines: 'Crimes against humanity whether committed in time of war or in time of peace as they are defined in the Charter of the International Military Tribunal, Nüremberg, of 8 August 1945 and confirmed by resolutions 3(I) of 13 February 1946 and 95(I) of 11 December 1946 of

the General Assembly of the United Nations, eviction by armed attack or occupation and inhuman acts resulting from the policy of apartheid, and the crime of genocide as defined in the 1948 Convention on the Prevention and Punishment of the Crime of Genocide, even if such acts do not constitute a violation of the domestic law of the country in which they were committed.' However, the Convention did not establish obligations with respect to international repression of the crime and, furthermore, still lacks widespread ratification.

18 (1987) 1465 UNTS 85, Article 2(2).
19 Declaration on the Protection of All Persons from Enforced Disappearance, GA Res. 47/133, preamble.
20 UN Doc. S/RES/827 (1993), annex, Article 5.
21 UN Doc. S/RES/955 (1994), annex, Article 4.
22 *Supra*, note 1, para. 141.
23 See generally, on crimes against humanity, La Rosa (1998, pp.17–26).
24 Geneva Convention Relative to the Protection of Civilians, (1950) 75 UNTS 287.
25 Protocol Additional to the 1949 Geneva Conventions of 12 August 1949, and Relating to The Protection of Victims of International Armed Conflicts, (1979) 1125 UNTS 3, Articles 85–86.
26 Study by the International Law Commission of the Question of an International Criminal Jurisdiction, GA Res. 216 B(III).
27 *Yearbook of the International Law Commission 1950*, Vol. II, pp.374–78.
28 GA Res. 3314(XXIX).
29 Report of the International Law Commission to the General Assembly on the work of its 46th session, UN Doc. A/CN.4/SER.A/1994/Add.1 (Part 2).
30 Report of the International Law Commission on the work of its 48th session, 6 May–26 July 1996, UN Doc. A/51/10.
31 Report of the Secretary-General Pursuant to Paragraph 2 of Security Council Resolution 808 (1993), UN Doc. S/25704.
32 *Prosecutor* v. *Erdemovic* (Case No. IT-96-22-A), Sentencing Appeal, 7 October 1997, (1998) 111 ILR 298.
33 *Prosecutor* v. *Furundzija* (Case No. IT-95-17/1-T), Judgment, 10 December 1998, (1999) 38 ILM 317.
34 *Velazquez Rodriguez* v. *Honduras*, Inter-Am. Ct. HR (ser. C), No. 4, para. 174.
35 General Comment No. 20(44), UN Doc. CCPR/C/21/Rev.1/Add.3, para. 7; *Bleir* v. *Uruguay* (Case No. 30/1978), UN Doc. CCPR/C/OP/1; *Baboeram* v. *Surinam* (Cases No. 146/1983 and No. 148–54/1983), UN Doc. A/40/40; *Barbato* v. *Uruguay* (Case No. 84/1981), UN Doc. A/38/40.
36 See generally Roht-Arriaza (1995).
37 UN Doc. E/CN.4/Sub.2/1997/20/Rev.1.
38 General Comment No. 20(44), UN Doc. CCPR/C/21/Rev.1/Add.3, para. 4.
39 Report No. 26/92 (El Salvador), OAS Doc. OEA/ser.L/V/II.82; Report 29/92 (Uruguay), OAS Doc. OEA/ser.L/V/II.82. Doc. 25; Report 24/92 (Uruguay), OAS Doc. OEA/ser.L/V/II.82. Doc. 24.
40 *A.G. Israel* v. *Eichmann*, (1968) 36 ILR 18 (District Court); *A.G. Israel* v. *Eichmann*, (1968) 36 ILR 277 (Supreme Court).
41 *R.* v. *Bow Street Stipendiary Magistrate and others, ex parte Pinochet Ugarte*, [1998] 4 All ER 897, [1998] 3 WLR 1456 (HL); *R.* v. *Bow Street Stipendiary Magistrate and others, ex parte Pinochet Ugarte* (Amnesty International and others intervening) (No. 3), [1999] 2 All ER 97, [1999] 2 WLR 825 (HL).
42 *Prosecutor* v. *Barayagwiza* (ICTR), Appeal Chamber Decision, 3 November 1999.

43   Question of the Death Penalty, CHR Res. 1997/12, preamble; Question of the
      Death Penalty, CHR Res. 1998/8, preamble; Question of the Death Penalty,
      CHR Res. 1999/61, preamble.
44   See Rolf Einar Fife, 'Penalties' in Lee (1999, pp.319–44).

BIBLIOGRAPHY

Askin, Kelly Dawn (1997), *War Crimes Against Women, Prosecution in International War Crimes Tribunals*, The Hague: Martinus Nijhoff.

Bassiouni, M. Cherif (ed.) (1999), *International Criminal Law*, 2nd rev. edn, New York: Transnational Publishers.

Beigbeder, Yves (1999), *Judging War Criminals, The Politics of International Justice*, New York: St Martin's Press.

Clark, Roger S. (1990), 'Crimes against humanity at Nuremburg', in G. Ginsburgs and V. N. Kudriavstsev (eds), *The Nuremburg Trial and International Law*, Dordrecht/Boston: Martinus Nijhoff, pp.177–212.

Dadrian, Vahakn N. (1989), 'Genocide as a problem of national and international law: the World War I Armenian case and its contemporary legal ramifications', *Yale Journal of International Law*, 14, pp.221–334.

Dinstein, Yoram and Tabory, Mala (1996), *War Crimes In International Law*, The Hague/Boston/London: Martinus Nijhoff.

German War Trials. Report of Proceedings before the Supreme Court in Leipzig (1921), London: HMSO.

Hayner, Priscilla (1994), 'Fifteen truth commissions – 1974 to 1994: a comparative study', *Human Rights Quarterly*, **16**, 597–632.

Kritz, Neil J. (ed.) (1995), *Transitional Justice, How Emerging Democracies Reckon with Former Regimes*, Washington, DC: United States Institute of Peace.

La Rosa, Anne-Marie (1998), *Dictionnaire de droit international pénal, Termes choisis*, Paris: Presses Universitaires de France.

Lee, Roy S. (ed.) (1999), *The International Criminal Court, The Making of the Rome Statute: Issues, Negotiations, Results*, The Hague/London/Boston: Kluwer Law International.

Lemkin, Raphael (1944), *Axis Rule in Occupied Europe: Laws of Occupation, Analysis of Government, Proposals for Redress*, Washington DC: Carnegie Endowment for World Peace.

McAdams, A. James (1997), *Transitional Justice and the Rule of Law in New Democracies*, Notre Dame/London: University of Notre Dame Press.

McCormack, Timothy L.H. and Simpson, Gerry J. (1997), *The Law of War Crimes, National and International Approaches*, The Hague/Boston/London: Martinus Nijhoff.

Meron, Theodor (1998), *War Crimes Law Comes of Age*, Oxford: Clarendon Press.

Minow, Martha (1998), *Between Vengeance and Forgiveness: Facing History After Genocide and Mass Violence*, Boston, MA: Beacon Press.

Rainer, Steven R. and Abrams, Jason S. (1997), *Accountability for Human Rights Atrocities in International Law: Beyond the Nuremberg Legacy*, Oxford: Clarendon Press.

Report of Robert H. Jackson, United States Representative to the International Conference on Military Trials, Washington DC: US Government Printing Office.

Roht-Arriaza, Naomi (1995), *Impunity and Human Rights in International Law and Practice*, New York/Oxford: Oxford University Press.

Schabas, William A. (2000), *Genocide in International Law: The Crime of Crimes*, Cambridge: Cambridge University Press.

Triffterer, Otto (ed.) (1999), *Commentary on the Rome Statute of the International Criminal Court: Observers' Notes, Article by Article*, Baden-Baden: Nomos Verlagsgesellschaft.

United Nations War Crimes Commission (1948), *History of the United Nations War Crimes Commission and the Development of the Laws of War*, London: HMSO.

10 Sanctions and Human Rights

KATARINA TOMAŠEVSKI

INTRODUCTION

Sanctions have created a range of human rights problems, many of which remain unsolved. In trying to punish a state for wrongdoing, formally imposed sanctions necessarily victimize its population. While it is easy to distinguish between the state, government and population in theory, the imposition of sanctions, in practice, obliterate this distinction. An even more intriguing problem has emerged where sanctions have been imposed as a response to human rights violations. Sanctions target the state because it is held responsible for violations, but the practical impossibility of distinguishing between the state and its population has resulted in double victimization – people victimized by human rights violations have been additionally harmed by sanctions.

At the conceptual level, the most important reason for problems created by sanctions in the field of human rights can be easily identified. Sanctions have been imported into international relations from criminal justice. At the domestic level, the state sanctions the criminal found guilty of an offence whereas the victim is not party to the process. The rights of the victim were only introduced into criminal justice recently, after centuries of disregard for him/her, and have not substantively altered the vertical relationship between the state and the criminal. When this criminal justice model is transposed to international relations, the state deemed guilty of a wrongful act is punished – sanctioned – by its peers, while the victims (who are also victims of the sanctions) tend to be forgotten. The personalization of punishment in domestic criminal justice confines punishment to the individual found guilty. The responsibility is personal and is established through due process of law before punishment can be imposed. At the international level, the responsibility of the state is institutional, while sanctions are more, often than not, imposed without due process of law. Punishing the state as an institution is difficult even in theory. Sanctions against a state thus victimize its population while often failing to affect those who make decisions in its name.

Gunnar Myrdal argued many years ago that research into any governmental policy should proceed '… in terms of means and ends rather than causes and effects'.[1] In analysing sanctions, one can scrutinize concordance or discordance between means and ends – between the objectives pursued through the imposition of sanctions and the means employed to attain them. From the human rights perspective, the ends that sanctions should accomplish do not undermine the necessity to evaluate the means used to attain them. Human rights analysis focuses on the employed means rather than on the professed ends, and human rights safeguards are necessary to prevent people from being punished for the sins of their rulers. While the criminal justice system could – and did – concentrate on the relations between the state and the perpetrator of a crime, the prerequisite of human rights is the recognition of the rights of the victim. The recognition of equal rights for all impedes treating victims as objects of victimization or protection; rather, it requires treating them as subjects of human rights.

The transfer of the criminal justice model from domestic to international relations has also created a great deal of confusion with regard to terminology. The term 'sanction' (as a noun) denotes 'enforcement', whose purpose is to exact forcibly an action from the targeted state. Conversely, 'to sanction' (as a verb) signifies approval. The linguistic potential of this peculiarity is immense because it endows 'sanction' (as a noun) with the authority of law from which it is assumed to derive, because the term is identical, whether used as a noun or a verb. The original meaning of 'to sanction' (as a verb) emphasizes authority rather than punishment; its ordinary meaning is 'to invest with legal or sovereign authority, to make valid or binding'.[2] At the domestic level, the state's monopoly over law enforcement combines authority with punishment, but this is not so on the international level. Sanctions are often imposed without the necessary authority derived from international law. The prevalent vocabulary does not reveal this lack of correspondence between the imposed sanctions and the necessary legal authority to resort to sanctions. They may appear to be endowed with the authority of law while lacking it. More often than not, sanctions have become an extralegal phenomenon, imposed without due process of law against a particular state by its peers.

Any analysis of sanctions thus requires crossing disciplinary boundaries between international relations and international law. A transdisciplinary bridge is necessary to discern how sanctions are decided upon and imposed, their justifications and objectives, and how these objectives are to be accomplished. The rationale for such an analysis is grounded in fundamental human rights precepts. Because law is symmetrical, freedom is correlated with responsibility; hence, the exercise of freedom to respond to wrongful acts entails responsibility. When sanctions are decided through internal political processes in one state as punishment for another, intended and unintended consequences flow from such a decision. The population of the target state is likely to be harmed unless explicit and effective safeguards are put in place. As Hubert Védrine put it, '… the dividing line is not between compassion and indifference, but between responsibility and irresponsibility'.[3] The choice of the means available to attain a particular objective entails weighing their consequences, in which human rights safeguards provide a ready-made corrective against punishing people for the sins of their rulers. The pursuit of those means which defy the professed ends is possible, even likely, if this choice is exercised irresponsibly. The rule of law aims to prevent such an irresponsible exercise of choice. Preventing the abuse of power is the main purpose of human rights. Subsuming sanctions under the rule of law is, therefore, a principal means for preventing the abuses of power made possible by sanctions as long as they remain an extralegal phenomenon.

DOMESTIC DECISION-MAKING ON INTERNATIONAL SANCTIONS

The state is routinely perceived as an actor (many would say 'the actor'), responding to positive or negative acts committed by its peers because enforcement of international law is largely left to individual states. Each state has a formally adopted policy for liaising with others, which increasingly includes a human rights component and thus a blueprint for responding to human rights violations by another state. Sanctions tend to be analysed within interstate relations, omitting intrastate processes which lead to their imposition. Beneath the veneer of conduct attributed to a state, often conflicting threads are interwoven, created by the acts and omissions of the many actors who formulate, interpret and execute a state's foreign policy. The mass media promptly broadcast newsworthy atrocities in faraway countries, demanding an instant reaction. Such a reaction is generated through domestic political processes which reflect a multitude of interwoven foreign policy concerns. The urge to punish perpetrators of an atrocity collides with the desire to help victims; pragmatic considerations of attaining either or both of these aims is routinely merged with a host of political and commercial considerations which foreign policy cannot disregard.

There is, moreover, a maze of non-state actors, ranging from political parties to trade unions, from exporters to development NGOs, from established churches to associations of exiles, whose visions differ with regard to what should be done in responding to human rights violations in other countries and how. Moreover, the 'state' comprises an executive and a legislature that often diverge in determining which human rights violations demand a punitive response in the form of sanctions. Foreign policy is a prerogative of the executive. The division of labour between different branches of the government, mandated by the separation of powers, exempts foreign policy decisions from judicial oversight[4] and, thus, also from human rights safeguards embodied in the rule of law. Foreign policy decisions have seldom been litigated, and this is unlikely to change. Domestic political processes do not provide for participation by populations of foreign countries, and foreign policy decisions are thus only partially constrained by democratic safeguards. These may include a concern for the fate of faraway populations but are not necessarily prioritized in domestic decision-making. Foreigners do not have political rights in another country and there is no means by which the population of the sanctioned country can demand their freedom from being sanctioned. Furthermore, the executive itself comprises various actors representing trade, aid, migration or suppression of drug trafficking that lay down varying priorities for bilateral or multilateral responses to actions by other states. Concerns for the plight of victims of human rights violations often clash with fears that they might seek refuge in other countries; many will readily condemn violations but will not provide refuge for victims. Geopolitical and geoeconomic criteria proverbially distort responses to human rights violations, small, poor and distant countries being much more frequent targets of condemnations and sanctions than powerful and commercially attractive ones. The priority attached to the human rights of the people whose states are the target of sanctions varies a great deal.

Foreign policy which results from the interplay of the existing multitude of governmental and non-governmental actors necessarily reflects their different interests and values. Underneath a coating of acceptable abstract principles in a formally adopted foreign policy, there is a maze through which information about violations attributed to other governments, particularly atrocities, and suggested courses of action is filtered, necessarily resulting in a labyrinthine pattern of responses. Attempts to clarify foreign policy with a single theory have thus far failed because of inevitable clashes between different, sometimes conflicting, interests and values in its creation. In the field of human rights, commercial interests or fears of mass immigration undermine human rights values, while both granting and withholding aid can – paradoxically – be defined in terms of promoting such values. After all, aid is routinely defined as a means for facilitating development; this often includes explicitly promoting human rights. Proponents of sanctions argue, however, that withholding aid from a government that violates human rights will benefit human rights by placing a price-tag on violations. Because foreign policy should accommodate a variety of interests and values, it can comprise both approaches, mutually contradictory as they are. In consequence, a state can appear to be pursuing several foreign policies simultaneously.

Foreign policy decisions are often made rapidly, particularly if they comprise symbolic statements (such as a verbal condemnation of an atrocity) and gestures (such as the suspension of a minuscule aid package) and typically accommodate a government's need to be seen to act. Outcomes of such decisions reflect the relative weight of influential domestic constituencies, necessarily having to balance their divergent interests and values. Sanctions consisting of cutting off aid may be opposed by the providers of aid; trade sanctions will be opposed by exporters and importers. Accommodating their different interests would be impossible were it not for the ample leeway between saying and doing, acting and being seen to act, which characterizes foreign policy. George Kennan has depicted the situation as follows:

Form means a great deal in international life. What is important, in other words, is not so much what is done as how it is done. And, in this sense, good form in outward demeanor becomes more than a means to an end, more than a subsidiary attribute: it becomes a value in itself, with its own validity and its own effectiveness, and – human nature being what it is – the greatest value of all.[5]

Such a view of foreign policy by one of its prominent practitioners allows for gesture politics (acts performed for the sake of acting), as well as for those acts that may not be achieving their professed goal but are symbolizing a government's commitment to it. Sanctions have been used as gesture politics when they are imposed and lifted with such lightning speed that no effects are likely to emerge, but they have also been imposed and kept in place regardless of their apparent deficiency in attaining the goals for which they were ostensibly imposed. What has not emerged, however, are sanctions that would have subordinated domestic self-interest to the human rights of others. An embargo impeding the import of oil from a repressive regime which happens to be the sole source of oil, for example, has never occurred nor is it likely to. Lisa Martin has argued that governments imposing sanctions routinely fail to demonstrate their willingness to suffer economic losses themselves.[6] David Leyton-Brown has taken this line of reasoning further by concluding that sanctions are used as a weapon of first resort – an easy way for governments to be seen to act.[7]

OBSTACLES TO SUBSUMING SANCTIONS UNDER THE RULE OF LAW

The authority of international law is not based on an international authority capable of governing but on the willingness of states to adjust their conduct to the requirements of the rule of law. International law has traditionally been interstate law and its enforcement was based historically on self-help. A state which was a target of wrongdoing had to react against harm inflicted upon it by another state. The development of substantive and procedural international law in past decades has provided alternatives to self-help. The institutionalization of collective enforcement, however, has only been developed for international peace and security. Forcible action to alter the conduct of states has been envisaged only when international peace and security is threatened and the powers are vested in the United Nations Security Council. Sanctions by the Security Council are extralegal, as the Council is endowed with power to define a situation as a threat to international peace and security and apply whatever means it finds suitable for fending off such a threat. Even the Security Council's sanctions depend on the willingness and ability of individual states to impose and enforce sanctions. The Council has the authority to impose sanctions but not the powers to enforce them. Enforcement is left to individual states and to pressure from peers. Where such pressure is strong, sanctions are enforced; where it is lacking, the Security Council's sanctions can be ignored.

Individual governments, acting on behalf of their states, have no authority to sanction each other. Nevertheless, the term 'sanctions' is used to denote such individual punitive measures and created much controversy in the work of the International Law Commission (ILC) when it attempted to codify the international law of state responsibility.

The ILC has chosen the term 'countermeasures' to differentiate between 'sanctions', which necessitate authority and are thus only imposed by an international organization, and 'countermeasures', which denote measures applied by one state against another and which are permitted in response to an internationally wrongful act of the target state. Freedom to resort to countermeasures in conditions of inequality favours the strong at the expense of the weak, and the ILC noted that:

> ... countermeasures were an exercise in power, wielded more often than not to the detriment of the principles of equality and justice and that by sanctioning unilateral resort to countermeasures, the Commission was opening the door to many possible abuses.[8]

This line of reasoning has opened the Pandora's Box of the eternal conflict between the rule of force and the rule of law within the international community. Continuing disagreements about the need to transfer sanctions from the rule of force to the rule of law have pre-empted the codification of international law of state responsibility relating to this issue, while the ensuing controversies have produced more heat than light. The continuing legal gap, however, reinforces the image of sanctions (this term will be used here regardless of its legal inaccuracy because it is used in practice) as an extralegal phenomenon.

Endless scholarly disputes testify to the diversity of opinion as to what the law is with regard to sanctions, while the few cases that could have led to incipient international jurisprudence reinforced the extralegality of sanctions. The Libyan Arab Jamahiriya challenged the legality of sanctions imposed on it by the Security Council before the International Court of Justice but did not obtain a decision by the Court that would have challenged them.[9] In addressing the sanctions imposed by Greece against the former Yugoslav Republic of Macedonia, the European Court of Justice acknowledged that national security concerns, regardless of how irrational they may seem to outsiders, may legitimately curtail any cooperation with a country seen to represent a threat.[10]

The imposition of sanctions by one government against another thus largely remains beyond the scope of law, with increasing exceptions embodied in international trade-and-investment law. Oscar Schachter has described the general legal *lacuna* that still prevails by saying that 'States are free to reduce trade, investment or aid with another State, whether or not the other State acted illegally'.[11] Similarly Theodor Meron has held that termination of 'discretionary aid' belonged to the sovereign discretion of the donors and was thus outside international law.[12] B.S. Brown has ventured to examine possibilities for a legal challenge to the 'politicization' of international development finance agencies but did not find much law to build upon.[13] Much as international trade law has reduced legal possibilities for resorting to unilateral sanctions in responding to human rights violations, the cases that have emerged in practice tend to be addressed through diplomatic negotiations rather than adjudication.[14]

With regard to the area for which sanctions have been legalized and institutionalized – namely, international peace and security – the 1990s brought both a proliferation of sanctions and increased challenges. At the beginning of 1992 an unprecedented summit meeting took place with the purpose of reaching a broad agreement on a post-Cold War role for the Security Council and the United Nations in general. A major stumbling-block was whether that role should encompass democracy and human rights, as proposed by the United States and endorsed by the United Kingdom and France. This was challenged by China (because of the proposed addition of electoral and human rights monitoring), Cape Verde, Ecuador, Morocco, Venezuela and Zimbabwe (because no mention was made of poverty and underdevelopment).[15] The Security Council noted that 'new favourable international circumstances' have enabled it to 'fulfil more effectively its primary responsibility for the maintenance of international peace and security'. The controversy about a role for the United Nations in democracy/human rights was solved by emphasizing that no international monitoring can be imposed upon a country, and it can only be undertaken as part of the maintenance of international peace and security:

> Election monitoring, human rights verification and the repatriation of refugees have in the settlement of some regional conflicts, at the request or with the agreement of the parties concerned, been an integral part of the Security Council's effort to maintain international peace and security.[16]

In its first 40 years, the Security Council imposed mandatory sanctions only twice (against Rhodesia and South Africa) – in both cases, for human rights violations.[17] In 1961 it also authorized the use of force in response to 'the systematic violations of human rights and fundamental freedoms and the general absence of the rule of law in the Congo'.[18] The Security Council was not created to deal with human rights, and thus human rights emerged on its agenda gradually and haphazardly. As early as 1963 the Soviet Union had raised problems concerning Iraqi Kurds; in 1976 the Council was invited to respond to Indonesia's annexation of East Timor. These and subsequent attempts to place human rights on the Security Council's agenda failed because of an implicit understanding that it was not meant to deal with human rights, and the attempts continued until 1990.[19]

With the proliferation of sanctions in the 1990s, different and often mutually opposed measures were put in place simultaneously – sanctions against states were imposed in order to restore or preserve international peace and security, while assistance to victimized populations had to be added in order to alleviate the effects of the sanctions. Attempts to punish the rulers of Haiti and Iraq failed while unleashing havoc on the populations because sanctions are an inherently blunt instrument. The break-up of states has created additional problems as to who to sanction, who to assist, and how. Sanctions were designed within the previous state-centred international order, state-created and state-enforced law, but when applied in situations where 'the government, the elite and the black marketeers are one and the same',[20] they have not proved effective in achieving their aims. Indeed, sanctions have sometimes proved futile, if not counterproductive, where wars have been 'financed by looting, racketeering and trafficking'.[21]

The post-Cold War Security Council contributed to the multiplication of sanctions and to increased references to human rights violations to justify them. Grounds for sanctions were broadened from breaches of international peace and security to internal repression, and targets widened from states to warring parties within states. That process highlighted the fact that the Security Council exercises discretion. The attempted challenge by the Libyan Arab Jamahiriya of the Security Council's sanctions before the International Court of Justice failed; another legal challenge attempted by Bosnia and Herzegovina, also failed to lead to an authoritative determination of the legal status of sanctions.[22] The Security Council's discretionary and final decisions about threats to peace and security and related responses were further manifested in an 'agreed Statement' which accompanied the Security Council decisions concerning Haiti. The Council had no evidence of a threat to international peace and security to support its decision as the United Nations Charter requires and therefore an agreed statement specified that that decision should 'not be regarded as constituting a precedent explicitly'.[23]

Inasmuch as sanctions imposed by the Security Council are an extralegal phenomenon and thus beyond international law, the effects of sanctions on the populations of sanctioned countries prompted a challenge on the grounds of human rights. However, the low priority for human rights within the United Nations was illustrated by the refusal of the Commission on Human Rights to permit a study into the human rights implications of United Nations enforcement actions. That refusal was based, *inter alia*, on 'the need for the Sub-Commission [Sub-Commission on the Promotion and Protection of Human Rights, formerly the Sub-Commission on Prevention of Discrimination and Protection of Minorities] to avoid making judgments on issues within the responsibility of other United Nations bodies'.[24]

In 1993 the Sub-Commission initiated a study into the human rights dimension of human rights enforcement, and one of its members, Claire Palley, carried out the preparatory work. Her working paper was endorsed by the Sub-Commission in 1994 and transmitted to the parent body, the Commission on Human Rights, asking for the issue to be placed on the agenda and to be followed by a comprehensive study. The Commission decided against that proposal. Claire Palley's preliminary overview of pertinent issues raised important but unpleasant questions because she argued that international enforcement could harm human rights. She pointed out that sanctions imposed by the Security Council allowed for humanitarian exceptions, but the sanctions committees had neither information on their human rights impact nor the power necessary to suspend sanctions when they resulted in the intolerable suffering of the population in the sanctioned country. She thus questioned international responsibility for the enforcement of human rights.[25] Obviously it would have been difficult, if not impossible, for one part of the United Nations to address the lack of human rights safeguards in the activities of another part of the same organization, so the topic was not pursued further.

The multiplication of sanctions coincided with a change in international relations. The United States' post-Cold War concept of a New World Order diverted attention from the need to cope with the disorder which accompanied the collapse of the previous system. International public order gave way to a realization that two crucial areas of international security – the military and finance – had escaped beyond the control of public international bodies. When the Security Council responded to internal conflicts by imposing sanctions, they proved futile because national public authorities could not (or would not) affect privatized flows of funds or weapons, or these flows simply did not exist. Although the privatization of international capital flows became a well-known feature of the 1990s, sanctions continued to target *public* finance and *public* authorities.

RESPONDING TO THE CHANGING PATTERN OF SANCTIONS

The collapse of the Cold War era increased opportunities for imposing sanctions, and their effects on human rights prompted a great deal of criticism. The process of dismantling existing states, conflict-prone by definition, was aggravated by international responses to the process of creating and re-creating states. The previous pre-human-rights rules granted external legitimacy to individual states on the basis of the capacity of the regime claiming statehood to govern the territorial entity which it aspired to represent internationally. These rules were altered with the entry of human rights into international policy, politics and law. The previous priority had been attached to effectiveness, while the internal legitimacy of the regime in question was rarely questioned. The new post-Cold War rules shifted attention to internal legitimacy. An unintended consequence of these new rules was the possibility for many 'collectivities' to claim a right to statehood and to use military force to attain it. The right of self-determination could be invoked as the collective right of peoples based on shared ethnicity, religion or language, although the international community has wavered in responding to such claims. The previous criterion of effective territorial control was replaced by judgements relating to the internal legitimacy of various regimes or aspirants. New criteria have been applied – sometimes even before they had been explicitly formulated – to determine whether a government came to power through free and fair multiparty elections, whether it was truly representative of the whole population, or whether new states created by ethnic minorities should be recognized. Such judgements have necessarily varied. The notion of human rights and their violations has thus continued to evolve, while unilateral and multilateral responses to viola-tions have proliferated and often encompassed sanctions.

Although the term 'sanctions' is a misnomer, and the law requires the use of the term 'countermeasures' as noted above, the continued use of the term 'sanctions' is not only a reflection of the unlikelihood of a legal term such as 'countermeasures' becoming accepted as a household word, but rather of the mobilizing power of 'sanctions' as a law-based response to an illegal act. The accompanying assumption is that everything labelled as a human rights violation for the purpose of justifying sanctions is a breach of inter-national human rights law. Phenomena for which international human rights law does not embody a clear-cut recipe (the death penalty, for example) have become a yardstick for assessing the human rights performance of individual states, as have minority rights, for which international human rights law, in fact, provides little guidance. Moreover, human rights protec-tion has been extended from times of peace to those of war, thus blurring the dividing line between human rights and humanitarian law. Because abuses during warfare are proverbially numerous, the label of violations could be stretched *ad infinitum*.

The broadening of the notion of human rights violations in international human rights politics has also broadened the possibilities for resorting to sanctions. Because it encompassed unilateral alongside multilateral sanc-tions, as well as targeting developing countries and those in transition, international policy-making on sanctions has revealed a deep split amongst the governments of the world. A government imposing sanctions implicitly creates for itself a right to punish, *ius puniendi*. This *ius puniendi* divides the international community along the line of sanctioning versus sanctioned, North versus South. The Commission on Human Rights has denounced coercive unilateral economic measures and proclaimed them to be in clear contradiction to international law,[26] singling out 'certain countries [which] using their predominant position in the world economy, continue to inten-sify the adoption of unilateral coercive measures'.[27] Such resolutions reflect the predictable anger of the South at the North's abuse of economic power. The voting pattern has revealed the split between the minority of govern-ments willing and able to resort to economic coercion, on the one hand, and the majority of those likely to become objects of sanctions, on the other. This abyss has prevented the forging of a shared United Nations policy but, even more importantly, prevented a focus on the effects and impact of sanctions on human rights.

THE RATIONALE OF SANCTIONS AND THE LOGIC OF HUMAN RIGHTS

The prerequisites for the recognition and protection of human rights em-phasize a bottom-up process, whereby human rights are articulated and safeguarded at the domestic level. International standards and procedures serve as a corrective to domestic human rights protection but can never replace it. Sanctions follow the opposite logic: being imposed against a state by its peers, they aim at enforcing a change in the behaviour of the targeted state from the outside. Sanctions thus result in the externalization of responsibility, situating both the specification of conditions for lifting sanctions and the assessment of compliance with them within the province of other states. Contrary to the insistence of international human rights law on domestic human rights protection, sanctions rely on foreign and/or international substantive and procedural standards, weakening the accountability of governments to their own populations.

Moreover, the profound long-term effect of sanctions is likely to increase the feeling of the affected population; it will consider itself as the object of foreign or international punitiveness rather than the subject of individual and collective rights. Anthony Hazlitt Heard has raised a crucial, and as yet unanswered, question about the long-term effect of sanctions: what sort of people will emerge when sanctions and repression end?[28] Ninety years ago, the Western sanctions against the Soviet Union following the October Revolution elicited this description:

> The continuance of the blockade of Russia renders helpless the quite innocent population, engenders in the people of Russia a feeling of hostility to the allies, and only serves to intensify the disordered state of the country.[29]

There have been many similar descriptions in the past nine decades, arguing that sanctions punish people for the sins of their rulers. Such descriptions do not vary for those sanctions that have been imposed ostensibly in the name of human rights.

The resort to human rights language to legitimize external policing and sanctioning undermines the very basis for human rights protection, which should be domestic. The implicit rationale for condemnations and sanctions is remote-controlled political development. A momentum for change that could not be generated within the country's domestic political processes is expected, as is the orientation of such change against the guilty government but in favour of human rights protection. That rationale remains implicit because it conflicts with what is known about the political effects of sanctions in the sanctioned countries – namely that they routinely strengthen the targeted government and often channel political changes in the direction of increased repression. Repression is then justified by the combination of impoverishment attributed to sanctions and the external enemy that caused that impoverishment.

Sanctions make the targeted government accountable to other governments, which are accountable to their own electorates. People in the sanctioned countries – in the name of whose rights sanctions are imposed – are not a factor in that equation. Human rights are thus removed from their grounding in the rule of law into the realm of politics. Human rights have developed as correctives for domestic political processes but exclude foreign policy. The design that has evolved during the past decades obliges each government to protect the human rights of its own population, but abuses of power by other governments are beyond the reach of the existing safeguards. Developing such safeguards is a challenge for the future.

DISCORDANCE BETWEEN THE ENDS AND THE MEANS

Alongside unanswered questions about the long-term effects of sanctions on the population of the targeted state, sanctions have also raised fundamental questions related to the orientation and purposes of human rights law. The pillar of human rights law is the state's obligation to protect human rights and its responsibility for failing to do so. Strengthening the state's willingness and the institutional capacity to guarantee human rights is therefore the primary objective of international human rights work. Breaches of human rights guarantees should be investigated, adjudicated and penalized by the state itself, lest it be found in breach of its basic human rights obligations. Just before international human rights law had started developing, an often quoted statement from the Nüremberg Trials put it differently:

> Crimes against international law are committed by men, not by abstract entities, and only by punishing individuals who commit such crimes can the provisions of international law be enforced.[30]

This assertion preceded the emergence of international human rights law and referred to the prosecution of genocide and war crimes. It was revived in the 1990s, however, within the area of human rights. Two different lines of argument have been pursued. The first is aimed at altering sanctions in order to avoid targeting a whole state and thus inflicting harm upon its population. Numerous proposals have been made to freeze the financial assets of political elites[31] rather than imposing sanctions against states. These have been supported by Kofi Annan, the Secretary-General of the United Nations, who has argued in favour of sanctions aimed at decision-makers and their families, including the freezing of personal and organizational assets, as well as restrictions on travel.[32] The second is directed at individualizing the responsibility for human rights violations, replicating the blueprint developed in international humanitarian law. This path has, however, implicitly questioned the role of the state in human rights by striving to identify and bring to court specific individuals deemed to have been responsible for ordering or committing abuses in the name of the state.

These parallel developments may well result in changing the future thrust of sanctions and alleviating some of their negative effects. They were founded on the awareness that, even though the aim of sanctions can be translated into preventing evil deeds, this only makes sanctions a lesser evil rather than something good in themselves. However justified, economic sanctions carry with them purposeful impoverishment which leads also to disempowerment. The population of the targeted country finds itself caught in the crossfire between its own government and those applying sanctions. Both sides are likely to point to the evil deeds of the other side and argue that their own represent a lesser evil.

When the spotlight is directed towards means rather than ends, the framework elaborated for regulating warfare provides ready-made guidance for assessing sanctions. Restrictions on warfare are intended to protect the civilian population against being targeted and to constrain the situations where civilian harm becomes 'collateral damage'. Prohibitions embodied in the law of armed conflicts protect civilians against purposeful destruction, intentional harm and collateral damage through gross negligence. By analogy, civilians should be at least equally protected in times of peace. Hans-Peter Gasser, then Legal Adviser of the International Committee of the Red Cross (ICRC) defined economic sanctions as instruments of warfare, arguing that humanitarian exceptions should apply as they do in warfare.[33] UNICEF has proposed that all sanctions should have an *ex ante* child impact assessment which would give details of the expected impact of proposed sanctions on children and include the offsetting measures proposed to be taken.[34] Graça Machel has noted that sanctions were seen '… as a safer recourse that can be applied at lower cost'[35] in comparison to waging war.

Indeed, economic sanctions follow the logic of warfare, aiming to 'deprive the enemy of the material means of resistance',[36] while simultaneously deterring potential providers of such means. The effects of sanctions that have been enforced, such as those against Iraq, Haiti or the former Yugoslavia, were found to have been the opposite of those intended – detrimental to the population and negligible (at best) for the government which was their real target. Sanctions against Haiti were at fault in their very design because neither the Organization of American States (OAS) nor the United Nations differentiated between legitimate and prohibited purposes of sanctions[37] as these can be inferred from the legal restrictions upon warfare.

The hardships imposed upon the population in the target country can be hidden behind legal rhetoric, whereby sanctions are imposed against the state rather than its population. The responsibility for protecting the population against the hardships created by sanctions falls into a legal gap. According to legal rules, this responsibility pertains to the government of the target state. Sanctions, however, aim to disempower the government of that state, to make it unable to perform ordinary governmental functions, even if it so wished. Those who have imposed sanctions do not have a legal responsibility towards the population of another country – hence this legal gap.

The costs of sanctions originating from this gap have raised a great deal of concern worldwide. While people are easily mobilized in favour of sanctions against a foreign dictator, when the effects of sanctions are seen to include the purposeful starvation of the children of that country, eyebrows are immediately raised, followed by questions and protests. The means used by the dictator, and by those working for his demise, become uncomfortably similar. The logic that triggers protests against sanctions can be thus simplified: a dictator, accused of violating the human rights of the population, is subjected to sanctions to hasten his demise; the sanctions inflict impoverishment and starvation upon the population so as to force the demise of that dictator in the hope that they will accomplish that aim and that the ensuing change will improve the respect of the human rights of the population. Since this rationale does not, in practice, work as intended, attention is shifted from means to ends. The means employed might be unpleasant, but are necessary to attain worthwhile ends.

The means are, however, the essential criteria used in conceptualizing such abuses of power as human rights violations. Every government's rhetoric promises worthwhile ends, domestically and internationally. The essential test is to determine whether the means employed lead to the professed ends and whether they are compatible with the declared ends. Alarm bells ring when the means employed apparently defy the professed ends, and prompt human rights defenders into action.

CHANGING HUMAN RIGHTS ACTIVISM

International human rights activism started with the maxim that people whose rights were protected should act for those who were less fortunate. During the 1960s its motto was formulated simply: exposing human rights violations was the first step towards opposing them. The globalization of human rights activism derived from the universality of human rights: the adjective *human* implied everybody's duty to defend the rights of all fellow human beings; allowing their violations to continue unexposed and unopposed undermined the very 'human' in human rights. A right to speak on behalf of victims of human rights violations was followed by a right to act on their behalf. 'Amnesty International does not consult the prisoners about whether they want to be adopted,' argued Cosmas Desmond in a critique that created quite a stir at the time, '… it assumes that if a person is in prison the most is to get him or her out, regardless of any wider political implications.'[38] The underlying dilemma has reached far beyond the political implications of activism to probe into its rationale, which can transform its postulated beneficiaries from subjects of rights into objects of protection.

A right to speak and act on behalf of victims was followed by a right to monitor their victimization, accompanied by lobbying for condemnations and sanctions and also, later, for military interventions. Applying a criminal justice model, such activism sought to condemn and punish victimizers, but neglected victims. As in criminal justice, the victim played no role. Condemnations of individual governments for human rights violations have sought to acknowledge victimhood by rejecting a state's self-granted right to abuse its population. The advocacy of sanctions has, however, implied a right to cause harm, to compound a population's victimization by its own government through economic hardship inflicted by another government.

The growth of human rights organizations started in earnest in the 1970s, when human rights entered the foreign policies of Western governments, creating demand for information on human rights violations in other countries. Responses to human rights violations have broadened from international political and/or legal judgements to economic sanctions, first bilateral and then multilateral. The institutionalization of human rights conditionality followed suit. Activism addressing human rights in other countries became part of domestic politics. Research was no longer purely academic because its findings could – and did – influence the foreign policy of a particular government, which often included responding to violations by resorting to sanctions. Advocacy could no longer be classified as international, foreign or domestic; human rights in other countries entered domestic politics with a view to influencing foreign policy to apply it in order to mould the policies, laws and practices of other countries.

The appeal of human rights to left-leaning parties, many of which define themselves as liberal, has led human rights into 'the fatal liberal combination of a lofty goal and inadequate resources'.[39] The moral crusade of putting the world to rights has obtained an ahistorical allure of instant universalism. Regardless of their past and present, it was an article of faith that any and every country could be remoulded into a human-rights-respecting state. A host of assumptions has been necessary to buttress this universalistic crusade. The first assumption is that individual rights and freedoms are already recognized and all that is needed is to constrain their violations; the second assumption, following on from this, is that human rights in other countries can be safeguarded at little or no cost; and a third assumption individualizes and personalizes victimizers and victims.

The exposure of abuses in other countries aimed to mobilize people into action against the government which was deemed responsible. This mobilization initially targeted one's own government to nudge it into action against another, embarrassing and publicly shaming it when it failed to act. A mere protest was rarely deemed to constitute a satisfactory response, condemnations and sanctions were urged, to be later followed by military interventions under some palatable name that included the adjective 'humanitarian' or rhetorically transformed bombing into an 'air campaign'.[40]

Human rights organizations, in spreading their activities from their nucleus in the West, have globalized their reach. The entry of human rights into Western foreign policies multiplied condemnations and sanctions. In contrast to the United Nations, individual Western governments needed no agreement or acquiescence from their non-Western peers. Aid-receiving countries were the most frequent target because they had more to lose and the wielding of the Western aid lever was expected to change their behaviour. Reports from non-governmental organizations (and the associated media coverage) were scheduled to coincide not only with annual sessions of the United Nations Commission on Human Rights or the General Assembly, but also with decision-making on development finance for countries that were the object of such reports. After non-Western sources of development finance had dwindled, conditionalities proliferated. Asymmetry was reinforced by marginalizing intergovernmental fora. Multilateralism was quietly but effectively redefined. The United Nations has often become marginalized in favour of an undefined term – the 'international community' – which could then be applied to a variety of intergovernmental fora (many of which do not include developing countries) or even to groups of states acting outside the United Nations system.

The audiences for reports from non-governmental organizations on human rights violations have multiplied with the increased linkages between violations and sanctions. Foreign ministries, development aid agencies, parliamentary foreign affairs committees, political parties, the mass media and many other actors have developed an insatiable demand for information about human rights in countries which were placed, or were likely to be placed, on the foreign policy agenda. Siegfried Pausewang has pointed out that allegations of human rights violations are not necessarily a tool for improving human rights protection but can be utilized to delegitimize a particular government.[41] The boundary between human rights work and political partisanship has thus become blurred.

BLURRED RESPONSIBILITIES

Sanctions require a trilateral analytical scheme to capture the multiple relations which ensue from responding to human rights violations through the imposition of sanctions:

- the horizontal relations between the two governments – the one imposing sanctions and the other being their target
- the vertical relations between each government and its own population, with the population in the country imposing sanctions often favouring them, at least until their effects on the population of the targeted countries become known, with that population being treated as an object of legal or illegal acts rather than the subject of rights
- diagonal relations between both governments and the population in another country.

No ready-made human rights framework exists for these cross-cutting relations because they were not anticipated, and no law exists to regulate them. Human rights guarantees were intended to regulate relations between the state and its own citizens, not the state's relations with citizens of other countries. These guarantees are an outcome of political processes from which citizens of other countries are excluded. As a consequence, a state cannot be brought to court for violating the human rights of citizens of another state.[42]

This legal lacuna exacerbates the complicated horizontal, vertical and diagonal relations which sanctions entail, posing questions which have thus far remained unanswered. Because human rights protection relies on the rule of law, the crucial question pertains to the responsibility for the effects and the impact of sanctions. This question has often been addressed with regard to the sanctions against Iraq, the longest and the most comprehensive imposed to date.

The facts relating to the detrimental effects of sanctions against Iraq on its population have not been denied, but the question – 'Who is responsible for these effects?' – has yielded different responses. Advocates of sanctions have argued their case as a legitimate international response to, *inter alia*, human rights violations. Opponents have argued that sanctions resulted in the double victimization of the Iraqi population. Jason Burke has summed up the debate as follows:

> President Saddam's enemies say he cynically spends less than he could on medicine because dying children are good propaganda material. His allies maintain that the money released by the United Nations is criminally insufficient. Either way, the effect is the same.[43]

The United Nations General Assembly has placed full responsibility for the sanctions and their effects on the Iraqi government by deploring Iraq's '... failure to provide the Iraqi population with access to adequate food and health care', through its refusal to implement pertinent Security Council resolutions.[44] In 1991 the Sub-Commission on the Promotion and Protection of Human Rights acknowledged the suffering of Iraq's population and appealed to all governments and international organizations to '... take urgent measures to prevent the death of thousands of innocent persons, in particular of children, and to ensure that their needs for food and health care were met'. One year earlier, the Sub-Commission had called upon '... all those participating in sanctions against Iraq not to prevent the delivery of necessary food and medicine'.[45] The Sub-Commission has avoided intra-United Nations conflicts by referring to a 'humanitarian situation' in Iraq, rather than to human rights.

The former United Nations Special Rapporteur on Iraq elaborated a two-pronged notion of human rights with his finding that '... the absence of respect for the rights pertaining to democratic governance is at the root of all the major violations of human rights in Iraq', but the absence of democratic governance has not impeded, in theory at least, '... the Government's responsibility to take all necessary action to ensure the full realization of the rights to food and health care for all'.[46]

CONCLUSION

The vicious circle in which the human rights debate has found itself when trying to find an entry point for the recognition and protection of human rights highlights the need to rethink sanctions. Responses to human rights violations have escalated from expressions of concern to condemnations and to various types of sanction and intervention. Such responses are not established and accepted state practice – at least, not yet. Traditional, if unwritten, norms of states' behaviour towards each other, developed over the centuries, endorse silence and inaction. Responses to human rights violations thus do not happen unless a political process has nudged, or forced, a government in this particular direction. This process is more often than not driven by domestic political concerns and constituencies, while its escalation from verbal condemnations to sanctions has taken place along this same path, without substantive and procedural rules to serve as guidance. The progression from non-response (that is, silence) and exposure and condemnation, to sanctions and, ultimately, intervention, maps out the range of possibilities out of which the collective governmental responses have rarely ventured beyond public exposure and condemnation. Western human rights policies have broadened the spectrum through extensive resort to economic sanctions and, more recently, military interventions.

Sanctions are generated through domestic and international political processes in which the legal grounding of human rights can be and is easily ignored. The price is arbitrariness, and challenging such arbitrariness is the principal means for reinstituting human rights protection into the realm of the rule of law.

NOTES

1 Myrdal (1957, p.vi).
2 *Compact Edition of the OED* (1971, Vol II, pp.82–83).
3 'Dans cette affaire, la ligne de clivage n'est pas entre sensibilité et insensibilité, mais entre responsabilité et irresponsabilité' (Védrine, 1996, p.637).
4 This is discussed in Tomaševski (1998).
5 Kennan (1967, p.408).
6 Martin (1992).
7 Leyton-Brown (1987, p.97).
8 International Law Commission, Draft articles on State responsibility, Report on the Work of the 33rd session, 1981, UN Doc. A/35/10, Article 30; Draft articles on State responsibility, *Yearbook of the International Law Commission 1979*, Vol. II, (Part 2), p.121; Report of the International Law Commission on the work of its 45th session, UN Doc. A/48/10, para. 228.
9 Martin (1993, p.20).
10 *Commission of the European Communities* v. *Hellenic Republic*, Case C-120/94 R, Application for interim measures ordering the Hellenic Republic to suspend, pending judgment in the main action, the measures adopted on 16 February 1994 with regard to the former Yugoslav Republic of Macedonia; Court of Justice of the European Communities, Order of 29 June 1994.
11 Schachter (1994, p.15).
12 Meron (1989, p.234).
13 Brown (1992).
14 In the best-known case of the US sanctions against Cuba, the apparent conflict between the Helms-Burton Act and free trade principles induced Europe to take the United States to the World Trade Organization (WTO), so as to obtain an authoritative determination of a breach of international trade law. The case was diverted to political negotiations. The acquiescence of the United States was sought for 'secure and lasting waivers' as well as a commitment not to continue trying to globalize US legislation. (Besides US sanctions against Cuba, those targeting Iran and Libya were also on the agenda.) Waivers were granted

against Europe's acknowledgment 'that many of the Castro nationalizations were illegal under international law and foreign investors might be investing in illegally acquired property'. *Démarche* by the Delegation of the European Commission of 5 March 1996, reproduced in *International Legal Materials*, **35** (1996), pp.398–99; European Communities – Proposal for a Council regulation protecting against the effects of the application of certain legislation of certain third countries, and actions based thereon or resulting therefrom, COM(96) 420 final of 31 July 1996; Buckley (1998); Cornwell (1998); Walker (1998).

15 Lewis (1992).

16 United Nations, Note by the President of the Security Council, UN Doc. S/23500 of 31 January 1992, p.2.

17 This is dealt with in Tomaševski (2000, chapter 2).

18 Security Council resolution 161 of 21 February 1961.

19 This is described and discussed in Tomaševski (1997, pp.135–54).

20 Christiansen and Powers (1993, p.42).

21 Jean (1993, p.5).

22 Cf. Orders of the International Court of Justice of 8 April and 13 September 1993.

23 UN Doc. S/PV/3238 of 16 June 1993.

24 Sub-Commission on Prevention of Discrimination and Protection of Minorities. Annotations to the provisional agenda for its forty-seventh session prepared by the Secretary-General, UN Doc. E/CN.4/Sub.2/1995/1/Add.1 of 21 June 1995, para. 303.

25 Sub-Commission on Prevention of Discrimination and Protection of Minorities. Further preparatory document submitted by Ms Claire Palley on the question of the role of the United Nations in international humanitarian activities and assistance and human rights enforcement, bearing in mind the principle of non-interference, UN Doc. E/CN.4/Sub.2/1994/39 of 15 June 1994, paras 14–16 and 30.

26 Resolution 1995/45 of the Commission on Human Rights of 5 March 1995, in positing that sanctions violated international law, cited as the authorities the United Nations Charter, the Declaration on the Principles of International Law concerning Friendly Relations and Cooperation among States in accordance with the Charter, the Charter of Economic Rights and Duties of States, and the Vienna Declaration and Programme of Action.

27 A series of resolutions, entitled 'Human rights and unilateral coercive measures', has been adopted by the Commission on Human Rights. The 1995/45 resolution was adopted by 24 votes in favour, 17 against and 12 abstentions, resolution 1994/47 was adopted by 23 delegations voting in favour, with 18 against and 12 abstaining. The voting pattern has changed and resolution 1999/21 was adopted by a vote 37–8–6, demonstrating a larger majority opposing report to sanctions without a single developing country voting against or abstaining. Commission on Human Rights – Report on the 55th session (22 March–30 April 1999), UN Doc. E/CN.4/1999/167, pp.332–33.

28 Hazlitt Heard (1993).

29 Berkenheim (1919, p.250).

30 Official documents of the trial of the major war criminals before the International Military Tribunal, Nüremberg, 14 November 1945–1 October 1946, 1947, p.223.

31 'Economic sanctions' (1993, p.162).

32 United Nations, 'The causes of conflict and the promotion of durable peace

and sustainable development in Africa', Report of the Secretary-General, UN Doc. S/1998/318 of 13 April 1998, para. 25.
33   In Post (1994, p.179).
34   Commission on Human Rights, 'Human rights and unilateral coercive measures', Report of the Secretary-General, UN Doc. E/CN.4/1995/43 of 13 January 1995, para. 83.
35   United Nations, 'Impact of armed conflicts on children', UN Doc. A/51/306 of 26 August 1996, para. 127.
36   Medlicott (1978, p.16).
37   Simunovic (1994, pp.14–15).
38   Desmond (1983, p.26).
39   Ferguson (1999).
40   Fisk (1999).
41   Pausewang (1995, p.206).
42   This assertion lays down the principle which, as all legal principles, allows exceptions. Before human rights entered the scene, foreigners had legal protection against abuses by whatever state might have abused them if their own state was strong enough to assert and protect their rights. Human rights attempted to derive the protection of individuals from their shared humanity and eliminate the power of the state of citizenship as the determining factor. This has remained an objective but has not become a binding rule.
43   Burke (1999).
44   United Nations, 'Situation of human rights in Iraq', General Assembly resolution 48/144 of 20 December 1993, preamble and para. 3.
45   Sub-Commission on Prevention of Discrimination and Protection of Minorities. Appeal concerning the civilian population in Iraq, decision 1991/108 of 29 August 1991, and decision 1990/109 of 24 August 1990.
46   Commission on Human Rights. Report on the situation of human rights in Iraq, submitted by the Special Rapporteur, Mr Max van der Stoel, UN Doc. E/CN.4/1998/67 of 10 March 1998, para. 7.

BIBLIOGRAPHY

Berkenheim, A. (1919), 'The economic blockade of Russia', *International Review*, **1** January–June.
Brown, B.S. (1992), *The United States and the Politicization of the World Bank. Issues of International Law and Policy*, London/New York: Kegan Paul International.
Buckley, N. (1998), 'Tough talking looms on US laws', *Financial Times*, 15 May.
Burke, J. (1999), 'Iraq sanctions fuel the politics of hate', *The Guardian Weekly*, 23–29 December.
Christiansen, D. and Powers, G.F. (1993), 'Sanctions: unintended consequences', *The Bulletin of the Atomic Scientists*, **49** (9), pp.101–23.
The Compact Edition of the Oxford English Dictionary (1971), Oxford: Oxford University Press.
Cornwell, R. (1998), 'Deal lets Europe trade with "pariahs"', *The Independent*, 19 May.
Desmond, C. (1983), *Persecution East and West: Human Rights, Political Prisoners and Amnesty International*, Harmondsworth, Penguin.
'Economic sanctions and international relations: an April 1993 Conference summary' (1993), *Scandinavian Journal of Development Alternatives*, **12** (4).

Ferguson, N. (1999), 'Bleeding hearts and bloody messages', *Financial Times*, 3–4 April.

Fisk, R. (1999), 'How to manipulate hearts and minds: Lies and more damned lies', *Le Monde diplomatique*, English edition, August.

Hazlitt Heard, A. (1993), 'Sanctions can work, but apply them with care', *International Herald Tribune*, 28 May.

Jean, F. (1993), *Life, Death and Aid. The Médecins Sans Frontières Report on World Crisis Intervention*, London: Routledge.

Kennan, George F. (1967), *Memoirs: 1925–1950*, Boston, MA: Little Brown.

Lewis, P. (1992), 'Security Council split on rights and arms issues', *International Herald Tribune*, 21 January.

Leyton-Brown, David (1987), 'Problems and prospects for economic sanctions', *Third World Affairs 1987*, London: Third World Institute.

Martin, I. (1993), 'The New World Order: opportunity or threat for human rights?', lecture by the Edward A. Smith Visiting Fellow, presented by the Harvard Law School Human Rights Programme.

Martin, Lisa (1992), *Coercive Cooperation: Explaining Multilateral Economic Sanctions*, Princeton, NJ: Princeton University Press.

Medlicott, W.N. (1978), *The Economic Blockade*, London: HMSO. First published 1952.

Meron, Theodor (1989), *Human Rights and Humanitarian Norms as Customary Law*, Oxford: Clarendon Press.

Myrdal, Gunnar (1957), *Economic Theory and Underdeveloped Regions*, London: Methuen & Co.

Pansewang, S. (1995), 'Ethiopia', in P. Baehr *et al.* (eds), *Human Rights in Developing Countries. 1996 Yearbook*, The Hague: Kluwer Law International and Nordic Human Rights Publications.

Post, H.H.G. (ed.) (1994), *International Economic Law and Armed Conflict*, Dordrecht: Martinus Nijhoff Publishers.

Schachter, Oscar (1994), 'United Nations law', *American Journal of International Law*, **88** (1), pp.1–23.

Simunovic, M. (1994), 'Sanctions studies pose dilemmas', *PHR Record*, **7** (1), Winter/Spring.

Tomaševski, K. (1997), *Between Sanctions and Elections*, London: Pinter/Cassell.

Tomaševski, K. (1998), 'Foreign policy and torture', in B. Duner (ed.), *An End to Torture: Strategies for Its Eradication*, London: Zed Books, pp.183–202.

Tomaševski, K. (2000), *Responding to Human Rights Violations, 1946–1999*, The Hague: Kluwer Law International.

Védrine, Hubert (1996), *Les Mondes de François Mitterrand à l'Elysée, 1981–1995*, Paris: Fayard.

Walker, M. (1998), 'Transatlantic deal placates EU', *Guardian Weekly*, 24 May.

11 Indicators for the Implementation of Human Rights

MICHAEL KIRBY

INTRODUCTION

The Intangible Sense of Freedom

Walk around the streets in a country new to you. No soldiers with rifles on the ready. Few police to exert civic control, the latter generally left to the self-discipline of the citizens. News-stands full of daily journals and weekly magazines, including some that criticize the politicians in power. School grounds full of happy children. Court houses teeming with lawyers with their serious faces. Prisoners in custody led into court, but still treated with respect for their human dignity. An elected government: not too visible, not too intrusive. Sport and culture readily available to the people. Plenty of associations in which ordinary individuals can meet together to exercise their freedoms. A sense of tolerance, of diversity. An underlying institutional strength essential if anarchy is to be replaced by the rule of law.

Walk the streets of such a country and the visitor will observe, even unconsciously, the indicators of the implementation of human rights. Of course, first impressions may be deceptive. Around the corner, in the back streets, may be the paraphernalia of oppression: close monitoring of civic activity, cruelty to minority groups and deprivation of fundamental human rights.

But, for the most part, the intangible sense of freedom which derives from general respect for human rights is resistant to mathematical measurement. Such things defy easy equations. Lawyers and social scientists may offer their checklists. Yet, in the end, the sense of freedom is an intangible thing. It is difficult to define. It is impossible to measure with precision. At different times, different aspects of human rights will be given different priorities by observers.

This was a point made tellingly by the Minister for Foreign Affairs of Singapore at the World Conference on Human Rights in Vienna.

> There may be a general consensus [about human rights]. But this is coupled with continuing and, at least for the present, no less important conflicts of interpretation. Singaporeans and people in many other parts of the world do not agree, for instance, that pornography is an acceptable manifestation of free expression, or that homosexual relationships are just a matter of lifestyle choice. Most of us will also maintain that the right to marry is confined to those of the opposite gender. Naturally, we do not expect everyone to agree with us. We should be surprised if anything were really settled once and for all. This is impossible. The very idea of human rights is historically specific. ... Take Britain for illustration ... Women only had the right to vote in 1928. Up to 1948, Oxbridge University graduates and businessmen had extra votes. The United States of America gained independence in 1776. Only those who paid poll tax or property tax had the right to vote from 1788. There were barriers of age, colour, sex and income. In 1860, income and property qualifications were abolished. But other barriers like literacy tests and poll tax still discriminated against African-Americans and other disadvantaged groups. Women only had the vote in 1920. It was not until 1965 that African-Americans could vote freely after the Voting Rights Act suspended literacy tests and other voter qualification devices which kept them out.[1]

Although the Vienna Conference rejected the notion of an exception to universal human rights for a particular country, region of the world or for different cultures, the Singapore Minister had a point. The history of the United Nations Statements on human rights, and of the development of international law in this regard, has been one of a journey of enlightenment. We are by no means at the end of that journey. Different states are at different points of the journey. Yet, by definition, the generally worded expressions of fundamental human rights are universal. Otherwise, the rights would not be classified as fundamental and universal.

One of the greatest achievements of the United Nations, building on the world's reaction to the horrors of the Second World War, has been the establishment of the framework by which universal human rights have been collected, written down and ushered into international law. This is a remarkable movement which has occurred in an incredibly short period of human history. It is all the more astonishing that it should have come about under the aegis of an international organization controlled by member states. A fundamental purpose of international human rights law is to put checks and limitations upon states so that tyranny is prevented and autocracy controlled. In the definition, expression, enforcement and furtherance of fundamental human rights, UNESCO, the UN Centre for Human Rights and other agencies of the United Nations system, have had a most honourable role.

The Systematic Measurement of Human Rights

My endeavour in this chapter is to collect indicators of the implementation of human rights. There have been many previous efforts to provide checklists against which the performance of different countries could be tested. Thus the Human Freedom Index (HFI) ranks selected countries according to criteria of specified freedoms. No country among the 88 covered observes all of the freedoms listed. Sweden and Denmark top the list with 38 of the measured freedoms, out of a possible total of 40. Among the high-ranking countries are New Zealand (36), Australia (33), Japan (32), Papua New Guinea (30) and Hong Kong (26). Amongst medium-ranking countries on the HFI are the Republic of Korea (14), Thailand (14) and Singapore (11). The low-ranking countries allegedly include Malaysia (9), Indonesia (5), Viet Nam (5) and China (2). Lowest of all in this list is Iraq.[2]

The HFI draws upon an earlier study by Charles Humana, who used his 40 indicators to measure cultural, social, economic and political freedom in a given country.[3] The difficulty with this approach, however, is that no observer of freedom would surrender the measurement to the criteria of another, however distinguished. Everyone has his or her own notions of what freedoms are important and how they should be weighted in the scale of things. Therefore, although measurement scales such as the HFI are useful as a stimulus to thinking and as criteria against which impressions may be judged, a more thorough investigation of the indicators is probably required, together with a healthy scepticism about superficial ranking of countries according to a measurement on a specified scale.

Allowing fully for such reservations, many distinguished workers in the field of promoting human rights stress the value of gathering information on the condition of human rights in particular countries and regions. They see this task as essential to furthering the universal protection and promotion of human rights. The late Martin Ennals observed, pointedly:

> The rapid increase in interest in human rights coincides with the rapid development of information technology. Unless a common and universal system of communication of human rights information is evolved, valuable information will be wasted, existing international machinery will not function, standards and codes agreed between governments and within professional bodies will not become known, and their implementation will not be monitored.[4]

It is this concept which, from the late 1970s, has caused a number of writers to suggest that enacting constitutions and laws and ratifying international human rights instruments is not enough. For such observers it is imperative to find out how well state, and non-state, participants live up to the standards for the protection of human rights and how large a gap exists between the universally acknowledged existence of human rights and their day-to-day exercise in different countries at different times. In this sense, the period which followed the adoption of the International Bill of Rights (comprising the Universal Declaration of Human Rights, the International

Covenant on Civil and Political Rights and the International Covenant on Economic Social and Cultural Rights) was an auditing phase. In the words of Sir Nigel Rodley, this function of human rights monitoring involved:

> ... nothing more complicated than the assembling, presentation and dissemination of pertinent data in a form that enables human rights performance to be assessed according to agreed-upon international standards.[5]

Impediments to Precise Measurement

Every writer in this field identifies the problems involved in the task of specifying the indicators of the implementation of human rights – namely:

- The volume of data is vast.
- The perception of the importance of, and the weight to be given to, particular indicators varies according to the observer.
- Reportage may depend upon the accuracy and honesty of reporters. Articulate advocacy groups, such as Amnesty International or the International Commission of Jurists, will have their own special perspectives and priorities. Particular governments will tend to concentrate upon some, rather than other, indicators of human rights, according to the urgencies expressed by their people.
- Substantial resources, evenly and fairly expended, would be necessary to secure a truly global approach to the task of identifying and then putting into operation the agreed indicators.
- A different set of indicators might be chosen for a simple task of comparative reporting. Such indicators would concentrate on fact-finding and reportage of particular violations of human rights or deprivations of fundamental entitlements under human rights law. On the other hand, a set of indicators to provide early warning of major breakdowns in human rights observance would concentrate upon different issues, providing more intensive study of human rights violations peculiar to the particular country under consideration.
- Forecasting is always difficult. Identifying indicators in a particular territory as most relevant to the condition of human rights will require judgement and an intensive knowledge of the place under consideration. Thus the 'fatal triangle' of political killings, torture and disappearances may be offered as a litmus test for the breakdown in human rights respect in countries in the most extreme positions.[6] In other countries, deprivations of cultural and linguistic rights, or of the right to self-determination of minority peoples, will be seen as more pressing.
- The content of human rights will itself be a controversy in some regions of the world. The so-called first-generation (civil and political) rights and the second-generation (economic, social and cultural) rights have now broadened to encompass a third generation of candi-

date rights for groups. These include peoples' rights, including to self-determination and, to enjoy, where a minority, their own culture, religion and language and to share information and communication. Some observers in developed countries continue to downplay the significance of economic, social and cultural rights. Some even regard them as a decoy or diversion from a proper concentration upon civil and political rights which tend to be more readily justiciable in courts and to have a longer lineage. In other societies, anxious about minorities and separatist movements, the claim to peoples' rights is disputed or, if acknowledged, confined to an exercise, strictly within the framework of the law of the country in question. For present purposes, I shall assume that the human rights of which indicators are to be identified are those which are contained in the major international instruments of the United Nations. UNESCO has published a compilation of the major universal and regional instruments for the protection of human rights, together with a schedule indicating the ratification by particular countries of these instruments.[7]

• Yet, even within these instruments, and confronted by their terms, there will be disputes about the meaning of the instrument. For example, some proponents (such as Amnesty International) regard capital punishment as a violation of the 'right to life' guaranteed by international human rights law. Others contend that the death penalty, properly executed and preceded by appropriate and effective legal safeguards, is not prohibited by international human rights law but is actually acknowledged by the International Covenant on Civil and Political Rights. The question is therefore posed, in devising the indicators for the implementation of human rights, 'Should the existence or abolition of capital punishment be one?'. To some observers of human rights in the world, the carrying out of the death penalty represents a most grave violation of fundamental human rights perpetrated by the state itself. To others, this is simply a punishment option of the particular legal regime. It is within the margin of appreciation accorded to any state in its interpretation of fundamental rights. Upon such a question it would be impossible, at least at this stage of human history, to obtain universal consensus. There are many similar questions. The demands by homosexuals to be treated without discrimination have presented quandaries of this kind to the Human Rights Committee of the United Nations established under the International Covenant on Civil and Political Rights. The responsible organ of the Finnish Broadcasting Corporation decided that it was not appropriate to permit discussion of issues related to homosexuality which could be interpreted as encouraging homosexual behaviour. The prohibition was eventually challenged in the Human Rights Committee. The Committee observed that public morals differed widely throughout the world. On this topic, there was no universally acceptable common standard. Therefore, a 'margin of discretion' had to be accorded to the responsible national authorities.[8] Contrast this decision with the later finding of the same Committee in the *Toonen* case. It upheld a complaint that the laws of Tasmania, Australia, criminalizing private adult homosexual behaviour, were contrary to Article 17 of the Covenant protecting individual privacy. The Committee did not accept the argument that moral issues were exclusively a matter of domestic concern '… as this would open the door to withdrawing from the Committee's scrutiny potentially large number of statutes interfering with privacy'.[9]

I hope that I have said enough in the foregoing to indicate the disputed nature of attempts to identify conclusively the indicators of the implementation of human rights. Inescapably, the task is controversial, because the subject-matter, observance of fundamental human rights, is inherently the subject of intense debate and of differences of opinion. The perceptions of all of us concerning the indicators of human rights observance are influenced by our upbringing, legal and social culture and life experience.

An observer from a developed country might be shocked at what is seen as the primitive conditions of a prison, or the unfair procedures of the military tribunal of a developing country. Human rights advocates of a developing country may denounce the poor, homeless beggars whom they see on the New York streets seeking refuge in cardboard packing boxes beside the marble and glass buildings opposite the United Nations Headquarters. Lawyers, brought up in the common law tradition, may be shocked at the superior status accorded to the public prosecutor in the legal procedures of a state of the civil law tradition. Professors of jurisprudence of civil law will be astonished at the absence of a modern constitutional bill of rights, enforceable in the courts, in countries of common law, such as Australia and the United Kingdom.

Even when the universal instruments are taken as our guide, there will be controversy and dispute about the meaning of the words, for that is the very nature of language and its operation in the law.

Within domestic jurisdiction, constitutional guarantees and legal texts may enshrine, with perfect clarity, the principles of universal human rights. By that test, the indicators will all be passed. But the reality, in practice, may be completely different. The law may not be respected. Exclusions may be allowed for political cases, or for proponents of minority rights. The judges may be independent in legal theory and guaranteed tenure under the constitution. But if, as in Cambodia, they were paid the equivalent of only about US$20 a month, the opportunity for true independence and economic certainty would be substantially lessened. The judicial officer may have the will to practise integrity and professional independence. But he or she will still have to house, feed, clothe and educate the family. Thus, a survey which listed only the legal instruments and the approximation of written texts to the international principles of human rights would run the risk of giving a misleading impression of the state of human rights in a given country. Indeed, such indicators could actually distort the true position. They could give a false image of human rights implementation. This is not to say that the existence of such texts is irrelevant, but it is only the start. The actual implementation, enforcement and observance of the law must also be judged, as must the teaching of the principles of human rights to all who live in the country, so that respect is semi-automatic and does not depend for its implementation on legal orders or disputed court cases.

I have now listed some of the chief problems which confront any attempt to collect the indicators of the implementation of human rights in a given country. Having alerted the reader to these difficulties, I will now turn to some of the existing institutional arrangements by which the condition of human rights implementation can be evaluated. These indicators should be considered with the foregoing warnings in mind.

INTERNATIONAL INDICATORS

From the outset, the establishing Charter of the United Nations took, as one of the purposes of the new organization, the achievement of respect for fundamental human rights. To this end, a great network of human rights treaties has been established, many of them negotiated under the auspices of the United Nations itself. The most important instruments include the two International Covenants previously mentioned and a series of other treaties concerning the prevention of discrimination, the outlawry of genocide, war crimes and crimes against humanity. Others were the conventions on the suppression of slavery, the traffic in persons and forced labour and instruments relating to the protection of particular groups, such as aliens, refugees and stateless persons, workers, women, children, prisoners and civilians.

This is a truly astonishing tapestry of international law. Most of it has been developed since the foundation of the United Nations.[10] Much of it is adhered to by many of the United Nations' member states. Some of it may be invoked by individual complaint mechanisms used by residents of a particular state complaining about human rights violations within that state.

One of the most important indicators of the implementation of human rights is, I believe, the adherence to the First Optional Protocol to the International Covenant on Civil and Political Rights.[11] By this instrument, member states, which agree, submit themselves to the jurisdiction of the Human Rights Committee. They accord to individual complainants a right of communication to the Committee. Such communications may assert that the participating state has failed to accord to the complainant the rights guaranteed by the Covenant. Only a minority of states have so far submitted to this jurisdiction. Unsurprisingly perhaps, many of the states which are reputed to be amongst the worst offenders against human rights, have failed to do so.

In Australia, immediately after ratification of this Protocol, a communication was lodged by Nick Toonen complaining about the failure of Australian law to provide, in Tasmania, proper protection of his human rights, under the International Covenant on Civil and Political Rights, including his right to privacy. The Human Rights Committee upheld his complaint.[12] This led to the enactment of a federal law in Australia, which in effect overrode the Tasmanian law complained about.[13] The power of the decision of the United Nations Human Rights Committee was not found in its binding force. In this respect, it was not like a judgment of the Privy Council in London, in days gone by, binding on Australian courts and enforceable by their sheriffs. But its persuasive influence and its determination of a fundamental and contested issue of human rights swiftly led to the Australian federal parliament almost unanimously approving a law aimed at bringing Australian domestic legislation, in all parts of the nation, into conformity with the found obligations of Australia under the Covenant.

This is why ratification of the First Optional Protocol can be seen as an important indicator of the implementation of human rights in a given country. In a sense, it is an indication of a state's confidence in its general adherence to the Covenant's human rights principles. It is willing to submit its laws and practices to the scrutiny, findings and persuasive advice of the members of the Human Rights Committee.

Apart from the work of the Human Rights Committee, it is important to mention the activities of the United Nations Commission on Human Rights and its Sub-Commission on the Promotion and Protection of Human Rights. Within the United Nations, a multitude of human rights activities are pursued by bodies created under the authority of the Charter, or under human rights treaties. The General Assembly and the Security Council, together with the Economic and Social Council and the Commission on Human Rights, are the principal bodies based on the Charter. The Human Rights Committee, the Committee on the Elimination of all Forms of Racial Discrimination, the Committee on Economic, Social and Cultural Rights, the Committee Against Torture, the Committee on the Rights of the Child and the Committee on the Elimination of Discrimination Against Women are all created under particular treaties. Specialized agencies of the United Nations, such as the International Labour Organization and bodies such as the United Nations High Commissioner for Refugees, have very important human rights functions. The relation between these bodies and individual states can often illustrate the situation of human rights in those states and provide visible indicators for the state of human rights.

An important indicator of human rights observance may thus be found in states' participation in the large network of United Nations-sponsored treaties relevant to human rights, in their timely provision of periodic reports on their compliance with these instruments, and in the extent to which they come through the reporting process under the searching questions of the various committees. The latter are quite frequently stimulated by information supplied to members by human rights NGOs critical of governmental performance.

Although acceding to an international human rights treaty has its complications,[14] accession alone is not enough. Nevertheless, accession can be an important symbolic acceptance of the standards laid down in the international instrument. It provides a criterion, both for national action and for international scrutiny. Submitting to the additional discipline of such scrutiny, on individual complaint, to the treaty bodies such as the Human Rights Committee, is generally a very good indication of human rights observance. An examination of the list of countries which have ratified international instruments and submitted to the individual complaint procedure will give at least some indication of the state of human rights in those countries. Certainly, it is rare to see the countries which have the worst reputation for human rights abuses submitting to the individual complaints procedure afforded by the First Optional Protocol to the International Covenant on Civil and Political Rights. As yet, there is no individual complaint procedure on the model of the Human Rights Committee for the Committee on the Economic, Social and Cultural Rights Covenant which was established in 1985. Its principal work is in the scrutiny of periodic reports of participating countries. Recently, there have been proposals for the establishment of facilities for direct communication by individuals, both to that Committee and to the Committee on the Elimination of All Forms of Discrimination Against Women. So far, none has been created.

A final indicator of the implementation of human rights on the international level can be mentioned. Concern about human rights should not stop at a state's borders. Living in an interdependent world, the concerns about human rights in other states must be shared by all member states of the United Nations. This feeling of concern has not only been evidenced in the political decisions of the General Assembly and Security Council, but also in the United Nations agencies which provide specialist assistance for building the infrastructures important for true human rights observance. It is also seen in participation in peacekeeping activities which provide the foundation for respect for human rights.

The work of the United Nations Transitional Authority for Cambodia (UNTAC) was a prerequisite for the conduct of a democratic election. The election which it initiated, in turn, laid the foundation for a constituent assembly and a national parliament to provide the source of civil government operating with respect to fundamental human rights.[15] An important ingredient of the UNTAC operation was the human rights component. It examined, investigated and reported upon complaints of human rights violation. It provided the foundation upon which was subsequently built the Office of the Centre for Human Rights in Phnom Penh – an office with which I work closely in my role as Special Representative of the Secretary-General.

A vital activity of the human rights component of UNTAC was the encouragement, protection and funding of human rights organizations designed to translate the aspirations of human rights in international law into the daily life of Cambodians, so long denied them. An important aspect of peacekeeping must be the establishment of human rights in the countries concerned. That is why it is essential to have clear criteria, found in the treaties of the United Nations. It is also a reason why it is essential that alleged abuse and exploitation on the part of United Nations troops and other officials should be vigilantly investigated and, where proved, redressed.[16]

NATIONAL GOVERNMENT INDICATORS

Independent Courts

History in many countries has shown the importance of the existence of independent courts for the protection of human rights. Courts, comprising judicial officers whose tenure is guaranteed and who work in a culture of integrity, neutrality and independence, afford protection for civil and political rights and the environment in which economic, social and cultural rights may also be advanced.

Without the guarantee of, and conventional obedience to, the independence of the courts, it is hard to see how the rule of law could be defended effectively. In its place all that would remain is the rule of power – whether the power from military guns, or of economic or political might, or of the lawless mob rampaging in the streets. Brave judicial officers who uphold fundamental human rights against the military or the mob, and even against popular opinion, are essential indicators of the implementation of human rights. To reinforce such courage, it is necessary to have procedures for the selection and training of judges, proper arrangements for receiving and impartially investigating complaints against judges, and constitutional provisions for their removal on proof of misconduct or incapacity, and that alone.

A good indicator of the role of the courts as implementors of human rights is to be found in the provision of a constitutional statement of human rights, or at least of core principles which are placed above the political fray, interpreted and, where necessary, enforced by the independent courts. Yet even this may not be absolutely essential. For example, in some countries which would be traditionally regarded as generally respectful of civil and political rights, the constitution (if it exists in writing at all) does not include a basic statement of human rights. In Australia for example, there is no such general constitutional charter. In Canada, the Charter of Fundamental Rights and Freedoms is of comparatively recent origin. In New Zealand and, most recently in the United Kingdom, it has no constitutional status as such. In the last mentioned countries there is an active debate concerning the desirability of having a constitutional guarantee of human rights.

Critics suggest that such charters tend to emphasize civil rights and to give inadequate attention to the less easily justiciable social and economic rights which may be of the greatest importance to the disadvantaged.[17] Other critics are fearful that a constitutional bill of rights will politicize the judiciary and transfer effective power on important social issues from elected representatives to non-elected judges.[18]

This is not the occasion to enter that debate. It is enough to say that, in most countries, the collection of fundamental rights in a constitutional document has proved useful in providing a reminder to the other branches of government, and a stimulus and guide to the judicial branch.

Even in those countries which do not have a constitutional charter covering the main rights typically found in United Nations treaties, the impact of international human rights law has recently produced the elaboration of implied legal rights, defensive of free speech and protective against discrimination. For example, without a guaranteed list of fundamental rights in the Australian Constitution, the courts have developed implied constitutional guarantees.[19] In addition, many common law countries are moving towards the application of the so-called Bangalore Principles.[20] Under these rules, devised by a meeting of senior judges sponsored by the Commonwealth Secretariat, a judge finding a gap in the common law or an ambiguity in a statute, may properly fill the gap or resolve the ambiguity by reference to international human rights jurisprudence.[21] This doctrine has received the cautious support of the High Court of Australia,[22] the Court of Appeal of New Zealand[23] and the English courts[24] and well illustrates the infectious impact of international human rights law on the courts. The growth of a culture of knowledge about, and respect for, international human rights principles in the judiciary of a country is an important indicator of the implementation of human rights at the judicial level.[25]

Notwithstanding these developments, in those countries which do not have constitutional bills of rights, there are numerous demands for the adoption of express guarantees enforceable by citizens.[26] Because constitutional reform is often difficult to achieve, and because human rights issues are often emotionally charged and disputed, such alterations of the basic texts are not easily procured, at least in most developed countries. But the value of a constitutionally stated and individually enforceable list of fundamental human rights is that it gives legitimacy to the protection of basic civil rights. It may protect those basic rights against the winds of popular sentiment which are not always sensitive to the rights of minorities. It is a truism that human rights matter most when they are demanded by unpopular or vulnerable minorities. That is why so many of the test cases in the courts are brought by members of such minorities – for example, indigenous peoples, religious and ethnic minorities, religious dissenters, specific racial groups and groups which traditionally suffer discrimination such as women, homosexuals, sex workers (prostitutes), people infected with HIV / AIDS, or the otherwise handicapped.

The mere existence of independent courts is just the prerequisite to the protection of human rights. Self-evidently there must be, in addition, an independent legal profession which has the courage to bring difficult and unpopular cases to the courts. One of the most important annual publications for monitoring the indicators of the implementation of human rights is *Attacks on Justice*. This report is produced every year by the Centre for the Independence of Judges and Lawyers (CIJL) in Geneva, established by the International Commission of Jurists. It chronicles the attacks, both physical and institutional, upon judges and lawyers in many lands. Few such attacks escape scrutiny under the watchful eye of the CIJL. Without an independent legal profession, willing to take on test cases and defend unpopular people, offering their services against official resistance, the courts, which cannot generally initiate proceedings, would be helpless. Without the provision of proper legal aid and financial assistance in appropriate cases, the promise of equality before the law would be false; the boast that the courts defend human rights would be an empty one. In many countries, including my own, the courts have upheld the state's obligation to provide legal aid for persons accused of serious crimes.[27]

Accountable Executive Government

Further indicators of the implementation of human rights can be found in the accountability of the executive government. Under constitutional arrangements, ministers and officials are ordinarily answerable, ultimately, to an elected parliament. But rendering them effectively answerable for the action of policemen on the street, the military at the borders and bureaucrats at administrative offices may be quite another thing. Translating the theory of accountability into practical reality has been one of the greatest challenges to the practice of public administration in the latter part of the twentieth century.

In many countries accountability has been improved by reforms of administrative law. Whereas the civil law countries have had a developed administrative law for many years, this has come slowly to countries of the common law tradition. In judging the implementation of human rights in the many activities of government, it is important to have regard to the institutions which have been established to enforce basic rights.

The courts themselves offer judicial review to keep administrators within the law, to ensure that their procedures are fair and that their ultimate decisions are not so unreasonable as to demand judicial intervention. The growth of judicial supervision of the executive government was described by a leading English judge, Lord Diplock, as the greatest advance in the English law in his lifetime. It is an advance which has spread throughout the common law world. It has ensured judicial review of administrative action which is much more vigilant to the 'three little words' which encompass an effective administrative law protective of human rights: legality, fairness and reasonableness.

In addition to judicial review, administrative review has been strengthened in many states to provide scrutiny of bureaucratic decisions. Thus, the office of the ombudsperson has been established in many countries to provide a cheap, effective and approachable guardian with power to investigate public complaints against administration. In many countries, law reform commissions have been established. In Australia, the Australian Law Reform Commission is obliged, by its statute,[28] to ensure that its proposals to parliament are, so far as possible, compatible with the International Covenant on Civil and Political Rights. This provision was enacted even before Australia had ratified the Covenant. It is an injunction which the Commission takes seriously.

Specialized protectors have also been established in many countries to receive public complaints, to investigate, conciliate and, where necessary, sanction, abuses of human rights. These frequently take the form of human rights commissions or committees, or anti-discrimination boards. Although such bodies may not have the power of the courts to impose sanctions or enforce orders, they will generally be more accessible to ordinary citizens, cheaper in their operation and less time-consuming in their procedures. They will also usually employ techniques of conciliation and education. They may extrapolate from their experience in particular cases and promote human rights education in schools and through the community, including by way of the media. The existence of effective procedures for administrative review, law reform bodies, human rights commissions, anti-discrimination boards, and specialist guardians (such as privacy or data protection commissioners) afford a rich panoply of institutional arrangements that are important indicators of the practical implementation of human rights in the vital sphere of modern government.

Unless there are effective and approachable bodies of this kind, easily accessible to citizens who claim that their human rights have been denied, the promise of human rights protection may be but empty words. Translating that promise into action requires a great deal of effort. Even the establishment of institutions of the kind which I have described will not ensure that individuals, if affected, have the determination, courage, knowledge and persistence to pursue their rights. These personal qualities are not easily inculcated in a community living in ignorance or fear. Yet at least by providing institutions of this kind, it may be hoped that vigorous individuals, supported by active NGOs and stimulated by modern procedures (for example, representative actions, class actions, test cases and so on) will bring important instances to the attention of courts, commissions and tribunals which can offer an effective human rights response.

If, therefore, one wishes to test the indicators of the implementation by executive governments of human rights, it is certainly relevant to look to the institutions of the kind that I have mentioned. Their absence tends to be a sign that the ministers and bureaucrats in their offices prefer to be left alone, untroubled by the complaints of human rights abuses, unanswerable to the people whom they 'serve'.

Vigilant Legislatures

With the twentieth-century shift of power to the executive and, to a lesser extent, the judiciary, elected parliaments have tended to lose much influence. The existence of free and fair elections is a prerequisite to the creation of a legislative body which is likely to be concerned about human rights. An important strategy of the United Nations in many countries in which it has offered assistance, notably through the United Nations Development Programme (UNDP), has been preparing for, underwriting, monitoring and following through the conduct of free and fair elections. In this regard, the

Inter-Parliamentary Union (IPU), the Commonwealth Parliamentary Association and other bodies also play a crucial role. A fairly elected legislature is likely to lift its voice against at least the worst cases of oppression and departures from human rights. The conduct of fair elections is therefore an important indicator of the likely implementation of human rights.[29]

Many parliamentary bodies have established human rights institutions of their own. Indeed, of the 164 parliaments which are members of the IPU, 52 have parliamentary bodies dealing specifically with human rights. Many also have informal groups of parliamentarians which meet together to discuss issues of relevance to human rights.

Even in a parliament, such as that of Australia, which does not have its own human rights commission or committee, there are legislative committees which have functions relevant to human rights. Thus, in the Australian Senate, the Committee on Regulations and Ordinances, established in 1932, is required to review subordinate legislation to ensure that it is:

> ... in accordance with the statute ... does not trespass unduly on personal rights and liberties ... does not unduly make the rights and liberties of citizens dependent upon administrative decisions which are not subject to review on the merits by a judicial or other independent tribunal ... and does not contain matter more appropriate for Parliamentary enactment.

In 1981 the Australian Senate also established a Committee for the Scrutiny of Bills. It examines primary legislation against the same criteria.

In many states such committees are now a common feature of parliaments and play an important role in the defence of fundamental human rights. Their operation in the states of the Pacific is regularly examined in the Australasian and Pacific Conference on Delegated Legislation.[30] There is similar cooperation in other regions.

The effective operation of a democratic legislature is thus a keystone in the arch of human rights. This point was stressed by Ibrahima Fall, then the Assistant Secretary-General of the United Nations Centre for Human Rights, in a speech to the Inter-Parliamentary Symposium in Budapest in May 1993 reflecting the views of the United Nations:

> Parliaments are one of the crucial elements in a democratic society and essential in ensuring the rule of law and protection of human rights. In fact, in their daily work of transforming the will of the people into law, and in controlling the Executive and public administration, Parliaments and Parliamentarians are often the unsung heroes of human rights ... . We in the United Nations pay tribute to the very important role of Parliaments in the field of human rights, and we are looking forward to establishing even closer contacts with them throughout the world, as we seek to assist in improving respect for human rights at the national level. The unique competence, experience and wisdom of Parliaments will be a precious contribution to achieving that objective.[31]

Sadly, some legislators are content to serve and draw their salaries and to allow the executive government or a military regime to ride roughshod over human rights. The existence of a legislature, and even of one fairly elected, is not necessarily a guarantee of respect for human rights. But the absence of such a guardian makes abuse of human rights easier, for in almost every elected legislative body there will be some who, even at personal risk, will raise their voices and denounce abuse, uphold principle and propose legislation to prevent wrongs and to redress them where they have occurred.

A culture of respect for diverse opinions, and an acceptance that sometimes those opinions may be right, are essential to the building of a legislative institution and party system protective of human rights. The privileges of members of parliament must be safeguarded and scrupulously protected by the legislators themselves. Legislators must see attacks on one as an attack on the institution. By the same token, they must not abuse their privileges, for that abuse can itself undermine the human rights of others.

OTHER INDICATORS

Beyond the institutional framework which I have mentioned, there are countless other indicators of the condition of freedom and the implementation of human rights in a given state. Amongst the most important are the economic indicators. Without a minimum level of economic progress, grinding poverty, uncontrolled population growth, malnutrition, disease and unmet wants will consume a society's potential to respond to the demands for basic human rights. In this regard, the achievement of economic and social rights is very much connected with the capacity of a government to provide an appropriate economic environment for the advances essential to an efficient, modern economy.[32]

Combating corruption and dealing with it at its source is a particular challenge in developing countries as they struggle to improve their economies and to reach the point of 'lift-off' which will have the beneficial effect of curbing excessive population growth and providing the kinds of human right which are acknowledged by the International Covenant on Economic, Social and Cultural Rights. The importance of those rights should not be underestimated.

Measuring enlightened leadership is difficult but obviously important. Quantifying respect for the values of neighbours is next to impossible. Evaluating the existence of a national, and even a global, civil ethic is hard indeed. Clearly relevant is the extent to which the state, or its leaders, are committed to demilitarizing their societies, spending less on arms and the military and ridding the environment of small arms and landmines which so threaten the human rights of ordinary people.

In most developing societies, ordinary citizens, minding their own business, will rarely, if ever, come into contact with the courts. They will have as little as possible to do with the executive government and probably no contact with the legislature, unless it be a very occasional vote at general elections. Yet, for the ordinary citizen, access to clean water, to health facilities when children are sick, to educational facilities for both girls and boys, and opportunities to enrich the spirit with religious instruction and cultural experience represent what such citizens will often see as the urgent priorities of human rights. Human rights are equal and interdependent. But the indicators of human rights in a given society go far beyond the courts, prisons and administrative offices where civil and political rights are typically measured. This is why, in classical studies of the monitoring of human rights and for judging the performance of particular countries, detailed attention is given to the right to food, the right to healthcare, the right to education, the right to fair working conditions and to be free from slavery and other rights respectful of the wishes of minorities to self-determination and to the integrity of their group identity.[33]

Because the right to free expression is also a vital indicator of the condition of human rights, the number of journals and the diversity of electronic media outlets is very important. To some extent, the advent of modern information technology makes it more difficult to restrict the free flow of ideas and information today. Satellites beam their messages down upon all of us. But with those messages have come new problems of cultural hegemony as the universal language and the entertainment empire of Hollywood and Rupert Murdoch reach out to swamp more vulnerable languages and cultures, the preservation of which is another important indicator of respect for human rights.

Every observer of the human rights indicators will have his or her own list of essential criteria by which the state of human rights can be judged. Mine, for example, would include most certainly the way in which a country responds to the human rights challenges of HIV/AIDS.[34] In many ways, the AIDS pandemic tests our respect for human rights and our resolve to deal compassionately and effectively with this unexpected and shocking challenge to humanity.

A connected theme of women's empowerment must also be mentioned. The Beijing Conference on Women in 1995 focused attention on the very many ways in which women have suffered gross disadvantages in the achievement of their human rights. The Conference also illustrated the diversity of viewpoints about just what those human rights involve. Although much common ground was discovered, there were important differences of perspective between representatives of women in different parts of the world.

The treatment of children has also become an important focus of human rights work following the adoption of the Convention on the Rights of the Child and its ratification by most countries of the world. Translating the fine words of the Convention into action for street children and other vulnerable minors is a different matter. The United Nations responded to that challenge by the appointment of a Special Rapporteur on the Sale of Children, Child Prostitution and Pornography (currently Mr Juan Miguel Petit of the Philippines).

A number of countries, including Australia, have enacted legislation to impose criminal sanction on nationals, whether at home or abroad, who engage in sexual exploitation of under-age children.[35] But the basic causes of child vulnerability must also be addressed. These include economic impoverishment of many societies in the world and the urgent need for birth-spacing and population control policies which are respectful of the fundamental human rights of all concerned.

There are many other identifiable indicators of respect for human rights. They include the treatment of indigenous minorities, a matter upon which Australia's record, at least until recently, has been less than perfect.[36] The protection of land rights of indigenous peoples and the redress of economic, social and cultural disadvantages of minority racial groups demonstrate the extent to which a country has sufficient self-respect to safeguard the interests of those who were living in the country before another dominant group (often of settlers) arrived.

The treatment of refugees and of displaced stateless persons is also a test providing an indicator of human rights respect for brothers and sisters from less fortunate circumstances. Some countries simply push the refugees away. They close their borders, prosecute and expel the few who gain entry. International human rights law imposes upon the international community of states duties of response to refugees. The enormous flows of population which occur in the wake of gross human rights deprivations have been seen recently in Rwanda, the former states of Yugoslavia, Kosovo, Chechnya, East Timor, Afghanistan and elsewhere. Xenophobia is by no means confined to advanced countries. A useful indicator of the respect of the rights of all human beings can be seen in the extent to which states accept refugees and offer them sanctuary and a new life for themselves and their families.

Increasingly, environmental issues are being recognized as relevant to fundamental human rights. The right to live in a sustaining environment is now acknowledged as one of the critical issues facing the global community. Uncontrolled logging without reforestation, the destruction of the natural beauties of the world, the despoliation of forest environments with consequent soil erosion, flooding and impoverishment, the destruction of the economic wherewithal of poor countries, the disappearance of the natural habitat of human communities and the elimination of precious varieties of flora and fauna all threaten the ecology of the world and its irreplaceable diversity. Fortunately, this has now been realized, and the United Nations has played a crucial role in the process of this realization. Contemporary indicators of the implementation of human rights will certainly include the extent to which states respect and protect the environment, not only of their own territory but also that of those whose economic resources they exploit. A truly modern list of the indicators of human rights will harshly judge those nations which put the global environment at risk by allowing marauding and the selfish exploitation of others' natural resources with little thought to sustained development and the long-term future. The notion of global commons demands consideration. The report of the Commission on Global Governance has called for a new trusteeship for global commons and for the reinforcement of the planet's civil society. The strengthening of

international law, the creation of an International Criminal Tribunal and
Code and the rendering of all persons, nationally and internationally, accountable to compliance with the Code are further goals of a world that
respects universal human rights.[37]

Limited space does not permit a detailed exploration of the delicate issue
of self-determination and the protection of minorities. This is also an issue
in which UNESCO has played a critical role, whilst most other agencies
have shied away. It is within UNESCO that the United Nations has sought
to describe the features of a 'people' for the purposes of the people's right
to self-determination guaranteed by the Covenants and now, more generally, by international law.[38] The respect for minority rights is one of the
most important issues for the future of human rights. Anyone in doubt
should look at the flashpoints of the recent challenges to the world's peace
and security. The lesson is obvious. New institutional arrangements are
needed within the United Nations. Meanwhile, the way in which countries
treat minorities living within their borders and respect the human rights of
such groups provide important indicators for their true commitment to
respect for human rights.

Relevant to all of the foregoing is the position of NGOs in both the
national and international communities. At the meetings of the organs of
the United Nations and the treaties which uphold human rights principles, international NGOs (such as Amnesty International, the International
Commission of Jurists, International Alert, Greenpeace, Global Witness,
the Watch Organizations among others) play a vital role in reporting
abuses of human rights, stimulating the advancement of remedial action
and of international law, encouraging the appointment of investigators
and scrutinizing their reports with a critical eye. The extent to which such
international bodies and their local counterparts are left alone to perform
their functions vital for human rights in any given state is a sure marker
of the health of human rights and the state's confidence in its own performance.

One study suggests that an important measure of liberty in a country is
to be found in the number of citizen groups, such as chess clubs, football
groups and choral societies. It is in ordinary collections of citizens, coming
together without fear or inhibition, that the ideas of freedom are shared and
the insistence on respect for human rights is nurtured. Belatedly, an attempt
is being made to provide a global framework for this 'third sector'. A new
international body, CIVICUS, has been established, with headquarters in
Washington, to give coherence to the free participation of citizens in civil
society in every land.

The future of human rights includes attention to the formal steps that are
necessary to make the human rights treaties work more effectively,[39] but it
also requires attention to the likely future issues for human rights. The
International Commission of Jurists (ICJ) has assisted by identifying the
likely target areas of future human rights activity. These, too, provide criteria by which the state of human rights in any country may be judged.
Included in the ICJ's list of future challenges to human rights are: the

human rights of drug users and drug-dependent persons; the human rights of sexual minorities; the human rights of persons infected with HIV/AIDS and similar disabilities; human rights and religious fundamentalism; human rights of women and of children; and the human rights challenges presented by new technologies such as informatics and the Human Genome Project.

The journey towards respect for human rights is, indeed, the journey of enlightenment. If some on the foregoing list might appear to include causes which are unpopular today, we should remember just how unpopular women's suffrage was when it was first propounded, as was also self-determination for colonial peoples, religious tolerance and diversity at the time of the Christian Reformation and equal voting rights to all races even in relatively advanced societies in very recent times.

No state has a monopoly on wisdom about human rights. Each of us can learn from others. The great advance of the past 50 years has been the acceptance by the international community and by international law of the fundamental principles of human rights and the national and international creation of bodies to give these statements effective operation, often for the first time. Although it is not possible to propose a simple formula for the measurement of human rights implementation in different states, it is perfectly feasible to suggest some indicators by which performance may be judged. It is also desirable to do this as a stimulus to every state to strive for higher attainment. Noble words are not enough. Action is needed. Action should be audited using the indicators for the implementation of human rights as the criteria. Each one of us is qualified, as a human being, to perform the audit. We should start at home. But we should not forget our sisters and brothers in other lands. And when, in our audit, the indicators for the implementation of human rights show that respect for human rights is wanting, we, the people, should not be slow to raise our voices. We should remember that the United Nations was created in our name. We, the people of the world, should assert our rights and insist that they are respected. One day, soon, that goal will be achieved. But it will only be achieved by our intelligent action and vigilant insistence.

NOTES

1   Wong Kan Seng, Minister for Foreign Affairs of the Republic of Singapore, 'The real world of human rights', address to the World Conference on Human Rights, Vienna, June 1993, in *Report of the World Conference*.
2   UNDP (1991). Noted in Jongman and Schmid (1994, p.2).
3   Humana (1992). For a critique, see Gupta, Jongman and Schmid (1994, p.131).
4   Martin Ennals, cited in Jongman and Schmid (1994, p.ix).
5   Rodley *et al*. (1979, p.119).
6   Jongman and Schmid (1994, p.7).
7   UNESCO (1994).
8   *Hertzberg* v. *Finland*, UN Human Rights Committee 61/1979, decided 2 April 1992.

9   *Toonen* v. *Australia*, UN Human Rights Committee 488/1992. See Selvanera (1994, p.331); Morgan (1992, p.77).
10   Exceptions are contained in certain of the conventions of the International Labour Organization which was established in 1919. See, for example, UNESCO (1994, p.11) referring to the ILO Convention (No. 11) Concerning the Rights of Association and Combination of Agricultural Workers, 1921, United Nations Treaties Series, Vol. 38, pp.153–59 (No. 594).
11   United Nations Treaties Series, Vol. 999, p.171. It entered into force on 23 March 1976.
12   See note 9 above.
13   See Human Rights (Sexual Conduct) Act 1994, Australia.
14   See, for example, Keith (1964, p.272).
15   McNamara (1995, p.57).
16   See, for example, Ramcharan (1992, p.24); Kirshenbaum (1993, p.11).
17   See Petter (1986, p.473); Petter (1987, p.857); Hutchinson and Petter (1990, p.365); cf. Sigurdson (1993, p.117).
18   See, for example, Mandel (1989).
19   See, for example, *Australian Capital Television* v. *The Commonwealth*, CLR 177 (1993) p.106 (High Court of Australia).
20   See CLR 14 (1988), p.1196; ALJ 62 (1988), p.531.
21   See, for example, Kirby (1988, p.514); also Kirby (1993a, p.363).
22   *Mabo* v. *State of Queensland* [No 2], CLR 175 (1992), No. 1 p.42 (High Court of Australia); *Minister of State for Immigration and Ethnic Affairs* v. *Teoh*, ALR 128 (1995), pp.353, 362 and 382 (High Court of Australia).
23   *Tavita* v. *Minister of Immigration*, NZLR 2 (1994), p.266 (Court of Appeal).
24   *Derbyshire County Council* v. *Times Newspapers Ltd*, QB (1992), pp.770 (Court of Appeal), 812 and 830.
25   See Higgins (1994, p.205).
26   See Wilcox (1993, pp.219 *et seq.*); O'Neil and Handley (1994, p.104); Bailey (1990, p.45).
27   See, for example, *Gideon* v. *Wainwright* 372 US 335; 9 Law Ed 2d 799 (1963) (US Supreme Court) at 344, 805; *McInnes* v. *The Queen*, CLR 143 (1979), p.575; *Dietrich* v. *The Queen*, CLR 177 (1993), p.292 (High Court of Australia).
28   Australian Law Reform Commission Act 1973 (Australia) s. 7.
29   Goodwin-Gill (1994).
30   Parliament of Victoria (1993). See also McKerihan (1995, p.30).
31   Fall (1993, p.4).
32   See Commission on Global Governance (1995, pp.26 *et seq*).
33   Jongman and Schmid (1994, pp.165 *et seq*).
34   See, for example, Sieghart (1989, p.107).
35   Australian Department of Foreign Affairs and Trade (1993, p.118).
36   See, for example, Hocking (1988).
37   Commission on Global Governance (1995, p.227).
38   See Kirby (1993b, p.27); Hannum (1993, p.5); Tomuschat (1993, p.1); Koskenniemi (1994, pp.241 and 245); Falk (1994, p.81).
39   Bayefsky (1992, p.229).

BIBLIOGRAPHY

Australian Department of Foreign Affairs and Trade (1993), *Human Rights Manual*, Canberra.

Bailey, P.H. (1990), *Human Rights – Australia in an International Context*, London: Butterworths.

Bayefsky, A.F. (1992) 'Making the human rights treaties work', in L. Henkin and J.L. Hargrove (eds), *Human Rights: An Agenda for the Next Century*, in *Studies in Transnational Legal Policy* of the American Society of International Law, p.229.

Commission on Global Governance (1995), *Our Global Neighbourhood*, Oxford: Oxford University Press.

Falk, R. (1994), 'The content of self-determination', in R. McCorquidale and N. Orosz (eds), *Tibet: The Position in International Law*, London: Serindia.

Fall, I. (1993), 'Address to the Inter-Parliamentary Symposium, Budapest, 1993', in *Inter-Parliamentary Union; Parliament: Guardian of Human Rights*, Geneva: Inter-Parliamentary Union, p.4.

Goodwin-Gill, G.S. (1994), *Free and Fair Elections – International Law and Practice*, Geneva: IPU.

Gupta, D.K., Jongman, A.J. and Schmid, A.P. (1994), 'Creating a composite index for assessing country performance in the field of human rights; proposal for a new methodology', *Human Rights Quarterly*, **16** (1), pp.131–63.

Hannum, R. (1993), 'Rethinking self-determination', *Virginia Journal of International Law*, **34**(1), pp.5–69.

Higgins, R. (1994), *Problems and Process – International Law and How We Use It*, Oxford: Clarendon Press.

Hocking, B. (ed.) (1988), *International Law and Aboriginal Human Rights*, Sydney: Law Book Co.

Humana, George (1992), *World Human Rights Guide*, Oxford: Oxford University Press.

Hutchinson, A.C. and Petter, A. (1990), 'Daydreaming believing: visionary formalism and the Constitution', *Ottawa Law Review*, 22, pp.365–97.

Jongman, A.J. and Schmid, A.P. (1994), *Monitoring Human Rights: Manual for Assessing Country Performance*, Leiden: PIOOM Leiden University.

Keith, K.J. (1964), 'New Zealand treaty practice: the executive and the legislature', *New Zealand University Law Review*, I, pp.272–95.

Kirby, M.D. (1988), 'The role of the judge in advancing human rights – by reference to human rights norms', *Australian Law Journal*, 62, pp.514–32.

Kirby, M.D. (1993a), 'People's rights and self-determination', *Bulletin of the Australian Society of Legal Philosophy*, 18(61), p.25.

Kirby, M.D. (1993b), 'The Australian use of international human rights norms; from Bangalore to Balliol – a view from the Antipodes', *University of New South Wales Law Journal*, (16), p.363.

Kirshenbaum, C. (1993), 'Who's watching the peace?', *MS*, May–June, pp.11–33.

Koskenniemi, M. (1994), 'National self-determination today: problems of legal theory and practice', *International Comparative Law Quarterly*, **43**, pp.241–65.

McKerihan, M. (1995), 'Unknown watchdog', *Australian Lawyer*, July, pp.30–56.

McNamara, D. (1995), 'Human rights activities in Cambodia: an evaluation', in *Honouring Human Rights and Keeping the Peace – Lessons from El Salvador, Cambodia and Haiti*, Aspen, CO: The Aspen Institute, pp.57–71.

Mandel, A. (1989), *The Charter of Rights and the Legalisation of Politics in Canada*, Toronto: Walt and Thompson.

Minnesota Advocates for Human Rights (1992), *Orientation Manual – The UN Commission on Human Rights, its Sub-Commission, and Related Procedures*, Minneapolis: Minnesota University Press.

Morgan, W. (1992), 'Sexuality and human rights: the first communication by an Australian to the Human Rights Committee under the Optional Protocol to the International Covenant on Civil and Political Rights', *Australian Yearbook of International Law* (14), pp.77–98.

O'Neil, N. and Handley, R. (1994), *Retreat from Injustice – Human Rights in Australian Law*, Sydney: Federation.

Parliament of Victoria, Australia (1993), *Proceedings of the Fourth Australasian and Pacific Conference of Delegated Legislation and First Australasian and Pacific Conference on the Scrutiny of Bills*, Melbourne.

Petter, A. (1986), 'The politics of the Charter', *Supreme Court Law Review*, 8, pp.473–95.

Petter, A. (1987), 'Immaculate deception: the Charter's hidden agenda', *Advocate*, 45, pp.857–78.

Ramcharan, B.G. (1992), 'The Security Council: maturing of international protection of human rights', *International Court of Justice Review* (48), pp.24–59.

Ravindran, D.J. *et al.* (ed.) (1994), *Handbook on Fact Finding and Documentation of Human Rights Violations*, Bangkok: Asian Forum for Human Rights and Development (Forum Asia).

Rodley, Nigel S. *et al.* (1979), *Monitoring Human Rights Violations in the 1980s – Enhancing Global Human Rights*, New York: McGraw-Hill.

Selvanera, G. (1994), 'Gays in private: the problems with the privacy analysis in furthering human rights', *Adelaide Law Review*, **16**.

Sieghart, P. (1989), *AIDS and Human Rights – A UK Perspective*, London: BMA.

Sigurdson, R. (1993), 'The left-legal critique of the Charter: a critical assessment', *Windsor Yearbook of Access to Justice*, 13, pp.117–33.

Tomuschat, C. (1993), 'Self-determination in a post-colonial world', in C. Tomuschat (ed.), *Modern Law of Self-Determination*, Dordrecht: Kluwer.

UNDP (1991), 'The Human Freedom Index', *Human Development Report*, New York: Oxford University Press and UNDP.

UNESCO (1994–2000), *Human Rights – Major International Instruments*, ed. J. Symonides and V. Volodin, Paris: UNESCO.

Wilcox, M.R. (1993), *An Australian Charter of Rights?*, Sydney: Law Book Co.

12 The Role of Non-Governmental Organizations (NGOs) in the Protection and Enforcement of Human Rights[1]

LAURIE S. WISEBERG

INTRODUCTION

On 29 April 1999 United Nations Secretary-General, Kofi Annan, addressed the NGO Forum on Global Issues in the following terms:

> In the United Nations a few decades ago, governments were virtually the sole players. Of course, NGOs helped found the United Nations and are mentioned in the Charter. Even before that, NGOs led the charge in the adoption of the Slavery Convention of 1926. And NGOs have a long and proud history of fighting against tyranny and providing humanitarian assistance to the victims of conflict and natural disaster.
>
> But it is only since the Earth Summit in 1992 that civil society groups have really made their mark on global society. You have played a key role at world conferences on such vital issues as human rights, population, poverty and women's rights.
>
> Thanks to you, the year 1997 was the year of the landmine – or should I say, the year of no more landmines? One thousand NGOs in 60 countries were linked together by a weapon that would ultimately prove more powerful than the landmine: e-mail and the Internet. And with that same weapon, and that same intensity, NGOs helped make 1998 the year of the International Criminal Court.
>
> The Nobel Committee has recognized this work, awarding its peace prize to NGOs, church and academic groups and others. But NGOs have also come in for a less welcome sort of recognition: you have been denied access to meetings and information; your representatives have been harassed, jailed and exiled, tor-

tured and murdered. It is to your credit that such acts have failed to deter you from your chosen causes.[2]

These remarks have particular resonance for human rights NGOs towards which governments and intergovernmental organizations frequently behave in a contradictory manner. On the one hand, they recognize the vital role that NGOs play in the protection and enforcement of human rights and, therefore, the importance of establishing a strong partnership with them; yet, on the other hand, they denigrate and vilify NGOs precisely because 'the *raison d'être* of many NGOs is to put pressure on governments and "hold their feet to the fire"'.[3]

This chapter presents the work of NGOs in the area of human rights, as it has been manifested over the past 50 years – that is, since the end of the Second World War and the creation of the United Nations. Moreover, since there have been dramatic changes in the environment in which NGOs function over this period – changes which have had a serious impact on what NGOs can do and how they do it – particular attention will be paid to elucidating the role of NGOs in the late 1990s.

It may be useful to note at the outset that we are talking about a world in which we now have a highly developed international human rights law (both treaties and declarations, universal and regional) which outlaws genocide, torture, slavery and other egregious violations; which recognizes that women's rights are human rights and prohibits discrimination and violence against women;[4] which prohibits religious intolerance and racial discrimination; and which seeks to protect the rights of children, minorities, indigenous peoples, refugees and migrant workers.[5] We now have, as presented in this volume, a multiplicity of fora, international and regional, in which to address human rights issues. We have a highly elaborated set of mechanisms (thematic and country-specific rapporteurs and working groups), treaty-body oversight committees, the Technical Assistance Programme of the Office of the High Commissioner for Human Rights (OHCHR), and local human rights offices of the OHCHR in over 20 countries, which can be used to protect and promote human rights.[6]

Moreover, human rights are now being addressed not only in conventional fora, such as the UN Commission on Human Rights or its Sub-Commission on the Promotion and Protection of Human Rights, but also before the international financial institutions (the World Bank and the International Monetary Fund), in the context of trade negotiations at the World Trade Organization (WTO) and in the development activities of the United Nations Development Programme (UNDP). This follows logically from the recognition in Vienna that 'the promotion and protection of human rights is a matter of priority for the international community'[7] and the corollary that human rights must be mainstreamed throughout the entire UN system.[8]

Most significantly, the human rights movement has become a universal movement, with human rights NGOs and people's organizations active – whether openly or underground – in every country in the world. Since the frontline of the human rights struggle is most frequently at the grassroots level, one should not underestimate this burgeoning energy. Moreover, modern communications technology has made it impossible to insulate societies from news and developments elsewhere in the world. Thus there are coalitions and/or networks of these organizations at the national, regional and international levels, which provide information, expertise and solidarity to those on the frontlines.

The 'human rights movement' is, admittedly, a nebulous concept that encompasses more than just NGOs. It includes legislators and executive policy-makers, journalists and leaders of opinion, foundations, academics, and other elements of what we today term 'civil society'. However, the core of this community is a mixture of 'pure type' non-governmental human rights organizations (local or grassroots, national, regional or international) and a multitude of other private associations (including trade unions, churches, professional associations and 'peoples' organizations') that have exhibited active concern for, and involvement in, the human rights struggle.[9]

More formally, a human rights NGO is a private association whose *raison d'être* derives from the promotion and/or protection of one or more internationally-recognized human rights. To a large extent, an NGO is defined by what it is not: it is not governmental, it is not controlled by government; stated positively, an NGO is independent or autonomous from government.[10] Typically, such organizations are led by human rights activists or human rights defenders – that is, individuals who make a major commitment to, and openly take up, the defence and protection of the human rights of others. Human rights defenders need not, however, be formally associated with an organization: they may be lawyers, journalists, writers, religious leaders, trade unionists, health workers or teachers; very frequently they are associated with broad-based 'peoples' organizations' of peasants, workers, slum dwellers, indigenous peoples or women. They are individuals who champion the human rights of others, often at great personal risk to their own lives and safety.[11] It is these human rights NGOs and human rights defenders that have been the spearhead of the human rights movement which began to coalesce into a major force in the late 1970s.

Although the universe of human rights NGOs is highly diverse, and all may not share the same common vision, what gives form and cohesion to it and makes it a human rights 'movement' is that all refer and appeal to the same set of international standards in holding governments accountable. The Vienna Declaration's reaffirmation of the universality, indivisibility, interdependence and interrelatedness of all human rights[12] was merely a reluctant recognition by states of this reality. Most striking in this regard was the fact that, in March 1993, Asian human rights NGOs met in Bangkok, where governments were holding a regional meeting prior to the 1993 World Conference on Human Rights, and produced the Bangkok NGO Declaration on Human Rights. While the governments were advancing arguments about Asian cultural values, the Asian NGOs unequivocally stated:

Universal human rights standards are rooted in many cultures. We affirm the basis of universality of human rights which afford protection to all of humanity, including special groups such as women, children, minorities and indigenous peoples, workers, refugees and displaced persons, the disabled and the elderly. While advocating cultural pluralism, those cultural practices which derogate from universally accepted human rights, including women's rights, must not be tolerated.

As human rights are of universal concern and are universal in value, the advocacy of human rights cannot be considered to be an encroachment upon national sovereignty.[13]

THE ROLES OR FUNCTIONS OF NGOS IN THE PROMOTION AND PROTECTION OF HUMAN RIGHTS

In the area of human rights promotion and protection, NGOs have performed – and continue to perform – a myriad roles or functions. There are a number of ways in which these can be analysed,[14] but I will treat them under the following eight headings:

- agenda-setting
- legislation
- fact-finding and analysis
- witnessing, denunciation or the mobilization of shame
- international solidarity and support to human rights defenders
- education
- expertise and policy analysis
- keeping the political system open.

Agenda-setting

Both historically and contemporaneously, NGOs have played a major role in bringing items for action on to the international agenda.[15] As Kofi Annan acknowledged in his address to the NGO Forum on Global Issues quoted above, NGOs played a major role in getting slavery inscribed into the international agenda. Prominent among these were the two antecedents of the London-based NGO now called Anti-Slavery: the Anti-Slavery Society founded in 1838 and the Aborigines' Protection Society founded in 1837.[16] Likewise, protection of the wounded on the battlefield, which then led to the elaboration of the entire body of humanitarian law, was conceived of, and shaped by, the International Committee of the Red Cross and, subsequently, the Red Cross movement.[17] Furthermore, it was NGOs that got human rights inscribed into the United Nations Charter.[18]

With the onset of the Cold War, the United Nations spent the first two decades of its existence focused almost exclusively on the drafting of international standards (the Universal Declaration of Human Rights, the Convention on the Prevention and Punishment of the Crime of Genocide, the International Covenant on Civil and Political Rights, the International Covenant on Social, Economic and Cultural Rights, the International Convention on the Elimination of All Forms of Racial Discrimination and so on), while denying that it had authority to act on violations.[19] It is now widely recognized that it was largely as a result of pressure from human rights NGOs that, in the late 1960s, states began to move very slowly from the promotion of human rights, focused on the drafting of international instruments and standards, to the protection of human rights, with an emphasis on implementation and enforcement. In other words, NGOs were forcing a significant change in the international agenda.

As late as October 1980, Theo van Boven and Bertie Ramcharan observed:

> ... notwithstanding their commitment in the Charter to achieve international cooperation in promoting and protecting human rights and fundamental freedoms, and notwithstanding, in many instances, their subsequent acceptance of other instruments ... there is still in practice a visibly discernible lack of commitment on the part of many governments either to protect human rights in their own countries, or to act for their protection at the international level.[20]

Throughout the 1970s and for much of the 1980s, a major consequence of this lack of commitment was the unwillingness of governments to monitor and to speak out against the human rights violations of other governments, unless there was a specific ideological, economic or military advantage in doing so. This point was underscored in 1978 by Louis Henkin when he observed that 'the early assumption that States might be prepared to scrutinize other States and be scrutinized by them' had not stood up, and that there had been little 'horizontal' enforcement.[21] Indeed, it has become clear that, to the extent that national governments or inter-governmental organizations were moved to express genuine concern for human rights, this was largely the result of pressures exerted upon them by the human rights community.

While we have come a considerable way from the 1970s, when states hid behind the domestic jurisdiction argument in order to sidestep scrutiny of their record, we continue to see what Roberta Cohen has called 'regional protectionism' in bodies such as the Commission on Human Rights. In essence, this is a strategy which involves protecting one's own; states in one region attempt to block the condemnation of other states from that same region.[22] A classic example of this (but one which failed) was the vote in the 4th Special Session of the Commission on Human Rights on East Timor in September 1999 where, with the exception of the Republic of Korea (which abstained), all Asian members of the Commission first voted against a special session, and then voted against establishing a commission of inquiry to gather information on possible violations of human rights and international humanitarian law in East Timor.[23]

A great many items have been placed on the international human rights agenda because of NGO pressure. It was Amnesty International that put the issue of torture on the international agenda when, in December 1972, it launched a worldwide 'Campaign for the Abolition of Torture'. The following year, the UN General Assembly approved a resolution inspired, by Amnesty International, which formally denounced torture. Amnesty International continued to spotlight the issue by publishing the first worldwide survey on torture in 1973, organizing conferences and circulating a petition of more than 1 million signatures, and it did not relax its pressure until the adoption of the Convention against Torture and Other Cruel, Inhuman or Degrading Treatment or Punishment in 1984.[24]

The issue of violence against women and the recognition that 'women's rights are human rights' was placed on the agenda of the World Conference on Human Rights (Vienna, 1993) as a result of a sustained campaign by women's rights organizations from around the world. Until that time, the former issue was largely ignored on the grounds that it occurred in the 'private' domain (that is, it was a family matter) and was not appropriate for 'public' regulation, while women's rights were treated as something apart from the mainstream of human rights concerns.[25] Now there is a United Nations Declaration on the Elimination of Violence Against Women (1993) and a Special Rapporteur on Violence against Women – Its Causes and Consequences. Similarly, women's rights groups have managed to get rape recognized as a war crime by the Ad Hoc International Criminal Tribunals for the former Yugoslavia and for Rwanda, and they have made election of women judges to the International Criminal Court a major agenda item.[26]

Other items that have been put on the agenda by NGOs in recent years include: a High Commissioner of Human Rights, a proposal by Amnesty International at the Vienna World Conference;[27] the International Criminal Court, another item pursued in Vienna, particularly by the International Commission of Jurists[28] and, subsequently, by the NGO Coalition for an International Criminal Court;[29] the issue of the commercial sexual exploitation of children, put on the international agenda by the NGO network End Child Prostitution, Pornography and Trafficking (ECPPAT);[30] the Landmines Convention by the International Campaign to Ban Landmines, which received the Nobel Peace Prize for its work;[31] and, recently, the issue of globalization and its impact on human rights standards, a major concern of the NGOs which participated at the Vienna Plus Five International NGO Forum (Ottawa, June 1998).[32] Indeed, 50 000 demonstrators converged in Seattle, Washington State, USA, for the opening of the next round of negotiations of the World Trade Organization (WTO). So strong has been NGO pressure on the WTO to take human rights, labour and environmental standards into account in trade talks, and to ensure that decisions are not made behind closed doors, that the Director-General of the WTO, Mike Moore, has taken the unprecedented step of agreeing to hold a full day of meetings with NGOs just before the WTO negotiations open.[33] Thereafter, the voice of NGOs was seriously taken into account by the WTO.

Drafting Legislation: International Treaties, Declarations and Programmes of Action

In the 1994–96 negotiations in the Open-ended Working Group established to revise ECOSOC resolution 1296 (XLIV)[34] which regulated how NGOs relate to the United Nations, a number of governments wanted to make quite clear the difference between government representatives and NGO representatives. Thus they were insistent on maintaining the principle that, while NGOs have the right to make statements and distribute communications according to set procedures, 'they cannot participate in negotiations'. According to these governments, 'Decision-making is a right that belongs only to Member States'.[35] From a legalistic perspective, they may be correct.[36] In recent years, however, NGOs have played a leading role in the drafting of both international treaties and/or declarations, as well as in the drafting of the declarations and programme of action that have emerged from the world conferences of the 1990s. The Canadian government, in explaining its position on this resolution, noted: 'The provision in para. 50 refers only to direct intergovernmental negotiation. NGOs can and should contribute to negotiations, and this provision should in no way be interpreted as more restrictive than the privileges enjoyed by NGOs in recent UN meetings'.[37]

The latitude given to NGOs in the various world conferences varied considerably from one meeting to another: at the Vienna World Conference on Human Rights, NGOs could attend the plenary sessions but were not permitted to observe the drafting sessions; at the Beijing World Conference on Women, NGOs could observe both the plenary and the drafting sessions but were not permitted to attend the informal meetings, where hard issues were negotiated; in Istanbul, at Habitat II, NGOs could not only attend all the meetings, they were even permitted to intervene in the negotiations and table material during the drafting, although within specific guidelines. Their statements had to be short and to the point and they could not support or oppose governments. But they could, and did, draw attention to specific texts, recommending changes, suggesting additions or proposing deletions.[38] A similar spirit of openness prevailed with respect to the drafting of the Statute of the International Criminal Court, where NGOs were even permitted to address the plenary.

Moreover, in most of the world conference processes, NGOs have participated fully in the Preparatory Committees and often in the pre-conference regional meetings. Thus, one commentator, talking about the lead-up to the Beijing Women's Conference, noted:

> Thousands of NGOs, representing the voices and concerns of hundreds of thousands more, contributed to the U.N. Platform for Action through regional and PrepCom meetings. At the actual conference, the 4,035 NGO delegates almost equaled the 4,995 government participants. … Because of NGO involvement, the Platform became an agenda reflective of women's voices around the world rather than a government-imposed plan.[39]

If there are some states that want to keep NGOs at arm's length, there are others that recognize the importance of partnership with NGOs, particularly in tackling global problems. The Canadian Foreign Minister, Lloyd Axworthy, addressed the Vienna Plus Five NGO Global Forum with the following words:

> In many ways … the real sea change at Vienna was in process, not substance. The massive, intense and well-coordinated involvement of non-governmental organizations was one of the great accomplishments of the World Conference. It meant that governments could no longer sit alone as the self-appointed protectors of human rights. … The partnerships forged at Vienna between civil society and like-minded governments were early examples of a new international dynamic. The collapse of the old bipolar world order, globalization, the information technology revolution – all these have changed the face of international relations beyond recognition. The ability of any one nation or group of nations to set the agenda is steadily dwindling. At the same time, the power of civil society to effect change is growing.[40]

In the area of international standard setting – or in what can be called international law-making – NGOs have made seminal contributions in recent years. Niall MacDermot, former Secretary-General of the International Commission of Jurists (ICJ), speaking on the occasion of receiving the Erasmus Prize in 1989, described four major efforts of the ICJ in this area: its work with regard to the African Charter of Human and Peoples' Rights, the European Convention on Torture, the reform of the Japanese Mental Health Law, and the first international instrument on the Independence of the Judiciary.[41] In introducing the subject, MacDermot noted that the work in this area is less dramatic than coming to the assistance of persons whose rights are being violated but, in the long run, it can give protection to many people.

Howard B. Tolley, Jr, in his study of the ICJ, also comments on this function: 'International lawmaking involves more collaboration than confrontation,' he points out. It involves 'elite contacts, expert testimony, workshops to draft proposals, reports documenting a need for action, NGO coalitions, and constituency pressure.' He then goes on to suggest that a few 'skilled ICJ lobbyists significantly influenced the adoption of global, regional and national standards'.[42] So, too, have other NGOs.

For example, the drafting of the Convention of the Rights of the Child – a ten-year process which began in 1979 – took place with sustained and systematic input from NGOs. In 1983 an Informal NGO Ad Hoc Group on the Drafting of the Convention began to meet twice a year and reported, in written form, the results of these consultations. These reports reviewed previously and newly proposed articles and, in some cases, produced entirely new texts or articles concerning rights that the NGO Group felt should be included in the draft Convention. As a consequence, Cynthia Price Cohen, who participated in the Ad Hoc Group as the representative of Human Rights Internet, concluded that 'the imprint of the NGO Group can be found in almost every article'.[43] There are many other international instruments which have been shaped by NGO input. The Statute on the International Criminal Court, for example, was drafted very much in partnership between NGOs and like-minded governments.[44] NGOs also played an important role in ensuring that the Declaration on the Right and Responsibility of Individuals, Groups and Organs of Society to Promote and Protect Universally Recognized Human Rights and Fundamental Freedoms (commonly known as the Declaration on Human Rights Defenders and which took 13 years to complete) was not undermined in the final stages of negotiation by governments wishing to limit severely the work of human rights defenders.[45]

Fact-finding or Information-gathering, Analysis and Dissemination

Perhaps the most important function that NGOs perform in the protection and promotion of human rights is that of information-gathering, evaluation and dissemination. While fact-finding by intergovernmental organizations increased quite dramatically during the 1990s – with more than 30 thematic and geographic mechanisms of the Commission on Human Rights (Special Rapporteurs, Special Representatives, Independent Experts or Working Groups), with six treaty bodies that regularly review the reports of States Parties, and with field offices of the High Commissioner for Human Rights in more than 20 countries – it is nonetheless clear that the intergovernmental human rights machinery would grind to a halt were it not fed by the fact-finding of human rights NGOs.

Diego Garcia-Sayan put it as follows:

> The United Nations Working Group on Forced Disappearances ... along with many intergovernmental organizations, relies basically upon NGOs and not the Governments themselves. The NGOs provide the Group with information, pressure it to act and clamour for results. This is true of all the United Nations specialized groups.
>
> Anyone who has ever attended a session of the United Nations Commission on Human Rights has seen the caution – to say the least – with which the government representatives act. Except in extreme cases or when dealing with countries which few or no Governments defend ..., it would seem that there exists a policy of not criticizing neighbouring countries directly or harshly. Strange but notorious silences can be understood simply as indicating geopolitical interests. The 'prosecutors' in these circumstances, that is to say those who hold human rights concerns above others, are the NGOs. They are the fuel and the lubricant which allow the machine to function and speed the working up. ... The NGOs contribute greatly to upholding the international community's ethics. If it were not for their efforts, this system of ethics would have been eroded a long time ago.[46]

Felice Gaer made a similar point:

> In fact, the mechanisms rely almost exclusively upon the information sent to them by non-governmental organizations. Although there is no detailed accounting of this, there are some significant indicators of the extent to which

non-governmental organizations fuel the special procedures of the Commission on Human Rights: at a June 1995 meeting of all the Special Rapporteurs and experts serving on Working Groups of the Commission, the group stated: 'We appeal to non-governmental organizations (NGOs) whose work and information is crucial to human rights protection and to the effective discharge of our own mandates to continue providing us with relevant information and ideas ...'.

... Amnesty International sends more than 500 such communications – covering thousands of cases – to the UN special procedures branch every year. Furthermore, the Working Group on Arbitrary Detentions reported in 1995 that 74% of the cases it took up in 1994 were brought by international NGOs, and another 23% came from national NGOs ... . The Special Rapporteur on Arbitrary Executions acknowledges the 'important' role of NGOs in alerting the international community about summary executions, and the Rapporteur on freedom of expression describes the NGO contribution as 'primordial'.[47]

With respect to the treaty bodies, NGOs are now commonly preparing 'shadow' or alternative reports which frequently challenge the facts or interpretations provided by governments. In some cases, NGOs are actually permitted to speak before the treaty body, as is the case with the Committee on Economic, Social and Cultural Rights. In a number of cases, members of the treaty body may contact NGOs about a forthcoming report, and ask them to provide them with a list of questions to put to the government representative. All of this comes into sharp focus if one considers that members of treaty bodies, like Special Rapporteurs, serve as 'volunteers' and receive no income for their work. Nor is the United Nations able to provide them with anything other than minimal staff assistance. On average, a staff member of the OHCHR must service at least two mechanisms, and frequently has other responsibilities. Thus, both the mechanisms and the treaty bodies are heavily dependent on NGO information. Amnesty International, with a research staff of several hundred, and Human Rights Watch, with a multi-million dollar budget for research, have a far greater capacity for seriously and systematically monitoring violations than do the special procedures of the United Nations or its treaty bodies.

The same situation prevails when a Special Rapporteur goes on a field mission. As Abid Hussain, Special Rapporteur on Freedom of Opinion and Expression recently commented, he relies heavily on NGOs in the countries that he visits to inform him who he ought to talk with and what questions he should ask; or, if he is going to a state where NGOs are unable to freely function, he will rely on NGOs outside the country to brief him. 'Let me also say that our success really depends on the NGOs.'[48]

Moreover, NGOs are frequently able to go in and gather information in places that bar admission to United Nations or other intergovernmental agents. This was the case with regard to the attempt of a United Nations joint mission, established by the Commission on Human Rights in April 1997, to investigate allegations of the slaughter of Hutu refugees in camps in eastern Zaire. The mission was totally blocked by President Laurent Kabila, who kept finding new reasons for refusing access to the United Nations team.[49] Meanwhile, in October 1997, Human Rights Watch was able to publish a report entitled *What Kabila is Hiding: Civilian Killings and Impunity in Congo*, documenting the attacks on the refugee camps in the former Zaire that began in late 1996 and continued in the ensuing seven months as war spread across the country.[50] In like manner, in 1994, the Centre on Housing Rights and Evictions (COHRE) was able to produce a report, *Destruction by Design. Housing Rights Violations in Tibet*, based on diverse sources, many directly from Tibetans in Tibet.[51] Given China's talent for blocking all action directed against its human rights record at the Commission on Human Rights, it is hard to conceive of a United Nations report of this genre. Nonetheless, it is precisely on evidence of this sort that the Committee on Economic, Social and Cultural Rights has been able to develop a General Comment on forced evictions, while a United Nations Expert Seminar was able to issue a set of *Comprehensive Guidelines on Development Based Displacement*.[52]

At the national level, while it is governments which are charged with investigating allegations of human rights abuses, there are only a handful of countries where the system for the administration of justice, together with national institutions (that is, governmental human rights commissions or ombudsmen), can be relied on to gather, analyse and act impartially on 'the facts'.[53] Even in the most democratic societies, it is often private associations and the media which first expose abuses of power.

Accurate and timely information is the main currency of human rights NGOs and the basis of their legitimacy. Amnesty International led the way by developing a research department to underpin all campaign work. When the objectivity of NGO information was challenged as being one-sided – a charge that was particularly levelled in the mid-1980s in the context of the civil war in El Salvador, NGOs took up the gauntlet, broadening their fact-finding to cover not only violations committed by government forces, but also violations committed by insurgents. They also began to document violations of humanitarian law as well as those of international human rights law.[54]

Over the course of two decades, such fact-finding has become the work of professionals rather than amateurs; it has developed its own methodology and it has demonstrated a strong concern for protecting those who provide the information. More recently, NGOs have begun to use videocameras as well as written affidavits to document abuses; they have begun to standardize data so that it can be computerized and/or statistically analysed; and they have developed specialized techniques for dealing with certain types of evidence – as with the application of forensic anthropology to mass graves, genetic matching to identify missing grandchildren, and techniques to confirm the application of torture. Much of the information on the basis of which truth commissions have written their reports, or prosecutions have been prepared against gross violators – for example, in Argentina, Brazil, Chile, El Salvador and Ethiopia – has been NGO data, increasingly computerized in highly sophisticated databases.[55] Such information has also been placed at the disposal of the International Criminal Tribunals for the former-Yugoslavia and Rwanda.

Finally, one might note a recent particularly impressive NGO monitoring effort on the implementation of the Convention on the Prohibition of the Use, Stockpiling, Production and Transfer of Anti-Personnel Mines and on Their Destruction (the Landmines Treaty), which has a weak state compliance mechanism (that is, the primary compliance is the provision that states voluntarily report once a year on measures they have taken to implement the Treaty).[56] To remedy that situation, in April 1999, the International Campaign to Ban Landmines published the first annual *Landmine Monitor Report*, a document of over 1000 pages with information on every country of the world with respect to landmine ban policy, use, production, transfer, stockpiling, mine clearance, mine awareness and survivor assistance. Compiled by a core group of five NGOs, but based on information supplied by NGOs in every region of the world, it is a truly professional product.[57]

Witnessing, Denunciation or the Mobilization of Shame

In dealing with human rights violators, witnessing or denunciation is a major NGO strategy. There are a multitude of tactics that can be, and have been, employed in different situations: issuing press releases and mounting press campaigns; publishing reports and disseminating these widely, especially to policy-makers; using the pulpit and the religious network for 'witnessing'; holding demonstrations, rallies and sit-ins; organizing people's tribunals at which witnesses testify to the violations; denunciations through videos, films, popular music or theatre; testifying before governmental or intergovernmental bodies; using fax networks; and most recently, using electronic mail (especially ListServes) and the World Wide Web to disseminate the information globally.

Informing all these tactics is the hope that, by exposing the violations to the harsh glare of public opinion, one can achieve one of several ends: the government can be shamed into putting a halt to the violations; domestic opposition can be mobilized to destabilize a rights-violating regime; and/ or international opposition can be generated leading to pressure and possibly open sanctions against the offending government.

Experience has shown that no regime, except the most insular, relishes being branded a human rights violator; hence the NGO emphasis on the mobilization of shame. However, governments often go on the offensive when their propriety and respectability (that is, their human rights record) are challenged, engaging in a host of tactics to counter such denunciations. These have ranged from blatant denial of the facts to impugning the reputation of the fact-finders (for example, labelling human rights NGOs as subversive, terrorist, or anti-nationalistic), pleading that special circumstances (that is, a threat to the nation) require special measures (for example, national security legislation); hiring high-powered public relations firms to give the dictatorship a different image; and creating their own government-organized non-governmental organizations (GONGOs) or national institutions to produce counter-reports.

During the Vienna World Conference on Human Rights (June, 1993), while governments met upstairs in an atmosphere of diplomatic affability to debate general principles, downstairs in the basement, where the NGO Forum took place, there were workshops, tribunals and panels exposing and denouncing government violations – the walls were plastered with photographs and posters graphically depicting scenes of torture, the faces of the disappeared, and the agony of the oppressed. Outside the conference centre, there were daily demonstrations. With the international media centred in Vienna, the NGOs could not pass up the opportunity for denunciation, although for many states this was anathema. Thus, they had initially attempted to prevent NGOs that would be critical of their human rights record from being accredited to the World Conference, to prohibit the NGO Forum from dealing with country-specific topics, and to restrict NGO access to the Vienna Conference itself.[58] They were not, however, successful in their attempts to silence their critics. It is, therefore, not surprising that the Chinese government, which hosted the Fourth World Conference on Women in September 1995, was more than a little concerned that the 30 000 women and journalists expected to attend the NGO Forum might have a destabilizing effect on their own domestic society. To forestall this eventuality, they decided to move the NGO Forum to a resort town some 60 kilometres from Beijing and at least an hour from the site of the United Nations Conference.[59]

International Solidarity and Support to Human Rights Defenders

A strategy of international solidarity and humanitarian relief has been evolved to provide protection to victims and potential victims under repressive regimes, and especially to human rights defenders at risk on the frontlines of the human rights struggle. This has included a wide range of tactics. One is the 'adoption' tactic of Amnesty International, which concerns Amnesty International groups adopting specific political prisoners and campaigning for their release, sometimes for years. A second is the 'Urgent Action (UA) Networks', also introduced by Amnesty, and now widely used by many NGOs (including churches, trade unions and professional associations), which organize hundreds of people around the world who are poised to respond immediately (by e-mail or fax) to prevent torture, disappearance, the application of the death penalty and, most recently, violence against women. Some of the United Nations Special Rapporteurs take action on the basis of these UAs, immediately contacting the government to request information about the case. A third tactic is 'accompaniment', developed by Peace Brigades International to deal with particularly dangerous situations. It involves providing a 24-hour a day 'bodyguard' to human rights activists at risk in the form of a foreign companion armed only with a camera, who lives with and goes everywhere with the defender. Pioneered in El Salvador and Sri Lanka, the premise has been substantiated that the authorities (whether military, paramilitary or civilian) are less likely to kill or abduct an activist under the glare of such international scrutiny.

International NGOs have also provided money and, in some cases, legal advice and/or lawyers, to defend political prisoners on trial for their life or liberty, and they have provided material and/or moral support to the families of detainees. It was NGOs that were also behind the establishment in the early 1980s of the United Nations Voluntary Fund for Torture, to support programmes that provide direct medical, psychological, social or other assistance to torture victims and their families. Furthermore, NGOs have assisted victims or their friends and relatives in preparing cases brought before intergovernmental human rights bodies (the Inter-American and European Commissions and Courts, and the Human Rights Committee).

Particularly innovative has been the strategy of using international standards in domestic courts to sue human rights violators. The 1988 decision of the United States Court of Appeals for the Second Circuit, in the case of *Filartiga* v. *Peña-Irala*, was a landmark victory. The Centre for Constitutional Rights (CRC) in New York filed the case in New York in 1984 on behalf of the Paraguayan activist and physician, Joel Filartiga, accusing the Inspector-General of Police of Asunción (who was then residing in the United States) in the death by torture of Filartiga's 17-year-old son. This involved the use of the Alien Tort Act as the basis for bringing a federal action for an alleged human rights violation of internationally recognized human rights law. While the District Court initially refused to hear the case, on appeal the case was both heard and decided in favour of Filartiga, awarding him a judgment of $10.3 million. While Filartiga would never see the $10.3 million, the case sent a clear message: that human rights torturers could not find safe haven in the United States.[60]

Subsequent to that case, American human rights groups lobbied for and saw a new law enacted, the *Torture Victim Protection Act*.[61] This Act permits anyone to sue any person living in the United States for torture committed anywhere in the world. In April 1995 another landmark victory was registered in the case brought against Guatemalan General Hector Alejandro Gramajo, responsible for the torture and murder of thousands of Guatemalans while he was Vice-Chief of Staff in the early 1980s and Defence Minister from 1987 to 1990. Gramajo was served with two law suits in 1991, as he was graduating from the John F. Kennedy School of Government at Harvard University. He left the country and refused to contest the case. Nonetheless, a judgment of $47.5 million was made in favour of eight Guatemalans and an American nun on whose behalf the suits were filed. 'In this case, plaintiffs have convincingly demonstrated that, at a minimum, Gramajo was aware of and supported widespread acts of brutality committed by personnel under his command resulting in thousands of civilian deaths,' wrote Judge Woodlock.[62]

The importance of such acts of international solidarity should not be underestimated. While dictatorships are usually overthrown or eroded from within, such international solidarity helps keep alive the indigenous leaders who are the only real hope for transformation.

Human Rights Education

A sixth function, which has become particularly relevant to societies in transition from authoritarian or dictatorial to democratic rule but which is important for all societies, is human rights education. Individuals and communities cannot adequately protect their rights if they do not know them. Moreover, those in positions of authority – particularly the army, the police and prison officials, as well as government officials and parliamentarians – must learn that there are limits to their power and that they cannot abuse others by virtue of their position. Judges and lawyers need to be educated about human rights so that the justice system is firmly grounded in the rule of law.

While human rights education tends to be the primary responsibility of national NGOs, since they can best interpret international standards in the local context, in recent years, international and regional NGOs have also begun to play an important role in this area. Human Rights Internet was able to identify and describe nearly 100 programmes in human rights education, many offered by universities but also numerous NGO programmes. These include courses/programmes offered by the African Centre for Democracy and Human Rights Studies in the Gambia, the Arab Institute of Human Rights in Tunisia, the Inter-American Institute of Human Rights in Costa Rica, the South Asian Forum for Human Rights in Nepal, and the Diplomacy Training Program in Australia.[63] One human rights scholar and activist commented that:

> In all regions of the globe, there are a multitude of initiatives on human rights education beyond the school setting, often propelled by non-governmental organizations. Of particular interest is the spread of courses and programmes aimed at difficult situations and specific groups who are the potential or actual victims of human rights violations, such as street children, their protectors and *animateurs*, such as non-governmental organizations, the mass media and community leaders.[64]

To further such efforts, a number of educational clearing houses have been established; for example, an Asian Regional Resource Center for Human Rights Education has existed in Bangkok since 1992.[65]

Experienced and well-established NGOs have been called upon to train and/or develop materials for fledgling national and local NGOs for the purpose of capacity-building or empowerment. For example, in 1994, the US-based Fund for Peace (FFP) published an extremely useful handbook on institution-building for NGOs, which was widely disseminated in Arabic, English, French and Spanish;[66] it covered such basic issues as determining an organization's mandate, writing by-laws, opening an office and generating resources. In 1999, FFP followed up with a *Handbook of Practical Strategies for Human Rights Groups*, which examines areas such as protection, generating publicity, utilizing the courts, responding to efforts to discredit local groups, and protection from surveillance.[67] Another US-based group, the Human Rights Law Group, largely funded by USAID, has undertaken major projects to support the work of, and to train, human rights NGOs in places as diverse as Bosnia-Herzegovina, Cambodia, the Democratic Republic of Congo, Nigeria, Romania and Yemen. The stated purpose of the Law Group's international advocacy training programme is to increase the skills of local activists and to broadcast their issues of concern globally.[68] Canadian NGOs have also been engaged in human rights education programmes. These notably include the Canadian Centre for International Cooperation (CECI), which has conducted training activities for lawyers and other professionals in order to increase their capacity to fight impunity in Haiti, and the Canadian Human Rights Foundation, which runs a summer programme for human rights activists from around the world, and has given training to the staff of human rights commissions and NGOs in various countries in Eastern Europe and in Asia.

Given the burgeoning of new NGOs wishing to work within United Nations arenas but lacking information about how to make an impact in such international fora, a number of older NGOs have undertaken to train or 'mentor' the new ones, among them Pax Romana and the Center for Woman's Global Leadership. At a more formal level, the International Service for Human Rights runs an internship programme which brings human rights advocates from the South and societies in transition to Geneva to monitor and learn how the United Nations Commission on Human Rights and/or its Sub-Commission on the Promotion and Protection of Human Rights operate.

The Asian Centre for Women's Human Rights (ASCENT), based in the Philippines, has been offering training to women's rights activists on how to document, monitor, investigate, campaign and intervene regarding the different human rights violations perpetrated on women, particularly violence against women.[69] In the face of the recent brutal civil wars, involving massive killings, mutilation, torture and rape, in Bosnia-Herzegovina, Liberia, Rwanda, Sierra Leone, Somalia and elsewhere, it has been necessary to train local activists to take affidavits from survivors, to be gender-sensitive in questioning witnesses, especially where rape is concerned, and to protect mass graves so that evidence, which may be used to prosecute perpetrators, is not destroyed.

NGOs have also been involved in provided training in areas as diverse as election monitoring, trial observation, how to establish a database of human rights violations, how to set up a human rights documentation centre, and how to connect to the Internet and to create websites.[70] Both national and international NGOs have also been involved in providing human rights training to judges, lawyers, parliamentarians, journalists, prison officials, the police and the military, and, for this purpose, they have been developing specialized human rights materials.[71] There have also been specific programmes and materials developed to teach different constituencies – women, workers, children, refugees, peasants, persons living with HIV/AIDS, persons with disabilities – about their rights and how to protect them. This has frequently involved the need to develop special methodologies and material, especially for working with illiterate populations – for example, teaching human rights through street theatre, song, videos, audios, posters and comics.

Expertise and Policy Analysis

A seventh function is one that has only recently become evident in the human rights sphere – namely, providing expertise to the United Nations and to other intergovernmental organizations (such as the Organization of Security and Cooperation in Europe or the African Commission on Human and Peoples' Rights) or to governments, to enable them to implement their programmes. This role was evident much earlier in other areas of ECOSOC's competence – for example, in development, environmental protection or humanitarian assistance. In terms of human rights, in the past NGOs were associated with providing information, rather than expertise. Now, they more and more frequently provide both.

Similar to the way in which NGOs have assisted the United Nations in drafting international legislation, as discussed above, at the national level they have assisted governments in bringing their legislation into line with international human rights standards. However, since the United Nations has established an extensive technical assistance programme, field offices and human rights monitors, as well as its extensive system of human rights mechanisms and treaty bodies, NGO expertise has been much in demand. A large number of the Special Rapporteurs of the United Nations Commission on Human Rights, of the experts who sit on the treaty bodies, and of those heading field offices, or leading investigative missions are individuals who received their training in non-governmental human rights organizations.

In a similar vein, to implement its programme of technical assistance to governments in the area of human rights, the OHCHR has increasingly employed experts from the human rights community: to undertake needs assessments; to train judges and police personnel; to establish national human rights commissions; and to develop programmes in human rights education. More recently, as the OHCHR has been nominating human rights monitors to countries such as Burundi, Guatemala, Haiti and Rwanda, individual monitors are being recruited through non-governmental human rights organizations. The human rights NGO movement, now over 20 years old, has trained professional cadres and equipped them with skills that are vital as the United Nations attempts to confront the new challenges of humanitarian intervention, conflict management, ending impunity and democratization. The expertise of seasoned human rights activists is needed by governments establishing truth commissions or prosecuting former perpetrators of human rights violations. NGOs are also being asked to engage in discussions on such difficult issues as the dissemination of hate propaganda and pornography on the Internet; how to hold non-state actors – whether guerrillas, terrorists, criminal syndicates or corporations – accountable under international human rights law; to find ways of protecting the intellectual property rights of indigenous peoples; how to deal with the HIV/AIDS epidemic by developing anti-discrimination guidelines; or ethical questions bearing on genetic engineering and cloning.[72]

This places human rights NGOs in a somewhat novel situation. Since they have become the primary source of information on the human rights violations committed by governments, they have been frequently perceived, especially by human rights violating regimes, as hostile protagonists of governments. Today, human rights NGOs – or at least some of them – are being cast in the role of implementing UN policies to assist governments, or of assisting governments directly. This is a fairly major shift in perspective, with considerable implications for them.

Keeping the Political System Open: Freedom of Association and Access to the United Nations

A final, but infrequently discussed, function that NGOs perform in the promotion and protection of human rights is one that is critical – namely, keeping the political system open to other elements of civil society. In working for freedom of association, freedom of opinion, freedom of expression and freedom of assembly, human rights NGOs make it possible for civil society to function; they create political space for democratic forces and, therefore, for democracy.

It is for this reason that protecting human rights defenders is so important. If a regime can kill off, or silence, those who speak out for human rights, they can more readily suppress the rights of everyone. This is why human rights defenders are often the first target of repressive regimes.[73] It is also why the United Nations is so important a forum for human rights organizations operating in repressive environments. When governments attempt to silence human rights activists at home – whether through intimidation or through the manipulation of laws regulating the registration or functioning of NGOs – they see the United Nations, especially its Commission on Human Rights, as a forum of last resort. It is, of course, for precisely this reason that repressive regimes have attempted to prevent human rights NGOs from having access to such arenas. Thus, freedom of association domestically, and access to the United Nations internationally, are two different dimensions of the same issue – the ability to give voice to human rights concerns.

This is what the Declaration on Human Rights Defenders seeks to address by stating clearly in its Article 1: 'Everyone has the right, individually and in association with others, to promote and to strive for the protection and realization of human rights and fundamental freedoms at the national and international levels.'

It must be recognized, however, that there is another way of silencing human rights defenders – different from repression, but sometimes just as effective – and that is by cooption. This speaks directly to the issue raised above: if human rights organizations begin to perceive themselves as service deliverers, whether for states or intergovernmental organizations, there is a danger that they will lose their independence and critical perspective which are essential for any objective monitoring of the implementation of human rights norms. At a recent consultation to consider how Canadian-based NGOs could more effectively ensure the implementation of international human rights treaties in Canada, Pierre Bosset addressed this problem:

> New mechanisms must be found to encourage the participation of civil society in the reporting and monitoring process. However, it is equally important for NGOs to keep some distance from the official reporting and monitoring process. The challenge of civil society participation lies perhaps, not so much in finding ways of allowing NGO involvement in the drafting of government reports, but in developing, through institutional means, the capacity of NGOs to conduct reporting and monitoring on their own terms.[74]

CONCLUSION

In a number of respects, it is easier to deal with dictatorial governments than with democratic ones. Thus, the world of the 1960s, 1970s and 1980s was simpler than that of the 1990s and the early 2000s. At that time we had 'good guys' and 'bad guys' – for example, Pinochet, Marcos and Idi Amin were indisputable villains with whom one could not work. Today, leaders are cast more in shades of grey than black and white. A human rights NGO must then ask whether it is compromising itself by working with, providing technical assistance or giving training to a regime that claims to want to improve its human rights record, but still has a long way to go in that regard. And, if it becomes financially beholden to such a government, its credibility and legitimacy will be at risk.

Thus, human rights NGOs face threats from two directions – from being embraced too closely or from being demonized by governments. They must be able to resist the inducements and temptations of power, while securing adequate resources to carry out the functions outlined above: placing new issues on the international agenda; participating in standard-setting; engaging in fact-finding and analysis; denouncing violations; offering international solidarity to those on the frontlines; educating about human rights; making their expertise available to the international community; and keeping the political system open. This is no small challenge.

NOTES

1   This chapter develops ideas introduced in earlier writings of the author, including the following: Wiseberg (1995a); Wiseberg (1991a); Wiseberg (1993); and Wiseberg (1989).
2   'Secretary-General calls partnership of NGOs, private sector, international organizations and governments powerful partnership for future', Text of remarks

made by United Nations Secretary-General Kofi Annan at the non-governmental organization (NGO) 'Forum on Global Issues', Berlin, 29 April 1999, Press Release SG/SM/6973.

3 Ibid.

4 This was first recognized in the Vienna Declaration and Programme of Action, June 1993, para. 18, and elaborated in the Beijing Platform for Action, *inter alia*, paras 210–23 and 112–130.

5 See United Nations (1993, Parts I and II); and United Nations (1997).

6 See Human Rights Internet (HRI), *For the Record: The UN Human Rights System* for the years 1997 and 1998, in hardcopy (6 vols each year), on CD-ROM, or on the Web at http://www.hri.ca/fortherecord.shtml. Vol. 1, 'Thematic Approaches' describes the various United Nations mechanisms.

7 Vienna Declaration on Human Rights, 1993, para. 1.

8 In 1998 the UNDP published a policy paper 'Integrating human rights with sustainable human development' which sets out UNDP guidelines in this area.

9 A 'pure-type' human rights NGO is one established specifically to carry out human rights work. Such groups may have a universal focus, like Amnesty International or Human Rights Internet (HRI) in Canada, or a regional or country-specific one, like the Inter-American Institute for Human Rights (IIDH) in Costa Rica or the Peoples' Union for Civil Liberties (PUCL) in India. It may have a mandate that is broad, like that of the Human Rights Watch Committees in New York, or narrowly focused on one issue, like the Minority Rights Group (MRG) in the UK or Defence for Children International (DCI) in Switzerland. All these groups exist solely to do human rights work. By way of contrast, trade unions, churches or professional associations were created for other purposes, although they may devote substantial resources to the defence of human rights.

10 The question of what is 'non-governmental' is not as straightforward as it appears at first sight, since organizations can be controlled to a greater or lesser degree by governments. We have many cases of governments actually creating GONGOs – that is, government-organized non-governmental organizations – to promote the government's positions in international arenas. Such groups obtain accreditation to international organizations or conferences and pass themselves off as genuine independent NGOs. For some useful insights into this problem, see Steiner (1991, pp.70–74).

11 For a more extended treatment of human rights defenders, see Wiseberg (1991b).

12 Vienna Declaration and Programme of Action, 1993, para. 5.

13 The text of the Declaration is available at http://www.hr-alliance.org/aphr-ft/bangkok.htm.

14 There is now extensive literature on the role or function of NGOs in the area of human rights. One recent and interesting study was published in 1997 by the Carter Center under the title *Human Rights, The United Nations and Non-governmental Organizations. A Report of the International Human Rights Council*, which is a collection of articles written by Council members. A major study is Korey (1998). Two important articles that appeared in the 1990s are Posner and Whittome (1994); and Gaer (1995). For earlier examinations, see Weissbrodt (1984); and Ermacora (1988, pp.180 *et seq.*).

15 NGOs also work to place items on to national agendas in the countries in which they are based, although this will not be discussed here.

16 See Archer (1967, pp.162–64); and Korey (1998, ch. 5).

17 Forsythe (1977, chs 1 and 2).

18   Korey (1998, ch. 1); Humphrey (1984, pp.12–13 and *passim*).
19   Rodley (1979, pp.161–72); and Tolley (1987, pp.16–19).
20   van Boven and Ramcharan (1980 p.10).
21   Henkin (1978, esp. n. on p.108).
22   Cohen (1992, pp.5–6).
23   Lafrenière and Wiseberg (1999).
24   Larsen (1978); and Power (1981, pp.59–70).
25   Parker and Comeau (1993).
26   See the following articles in the *Human Rights Tribune*: Oosterveld and Copelon (1997); Dufraimont and Hammell (1999); and Steward (1998).
27   'A Special Commissioner could move quickly on urgent human rights situations', *Human Rights Tribune*, **2** (1), (1993), p.18.
28   Comeau (1993), pp.24–25.
29   See their publication, *The International Criminal Court Monitor*, New York, which began with Issue No. 1 in June/July 1996 and/or their website, http://www.iccnow.org.
30   Hecht (1997).
31   Jenish (1997).
32   *Human Rights Tribune*, **5** (3), Special Issue on Vienna Plus Five International NGO Forum; see especially pp.17–18.
33   This was reported on CBC radio on 29 November 1999. On the eve of the Conference, the *New York Times*, the Toronto *Globe and Mail*, the Seattle newspapers and all the wire services carried stories of NGOs' demands on the WTO, most notably, the demand for 'transparency'.
34   Ryan and Wiseberg (1997).
35   ECOSOC resolution 1996/31, para. 50 – a revision of resolution 1296 (XLIV).
36   See Wiseberg (1995b, p.35); and Wiseberg (1996, p.11).
37   Wiseberg (1996, p.11).
38   'A bird's eye view' (1996).
39   Ryan and Kambayashi (1997, p.65).
40   Notes for an address by the Honourable Lloyd Axworthy, Minister of Foreign Affairs, to the NGO Global Forum on the Five-year Review of the Vienna World Conference on Human Rights, Ottawa, Ontario, 23 June 1998. Available online at http://www.dfait-maeci.gc.ca.
41   MacDermot (1989). In the same publication, see also van Boven (1989).
42   Tolley (1994, p.275).
43   Price Cohen (1990, p.142).
44   At the Rome Conference, there were delegates from 160 nations, 14 UN agencies, 17 other intergovernmental organizations, and 124 NGOs. See Austin and Stewart in Rome: (1998); see also the numerous documents, reports and position papers relating to the creation of the ICC which were mounted on the Web by the NGO Coalition for the ICC at www.igc.org/icc.
45   In 1996, 1997 and 1998, NGOs were seriously concerned that a number of states were deliberately delaying the adoption of the Declaration and/or attempting to seriously undermine universal human rights standards. They, therefore, mounted a Defenders Campaign to ensure that NGO pressure was brought to bear on the Working Group to complete a strong text in time for adoption in 1998 on the 50th anniversary of the Universal Declaration of Human Rights. In the *Human Rights Tribune*, see McCheshney (1996); Wiseberg (1997); 'Draft Declaration' (1997); and Ryan (1998).
46   Garcia-Sayan (1991, pp.38–39).

47   Gaer (1995, p.8).
48   Wiseberg (1999, p.10), Mr Hussain discussed the preparation of his fact-finding missions at a June 1999 meeting in Ottawa, Canada.
49   Williams (1997).
50   *Human Rights Watch*, **9** (5(A)), October 1997, available on the Web at http://www.hrw.org/hrw/reports97/congo/.
51   Leckie, February (1994).
52   Leckie and Farha (1997).
53   That is, there are still very few states whose national institutions meet the criteria of independence and impartiality set out in the Paris Principles. See 'National institutions for the promotion and protection of human rights', UN General Assembly document A/RES/48/134, 4 March 1994.
54   For an elaboration on this, see Wiseberg (1986).
55   Interview with Patrick Ball (1997/98).
56   Human Rights Internet (1997).
57   International Campaign to Ban Landmines (1995).
58   For more detailed information, see Wiseberg (1995); and *Human Rights Tribune*, **2** (2) (1993).
59   Comeau (1995).
60   Lillich (1993, pp.207–208 and pp.217–18).
61   Drinan and Kuo (1993, pp.605–24).
62   *Globe and Mail*, 13 April 1995, pp.A2.
63   Human Rights Internet, *HRI Reporter, Special Issue on Human Rights Education*, **16** (2), January 1999, Ottawa, Canada. This is being updated regularly on the Internet at http://www.hri.ca/.
64   Muntarbhorn (1998, p.293).
65   Information on this, and other NGOs active in human rights education, can be found in HRI's database of organizations concerned with human rights, at http://www.hri.ca/.
66   Fund for Peace (1994).
67   Fund for Peace, New York (1999).
68   Their programme is described in greater detail on their website at http://www.hrlawgroup.org/site/-programs.html.
69   See HRI's *Directory of Programmes of Human Rights Education*. A description of ASCENT's programme is found at http://www.hri.ca/coldfusion/cfteac/viewrecord.cfm?ID=23.
70   In June 1999, Human Rights Internet ran its first training programme on using the Internet for human rights work, training 12 human rights advocates from countries in Asia, Africa, Latin America and Eastern Europe.
71   For example, a recent resource developed for the media is *A Journalist's Handbook: Reporting Human Rights and Humanitarian Stories*, produced by Jo-Anne Velin, Geneva, Switzerland (1997).
72   Whenever the UN or its specialized agencies hold meetings on such critical issues, they almost invariably involve NGOs in the discussions.
73   For a further development of this theme, see Wiseberg (1993).
74   Bosset, 1999.

BIBLIOGRAPHY

'A bird's eye view – how it worked in Istanbul', *Human Rights Tribune*, 3(4), pp.31–32.

Archer, Peter (1967), 'Action by unofficial organizations on human rights', in Evan Luard (ed.), *Protection of Human Rights*, London, Thames and Hudson, pp.160–82.

Austin, Karen and Stewart, Nell (1998), 'Courting justice in Rome: International Criminal Court Treaty signed', *Human Rights Tribune*, 5(4), p.6.

Bosset, Pierre (1999), 'Civil society participation in the process of reporting and monitoring implementation of international human rights: the domestic dimension', paper prepared for Human Rights Linkage Initiative, National Consultation on Human Rights, Ottawa, 26–27 October.

Cohen, Roberta (1992), *Human Rights and Humanitarian Emergencies: New Roles for U.N. Human Rights Bodies.* Washington, DC: Refugee Policy Group.

Comeau, Pauline (1993), 'A permanent criminal court is central to ICJ agenda', *Human Rights Tribune*, 2(1), pp.24–25.

Comeau, Pauline (1995), ' Access becomes the key issue for the UN World Conference on Women', *Human Rights Tribune*, 3(2), pp.7–11.

'Draft Declaration on the Rights of Human Rights Defenders: an update', *Human Rights Tribune*, 4(2–3), p.45.

Drinan, Robert F. and Kuo, Teresa T. (1993), 'Putting the world's oppressors on trial: the Torture Victim Protection Act', *Human Rights Quarterly*, 15(3), pp.605–24.

Dufraimont, Lisa and Hammell, Andrea (1999), 'Rwanda – the Akayesu verdict. Tribunal breaks new ground in recognizing rape as genocide', *Human Rights Tribune*, 6(1).

Ermacora, Felix (1988), 'Non-governmental organizations as promoters of human rights', in Franz Matscher and Herbert Petzold (eds), *Protecting Human Rights: The European Dimension*, Cologne: Carl Heymanns Verlag KG.

Forsythe, David (1977), *Humanitarian Politics: The International Committee of the Red Cross*, Baltimore/London: The Johns Hopkins University Press.

Fund for Peace in association with the Jacob Blaustein Institute for the Advancement of Human Rights (1994), *Human Rights Institution-Building: A Handbook on Establishing and Sustaining Human Rights Organizations*, New York.

Fund for Peace in association with the Jacob Blaustein Institute for the Advancement of Human Rights (1999), *A Handbook of Practical Strategies for Local Human Rights Groups*, New York.

Gaer, Felice D. (1995), 'Reality checks: human rights non-governmental organizations confront governments at the United Nations', unpublished paper presented to a Conference on 'Non-governmental Organizations: The United Nations and Global Governance', Academic Council on the United Nations System, April.

Garcia-Sayan, Diego (1991), 'Non-governmental organizations and the human rights movement in Latin America', *Bulletin of Human Rights*, 90(1), New York: United Nations, pp.31–41.

Hecht, Hans-Erik (1997), 'The World Congress against the commercial sexual exploitation of children', *Human Rights Tribune*, 4(1), pp.7–9.

Henkin, Louis (1978), *The Rights of Man Today*, Boulder, CO: Westview Press.

Human Rights Internet (1997), 'The role of civil organizations in monitoring the Convention on the Prohibition of the Use, Stockpiling, Production and Transfer of Anti-Personnel Mines and on Their Destruction: a proposal for a cooperative compliance mechanism', unpublished paper prepared for the Office of Non-Proliferation, Arms Control and Disarmament of the Department of Foreign Affairs and International Trade, Government of Canada, November.

Human Rights, the United Nations and Non-governmental Organizations. A Report of the International Human Rights Council (1997), Atlanta, GA: Carter Center.

Humphrey, John (1984), *Human Rights and the United Nations: A Great Adventure*, Dobbs Ferry, NY: Transnational Publishers.

International Campaign to Ban Landmines (1999), *Landmine Monitor Report: Towards a Mine-free World*, New York: Human Rights Watch.

Interview with Patrick Ball (1997/98), 'Who did what to whom? Building violations databases', *Human Rights Tribune*, 4(4), pp.33–36 and 5(1–2), pp.40–42.

Jenish, D'Arcy (1997), 'Landing the prize. Peace activists share in the 1997 Nobel', *McLean's*, 20 October, pp.32–33.

Korey, William (1998), *NGOs and the Universal Declaration of Human Rights. 'A Curious Grapevine'*, New York: St Martin's Press.

Lafrenière, Julie and Wiseberg, Laurie S. (1999), 'UN Special Session on East Timor', *Human Rights Tribune*, 6(4), pp.6–14.

Larsen, Egon (1978), *A Flame in Barbed Wire: The Story of Amnesty International*, New York: W.W. Norton & Co.

Leckie, Scott (1994), *Destruction by Design. Housing Rights Violations in Tibet*, The Netherlands: Centre on Housing Rights and Eviction (COHRE).

Leckie, Scott and Farha, Leilani (1997), 'Glimmer of hope: building new standards on forced evictions at the UN', *Human Rights Tribune*, 4(4), pp.24–26.

Lillich, Richard B. (1993), 'Damages for gross violations of international human rights awarded by US courts', *Human Rights Quarterly*, 15(2), pp.207–29.

McCheshney, Allan (1996), 'Human Rights Defenders Declaration still on hold', *Human Rights Tribune*, 3(4).

McDermot, Niall (1989), 'The role of NGOs in the promotion and protection of human rights', in *The Role of Non-Government Organizations in the Promotion and Protection of Human Rights*, Symposium organized on the occasion of the award of the *Praemium Erasmianum* to the International Commission of Jurists, Leiden: Stichting NJCM-Boekerij, pp.45–52.

Muntarbhorn, Vitit (1998), 'Education for human rights', in Janusz Symonides (ed.), *Human Rights Dimensions and Challenges: Manual on Human Rights*, Aldershot: Ashgate Publishing/UNESCO, pp.281–99.

Oosterveld, Valerie and Copelon, Rhonda (1997), 'First rape charges brought at the Rwanda Tribunal', *Human Rights Tribune*, 4(4), pp.16–18.

Parker, Wendy and Comeau, Pauline (1993), 'Women succeed in Vienna where others fail', *Human Rights Tribune*, 2(2), pp.22–26.

Posner, Michael M. and Whittome, Candy (1994), 'The status of human rights NGOs', *Columbia Human Rights Law Review*, 25, pp.269–90.

Power, Jonathan (1981), *Against Oblivion: Amnesty International's Fight for Human Rights*, London: Fontana Paperbacks.

Price Cohen, Cynthia (1990), 'The role of non-governmental organizations in the drafting of the Convention on the Rights of the Child', *Human Rights Quarterly*, 12(1), pp.137–47.

Rodley, Nigel S. (1979), 'Monitoring human rights by the U.N. System and non-governmental organizations', in Donald Kommers and Gilburt D. Loescher (eds), *Human Rights and American Foreign Policy*, Notre Dame/London: University of Notre Dame Press, pp.157–78.

Ryan, Karin D. (1998), '13 years in the making – not perfect but not bad', *Human Rights Tribune*, 5(1–2), p.13.

Ryan, Karin D. and Kambayashi, Makiko (1997), 'Women's human rights NGOs and the U.N. system', in *Human Rights, the United Nations and Non-government*

Organizations: A Report of the International Human Rights Council, Atlanta, GA: Carter Center, pp.6–177.

Ryan, Karin D. and Wiseberg, Laurie S. (1995), 'ECOSOC resolution 1996/31: the end result of the ECOSOC Review Process of the Rules Governing NGO Relations with the United Nations', in *Human Rights, the United Nations and Non-government Organizations: A Report of the International Human Rights Council*, Atlanta, GA: Carter Center, pp.9–24.

Steiner, Henry J. (1991), *Diverse Partners: Non-Governmental Organizations in the Human Rights Movement*, Cambridge, MA: Harvard Law School Human Rights Program and Human Rights Internet.

Steward, Nell (1998), 'Guarded borders. Gender at the International Criminal Court Conference', *Human Rights Tribune*, 5(4), p.11.

Tolley, Howard B. Jr (1987), *The U.N. Commission on Human Rights*, Westview Special Studies in International Relations, Boulder, CO/London: Westview Press, pp.10–12.

Tolley, Howard B. Jr (1994), *The International Commission of Jurists: Global Advocates for Human Rights*, Philadelphia, PA: University of Pennsylvania Press.

United Nations (1993), *A Compilation of International Instruments*, Vol. I, Geneva: United Nations.

United Nations (1997), *A Compilation of International Instruments*, Vol. II: Regional Instruments, Geneva: United Nations.

van Boven, Theo C. (1989), 'The role of NGOs in international human rights standard-setting: non-governmental participation a perquisite of democracy?', in *The Role of Non-Government Organizations in the Promotion and Protection of Human Rights*, Symposium organized on the occasion of the award of the *Praemium Erasmianum* to the International Commission of Jurists, Leiden: Stichting NJCM-Boekerij, pp.53–72.

van Boven, Theo C. and Ramcharan, B.G. (1982), 'Problems in the protection of human rights at the international level', in I. Kuçuradi (ed.), *The Philosophical Foundation of Human Rights*, Ankara, pp.105–11.

Velin, Jo-Anne (1997), *A Journalist's Handbook: Reporting on Human Rights and Humanitarian Stories*, Geneva: Human Rights Internet/International Centre for Humanitarian Reporting.

Weissbrodt, David (1984), 'The contribution of international non-governmental organizations to the protection of human rights', in Theodor Meron (ed.), *Human Rights in International Law: Legal and Policy Issues*, Oxford: Clarendon Press, pp.403–38.

Williams, Paul ((1997), 'Kabila blocks UN investigation into massacres', *Human Rights Tribune*, 4(4), pp.18 and 23.

Wiseberg, Laurie S. (1986), 'Human rights reporting', *Human Rights Internet Reporter*, 11(4), pp.3–6.

Wiseberg, Laurie S. (1989), 'Human rights NGOs', in *The Role of Non-Governmental Organizations in the Promotion and Protection of Human Rights*, Symposium organized on the occasion of the award of the *Praemium Erasmianum* to the International Commission of Jurists. Leiden, Stichting NJCM-Boekerij.

Wiseberg, Laurie S. (1991a), 'The role of non-governmental organizations', in *Put our World to Rights*, London: Commonwealth Human Rights Initiative, pp.151–72.

Wiseberg, Laurie S. (1991b), 'Protecting human rights activists and NGOs: what more can be done?', *Human Rights Quarterly*, 13 (4), pp.525–44.

Wiseberg, Laurie S. (1993), *Defending Human Rights Defenders: The Importance of Freedom of Association for Human Rights NGOs*, Essays on Human Rights and

Democratic Development No. 3. Montreal: International Centre for Human Rights and Democratic Development.

Wiseberg, Laurie S. (1995), 'The Vienna World Conference on Human Rights', in Eric Fawcett and Newcombe, Hanna (eds), *United Nations Reform: Looking Ahead after Fifty Years*, Toronto: Science for Peace, pp.173–82.

Wiseberg, Laurie S. (1995a), 'Frivilligorganisationernas roll' (The role of NGOs in the United Nations system), in Bertil Bruner (ed.), *FN och de manskliga rattigheterna*, London: Juridik & Samhalle, pp.141–60.

Wiseberg, Laurie S. (1995b), 'Consultative status review stalled', *Human Rights Tribune*, 3(2), pp.32–37.

Wiseberg, Laurie S. (1996), 'Resolution 1296 revised. A done deal on consultative status', *Human Rights Tribune*, 3(4), pp.7–11.

Wiseberg, Laurie S. (1997), 'Editorial: act now to defend your right to defend human rights', *Human Rights Tribune*, 4(1), p.5.

Wiseberg, Laurie S. (1999), 'A conversation with the Special Rapporteur on freedom of opinion and expression', *Human Rights Tribune*, 6(3), p.10.

Index